Lecture Notes in Computer Science 5455

Commenced Publication in 1973
Founding and Former Series Editors:
Gerhard Goos, Juris Hartmanis, and Jan van Leeuwen

Editorial Board

David Hutchison
  Lancaster University, UK
Takeo Kanade
  Carnegie Mellon University, Pittsburgh, PA, USA
Josef Kittler
  University of Surrey, Guildford, UK
Jon M. Kleinberg
  Cornell University, Ithaca, NY, USA
Alfred Kobsa
  University of California, Irvine, CA, USA
Friedemann Mattern
  ETH Zurich, Switzerland
John C. Mitchell
  Stanford University, CA, USA
Moni Naor
  Weizmann Institute of Science, Rehovot, Israel
Oscar Nierstrasz
  University of Bern, Switzerland
C. Pandu Rangan
  Indian Institute of Technology, Madras, India
Bernhard Steffen
  University of Dortmund, Germany
Madhu Sudan
  Massachusetts Institute of Technology, MA, USA
Demetri Terzopoulos
  University of California, Los Angeles, CA, USA
Doug Tygar
  University of California, Berkeley, CA, USA
Gerhard Weikum
  Max-Planck Institute of Computer Science, Saarbruecken, Germany

Mladen Berekovic
Christian Müller-Schloer
Christian Hochberger   Stephan Wong (Eds.)

Architecture of Computing Systems – ARCS 2009

22nd International Conference
Delft, The Netherlands, March 10-13, 2009
Proceedings

Springer

Volume Editors

Mladen Berekovic
Institut für Datentechnik und Kommunikationsnetze
Hans-Sommer-Str. 66, 38106 Braunschweig, Germany
E-mail: berekovic@ida.ing.tu-bs.de

Christian Müller-Schloer
Leibniz University
Appelstr. 4, 30167 Hannover, Germany
E-mail: cms@sra.uni-hannover.de

Christian Hochberger
Technical University of Dresden
Nöthnitzer Str. 46, 01187 Dresden, Germany
E-mail: christian.hochberger@inf.tu-dresden.de

Stephan Wong
Delft University of Technology
Mekelweg 4, 2628 CD Delft, The Netherlands
E-mail: j.s.s.m.wong@tudelft.nl

Library of Congress Control Number: 2009921822

CR Subject Classification (1998): C.2, C.5.3, D.4, D.2.11, H.3.5, H.4, H.5.2

LNCS Sublibrary: SL 1 – Theoretical Computer Science and General Issues

ISSN	0302-9743
ISBN-10	3-642-00453-9 Springer Berlin Heidelberg New York
ISBN-13	978-3-642-00453-7 Springer Berlin Heidelberg New York

This work is subject to copyright. All rights are reserved, whether the whole or part of the material is concerned, specifically the rights of translation, reprinting, re-use of illustrations, recitation, broadcasting, reproduction on microfilms or in any other way, and storage in data banks. Duplication of this publication or parts thereof is permitted only under the provisions of the German Copyright Law of September 9, 1965, in its current version, and permission for use must always be obtained from Springer. Violations are liable to prosecution under the German Copyright Law.

springer.com

© Springer-Verlag Berlin Heidelberg 2009
Printed in Germany

Typesetting: Camera-ready by author, data conversion by Scientific Publishing Services, Chennai, India
Printed on acid-free paper   SPIN: 12626823   06/3180   5 4 3 2 1 0

Preface

The ARCS series of conferences has over 30 years of tradition reporting top-notch results in computer architecture and operating systems research. It is organized by the special interest group on "Computer and System Architecture" of the GI (Gesellschaft für Informatik e.V.) and ITG (Informationstechnische Gesellschaft im VDE - Information Technology Society). In 2009, ARCS was hosted by the Delft University of Technology, which has one of the leading information technology schools in Europe.

This year's special focus was set on energy awareness viewed from two different perspectives. Firstly, this deals with the improvement of computer systems to be as energy-efficient as possible (particularly for specific applications). One can think of heterogeneous multi-core architectures or reconfigurable architectures for this purpose. Secondly, this addresses the usage of computer systems to reduce the energy consumption of other systems, which might lead to problems of communication and cooperation. Like the previous conferences in this series, it continues to be an important forum for computer architecture research.

The call for papers resulted in a total of 57 submissions from around the world. Each submission was assigned to at least three members of the Program Committee for review. The Program Committee decided to accept 21 papers, which are arranged into eight sessions. The accepted papers are from: Finland, France, Germany, Japan, The Netherlands, Singapore, Spain, UK, and USA. Three intriguing keynotes from academia and industry complemented the strong technical program.

We would like to thank all who contributed to the success of this conference, in particular the members of the Program Committee (and the additional reviewers) for carefully reviewing the contributions and selecting a high-quality program. Our Workshop and Tutorial Chair Jörg Hähner did a perfect job in organizing the tutorials and coordinating the workshops. Our special thanks go to the members of the Organizing Committee for their numerous contributions: Thomas B. Preußer set up the conference software and designed and maintained the conference website. Dimitris Theodoropoulos took over the laborious task of preparing this volume. We would like to especially thank Carlo Galuzzi for taking care of the local arrangements and many other aspects in the organization of the conference.

We hope that all participants enjoyed a successful conference, made many new contacts, engaged in fruitful discussions, and had a pleasant stay in Delft.

March 2009

Christian Hochberger
Stephan Wong
Mladen Berekovic
Christian Müller-Schloer

Organization

General Chairs

Mladen Berekovic   Technical University of Braunschweig, Germany
Christian Müller-Schloer University of Hannover, Germany

Program Chairs

Christian Hochberger   Technical University of Dresden, Germany
Stephan Wong   Delft University of Technology, The Netherlands

Workshop and Tutorial Chair

Jörg Hähner   University of Hannover, Germany

Proceedings Chair

Dimitris Theodoropoulos Delft University of Technology, The Netherlands

Financial and Local Arrangements Chair

Carlo Galuzzi   Delft University of Technology, The Netherlands

Web Chair

Thomas Preußer   Technical University of Dresden, Germany

Program Committee

Wael Adi   Technical University of Braunschweig, Germany
Tughrul Arslan   University of Edinburgh, UK
Nader Bagherzadeh   University of California Irvine, USA
Michael Beigl   Technical University of Braunschweig, Germany
Guillem Bernat   Rapita Systems and University of York, UK
Arndt Bode   Technical University of Munich, Germany
Koen De Bosschere   Ghent University, Belgium
Uwe Brinkschulte   University of Karlsruhe, Germany
Jiannong Cao   The Hong Kong Polytechnic University, China
João Cardoso   NESC-ID, Lisbon, Portugal, Portugal

Luigi Carro	Universidade Federal do Rio Grande do Sul, Brazil
Henk Corporaal	Technical University of Eindhoven, The Netherlands
Francisco J. Cazorla	Universitat Politècnica de Catalunya (UPC), Spain
Steven Derrien	INRIA-Rennes, France
Nikitas Dimopoulos	University of Victoria, Canada
Alois Ferscha	University of Linz, Austria
Fabrizio Ferrandi	Politecnico di Milano, Italy
Björn Franke	University of Edinburgh, UK
Werner Grass	University of Passau, Germany
Soonhoi Ha	Seoul National University, Korea
Andreas Herkersdorf	Munich University of Technology, Germany
Seongsoo Hong	Seoul National University, Korea
Paolo Ienne	Ecole Polytechnique Fédérale de Lausanne, Switzerland
Tohru Ishihara	Kyushu University, Japan
Jadwiga Indulska	University of Queensland, Australia
Murali Jayapala	IMEC, Belgium
Gert Jervan	Tallinn University of Technology, Estonia
Ben Juurlink	Technical University of Delft, The Netherlands
Wolfgang Karl	University of Karlsruhe, Germany
Manolis Katevenis	FORTH and University of Crete, Greece
Andreas Koch	Technical University of Darmstadt, Germany
Krzysztof Kuchcinski	Lund University, Sweden
Spyros Lalis	University of Thessaly, Greece
Paul Lukowicz	University of Passau, Germany
Jianhua Ma	Hosei University, Japan
Erik Maehle	University of Lübeck, Germany
Jan Madsen	Technical University of Denmark, Denmark
Tom Martin	Virginia Tech, USA
Peter Marwedel	University of Dortmund, Germany
Dragomir Milojevic	Université Libre de Bruxelles, Belgium
Nacho Navarro	Universitat Politècnica de Catalunya (UPC), Spain
Alex Orailoglu	University of California San Diego, USA
Emre Özer	ARM, UK
Andy Pimentel	University of Amsterdam, The Netherlands
Burghardt Schallenberger	Siemens AG, Germany
Pascal Sainrat	Paul Sabatier University, Toulouse, France
Yiannakis Sazeides	University of Cyprus, Cyprus
Hartmut Schmeck	University of Karlsruhe, Germany
Karsten Schwan	Georgia Tech, USA
Gerard Smit	University of Twente, The Netherlands

Leonel Sousa	Technical University of Lisbon, Portugal
Rainer G. Spallek	Technical University of Dresden, Germany
Peter Steenkiste	Carnegie-Mellon University, USA
Bassel Soudan	University of Sharjah, UAE
Jarmo Takala	Tampere University of Technology, Finland
Jürgen Teich	University of Erlangen-Nuremberg, Germany
Lothar Thiele	ETH Zürich, China
David Thomas	Imperial College London, UK
Pedro Trancoso	University of Cyprus, Cyprus
Gerhard Tröster	ETH Zürich, China
Theo Ungerer	University of Augsburg, Germany
Mateo Valero	Universitat Politècnica de Catalunya (UPC), Spain
Stephane Vialle	Supelec, France
Lucian Vintan	Lucian Blaga University of Sibiu, Romania
Klaus Waldschmidt	University of Frankfurt, Germany
Laurence T. Yang	St. Francis Xavier University, Canada
Sami Yehia	Thales Group, France

List of all Reviewers Involved in ARCS 2009

Adi, Wael
Andersson, Per
Antonopoulos, Christos
Arslan, Tughrul
Bagherzadeh, Nader
Bauer, Lars
Beck, Antonio
Beigl, Michael
Bernat, Guillem
Bode, Arndt
Brinkschulte, Uwe
Cao, Jiannong
Cardoso, João
Carro, Luigi
Cazorla, Francisco J.
Chen, Jian-Jia
Claus, Christopher
Corporaal, Henk
De Bosschere, Koen
Derrien, Steven
Dias, Tiago
Dimopoulos, Nikitas
Dutta, Hritam
Ellervee, Peeter

Ferrandi, Fabrizio
Ferscha, Alois
Franke, Björn
Galuzzi, Carlo
Georges, Andy
Gladigau, Jens
Grass, Werner
Gruian, Flavius
Guzma, Vladimir
Ha, Soonhoi
Hartl, Robert
Herkersdorf, Andreas
Hong, Seongsoo
Ienne, Paolo
Ilic, Aleksandar
Indulska, Jadwiga
Isaza, Sebastian
Ishihara, Tohru
Jahr, Ralf
Jayapala, Murali
Jervan, Gert
Jovanovic, Olivera
Juurlink, Ben
Karl, Wolfgang

Katevenis, Manolis
Kellomäki, Pertti
Kim, Deokkoo
Kissler, Dmitrij
Kleanthous, Marios
Kluter, Theo
Koch, Andreas
Kramer, David
Kuchcinski, Krzysztof
Kumar, Manish
Lalis, Spyros
Lange, Holger
Lee, Je Hyun
Loukopoulos, Thanasis
Lukowicz, Paul
Ma, Jianhua
Madsen, Jan
Maehle, Erik
Martin, Tom
Marwedel, Peter
Meenderinck, Cor
Membarth, Richard
Metzlaff, Stefan
Mhamdi, Lotfi
Milojevic, Dragomir
Navarro, Nacho
Nowak, Fabian
Orailoglu, Alex
Özer, Emre
Park, Juwon
Pereira, Monica
Pericas, Miquel
Pimentel, Andy
Plazar, Sascha
Pratas, Frederico

Preußer, Thomas
Rutzig, Mateus
Sainrat, Pascal
Sazeides, Yiannakis
Schallenberger, Burghardt
Schindewolf, Martin
Schmeck, Hartmut
Schranzhofer, Andreas
Schwan, Karsten
Sick, Bernhard
Smit, Gerard
Soudan, Bassel
Sousa, Leonel
Spallek, Rainer G.
Steenkiste, Peter
Steinfeld, Leo
Takala, Jarmo
Teich, Jürgen
Thiele, Lothar
Thomas, David
Trancoso, Pedro
Tröster, Gerhard
Ungerer, Theo
Valero, Mateo
Verdú, Javier
Vialle, Stephane
Vintan, Lucian
Waldschmidt, Klaus
Yang, Laurence T.
Yehia, Sami
Zabel, Martin
Zeppenfeld, Johannes
Zhang, Ji
Zhang, Shigeng

Table of Contents

Keynotes

Life on the Treadmill 1
  Krisztián Flautner

Key Microarchitectural Innovations for Future Microprocessors 2
  Antonio González

The Challenges of Multicore: Information and Mis-Information 3
  Yale Patt

Compilation Technologies

Extracting Coarse-Grained Pipelined Parallelism Out of Sequential
Applications for Parallel Processor Arrays 4
  Dimitris Syrivelis and Spyros Lalis

Parallelization Approaches for Hardware Accelerators – Loop Unrolling
Versus Loop Partitioning 16
  Frank Hannig, Hritam Dutta, and Jürgen Teich

Evaluating Sampling Based Hotspot Detection 28
  Qiang Wu and Oskar Mencer

Reconfigurable Hardware and Applications

A Reconfigurable Bloom Filter Architecture for BLASTN 40
  Yupeng Chen, Bertil Schmidt, and Douglas L. Maskell

SoCWire: A Robust and Fault Tolerant Network-on-Chip Approach for
a Dynamic Reconfigurable System-on-Chip in FPGAs 50
  Björn Osterloh, Harald Michalik, and Björn Fiethe

A Light-Weight Approach to Dynamical Runtime Linking Supporting
Heterogenous, Parallel, and Reconfigurable Architectures 60
  Rainer Buchty, David Kramer, Mario Kicherer, and Wolfgang Karl

Ultra-Fast Downloading of Partial Bitstreams through Ethernet 72
  *Pierre Bomel, Jeremie Crenne, Linfeng Ye,
  Jean-Philippe Diguet, and Guy Gogniat*

Massive Parallel Architectures

SCOPE - Sensor Mote Configuration and Operation Enhancement 84
  Harun Özturgut, Christian Scholz, Thomas Wieland, and Christoph Niedermeier

Generated Horizontal and Vertical Data Parallel GCA Machines for the N-Body Force Calculation 96
  Johannes Jendrsczok, Rolf Hoffmann, and Thomas Lenck

Hybrid Resource Discovery Mechanism in Ad Hoc Grid Using Structured Overlay 108
  Tariq Abdullah, Luc Onana Alima, Vassiliy Sokolov, David Calomme, and Koen Bertels

Organic Computing

Marketplace-Oriented Behavior in Semantic Multi-Criteria Decision Making Autonomous Systems 120
  Ghadi Mahmoudi, Christian Müller-Schloer, and Jörg Hähner

Self-organized Parallel Cooperation for Solving Optimization Problems 135
  Sanaz Mostaghim and Hartmut Schmeck

Memory Architectures

Improving Memory Subsystem Performance Using ViVA: Virtual Vector Architecture 146
  Joseph Gebis, Leonid Oliker, John Shalf, Samuel Williams, and Katherine Yelick

An Enhanced DMA Controller in SIMD Processors for Video Applications.. 159
  Guillermo Payá-Vayá, Javier Martín-Langerwerf, Sören Moch, and Peter Pirsch

Cache Controller Design on Ultra Low Leakage Embedded Processors 171
  Zhao Lei, Hui Xu, Naomi Seki, Saito Yoshiki, Yohei Hasegawa, Kimiyoshi Usami, and Hideharu Amano

Energy Awareness

Autonomous DVFS on Supply Islands for Energy-Constrained NoC Communication... 183
  Liang Guang, Ethiopia Nigussie, Lauri Koskinen, and Hannu Tenhunen

Energy Management System as an Embedded Service: Saving Energy
Consumption of ICT 195
  Francisco Maciá-Pérez, Diego Marcos-Jorquera, and
  Virgilio Gilart-Iglesias

Java Processing

A Garbage Collection Technique for Embedded Multithreaded
Multicore Processors 207
  Sascha Uhrig and Theo Ungerer

Empirical Performance Models for Java Workloads 219
  Pradeep Rao and Kazuaki Murakami

Chip-Level Multiprocessing

Performance Matching of Hardware Acceleration Engines for
Heterogeneous MPSoC Using Modular Performance Analysis 233
  Hritam Dutta, Frank Hannig, and Jürgen Teich

Evaluating CMPs and Their Memory Architecture 246
  Chris Jesshope, Mike Lankamp, and Li Zhang

Author Index 259

Life on the Treadmill

Krisztián Flautner

ARM Ltd

Abstract. Silicon technology evolution over the last four decades has yielded an exponential increase in integration densities with steady improvements of performance and power consumption at each technology generation. This steady progress has created a sense of entitlement for the riches that future process generations would bring. Today, however, classical process scaling seems to be dead and living up to technology expectations requires continuous innovation at many levels, which comes at steadily progressing implementation and design costs. Solutions to problems need to cut across layers of abstractions and require coordination between software, architecture and circuit features.

Key Microarchitectural Innovations for Future Microprocessors

Antonio González

Intel Barcelona Research Center, Intel Labs   UPC, Barcelona

Abstract. Microprocessors have experienced tremendous performance improvements generation after generation since its inception. Moores law has fueled this evolution and will keep doing it in forthcoming generations. However, future microprocessors are facing new challenges that require innovative approaches to keep delivering improvements comparable to those that we have enjoyed so far. Power dissipation is a main challenge in all segments, from ultra-mobile to high-end servers. Another important challenge is the fact that we have relied on instruction-level parallelism (ILP) as a main lever to improve performance, but after more than 30 years of enhancing ILP techniques we are approaching a point of diminishing returns. In this talk we will discuss these challenges and propose some solutions to tackle them. Multicore is a recently adopted approach in most microprocessors that offers significant advantages in terms of power and exploits a new source of parallelism: thread-level parallelism. In this talk we will discuss the benefits of multicore and also show its limitations. We will also describe some other technologies that we believe are needed to complement the benefits of multicore and offer all together a foundation for future microprocessors.

The Challenges of Multicore: Information and Mis-Information

Yale Patt

The University of Texas at Austin

Abstract. Now that we have broken the threshold of one billion transistors on a chip and multi-core has become a reality, a lot of buzz has resulted – from how/why we got here, to what is important, to how we should determine how to effectively use multicore. In this talk, I will examine a number of these new "conventional wisdom" nuggets of information to try to see whether they add value or get in the way. For example: what can we expect multicore to do about saving power consumption? is ILP dead? should sample benchmarks drive future designs? is hardware sequential? should multicore structures be simple? is abstraction a fundamental good? Hopefully, our examinations will help shed some light on where we go from here.

Extracting Coarse-Grained Pipelined Parallelism Out of Sequential Applications for Parallel Processor Arrays

Dimitris Syrivelis and Spyros Lalis

Dept of Computer & Communication Engineering, University of Thessaly, Hellas
`jsyr@inf.uth.gr,lalis@inf.uth.gr`

Abstract. We present development and runtime support for building application specific data processing pipelines out of sequential code, and for executing them on a general purpose platform that features a reconfigurable Parallel Processor Array (PPA). Our approach is to let the programmer annotate the source of the application to indicate the desired pipeline stages and associated data flow, with little code restructuring. A pre-processor is then used to transform the annotated program into different code segments according to the indicated pipeline structure, generate the corresponding executable code, and produce a bundled application package containing all executables and deployment information for the target platform. There are special mechanisms for setting up the application-specific pipeline structure on the PPA and achieving integrated execution in the context of a general-purpose operating system, enabling the pipelined application to access the usual system peripherals and run concurrently with other conventional programs. To verify our approach, we have built a prototype system using soft processor arrays on an embedded FPGA platform, and transformed a well-known application into a pipelined version that executes successfully on our prototype.

1 Introduction

The advent of embedded distributed memory Parallel Processor Array (PPA) solutions like Ambric [1] introduces new workload acceleration possibilities. Application logic can be now implemented as a program that executes on a CPU-based subsystem, which in turn plays the role of an application-specific co-processor for the platform main CPU. However, developing applications that can exploit the potential of such a system is far from trivial. One encounters most of the challenges faced when trying to write parallel programs for conventional multi-processor systems; above all, to structure the code in a way that enables its efficient parallel execution on top of the underlying hardware. Moreover, the PPA CPUs may not have enough resources to run a complex runtime with support for multi-threaded execution, thread placement and thread migration. It is also important to reuse the existing (sequential) codebase of applications instead of developing them from scratch for this particular type of system.

In this paper, we present a framework for supporting the development and execution of applications in conjunction with reconfigurable PPA subsystems, specifically for programs that are amenable to pipelining. From a development perspective, our approach is to let the programmer specify the desired pipeline structure in an explicit fashion, by annotating the original source code, without having to move code around or redefine function boundaries. A preprocessor reads the annotated code, extracts the corresponding multi-core structure, generates the different program segments for each core, inserts additional code for their communication/synchronization, and compiles them for execution on the target platform.

We have implemented a prototype PPA system that is capable of dynamically loading and running such applications, on a Xilinx Spartan FPGA board featuring Microblaze soft processor arrays and a largely standard Linux environment. We provide the runtime support for reconfiguring the FPGA to set up the application-specific network of CPUs, loading the pipeline segments on the corresponding CPUs, and executing the application. Notably, pipelined applications may run concurrently to other conventional programs. To enable a straightforward testing of the pipelined program without employing any special hardware, the preprocessor also generates code for a Linux-based emulation environment which can be used to profile program execution, e.g., in order to determine whether the pipeline structure is well-balanced or needs adjustment.

2 Pipeline Architecture for Reconfigurable PPAs

Our high-level objective is to support the coarse-grained pipelining of existing applications for reconfigurable PPAs in a straightforward and efficient way. Most importantly, we wish to do this in the context of a proper operating system that can be used to execute other (conventional) applications as well, concurrently to the pipelined application.

2.1 Concept

We propose a heterogeneous architecture that comprises a distinct *main CPU* and several *coCPUs* used to run the stages of the application pipeline, connected in a unidirectional data flow network. The main CPU is interfaced with the bulk of memory resources and all system peripherals. It runs a proper (single-processor) operating system together with the usual system and application programs. A coCPU has not access to system resources and peripherals, except for its private local memory and links to other CPUs. CoCPUs are used exclusively for processing stages of pipelines.

Each pipelined application employs its own dedicated coCPU network, which can be viewed as a private application-specific accelerator that can be dynamically instantiated on the PPA. Provided there are enough hardware resources on the PPA, several different coCPU networks (accelerators) can be accommodated at the same time, enabling the parallel execution of different pipelined applications. Figure 1 shows an indicative configuration with two coCPU networks.

Besides configuring the PPA to connect the coCPUs as needed, additional customization can be introduced to optimize the coCPUs for the task at hand. For instance in the Ambric [1] architecture, the frequency of each coCPU can be configured independently. Soft architectures enable even more radical customization for each core, but for the time being the large performance gap between hard and soft processors typically makes the latter an overall less attractive solution.

The main drawback of the proposed organization is that only the part of the application which executes on the main CPU may invoke system calls, perform standard

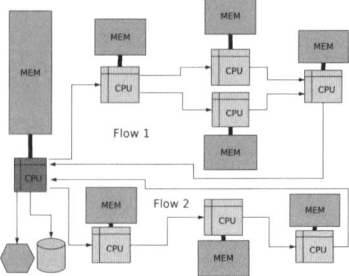

Fig. 1. Indicative hardware configuration with two pipelines

I/O and access the usual system resources and peripherals. It is therefore only this part which can be assigned the task of pushing data into and pulling data out of the coCPU pipeline. This in turn implies that all pipelines must have the main CPU as both their *root* and *sink*, as illustrated in Figure 1.

2.2 FPGA-Based Prototype

The proposed architecture is prototyped on an FPGA, used to install multiple identical softcore CPUs and setup the interconnections between them. The platform is the Atmark Techno Suzaku [2], featuring a Xilinx Spartan 3 FPGA along with off-chip 16MB RAM, 8MB flash, a MAC core and a configuration controller. For the softcore main CPU and coCPUs we choose the Xilinx Microblaze, operated at $100Mhz$. The Microblaze supports a fast bus architecture named FSL (Fast Simplex Links), which can be used to setup dedicated 32-bit wide unidirectional point-to-point communication channels. Data transfer can be done directly from/to the register file via special instructions that have blocking (they stall the processor) and non-blocking versions. The current Microblaze implementation can have up to 8 read and 8 write FSL interfaces, enabling the implementation of quite complex interconnects.

The main CPU is interfaced to all platform peripherals and runs a customized version of uClinux [3]. The coCPUs have access only to their local memory and are connected to each other and the main CPU using FSL links, reflecting the topology that is specified by the application developer (see Section 3). The runtime for coCPUs is a small basic input/output system we have developed that must be statically linked to the application code to be loaded on the coCPU (the coCPUs do not feature a proper runtime nor any kind of support for multi-programming, multi-threaded execution, thread migration, etc). The BIOS is about 512 bytes long, keeping the memory requirements of coCPUs low; of course, the amount of memory each coCPU will ultimately be equipped with depends on the complexity of the pipeline stage that will run on it.

Loading is done using a custom program we developed for this purpose. The loader reads the application deployment file and passes information about the coCPU network to a system process that is responsible for managing the hardware reconfiguration. If the required configuration is not already installed, the system reconfigures to deploy it on the FPGA. Runtime reconfiguration is based on existing support that we have built in previous work [4]. Then, the binary for each pipeline stage is extracted from the deployment file and loaded on the corresponding coCPU (coCPUs are preloaded with logic to dynamically load application code). When the loading of all coCPUs completes, the binary that will run on the main CPU is loaded using the standard uClinux procedure, and the execution of the application commences. The entire process is transparent for the user, who is given the illusion of loading and running a conventional application.

As already mentioned, the main CPU serves both as the root and sink of all pipelines. It must also run all other (conventional) applications. Given this bottleneck situation, it is crucial to avoid any busywaiting on the main CPU while waiting for the pipeline to get ready to accept data and/or deliver data. For this reason, we developed an FSL *Slave Interrupt Generator* (SIG) peripheral that is interfaced to the *first* and *last* coCPU of each pipeline and the Interrupt Controller of the main CPU. The interrupts are generated by the coCPUs using standard FSL instructions, when they are ready to accept data from and respectively deliver data to the main CPU. On the uClinux side, we developed a *FlowControl* driver that handles the respective IRQs. Applications register with this driver in order to get notified via a SIGUSR1 signal as soon as it becomes possible to push/pull data into/from their pipeline.

3 Application Development Framework

In terms of programming methodology, we let the programmer specify the pipeline structure in the original application source code, using a small set of annotations. This makes it possible to reuse existing sequential code with little re-structuring. When done, a preprocessor is employed to transform the annotated code into separate compilation units, generate the corresponding executables, and bundle them into a deployment package for the target system. We have implemented support for two (radically) different platforms: (i) a process-based execution environment for a standard Linux system, and (ii) our FPGA-based prototype (see Section 2.2). The most important aspects of our development framework are discussed in the following.

3.1 Annotation Primitives

The annotations for marking the stages of the application pipeline and the data exchange between them are introduced as extensions of *OpenMP* [5]. They are described in more detail below.

The region directive *#pragma omp stage (<stage no>, <path no>, <function name>)* defines a pipeline stage. It takes as arguments the stage number, the path number and the entry function name. The function name can be left blank if the directive is used inside a function body, in which case its location indicates the boundary between two stages. The region directive *#pragma omp path (<path no>)*, taking as an optional argument a path number, is used to define a path entry point in the pipeline. The declarative directive *#pragma omp threadprivate (<variable name>)* already exists in the *OpenMP* specification. In our case, it is used to identify the variables that are shared among the root and sink segments, for which different "copies" need to be managed properly (as will be discussed in Section 3.2). Finally, the library templates

#pragma omp push(<stage>, <path no>, <data pointer>, <size>) and its counterpart #pragma omp pull are used to transfer data between two pipeline stages. The location of these annotations in the source code is of key importance, because they implicitly define a boundary between two or more stages (also forks and joins). Also, when a *pull* is used in isolation, without an accompanying *stage* or *path* directive, it indicates the end of the pipeline, i.e., the boundary with the sink of the pipeline.

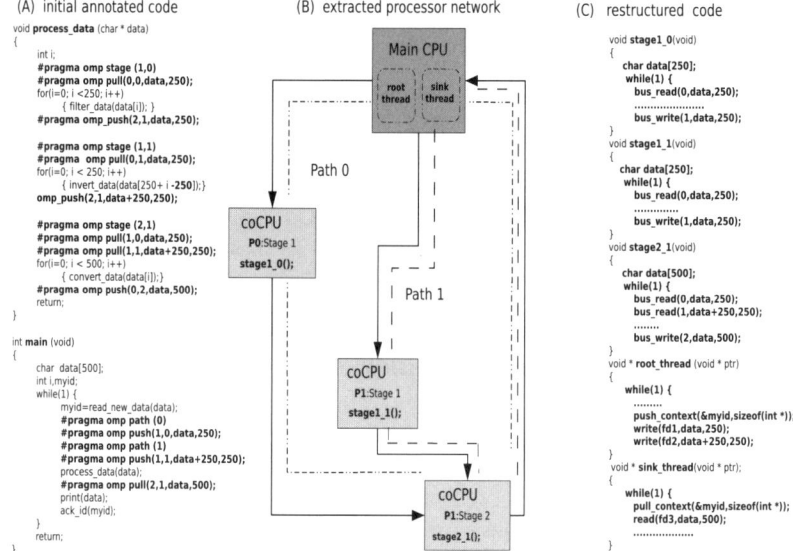

Fig. 2. Code annotation example

Figure 2-A shows a simple program with annotations denoting a pipelined execution whose structure is depicted in Figure 2-B. Figure 2-C shows the most relevant parts of the code generated for each segment, after going through the transformation explained in the sequel.

3.2 Code Transformation

Based on the location of the annotations in the source code, the program text is split into distinct segments that can be compiled separately. One segment is produced for each pipeline stage, to be executed on a separate coCPU. In addition, special *root* and *sink* segments are created to host the code before the first pipeline stage and after the last pipeline stage, respectively, as well as the code for loading and unloading the pipeline. The root and sink execute on the main CPU via two separate threads (it is possible to rely on standard multithreading support on the main CPU).

The original source code of the application may be structured using several functions which invoke each other along a conventional call chain. This does not pose a problem because there are no restrictions concerning the placement of annotations. It is namely possible to define more than one pipeline stages within a single function body as well as to define stages that cross function boundaries. Moreover, the first stage of the pipeline may be defined inside a function deep into the call chain. To deal with this case, each of the functions invoked until the first stage is reached, is split in two parts: the so-called *pre-subroutine* and *post-subroutine* which contains code to be executed before pushing data into the pipeline and after pulling data out of the pipeline, respectively. The generated root and sink segments contain these pre-subroutines and respectively post-subroutines in a suitably arranged call tree. The last stage may end within a function body, in which case the corresponding post-subroutine is executed by the sink; which may include additional function calls, if the programmer decides to end the last stage of the pipeline deep inside the call chain of the original program.

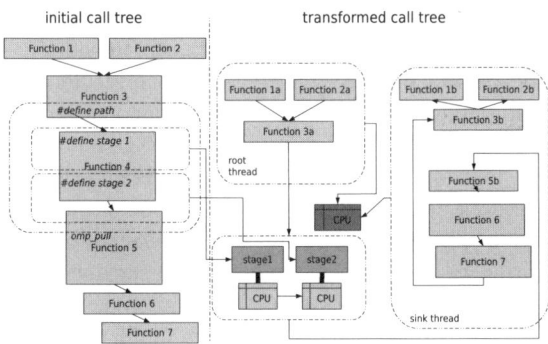

Fig. 3. Function separation; suffixes a and b denote pre- and post-subroutines, respectively

Figure 3 illustrates the approach. It shows a program with two call chains starting from f1 and f2, respectively, each involving five nested invocations of f3, f4, f5, f6 and f7. The annotations denote a 2-stage pipeline (without branches), the first stage defined from the beginning of f4 until the midst of f4, and the second stage defined from the midst of f4 until the midst of f5. As a result, four segments are produced: (i) the root containing f1a and f2a calling into f3a; (ii) the first stage containing the upper part of f4; (iii) the second stage containing the lower part of f4 and the upper part of f5; and (iv) the sink containing a call chain with f5b, f6 and f7 as well as the return chain, with f3b invoking either f1b or f2b depending on the flow taken by the root.

The transformation of the sequential code into a pipelined version makes it necessary to duplicate and properly update in every segment each variable referenced in the original program under the regime of sequential execution. For the segments that execute on the coCPUs, the programmer must explicitly transfer the values of such variables via the *push* and *pull* primitives, together with the rest of the data travelling downstream. For the pre- and post-subroutines in the root and sink segments, which execute in different threads on the main CPU, a FIFO *context queue* is employed for keeping the values of "shared" variables in sync between these two threads. When starting a new instance (iteration) of the computation, before pushing data into the pipeline, the root adds a new context entry in the queue with the proper values, and, conversely, the sink retrieves the next context entry from the queue and updates the corresponding variables before pulling data out of the pipeline.

The context queue mechanism is further exploited to handle call trees with branches. For example, in Figure 3, f3 can be called either from f1 or f2. In this case, the pre- and post-subroutines (f1a-f1b and f2a-f2b) are generated as usual, and a different integer value is assigned to each option. The value of the option taken at runtime by the root (f1a or f2a) is stored in the entry added to the context queue. When the sink retrieves the next context entry, it consults that value to pick the corresponding post-subroutine (f1b or f2b), using a switch statement properly placed in the returning function (f3b).

3.3 The Preprocessor

The transformation of the annotated source code and the generation of executable code for each application segment is performed using a 2-pass preprocessor. In the first pass, the preprocessor builds the function call tree, determines the number of pipeline paths and stages, and marks the functions associated with the corresponding entry/exit points. It also performs basic sanity checks to verify that the annotations are placed in a logically correct order, contain proper arguments and that the data exchanges between the stages are consistent. If errors are found, a report is generated and the tool exits. In the second pass, the preprocessor makes the changes to the source code, i.e., splits functions as needed, adds calls to properly manage the context information between the root and sink segment, and arranges for their execution via two separate *POSIX* threads. Also, the abstract data transfer directives found in the various code segments are substituted with the appropriate code (library calls) for performing the necessary communication between the CPUs on the target platform.

A separate source file that can be compiled independently is generated for each segment. This makes it possible to employ a customized CPU architecture and different runtime environment for each pipeline stage, subject to the capabilities and flexibility of the target platform. In any case, the preprocessor produces the executable for each stage by compiling and linking against the corresponding runtime. Finally, all executables along with corresponding platform configuration information are bundled in a single deployment unit.

The processing of annotations and most of the code transformation is orthogonal to the particular characteristics of the target platform. The main platform-specific part is the code that needs to be injected for sending and receiving data between segments, and the compiler that needs to be invoked for generating the executable for each segment. This allows the preprocessor to be implemented in a structured way so that it can be extended to support more targets, e.g., by adding "backends" for different multi-core systems (hard or soft, shared or distributed memory). In fact, support for the emulation and prototype FPGA-based platforms, discussed in Section 3.5 and Section 3.6, is implemented via such extensions.

3.4 Coding Restrictions

Besides using annotations in the expected way, the application code must conform to a few additional restrictions. Firstly, function invocation should be *explicit* so that the preprocessor can properly resolve the respective call tree at source level. Any function pointers in the code must be replaced by hand. Secondly, system calls may be issued *only* from code that will execute on the main CPU, i.e., the root and sink segments. This is because, according to our architecture model (Section 2.1), coCPUs are not connected to system peripherals and do not feature a full-fledged runtime environment.

One of the consequences of the latter restriction is that a pipeline segment is not allowed to invoke the standard dynamic memory allocation primitives. This is not as crucial as it seems though, for applications that are typically attractive to pipelining. In most cases, such programs simply allocate a fixed amount of memory in the beginning of the computation, hence the maximum required memory can be figured out by reading the source code. Else, a memory usage trace tool like *valgrind* [6] can be used to determine the memory requirements for typical inputs; but of course this does not guarantee error-free operation for all inputs. To make execution robust against memory overflows, one could introduce a dynamic memory management library especially crafted for the coCPU runtime, and let the preprocessor substitute the original invocations with calls to this API. So far we have managed to do without placing such support on the coCPUs, but this could be easily done, if needed.

3.5 Support for the Emulation Platform

To test a pipelined application and to assess the expected performance without running it on the target hardware, we have developed support for an emulation platform. This is implemented on top of an off-the-shelf Linux environment, by letting each pipeline segment run as a separate process. The *push* and *pull* annotations are replaced with functions that perform the data transfer via pipes. The preprocessor also inserts profiling routines at the proper locations in the source code. The executables for each segment are produced by invoking the off-the-shelf system compiler. Finally, a script is generated for initializing the corresponding process configuration and starting the application.

Code execution can be done on top of *GNU debugger* to catch and analyze runtime errors. One may use the *strace* tool to double check that system calls are issued only from within the root and sink segments. It is also possible to generate profiling data, providing feedback on how well-balanced the workload distribution is among the pipeline stages as well as the respective computation-to-communication ratios. The developer can use this information to re-partition the computation.

It is important to note that profiling data is only a hint, given that the ultimate target platform will typically have a different operating/runtime system for the main CPU and coCPUs, different main CPU and coCPU architectures, and a different data transfer mechanism (between CPUs). To improve the usefulness of profiling, we adjust data by taking into account the differences in the communication overhead and CPU computing capacity between the emulation and the target platform. Nevertheless, the reported figures continue to be a rough approximation because we do not take into account many other performance-related aspects, like CPU instruction set, instruction pipeline, data and instruction cache and peripheral access times.

3.6 Support for the FPGA-Based Prototype

Based on the pipeline structure defined by the programmer, the preprocessor generates information about the coCPU interconnection network along with the corresponding

FSL channel numbers and data transfer directions. The *push* and *pull* annotations are replaced with instructions for accessing the FSL. Also, code for registering with the *FlowControl* driver and properly blocking on the SIGUSR1 signal (see Section 2.2) is injected at the proper locations of the root and sink. The executables for the different code segments are generated for the respective CPUs and runtime environments. Specifically, the binary for the root and sink is linked to the uClinux system image and libraries. The binaries for the rest of the segments are generated for the coCPUs and are linked to our basic I/O system.

We have also developed a special platform mapper tool, which uses the initial platform description report to build a single deployment file, akin to the elf format, with all the binaries and the description for the coCPU configurations. The tool determines the required local memory size for each coCPU and transforms the initial platform description file to a Microblaze Hardware Specification (MHS) file. This is then used by the Xilinx Platform Studio toolchain to build the FPGA configuration bitstream.

4 Proof-of-Concept Application

We have used our framework to develop and test a pipelined version of *Tremor*, a fixed-point version of the *Ogg Vorbis* decoder [7] targetted at integer cores. The partitioning and execution of the pipelined version of *Tremor* are discussed in the sequel.

4.1 Profiling and Partitioning

The first step was to compile *Tremor* with profiling extensions for a normal Linux environment and run it to decode a variety of input sample files. *GNU prof* was used to analyze the generated information, revealing that 80% of the CPU cycles are spent on the inverse discrete cosine transform (DCT) related functions. The rest of the CPU cycles are spent on file processing and soundcard interaction, which cannot be accelerated using our approach. The DCT-related processing comprises two main parts, the butterflies calculations and the bit reverse calculations, which can be naturally processed via two different pipeline stages. To balance the workload, the first calculation was further split in two parts, giving a total of three stages.

We subsequently changed the *Tremor* source by removing function pointers and annotating the code to define the desired pipeline structure. The preprocessor was used to generate executables for the emulation platform. The profiling information that was generated when running this code for various inputs indicated that the root and sink accounted for 20% of the workload whereas the three pipeline stages accounted for 28%, 25.4% and $26,6\%$, respectively. The communication to computation ratio was reported to be $1.8*10^{-2}$ for the root and sink, $1*10^{-2}$ for the first and third stage, and $0.8*10^{-2}$ for the second stage. Given this profile, the pipelined version of *Tremor* would be expected to achieve a $3.57x$ speedup in a homogeneous 4-processor system, such as our FPGA-based prototype (the main CPU and all coCPUs are Microblazes).

4.2 Performance Measurements

We have measured the performance of the original sequential version vs the pipelined version of *Tremor* for decoding an indicative input file holding 102656 data samples

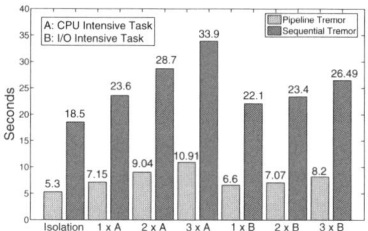 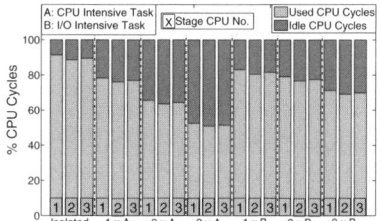

Fig. 4. Performance of pipelined vs sequential *Tremor* for isolated & mixed executions

Fig. 5. CPU utilization of the pipelined *Tremor* for isolated and mixed executions

(the file resides on the flash). To outline the performance impact of concurrent workload on the main CPU we use two types of dummy tasks: type A that performs CPU intensive computations, and type B that performs periodic I/O access to the flash (reads-writes for $50ms$, every $100ms$). Note that flash I/O is CPU driven, using polling, thus it also occupies the CPU. The execution time of each such task is set to $5secs$, approximately matching the execution time of the pipelined *Tremor* version. Figure 4 shows the times for executing Tremor in isolation as well as concurrently with one, two and three instances of each task type. The recorded utilization of the coCPUs (for the pipelined version) during these executions is shown in Figure 5.

When executing in an unloaded system, the pipelined version is $3.49x$ faster than the sequential version, which is close to the $3.57x$ speedup that was estimated using the profiling data of the emulation environment. The performance of the pipelined version drops when loading the main CPU with extra (dummy) work, with CPU intensive tasks having a more negative effect than I/O intensive tasks. This degradation is confirmed by the respective idleness of the pipeline stages; as the main CPU gets increasingly loaded, the number of pipeline stalls (failure to push data into or pull out of the pipeline) grows as well, leading to more idle cycles in the coCPUs. Notably, the extra load on the main CPU also affects the performace of the sequential version, but (in our experiments) this impact is less noticeable than for the pipelined version because dummy tasks finish before the completion of the sequential version, which can fully exploit the main CPU thereafter. Overall, the pipelined version outperforms the sequential version as expected, but it is also sensitive to other tasks executing on the main CPU.

Taking a second look at the results of the pipelined version in the case of isolated execution, it can be seen that the idleness of the coCPUs closely follows the load distribution recorded using the emulation environment for an unloaded system. However, contrary to the profiling data which indicate that the first stage is the bottleneck of the computation, i.e., works at full speed, in reality the first stage coCPU remains idle for 8.6% of the execution time. Further investigating into this matter, we confirmed that the *root* thread is burdened with extra overheads such as time consuming memory allocation on our MMU-less platform and access to the flash (concurrently to the *sink* thread), which are not captured in the emulation environment. As a consequence, the main CPU becomes the actual bottleneck and cannot feed the pipeline fast enough, leading to the idleness of the first stage coCPU. This also explains the difference between the estimated vs actual speedup. Of course, this situation deteriorates as the load on the main CPU increases.

5 Related Work

The ideal target for our framework would be the Ambric PPA architecture [1] integrated with a master CPU that can run a full-fledged OS. Currently on Ambric, the programmer separates the application into high-level processing objects which can be developed independently and can execute asynchronously with each other, at their own speed, on their own dedicated processor core and defines their interconnections. Our framework extracts programmer identified pipeline flows out of existing sequential applications and each independent stage could be mapped to an Ambric object with proper backend changes. This way our approach could be used to quickly transform existing codebase for the Ambric architecture rather than coding everything from scratch. Since Ambric building blocks are processor cores, we believe that the integration of PPA functionality in an OS context is also important. Cell processor [8] could have been another possible target for our framework. But in this case, given that all cores, apart from private local memories, share the main system memory, the code transformation approach can be explored in the context of more appropriate programming models [9] instead of distributed memory pipelines.

StreamIt [10] is a high-level programming model which enables the compiler to automate tasks such as partitioning, load balancing, layout and memory management. This approach is radically different from conventional sequential programming, thus applications have to be developed from scratch, in terms of both logic and code. Message-passing [11] and POSIX threads [12] are widely used to implement parallel programs, but do not directly support pipeline- or stream-based applications. Taking a different approach, *OpenMP* [5] is a specification for a set of compiler directives, library routines and environment variables which can be used to specify the desired level of parallelism. Inserting annotations to build parallel versions of a sequential program requires minimal changes to the source code.

In [13] code annotations are proposed to achieve coarse grained pipelined parallelism. A dynamic analysis tool is used to help the programmer balance pipeline stage workload, and the underlying runtime support is used to fork the pipeline stages as different private memory processes that communicate via *Unix* pipes. Pipeline parallelism is also exploited in [14] using the techniques of Decoupled Software Pipelining [15], in conjunction with thread-level speculation to opportunistically execute multiple loop iterations in parallel. Both approaches seemingly assume a dedicated execution environment where all system resources are used to serve one pipelined application at a time, without any contention due to other concurrently executing applications.

6 Conclusions

We have presented support for developing and executing coarse-grained application pipelines for PPAs in conjunction with a general purpose OS, and discussed a proof-of-concept application which was developed using our tools and executes successfully on our FPGA-based prototype platform. The main contributions of our work are: (i) annotations that can be used to indicate the desired pipeline structure in the source code; (ii) a preprocessor that performs the necessary code transformations to produce code segments that can be compiled separately for execution on different CPUs, with the necessary hooks for plugging platform-specific backends; (iii) a complete working prototype platform on an FPGA, with the necessary preprocessor extensions and all the mechanisms in place that are needed to load and execute such pipelined programs.

Acknowledgments. This work is part of the 03ED918 research project implemented within the framework of the "Reinforcement Programme of Human Research Manpower" (PENED) (75% from E.U. Fund and 25% from the Greek GSRT).

References

1. Butts, M., Jones, A.M., Wasson, P.: A structural object programming model, architecture, chip and tools for reconfigurable computing. In: FCCM 2007 (2007)
2. Atmark Techno Inc., http://www.atmark-techno.com Suzaku Series
3. Williams, J.: The Microblaze-uClinux kernel port Project, http://www.itee.uq.edu.au
4. Syrivelis, D., Lalis, S.: System- and application-level support for runtime hardware reconfiguration on soc platforms. In: USENIX ATC, General Track, pp. 315–327 (2006)
5. Mattson, T.G.: How good is openmp. Sci. Program. 11(2), 81–93 (2003)
6. Nethercote, N., Seward, J.: Valgrind: a framework for heavyweight dynamic binary instrumentation. SIGPLAN Not. 42(6), 89–100 (2007)
7. xiph open source community, T.: Tremor Ogg Vorbis decoder, http://wiki.xiph.org
8. Gschwind, M.: Chip multiprocessing and the cell broadband engine. In: CF 2006: Proceedings of the 3rd conference on Computing frontiers, pp. 1–8 (2006)
9. Gschwind, M., Erb, D., Manning, S., Nutter, M.: An open source environment for cell broadband engine system software. Computer 40(6), 37–47 (2007)
10. Thies, W., Karczmarek, M., Amarasinghe, S.P.: Streamit: A language for streaming applications. In: Computational Complexity, pp. 179–196 (2002)
11. Forum, M.P.I.: MPI: A message-passing interface standard. Technical Report UT-CS-94-230 (1994)
12. Mueller, F.: A library implementation of posix threads under unix. In: In Proceedings of the USENIX Conference, pp. 29–41 (1993)
13. Thies, W., Chandrasekhar, V., Amarasinghe, S.: A practical approach to exploiting coarse-grained pipeline parallelism in c programs. In: MICRO, pp. 356 369 (2007)
14. Bridges, M.J., Vachharajani, N., Zhang, Y., Jablin, T., August, D.I.: Revisiting the sequential programming model for multi-core. In: MICRO (2007)
15. Vachharajani, N., Rangan, R., Raman, E., Bridges, M.J., Ottoni, G., August, D.I.: Speculative decoupled software pipelining. In: PACT (2007)

Parallelization Approaches for Hardware Accelerators – Loop Unrolling Versus Loop Partitioning

Frank Hannig, Hritam Dutta, and Jürgen Teich

Hardware/Software Co-Design, Department of Computer Science,
University of Erlangen-Nuremberg, Germany

Abstract. State-of-the-art behavioral synthesis tools barely have high-level transformations in order to achieve highly parallelized implementations. If any, they apply loop unrolling to obtain a higher throughput. In this paper, we employ the PARO behavioral synthesis tool which has the unique ability to perform both loop unrolling or loop partitioning. Loop unrolling replicates the loop kernel and exposes the parallelism for hardware implementation, whereas partitioning tiles the loop program onto a regular array consisting of tightly coupled processing elements. The usage of the same design tool for both the variants enables for the first time, a quantitative evaluation of the two approaches for reconfigurable architectures with help of computationally intensive algorithms selected from different benchmarks. Superlinear speedups in terms of throughput are accomplished for the processor array approach. In addition, area and power cost are reduced.

1 Introduction

Industrial, scientific, and multimedia applications are characterized by a growing need for computational power and stringent constraints on power consumption. Standard desktop, server, or embedded processors are often not suitable for these applications, because they are either expensive, have a too high power consumption, or do not provide enough performance in order to fulfill the user's requirements. For that reason, there has always been the idea to accelerate the execution by means of special hardware support. In this regard, several different solutions have been proposed over time. Since most computationally intensive algorithms feature a high inherent parallelism, many techniques were developed that focus on exploiting parallel processing capabilities in order to accelerate the execution of an application. All standard processors provide fine-grained parallelism by executing a small amount of machine instructions in parallel. The parallelization is done either implicitly by the processor or explicitly by the compiler for so-called very long instruction word (VLIW) processors. Furthermore, many processors provide a set of instructions that work on several data words concurrently (single instruction multiple data, SIMD). The availability of reconfigurable logic platforms like field programmable gate arrays (FPGAs) allows for implementation of custom hardware accelerators. In contrast to the general purpose architectures, these systems are usually application-specific, that is, they can only execute a single program or are only programmable to a very limited extent.

The importance of time-to-market considerations and time-consuming and error-prone manual implementations of special-purpose hardware accelerators motivates the need for high-level synthesis tools. The major aim of such tools is to automatically generate the dedicated accelerators subject to performance, cost, and power constraints from their corresponding algorithm description. The existing transformations in many such tools are based on compilation approaches from the DSP world. *Loop unrolling* is a major optimization transformation which exposes parallelism in a loop program. Loop unrolling by a factor n expands the loop kernel by copying $n - 1$ consecutive iterations. Then, the mapping tools schedule and synthesize the unrolled dataflow graphs for generating the hardware accelerators. This also leads to a design space exploration problem because of different factors available for partial loop unrolling [1].

Another approach for generating a special class of hardware accelerators called VLSI processor arrays for computation intensive algorithms borrows ideas from parallelization in the polytope model [2] and the generation of array architectures. These architectures consist of a regular arrangement of rather simple processor elements. The *projection* is an important transformation in this approach for obtaining full-size processor array descriptions from a given nested loop program. This corresponds to full loop unrolling in terms of resource usage. *Partitioning* is another necessary transformation for mapping loops onto reduced-size arrays in order to meet the resource constraints. Well known partitioning techniques are *tiling* and *clustering* [3]. Partitioning corresponds to partial loop unrolling.

In this paper, we study and compare the two different methodologies of loop unrolling from the high-level synthesis approach and loop partitioning (processor array approach). In the next section, a brief overview of related work and state-of-the-art in hardware synthesis is presented. In Section 3, the PARO design flow and tool is introduced. A concise description of the two loop transformations follows in Section 4. In Section 5, the quantitative analysis of the transformations with help of benchmarks is presented. Finally in Section 6, conclusions and an outlook are given.

2 Related Work

While software compilers are used in every day life by engineers, there still exist only few and restricted tools for the synthesis of hardware implementations from high-level algorithm descriptions. Commercial examples of such systems are Catapult-C from Mentor Graphics [4], Forte Cynthesizer [5], or PICO Express from Synfora [6]. Apart from commercial systems, there exist several C-based synthesis approaches in academia. For instance, the SPARK [7] synthesis methodology which is particularly targeted to control-intensive signal processing applications. All aforementioned design tools start from a subset of sequential C or C++ code. Starting with sequential languages has the disadvantage that their semantics force a lot of restrictions on the execution order of the program and language subset. Furthermore, most existing tools do not allow high-level program transformations in order to match the input program to given architecture constraints (like maximum available memory or I/O bandwidth), or only to a limited extend. Other academic behavioral synthesis approaches try to avoid the restrictions of sequential languages by using different programming and execution models [8, 9].

Loop unrolling has been studied in detail with respect to resource usage and performance in [1]. In [10], the authors study loop unrolling in high-level synthesis taking the controller delay into account.

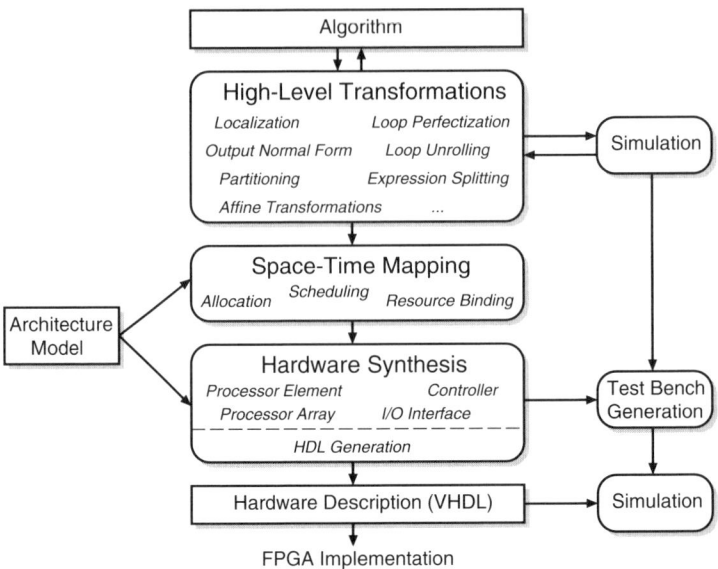

Fig. 1. Design flow for mapping algorithms to hardware accelerators

3 Design Flow

PARO [11] is a design system project for modeling, transformation, optimization, and hardware synthesis for a class of computationally intensive loop programs. The goal of the project is the automatic synthesis of dedicated, massively parallel processor arrays which may be implemented on fine-grained reconfigurable platforms like FPGAs or custom application-specific integrated circuits (ASIC).

An overview of the PARO design flow design flow is depicted in Fig. 1. As design entry we developed a functional programming language. The class of algorithms that can be expressed by a PARO program is based on the mathematical model of *dynamic piecewise linear/regular algorithms (DPLA)* [12]. The language consists of a set of recurrence equations defined for a multi-dimensional iteration space as it occurs in nested loop programs. When modeling signal processing algorithms, a designer naturally considers mathematical equations. Hence, the programming is very intuitive. To allow irregularities in a program, an equation may have iteration and run-time dependent conditions. Furthermore, big operators (also often called reductions) which implement mathematical operators such as $\sum$ or $\prod$ can be used. In contrast to the common mathematical notation, the iteration space is not required to be 1-dimensional, as the following image processing code fragment of a 2-D Gaussian window filter demonstrates.

```
w[0,0] = 1; w[0,1] = 2; w[0,2] = 1;
w[1,0] = 2; w[1,1] = 4; w[1,2] = 2;
w[2,0] = 1; w[2,1] = 2; w[2,2] = 1;
h[x,y] = SUM}[i>=0 and i<=2 and j>=0 and j<=2](pic_in[x+i,y+j] * w[i,j]);
pic_out[x,y] = h[x,y] >> 4;   // divided by 16
```

A program is thus a system of quantified equations that implicitly defines a function of output variables in dependence of input variables. Some other semantical properties are particular to the input language. *Single assignment property*: Any instance of an indexed variable appears at most once on the left hand side of an equation. *Computability*: There exists a partial ordering of equations such that any instance of a variable appearing on the right side of an equation earlier appears in the left hand side in the partial ordering.

A given program is fed to the PARO system where first a set of equivalence preserving high-level transformations is applied. Examples of such transformations are:

- *Localization* [13], which replaces global data dependencies that usually introduce high hardware cost into local dependencies where data is *propagated* through the processor array.
- *Partitioning* and *loop unrolling*, in order to match the algorithm to given hardware constraints like area, available memory, or I/O bandwidth.
- *Loop perfectization* [14] to transform non-perfectly nested loop programs in perfectly nested loop programs.
- Well-known algorithmic optimizations [15] like affine transformations of the iteration space, dead-code elimination, common sub-expression elimination, strength reduction of operators (usage of shift and add instead of multiply or divide), constant/variable propagation, and others.

During the transformation step, the program may be simulated in order to verify the algorithm and also the correctness of the transformations that were applied. Next *space-time mapping* is performed, that is, every computation in the algorithm is assigned a processor element and a functional unit within that processor element (space), as well as the start time for execution. A prerequisite of space-time mapping is a model of the target architecture, for example, which functional units are available and what are their execution times. Afterwards, the space-time mapped program is synthesized. The hardware synthesis step generates a completely platform and language independent register transfer level (RTL) description of the hardware. This RTL model is further optimized and, depending on the selected backend and target platform (e.g., FPGA type), finally converted into HDL code of choice.

4 Problem Statement

The synthesis of loop programs on hardware has been a deeply studied problem. The two different parallelization approaches for resource constrained mapping onto hardware are loop unrolling and partitioning (e.g., tiling and clustering). Fig. 2(a) shows the iteration space without data dependencies of a 4-tap FIR filter which is used to illustrate the fundamental difference between the two approaches. The pseudo-code of an N-tap FIR filter is given in Fig. 3.

Figure 2(b) shows the loop unrolling approach, where the innermost loop is completely unrolled and mapped onto a processor element (PE) with 4 MUL and ADD units. In addition to full loop unrolling, one can partially unroll the loop nest for an iteration variable. The unroll factor u denotes how often the loop body is duplicated. In

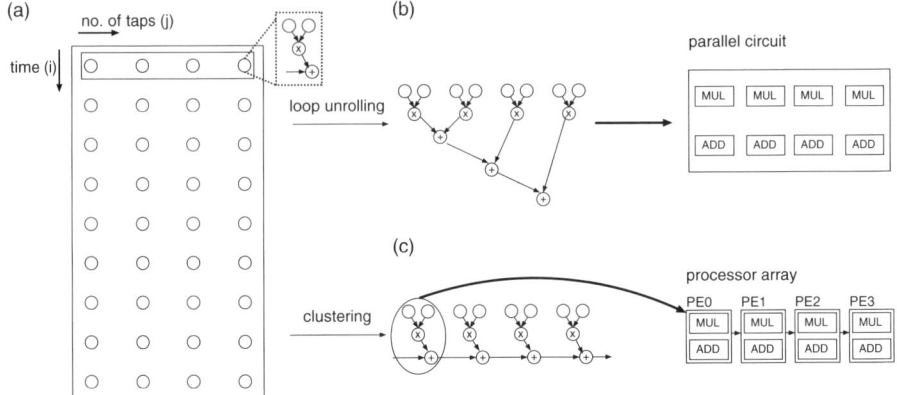

Fig. 2. (a) Iteration space of a loop program. (b) Synthesis problem for partially unrolled loop. (c) Synthesis problem for the loop program on clustering.

```
FORALL (i >= 0 and i <= T-1)           // T: number of input samples
{ FORALL (j >= 0 and j <= N-1)         // N: number of filter taps
  { IF (i==0) THEN a[i,j] = a_in[j];   // Read filter coefficient
           ELSE a[i,j] = a[i-1,j];
    IF (j==0) THEN
    { u[i,j] = u_in[i];                // Read input sample
      y[i,j] = a[i,j] * u[i,j];
    }
    ELSE
    { y[i,j] = y[i,j-1] + a[i,j] * u[i,j];
      IF (i==0) THEN u[i,j] = 0;
             ELSE u[i,j] = u[i-1,j-1]; // Enables data reuse
    }
    IF (j == N-1) y_out[i] = y[i,j];   // Write output
  }
}
```

Fig. 3. Pseudo-code of an N-tap FIR filter

Fig. 4, the iteration variable j of the N-tap FIR filter is unrolled by a factor of 2. The IF conditions in the pseudo-code are to enable data-reuse within the generated hardware. This helps to combat the memory bottleneck for compute intensive applications.

Partitioning is a well known transformation which covers the index space of computation using congruent hyperplanes, hyperquaders, or parallelepipeds called *tiles* [3,16]. Well known partitioning techniques are multiprojection, LSGP (local sequential global parallel, often also referred as clustering or blocking) and LPGS (local parallel global sequential, also referred as tiling). Fig. 2(c) shows the partitioning approach with help of clustering, where the iterations within the tile are processed in parallel by 4 PEs. Each

```
FORALL (i >= 0 and i <= T-1)
{ FORALL (j >= 0 and j <= N/2-1)
  { IF (i==0) THEN
     { a0[i,j] = a_in0[j];
       a1[i,j] = a_in1[j];
       u1[i,j] = 0;
     }
    ELSE
     { a0[i,j] = a0[i-1,j];
       a1[i,j] = a1[i-1,j];
       u1[i,j] = u0[i-1,j];
     }
    IF (j==0) THEN
     { u0[i,j] = u_in[i];
       y0[i,j] = a0[i,j] * u0[i,j];
     }
    ELSE
     { y0[i,j] = y1[i,j-1] + a0[i,j] * u0[i,j];
       IF (i==0) THEN u0[i,j] = 0;
                 ELSE u0[i,j] = u1[i-1,j-1];
     }
    y1[i,j] = y0[i,j] + a1[i,j] * u1[i,j];
    IF (j == N-1) y_out[i] = y1[i,j];
  }
}
```

Fig. 4. FIR filter unrolled by a factor of $u=2$

```
FORALL (i >= 0 and i <= T-1)
{ FORALL (j >= 0 and j <= P-1)          // P: number of PEs
  { FORALL (k >= 0 and k <= N/P-1)      // Iteration over different tiles
    { IF (i==0) THEN
       { a[i,j,k] = a_in[j+k];
       }
      ELSE
       { a[i,j,k] = a[i-1,j,k];
         IF (j>0)      THEN u[i,j,k] = u[i-1,j-1,k];      // Intra-tile comm.
         ELSEIF (k>0) THEN u[i,j,k] = u[i-1,j+P-1,k-1];  // Inter-tile comm.
       }
      IF (j==0 and k==0) THEN
       { u[i,j,k] = u_in[i];
         y[i,j,k] = a[i,j,k] * u[i,j,k];
       }
      ELSEIF (i==0) THEN u[i,j,k] = 0;
      IF (j>0)      THEN y[i,j,k] = y[i,j-1,k] + a[i,j,k] * u[i,j,k];
      ELSEIF (k>0) THEN y[i,j,k] = y[i,j+P-1,k-1] + x[i,j,k];
      IF (j==P-1 and k==N/P-1) y_out[i] = y1[i,j,k];
    }
  }
}
```

Fig. 5. Partitioned FIR filter

PE contains one MUL and one ADD unit. The tiles are processed *global sequentially*. The partitioned FIR filter is shown in Fig. 5.

The major questions that need to be answered on basis of several algorithms are:

- What is the quantitative trade-off in terms of hardware cost, performance, and power between loop unrolling and partitioning?
- What should be the optimal granularity of resources in parallel processors for efficient mapping?

In the next section, we answer the above questions by quantitative analysis of reconfigurable hardware generated for the transformed loop programs by the PARO design system. The resource constrained scheduling problem for the dataflow graph for both the variants is solved by the same mixed integer linear programming (MILP) approach [12] which leads to minimal latency.

5 Experiments and Quantitative Evaluation

In this section, we compare the two methods described before with respect to resource usage, performance (clock frequency and throughput), and power. Several experiments with different setups have been performed. Also the difference between the usage of dedicated DSP elements of the target devices or the synthesis purely in LUTs has been studied. The synthesis results were obtained from *Xilinx ISE 9.1* for a *Xilinx Virtex 4* FPGA (xc4vlx100-12ff1513). For the estimation of the dynamic power, *Xilinx XPower* was used in combination with the *post-place & route simulation models* of the designs. The usage of BRAMs was disabled throughout all experiments except for the matrix multiplication where we allowed BRAMs for the storage of intermediate data.

In the first experiment a 8-bit 64-tap FIR filter is considered. The coefficients of the filter are reconfigurable, that means, they were implemented as inputs. The results are shown in Table 1, where the first column denotes the unroll factor u in case of the standard high-level synthesis (HLS) approach and in case of a processor array implementation the number of processing elements. This number corresponds also to the total number of available multipliers and adders for the data-path implementation in both variants. The results for the HLS approach and for the processor follows in the

Table 1. Resource usage and performance of different 64-tap FIR filter implementations

u / #PE [no.]	HLS					Processor Array									DSP48 slices [no.]
	LUTs [no.]	FFs [no.]	Clock [MHz]	Through-put [MB/s]	Power [mW]	LUTs [no.]	Diff. [%]	FFs [no.]	Diff. [%]	Clock [MHz]	Diff. [%]	Through-put [MB/s]	Power [mW]	Diff. [%]	
2	207	152	189	5.6	19	242	16.9	154	1.3	218	15.3	6.5	23	21.1	0
4	366	252	197	11.7	24	395	7.9	256	1.6	219	11.2	13.1	29	20.8	0
8	723	501	201	24.0	37	734	1.5	471	-6.0	224	11.4	26.7	41	10.8	0
16	1428	999	168	40.1	49	1401	-1.9	861	-13.8	218	29.8	52.0	62	26.5	0
32	3037	2143	164	78.2	93	2748	-9.5	1698	-20.8	210	28.0	100.1	103	10.8	0
64	6681	4540	156	148.8	189	4907	26.6	4321	-4.8	222	42.3	211.7	187	-1.1	0
2	150	126	163	4.9	18	185	23.3	140	11.1	231	41.7	6.9	27	50.0	2
4	215	192	192	11.4	27	249	15.8	224	16.7	213	10.9	12.7	32	18.5	4
8	347	324	193	23.0	38	413	19.0	396	22.2	218	13.0	26.0	47	23.7	8
16	636	727	185	44.1	60	738	16.0	736	1.2	185	0.0	44.1	64	6.7	16
32	1471	1623	182	86.8	114	1382	-6.1	1418	-12.6	212	16.5	101.1	130	14.0	32
64	3284	3333	143	136.4	240	2631	-19.9	2794	-16.2	192	34.3	183.1	219	-8.8	64

table. Finally, in the last column of the table, the number of consumed DSP48 slices is given. Two columns depict the cost in terms of number of look-up tables (LUTs) and slice flip-flops (FFs), two other columns represent the performance metrics clock frequency and throughput followed by the dynamic power consumption. Next to each column (LUTs, FFs, clock, power) of the processor array implementations, the relative difference compared with the HLS approach is given. Since the throughput is proportional to the clock frequency, the relative difference is the same and is omitted in the table.

In the upper half of Table 1, the usage of dedicated DSP48 slices was disabled. Here, for the lowest resource usage ($u = 2$), the processor array implementation is more than 15% faster than the unrolled variant but also for a higher price, 16.9% more LUTs and 1.3% more flip-flops. Note that the power dissipation is directly related to the clock frequency. It can be noticed that for increasing u, the clock frequency of the HLS approach is decreasing whereas for the processor array implementations it is almost constant. It seems that the place and route routines do not perform so well for larger designs (flattened register-transfer circuits), whereas the clustering of operations into several processor elements performs much better in terms of clock speed. A closer look at the placed and routed designs shows the reasons for the lower clock frequency and for the higher amount of LUTs for the loop unrolled versions compared with the partitioned versions. The reasons are longer wires and more multiplexing.

In a second run of experiments the multiplications in the FIR algorithms were implemented by the Xilinx DSP48 slices. The results for different unroll factors and number of processing elements, respectively, are also shown in Table 1. Because of the predetermined location of the DSP48 slices, the values fluctuating more than in the previous case (no DSP48 slices). However, apart from one outlier, the throughput of the processor array approach is 11 to 42% higher as compared with the unrolled approach. In Fig. 6, the throughput itself, normalized by the gate count, and the throughput per mW is shown.

In Fig. 7, the speedup characterizes the performance gain with respect to the throughput for the FIR filter algorithm. The cost increase is related to the gate count of the designs. In the single PE solution of the FIR filter, the 64 iterations are executed sequentially within one PE. For this solution both throughput and cost are normalized to 1.0. Partitioning the algorithm to 2, 4, ..., 64 PEs theoretically enables also a higher throughput by the same factor. The superlinear speedup in case of the processor array implementations is because of the increasing clock frequency for larger numbers of PEs. The moderate cost and power increase is caused by the decreasing amount of intermediate data which have to be stored internally in the processor array.

Since the difference for the $u = 64$ implementations was tremendous, several other fully unrolled/full size versions have been studied. The results are shown in Fig. 8. In case when enabling the DSP48 slices, the throughput for the unrolled approach sharply falls for higher numbers of taps. Note, that these results should not be used to compare the achievable throughput between DSP48 and LUT-based implementations since an optimal pipelined version of the DSP48 slices had not been used in the experiments.

As second algorithm a DCT width 8-bit I/O and internally up to 16 bits datapath was studied. The results for different numbers of available multipliers implemented in

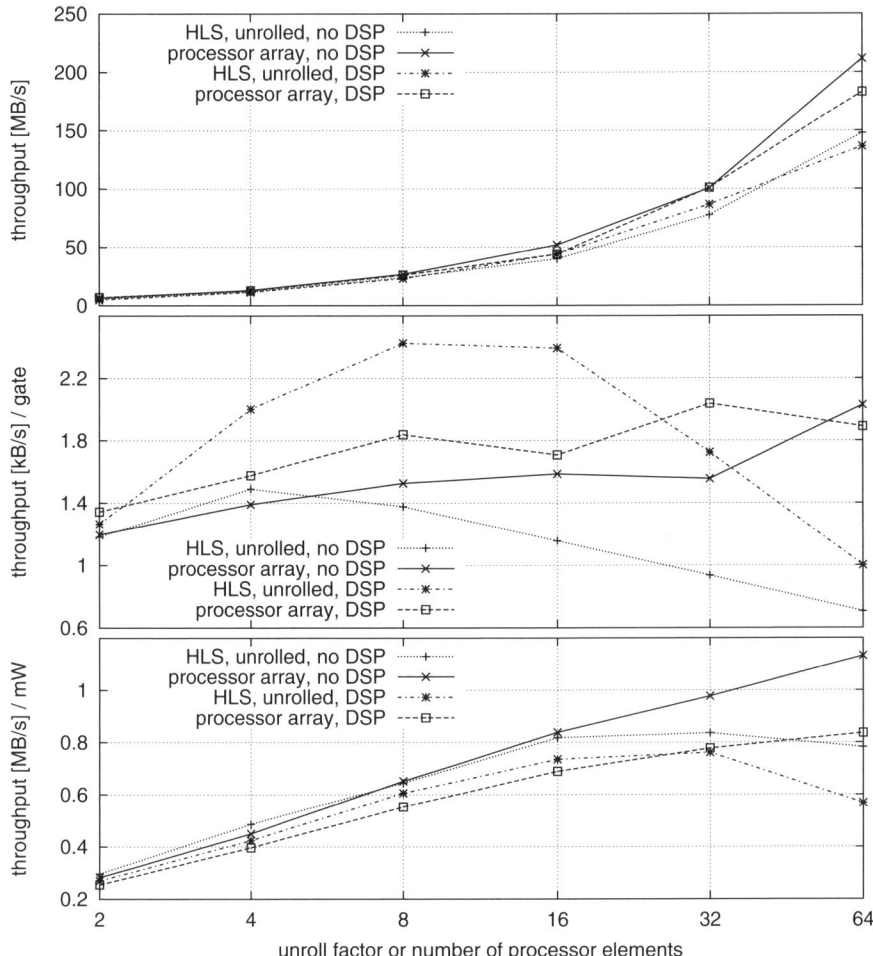

Fig. 6. Throughput, throughput per gate, and the throughput per mW for different unroll factors and numbers of processor elements, respectively

DSP48 slices are shown in Table 2. Unlike the FIR filter, the DCT has no loop carried data dependencies. The loop body of the DCT was unrolled four times and a processor array consisting of 4 processing elements was considered, respectively. The unrolled loop body contains 96 multiplications therefore the results for the cost (LUTs, FFs) of the last experiment, where 96 multipliers were available, are quite close. However, the processor array implementation has in three of four cases a better throughput, up to 21% along with a power dissipation increased only by 11%.

Lastly, an algorithm for the multiplication of two 64×64 matrices was considered. Using the processor array approach, again a higher clock frequency and throughput as compared with the loop unrolling approach using the same number of resources (multipliers and adders) is achieved (see Table 3). The higher area cost in terms of LUTs

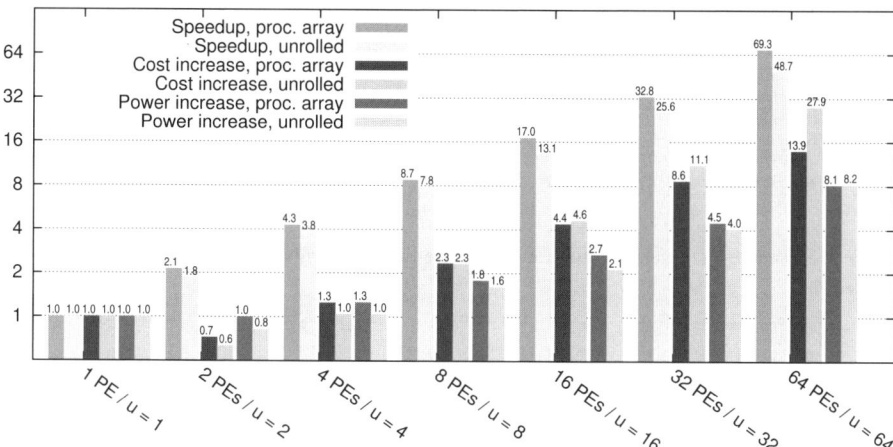

Fig. 7. Speedup, cost and power increase for different FIR filter implementations

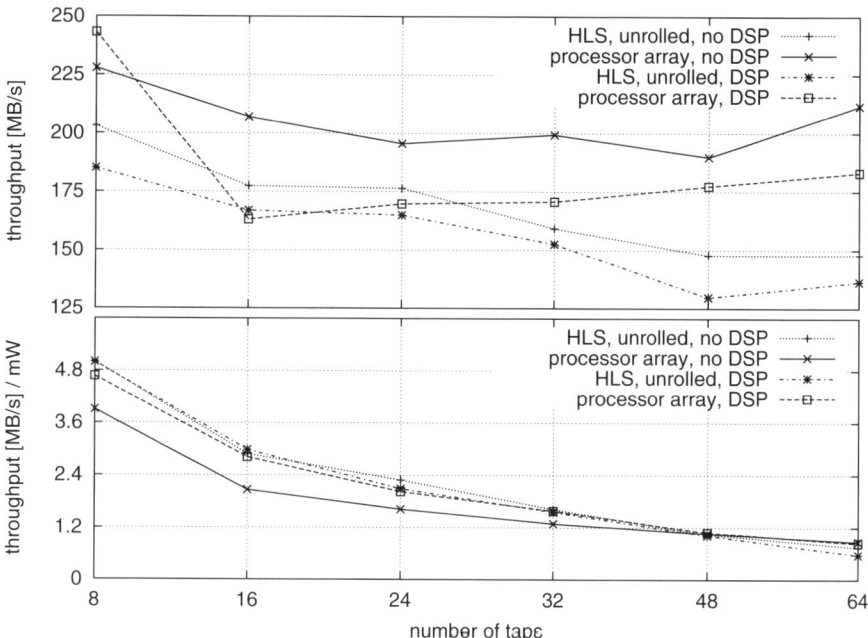

Fig. 8. Throughput of different fully unrolled and full size FIR filter implementations

for the processor array approach is caused by the control overhead when partitioning the algorithm onto several processor elements. 8 BRAMs are instantiated for data reuse for both the variants.

Table 2. Resource usage and performance of different DCT implementations

no of mult.	HLS					Processor Array									DSP48 slices [no.]
	LUTs [no.]	FFs [no.]	Clock [MHz]	Through-put [MB/s]	Power [mW]	LUTs [no.]	Diff. [%]	FFs [no.]	Diff. [%]	Clock [MHz]	Diff. [%]	Through-put [MB/s]	Power [mW]	Diff. [%]	
16	3935	1717	152	48.3	438	3811	-3.2	1760	2.5	163	7.2	51.8	483	10.3	16
32	3944	2644	186	118.3	528	3808	-3.4	2543	-3.8	175	-5.9	111.3	638	20.8	32
48	3590	3141	185	176.4	700	3457	-3.7	3080	-1.9	224	21.1	213.6	778	11.1	48
96	3023	3556	190	362.4	867	3067	1.5	3600	1.2	207	8.9	394.8	880	1.5	96

Table 3. Resource usage and performance of different matrix multiplication for $N = 64$ implementations

u #PE [no.]	HLS				Processor Array						
	LUTs [no.]	FFs [no.]	Clock [MHz]	Throughput [MB/s]	LUTs [no.]	Diff. [%]	FFs [no.]	Diff. [%]	Clock [MHz]	Diff. [%]	Throughput [MB/s]
2	784	474	148	9.2	895	14.2%	603	27.2%	153	3.4%	9.5
4	1459	812	145	18.2	1629	11.7%	1082	33.3%	149	2.8%	18.6
8	3049	1724	123	30.8	3030	-0.1%	2038	18.2%	152	23.6%	38.1
16	5937	3166	125	62.4	5895	-0.1%	3991	26.0%	172	37.6%	85.8

6 Conclusions and Future Work

In existing behavioral synthesis tools, loop unrolling is applied in order to achieve higher throughput. Unique to the PARO system is the ability to consider both loop unrolling and processor array designs. The usage of the same design tool enabled, for the first time, a fair quantitative evaluation of the two approaches for a set of computational intensive algorithms. Because of its regularity and the clustering of resources into several processing elements, the processor array approach achieves in all experiments a far better throughput, up to 42% more compared with loop unrolling. For the cost and power metrics it can be noted that for smaller designs the loop unrolling results are better whereas for larger designs the processor array approach is better.

In the future, we would like to automatically elaborate when loop unrolling and when the processor array approach should be applied. This is important to obtain for small as well as for large problem instances and different requirements (throughput, cost, power) optimal designs. Since the considered metrics are contradicting, the automatic exploration of different mapping and transformation variants will be of great importance to further shorten the design process of hardware accelerators.

The PARO design flow is also capable of targeting a new class of architectures, so-called *weakly programmable processor arrays* (WPPA) [17]. WPPAs are a generic architecture template consisting of a tightly coupled, reconfigurable VLIW processor arrays. In this context, we would like to study the trade-off between VLIW word size and number of processors.

References

1. Cardoso, J.M.P., Diniz, P.C.: Modeling Loop Unrolling: Approaches and Open Issues. In: Pimentel, A.D., Vassiliadis, S. (eds.) SAMOS 2004. LNCS, vol. 3133, pp. 224–233. Springer, Heidelberg (2004)
2. Lengauer, C.: Loop Parallelization in the Polytope Model. In: Best, E. (ed.) CONCUR 1993. LNCS, vol. 715, pp. 398–416. Springer, Heidelberg (1993)

3. Wolfe, M.: High Performance Compilers for Parallel Computing. Addison-Wesley Inc., Reading (1996)
4. Mentor Graphics Corp., http://www.mentor.com
5. Forte Design Systems, http://www.forteds.com
6. Synfora, Inc., http://www.synfora.com
7. Gupta, S., Dutt, N., Gupta, R., Nicolau, A.: SPARK: A High-Level Synthesis Framework for Applying Parallelizing Compiler Transformations. In: Proceedings of the International Conference on VLSI Design, pp. 461–466 (January 2003)
8. Guillou, A., Quinton, P., Risset, T.: Hardware Synthesis for Multi-Dimensional Time. In: Proceedings of IEEE 14th International Conference on Application-specific Systems, Architectures, and Processors (ASAP), Los Alamitos, CA, USA, pp. 40–50 (2003)
9. Zissulescu, C., Kienhuis, B., Deprettere, E.: Expression Synthesis in Process Networks generated by LAURA. In: Proceedings IEEE 16th International Conference on Application-specific Systems, Architectures, and Processors (ASAP), Island of Samos, Greece, pp. 15–21 (July 2005)
10. Kurra, S., Singh, N.K., Panda, P.R.: The Impact of Loop Unrolling on Controller Delay in High Level Synthesis. In: Proceedings of Design, Automation and Test in Europe (DATE), Nice, France, pp. 391–396 (April 2007)
11. Hannig, F., Ruckdeschel, H., Dutta, H., Teich, J.: PARO: Synthesis of Hardware Accelerators for Multi-Dimensional Dataflow-Intensive Applications. In: Woods, R., Compton, K., Bouganis, C., Diniz, P.C. (eds.) ARC 2008. LNCS, vol. 4943, pp. 287–293. Springer, Heidelberg (2008)
12. Hannig, F., Teich, J.: Resource Constrained and Speculative Scheduling of an Algorithm Class with Run-Time Dependent Conditionals. In: Proceedings of the 15th IEEE International Conference on Application-specific Systems, Architectures, and Processors (ASAP), Galveston, TX, USA, pp. 17–27 (September 2004)
13. Thiele, L., Roychowdhury, V.: Systematic Design of Local Processor Arrays for Numerical Algorithms. In: Deprettere, E., van der Veen, A. (eds.) Algorithms and Parallel VLSI Architectures, Tutorials, Amsterdam, vol. A, pp. 329–339 (1991)
14. Xue, J.: Unimodular Transformations of Non-Perfectly Nested Loops. Parallel Computing 22(12), 1621–1645 (1997)
15. Muchnick, S.: Advanced Compiler Design and Implementation. Morgan Kaufmann, San Francisco (1997)
16. Dutta, H., Hannig, F., Teich, J.: Hierarchical Partitioning for Piecewise Linear Algorithms. In: Proceedings of the 5th International Conference on Parallel Computing in Electrical Engineering (PARELEC), Bialystok, Poland, pp. 153–160 (September 2006)
17. Kissler, D., Hannig, F., Kupriyanov, A., Teich, J.: A Highly Parameterizable Parallel Processor Array Architecture. In: Proceedings of the IEEE International Conference on Field Programmable Technology (FPT), Bangkok, Thailand, pp. 105–112 (December 2006)

Evaluating Sampling Based Hotspot Detection*

Qiang Wu and Oskar Mencer

Department of Computing, Imperial College London,
South Kensington, London SW7 2AZ, UK
{qiangwu,oskar}@doc.ic.ac.uk
http://comparch.doc.ic.ac.uk

Abstract. In sampling based hotspot detection, performance engineers sample the running program periodically and record the Instruction Pointer (IP) addresses at the sampling. Empirically, frequently sampled IP addresses are regarded as the hotspot of the program. The question of how well the sampled hotspot IP addresses match the real hotspot of the program is seldom studied by the researchers. In this paper, we use instrumentation tool to count how many times the sampled hotspot IP addresses are executed, and compare the real execution result with the sampled one to see how well they match. We define the normalized root mean square error, the sample coverage and the order deviation to evaluate the difference between the real execution and the sampled results. Experiment on the SPEC CPU 2006 benchmarks with various sampling periods is performed to verify the proposed evaluation measurements. Intuitively, the sampling accuracy decreases with the increase of sampling period. The experimental results reveal that the order deviation reflects the intuitive relation between the sampling accuracy and the sampling period better than the normalized root mean square error and the sample coverage.

Keywords: hotspot detection, sampling, accuracy, performance event counters, instrumentation.

1 Introduction

Sampling based hotspot detection is a common practice to locate the frequently executed part of a program in performance analysis. With the help of hardware performance event counters built in the processors, sampling can be done efficiently with a low overhead. Most performance monitor tools provide the functionality to count the Instruction Pointer (IP) addresses encountered during the sampling, revealing a runtime profile of the program [1][2][3][4]. By analyzing the collected counts of IP addresses, performance engineers can figure out which part in the program is most frequently executed, in a statistical manner. Intuitively, the more the IP address is encountered in the sampling, the likelier the IP address is a hotspot of the program.

---

* This work is supported by EPSRC grant - Liquid Circuits: Automated Dynamic Hardware Acceleration of Compute-Intensive Applications.

However, the periodical sampling may not match with the real execution of the program due to its statistical nature. Fig. 1 shows the comparison of the sampled counts and the real execution counts of IP addresses for the SPEC CPU 2006 benchmark 403.gcc with one of the input data sets. For legibility, the counts are displayed in their percentages against the total sample number and the total instruction number respectively. From the figure, we can see that the sampled counts are different from the real execution counts of the IP addresses. Basically, the most frequently sampled IP address is not the same as nor even close to the most frequently executed IP address.

So the question arises that how well the sampled hotspot IP addresses match the real hotspot of the program. Since the hotspot detection is the starting step of the performance engineering, we don't want to be diverted too far from the real hotspot at the beginning.

In this paper, we address the issue of sampling accuracy by proposing evaluation method to compare the sampled hotspot IP addresses with the real execution hotspot of the program. Main contributions of our work are outlined as follows:

1. Three measurements, normalized root mean square error, sample coverage and order deviation, are proposed to evaluate the accuracy of sampling based hotspot detection;
2. Experiment on SPEC CPU 2006 benchmarks with various sampling periods is performed to verify the proposed evaluation measurements;

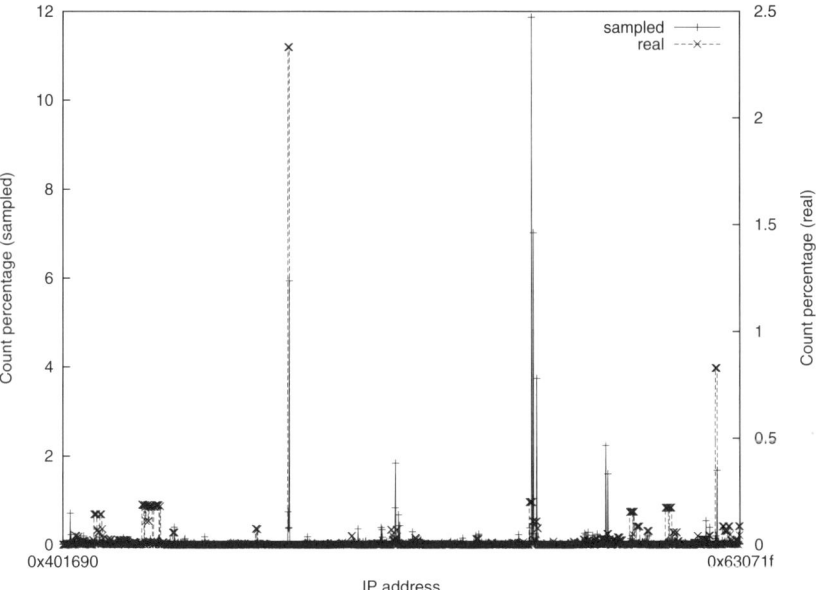

Fig. 1. Count percentages of 403.gcc with input set 1 sampled at 16M unhalted clock cycles (percentages are calculated by dividing the sampled and real execution counts with the total sample number and total executed instruction number respectively)

3. Based on the intuitive relation between the sampling accuracy and the sampling period, order deviation is regarded as the most appropriate measurement to evaluate sampling accuracy.

2 Related Work

Sampling based hotspot detection with hardware performance event counters is widely used in performance analysis. [5] introduces the method of using performance event counters to analyze the performance of running programs. In addition, [5] investigates the accuracy of event counting with multiplexing of performance event counters, which is also studied in [6]. They compare the event counts with those estimated from the incomplete samples with performance event counter multiplexing, to figure out how much error is introduced by the multiplexing technique.

Another accuracy issue is indicated by Korn W., Teller P.J. and Castillo G. in [7], which discusses the error introduced by the overhead of the event counting module itself. They compare the event counts collected by the performance event counters with the predicted ones. [8] and [9] look into this issue further. Both counting and sampling modes of the performance event counters are tested, and the measured counts are compared with the predicted ones. Statistical error in sampling mode is mentioned in [8], with a brief description of the difference between the counts obtained from sampling results and the real execution counts. No further investigation of the issue is made. In [10] and [11] simulation accuracy is studied. [10] uses Euclidean distance to compare the difference of frequency vectors and calculates the error with the distance between simulated results and real execution, and the variance with the average squared distances. In [11] the accuracy of some cumulative property estimated from samples, such as CPI (Cycles Per Instruction), is evaluated based on the statistical mathematics.

3 Method

We notice that processors with built-in hardware event counters always support the CPU clock cycles (unhalted clock cycles) event. The unhalted clock cycles event is often used for determining the sampling period in sampling based hotspot detection. In the information recorded during the sampling, IP address is usually available. Taking the above observations into account, we focus on the sampling period in terms of unhalted clock cycles in this paper. And we assume the IP address is recorded during the sampling. With as few as possible assumptions, our method is generic for different architectures.

3.1 Definitions

The sampling procedure records IP address with the sampling period T, resulting in a list of paired values (t_1, IP_1), (t_2, IP_2), ..., (t_n, IP_n), where n is the number of samples obtained during the sampling. We use $t_1, t_2, ..., t_n$ instead of $T, 2T, ..., nT$ for two reasons. One is that the actual time of sampling is hardly $T, 2T, ..., nT$ due to the uncertainty in the handling of sampling interrupts. The other is that randomization of the sampling period is often used in sampling to avoid biased sampling result.

Aggregate the sampling records $(t_1, IP_1), (t_2, IP_2), ..., (t_n, IP_n)$ to IP addresses, we can get a count histogram of IP addresses, $S = \{(IP_1, c_1), (IP_2, c_2), ..., (IP_m, c_m)\}$, where c_i indicates the count of IP_i in the sampling, and m is the number of different IP addresses collected in the sampling.

On the other hand, we can use instrumentation tool to get the execution count of all the basic blocks of the program with the specific input set. Suppose $B = (BBL_1, bc_1), (BBL_2, bc_2), ..., (BBL_l, bc_l)$ be the counts of all basic blocks of the program with the specific input set, where bc_i is the execution count of the basic block BBL_i, and l is the number of different basic blocks. With the above basic block counts, we can find out the real execution counts of the IP addresses collected in the sampling by simply looking up the corresponding execution count of the basic block that the IP address falls in. Let $R = \{(IP_1, r_1), (IP_2, r_2), ..., (IP_m, r_m)\}$ denote the real execution counts of all the sampled IP addresses.

To compare the sampled hotspot with real hotspot of the program, we need some measurements to evaluate the difference between the two sets of values, S and R with the additional basic block counts B.

3.2 Measurements

Normalized Root Mean Square Error. To evaluate the difference between the predicted and real values, the root mean square error is often employed [12]. We normalize it with the range of the values involved to balance among difference tests:

$$NRMSE = \frac{\sqrt{\sum_{i=1}^{m} \frac{1}{m}(x_{1,i} - x_{2,i})^2}}{x_{max} - x_{min}}$$

where $\{x_{1,i}\}$ and $\{x_{2,i}\}$ are two sets of values.

Considering the particulars of the sampled counts and the execution counts of IP addresses, we make two modifications to the above formula. The first is the scaling of the sampled counts of IP addresses. Since the sampled count is always far less than the execution count of an instruction at the specific IP address, directly subtracting the sample count with the execution count leads to a difference too large to evaluate. In particular, this large difference makes the variations among different sampling periods hidden behind the big numbers. So, instead of subtracting the count values directly, we calculate the difference between the count fractions. That is, we place $(\frac{c_i}{NS} - \frac{r_i}{NI})$ instead of $(c_i - r_i)$ inside the NRMSE formula, where NS is the number of all samples and NI is the number of all instructions executed.

The second is the weighting of the count differences. In normal NRMSE formula, $\frac{1}{m}$ is used for all squared differences, which means the same weight for all differences. However, in hotspot detection, the larger the count is, the more important it is. So we replace the $\frac{1}{m}$ with the $\frac{c_i}{NS}$, where $\sum_{i=1}^{m} \frac{c_i}{NS} = 1$.

The resultant normalized root mean square error formula to compare sample counts S and real execution counts R is:

$$NRMSE_{SR} = \frac{\sqrt{\sum_{i=1}^{m} \frac{c_i}{NS}(\frac{c_i}{NS} - \frac{r_i}{NI})^2}}{\max_{i=1}^{m}(\{\frac{c_i}{NS}\} \cup \{\frac{r_i}{NI}\}) - \min_{i=1}^{m}(\{\frac{c_i}{NS}\} \cup \{\frac{r_i}{NI}\})}$$

In the above formula, c_i and r_i are the sample count and real execution count for IP address IP_i respectively. NS is the number of all samples which is equal to $\sum_{i=1}^{m} c_i$. NI is the number of all executed instructions.

Sample Coverage. It is a well-known rule of thumb that 80% time of the execution is spent on 20% of the program code. This sparks the measurement of the sample coverage to evaluate the sampling based hotspot detection. In this paper, the sample coverage is simply defined to be the total real execution count of sampled IP addresses over the number of all the instructions executed.

$$SC = \frac{\sum_{i=1}^{m} r_i}{NI}$$

Since r_i represents the real execution count of the instruction at the address IP_i, the SC indicates the portion of the instructions at sampled IP addresses in the whole execution of the program.

Order Deviation. In hotspot detection, we care more about the order of the counts of IP addresses than their actual values. It is a common practice in hotspot detection to pick the top IP addresses from the list sorted by the sampled count. The picked IP addresses, or the IP addresses with largest sampled count, may correspond to the most frequently executed instructions in the program, or may not, as we have seen in Fig. 1.

The difference between the order of IP addresses in the sampled count list and the order of these IP addresses in the real execution count list is an interesting issue to investigate. We propose the order deviation to measure the difference between the orders of the IP addresses in the sampled count and real execution count lists. Since we utilize the basic block counts to sort out the real execution count list, the basic block count is used to represent the real execution count in the following text.

Before computing the order deviation, it should be noted that there may be several IP addresses having the same count value. For these IP addresses, we assume them having the same order level. This means that the IP addresses with the same count value have no difference in order inside the involved list. The following is an example of the sorted list of IP addresses and sampled counts illustrating the meaning of the order level.

$$\underbrace{(IP_{i_1}, c_{i_1})(IP_{i_2}, c_{i_2})...}_{\substack{\text{order level 1} \\ c_{i_1} = c_{i_2} = ... = v_1}}, ..., \underbrace{(IP_{i_j}, c_{i_j})(IP_{i_{j+1}}, c_{i_{j+1}})...}_{\substack{\text{order level } j \\ c_{i_j} = c_{i_{j+1}} = ... = v_j}}, ...$$

Here v_1, ..., v_j, ... represent different values in the counts c_1, c_2, ..., c_m.

Suppose the $SOLevel(IP_i)$ returns the order level of IP_i in the list of IP addresses sorted by sampled count. $ROLevel(IP_i)$ returns the order level of the basic block where IP_i locates, in the list of basic blocks sorted by the execution count of the basic blocks. The order deviation is defined as:

$$OD = \frac{\sqrt{\sum_{i=1}^{m} \frac{c_i}{NS}(SOLevel(IP_i) - ROLevel(IP_i))^2}}{m}$$

Here m is the number of different IP addresses, c_i is the sampled count for IP_i, NS is the number of all samples equal to $\sum_{i=1}^{m} c_i$. The OD formula gives the weighted root mean square error of the order level per IP address.

3.3 Tool

We use pfmon in [4] as the sampling tool. pfmon provides the thread-specific sampling and the feature of the randomization of the sampling period. By default, pfmon supports the unhalted clock cycles event for different processors. It comes with a sampling module that can record the IP address during sampling and print out the count histogram of the IP addresses.

For the instrumentation, we employ the Pin [14] tool. Pin is able to instrument executable files and even the running program on the fly. It supports image level, routine level, basic block level and instruction level instrumentation. We utilize the basic block level instrumentation to record the execution counts of basic blocks.

4 Experiment

We perform the experiment on SPEC CPU 2006 [13] benchmarks with various sampling periods. All benchmarks with different input sets in SPEC CPU 2006 have been tested, totally 55 test cases.

4.1 Test Platform

The test platform is a workstation with 2 AMD opteron dual core processors running at 2210 MHz. The size of the system RAM is 2 GB.

SPEC CPU 2006 version 1.0 benchmarks are installed on the system, and are built by GCC and GFortran 4.1.2 with -O2 switch.

The operating system is Ubuntu Linux 7.10 with kernel 2.6.24.3, running in 64-bit mode. The kernel is patched with perfmon [4] to interface the performance event counters. The version of perfmon kernel patch is 2.8 which is required for pfmon [4] tool version 3.3. pfmon is used to perform the sampling and print out the counts histogram of IP addresses.

Instrumentation is done with the Pin [14] tool, which figures out the execution counts of basic blocks. The version of Pin is 2.4 for Linux x86_64 architecture.

4.2 Test Results

We use pfmon to sample the SPEC CPU 2006 benchmarks and get the histograms of the sampled counts of IP addresses. Sampling periods are set to be 9 different values: 64K, 128K, 256K, 512K, 1M, 2M, 4M, 8M and 16M unhalted clock cycles. To avoid biased sampling results, sampling period randomization provided by pfmon is used for all the tests. The randomization mask value is set to be one eighth of the sampling period. That is to say, at the time of sampling, a random value up to one eighth of the sampling period is added to the original value. The resultant value is used as the count-down value for the next sampling.

We have carried out the tests on three evaluation measurements: normalized root mean square error (NRMSE), sample coverage (SC) and order deviation (OD). An intuitive rule is adopted to evaluate the above measurements:

– The longer the sampling period is, the less accurate the sampling result is.

This intuitive rule means that the difference between the sampling result and the real execution, in our case, the normalized root mean square error and order deviation, should rise with the increase of the sampling period. On the contrary, the sample coverage should fall with the increase of the sampling period. The test results are shown and discussed in below.

Normalized Root Mean Square Error (NRMSE): Fig. 2 shows the NRMSE values for SPEC CPU 2006 benchmarks with various sampling periods. NRMSE values are displayed with one clustered bars for each benchmark, and one color for one sampling period. Bars are lined from left to right in the ascending order of sampling periods, from 64K to 16M unhalted clock cycles.

It can be seen from the figure that most benchmarks have a normalized root mean square error (NRMSE) value around or below 0.2. NRMSE values of benchmarks 401.bzip2 with input set 4, 403.gcc with input sets 3, 4, 5, 6 and 8 and 465.tonto with input set 1 are around or above 0.3.

The more noticeable feature of the figure is the variation pattern of each cluster of bars, which represents the NRMSE values corresponding to different sampling periods of each benchmark. We expect to see a rising trend of the bars with the increase of the sampling periods. However, it should be admitted that in Fig. 2, there is no obvious trend of ascending witnessed in the clusters of bars.

Sample Coverage (SC): Fig. 3 shows the sample coverage values for SPEC CPU 2006 benchmarks with various sampling periods. Sample coverage values are displayed in a similar way as Fig. 2, with one color bar for one sampling period and a cluster of bars for one benchmark.

We can see in Fig. 3 that most benchmarks have a sample coverage (SC) value above or around 0.5. Benchmark 403.gcc with input sets 1, 2, 3 and 9, 410.bwaves with input set 1 and 465.tonto with input set 1 fall below 0.5.

For the variation inside each bar cluster, we can find a trend of descending in most of the clusters, with some exceptions such as 401.bwaves, 416.gamess with input set 3, 447.dealII, 454.calculix, 456.hmmer, and 473.astar. The descending

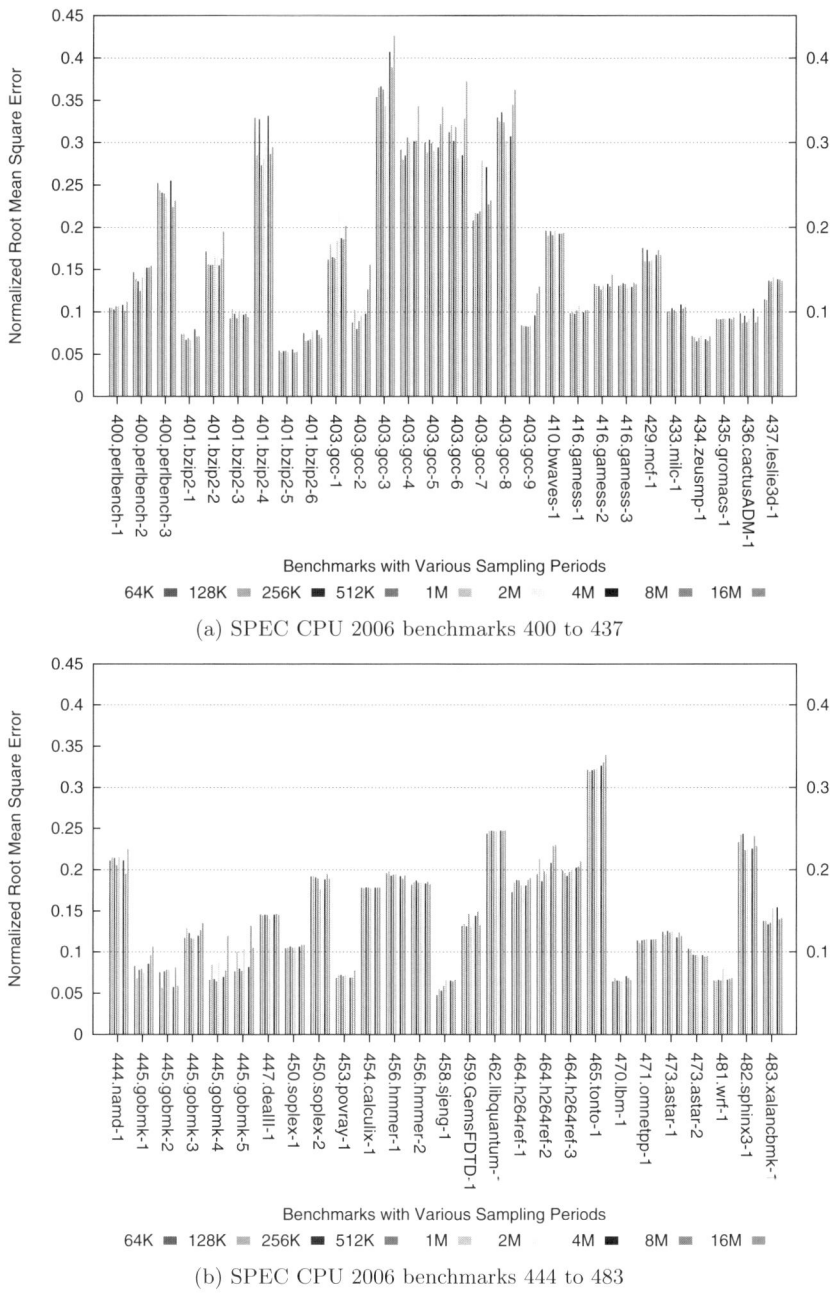

Fig. 2. Normalized Root Mean Square Error (NRMSE) of SPEC CPU 2006 benchmarks with various sampling periods (NRMSE values of each benchmark are displayed from left to right with a cluster of bars in the order of sampling periods from 64K to 16M unhalted clock cycles)

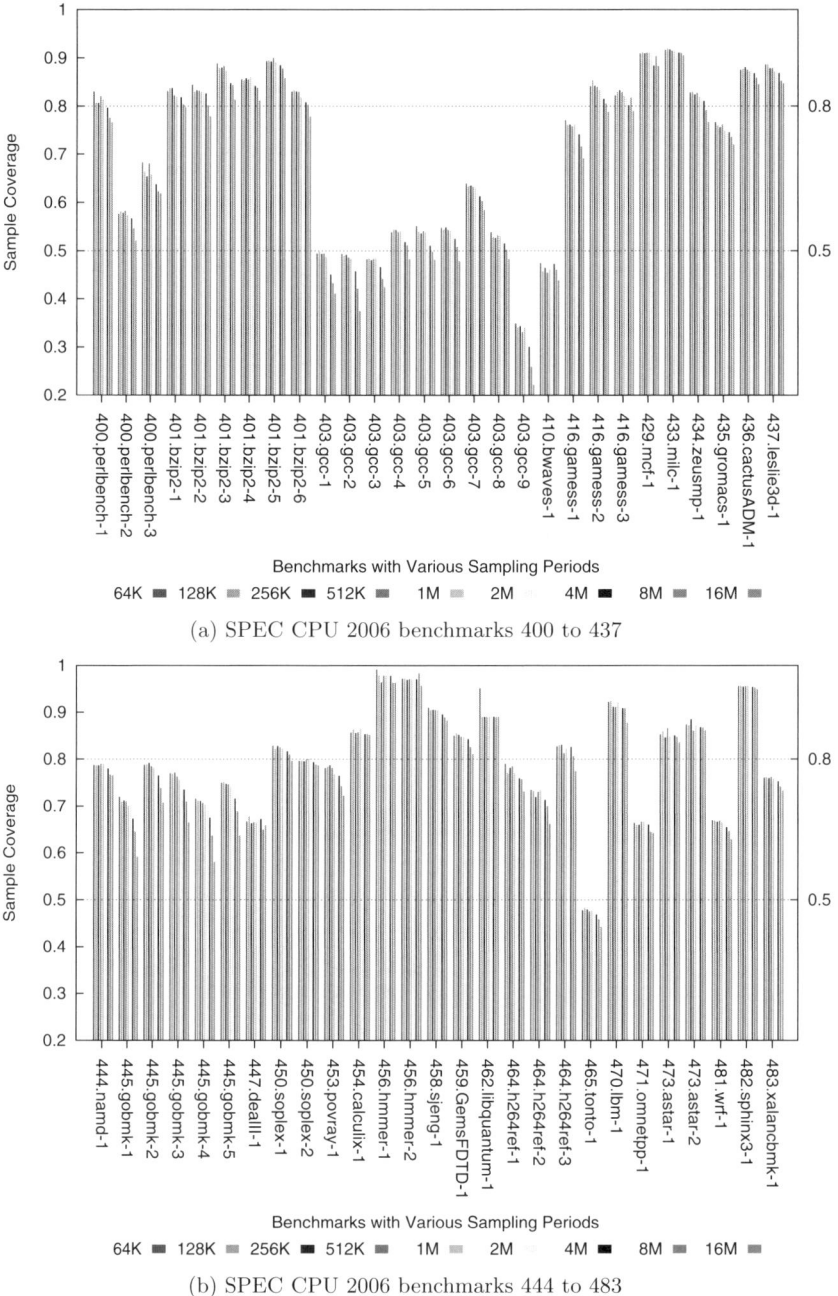

Fig. 3. Sample coverage (SC) values of SPEC CPU 2006 benchmarks with various sampling periods (SC values of each benchmark are displayed from left to right with a cluster of bars in the ascending order of sampling periods from 64K to 16M unhalted clock cycles)

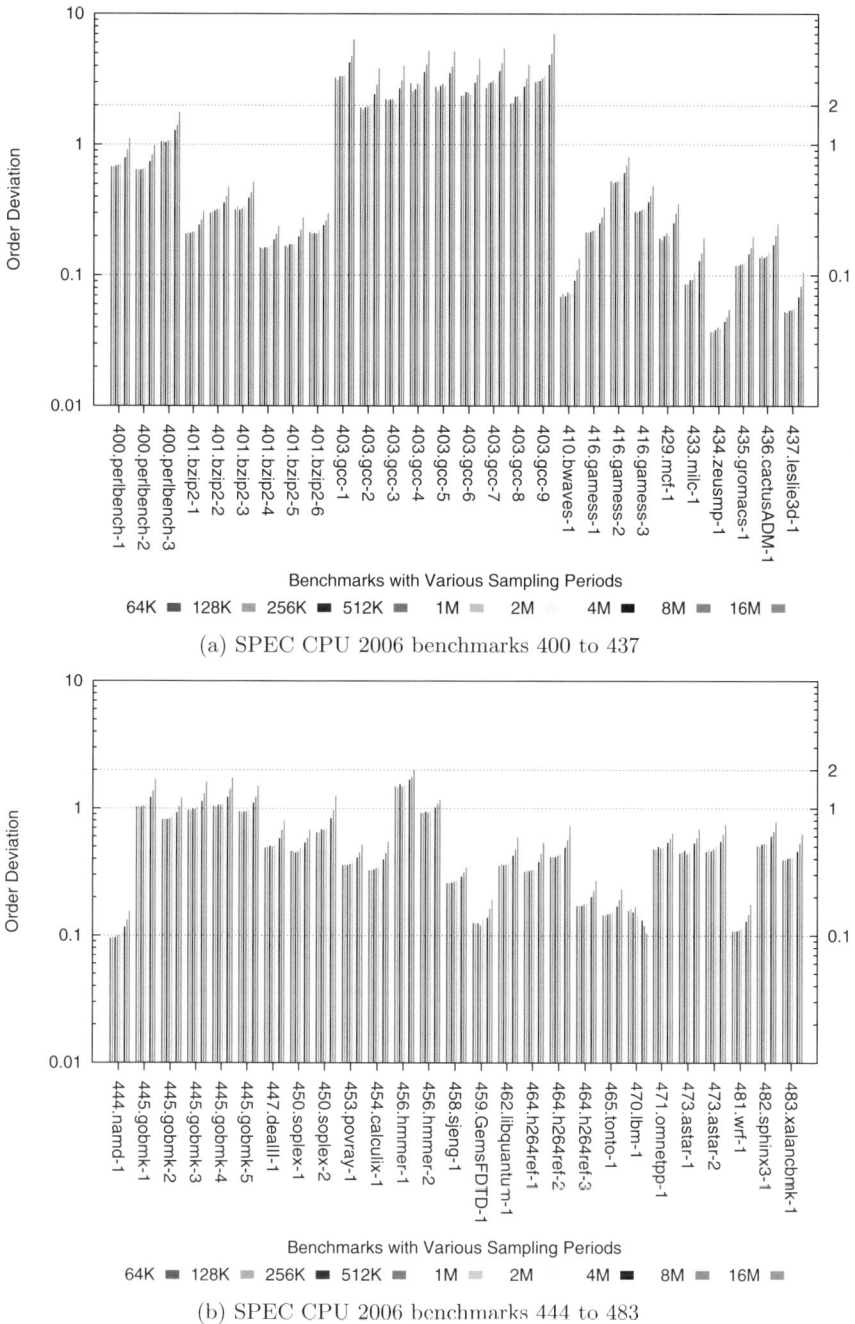

Fig. 4. Order Deviation (OD) of SPEC CPU 2006 benchmarks with various sampling periods in logscale (OD values of each benchmark are displayed from left to right with clustered bars in the order of sampling periods from 64K to 16M unhalted clock cycles)

trend means that with the increase of the sampling period, the sample coverage is decreasing, i.e. the IP addresses recorded in the sampling covers less instructions in the program execution.

Order Deviation (OD): Fig. 4 shows the order deviation (OD) values for SPEC CPU 2006 benchmarks with various sampling periods. Each cluster of color bars corresponds to a set of OD values for one benchmark with different sampling periods. It should be noted that the order deviation values are displayed in logarithmic scale for a better visual effect.

In the Fig. 4, despite the actual order deviation values, the most interesting discovery is that nearly all the bar clusters show a trend of ascending with the increase of the sampling period. The only exception is the bar cluster corresponding to 470.lbm with input set 1, which has a descending trend. As we mentioned before, intuitively the accuracy of sampling should fall with the increase of the sampling period. Obviously, the order deviation reflects this intuitive rule better than the sample coverage and the normalized root mean square error.

For the actual values, we can see that order deviations (OD) for most benchmarks are around or below 1.0. The outstanding ones are the OD values of benchmark 403.gcc with input sets 1 to 9, which are above 2.0. Roughly speaking, an OD value of 2.0 means that in average the order of each sampled IP address is deviated by 2 from the real execution order of the IP address in the whole program. We regard that the order deviation above 2 is not good for identifying hotspots. Considering that benchmark 403.gcc is a control dominant program, which has lots of branches in its code, this suggests that the sampling based hotspot detection has an accuracy degradation for the control dominant programs.

5 Conclusion

In this paper, we investigate the accuracy of sampling based hotspot detection. Three measurements, normalized root mean square error, sample coverage and order deviation are proposed to evaluate how well the sampled hotspot matches the real hotspot of the program. These measurements are adopted in the consideration of the experiences of previous research work and our observations. We test the proposed measurements on SPEC CPU 2006 benchmarks with different sampling periods. To verify and compare the proposed measurements, we exploit an intuitive relation between the sampling accuracy and sampling period. The longer the sampling period is, the less accurate the sampling result is. From the experimental results, we find that the order deviation fits the intuitive relation best, with only 1 significant exception out of 55 test cases. We also notice that the control dominant benchmark 403.gcc has relatively lower sampling accuracy indicated by the order deviation measurement which are generally above 2.0, a level of value that is regarded as acceptably different in our point of view. This suggests that control dominant programs usually degrade the sampling accuracy to some extent. Our future plan is to investigate the relation between the program code characteristics and the sampling accuracy.

References

1. Intel Corporation. Intel VTune Performance Analyzer,
   http://www.intel.com/cd/software/products/asmo-na/eng/239144.htm
2. AMD Inc. AMD CodeAnalyst Performance Analyzer,
   http://developer.amd.com/CPU/Pages/default.aspx
3. OProfile - A System Profiler for Linux, http://oprofile.sourceforge.net
4. perfmon project, http://perfmon2.sourceforge.net
5. Azimi, R., Stumm, M., Wisniewski, R.W.: Online performance analysis by statistical sampling of microprocessor performance counters. In: Proc. of the Intl. Conf. on Supercomputing, pp. 101–110. ACM Press, New York (2005)
6. Mathur, W., Cook, J.: Towards Accurate Performance Evaluation using Hardware Counters. In: Proc. of the ITEA Modeling and Simulation Workshop, Las Cruces, NM (2003)
7. Korn, W., Teller, P.J., Castillo, G.: Just How Accurate Are Performance Counters? In: Proc. of the Intl. Conf. on Performance, Computing, and Communications, pp. 303–310. IEEE Press, New York (2001)
8. Maxwell, M.E., Teller, P.J., Salayandia, L., Moore, S.V.: Accuracy of Performance Monitoring Hardware. In: Proc. of the Los Alamos Computer Science Institute Symposium, Santa Fe, NM (2002)
9. Moore, S.V.: A Comparison of Counting and Sampling Modes of Using Performance Monitoring Hardware. In: Sloot, P.M.A., Tan, C.J.K., Dongarra, J., Hoekstra, A.G. (eds.) ICCS-ComputSci 2002. LNCS, vol. 2330, pp. 904–912. Springer, Heidelberg (2002)
10. Hamerly, G., Perelman, E., Lau, J., Calder, B.: SimPoint 3.0: Faster and More Flexible Program Analysis. Journal of Instruction-Level Parallelism 7, 1–28 (2005)
11. Wunderlich, R.E., Wenisch, T.F., Falsafi, B., Hoe, J.C.: SMARTS: Accelerating Microarchitecture Simulation via Rigorous Statistical Sampling. In: Proc. of ISCA, pp. 84–95. IEEE Press, New York (2003)
12. Hamad, H.: A new metric for measuring metamodels quality-of-fit for deterministic simulations. In: Proc. of the Conf. on Winter Simulation, pp. 882–888. ACM Press, New York (2006)
13. Standard Performance Evaluation Corporation, http://www.spec.org
14. Pin - A Dynamic Binary Instrumentation Tool, http://rogue.colorado.edu/pin

A Reconfigurable Bloom Filter Architecture for BLASTN

Yupeng Chen, Bertil Schmidt, and Douglas L. Maskell

School of Computer Engineering, Nanyang Technological University, Singapore
{CHEN0511,ASBSchmidt,ASDouglas}@ntu.edu.sg

Abstract. Efficient seed-based filtration methods exist for scanning genomic sequence databases. However, current solutions require a significant scan time on traditional computer architectures. These scan time requirements are likely to become even more severe due to the rapid growth in the size of databases. In this paper, we present a new approach to genomic sequence database scanning using reconfigurable field-programmable gate array (FPGA)-based hardware. To derive an efficient mapping onto this type of architecture, we propose a reconfigurable Bloom filter architecture. Our experimental results show that the FPGA implementation achieves an order of magnitude speedup compared to the NCBI BLASTN software running on a general purpose computer.

Keywords: genomic sequence analysis, Bloom filter, bioinformatics, reconfigurable computing.

1 Introduction

Scanning genomic sequence databases is a common and often repeated task in molecular biology. The need for speeding up these searches comes from the rapid growth of the bio-sequence banks: every year their size is scaled by a factor 1.5 to 2. The scan operation consists of finding similarities between a particular query sequence and all sequences of a bank. This allows biologists to identify sequences sharing common subsequences, which from a biological viewpoint have similar functionality. Dynamic programming based alignment algorithms whose complexities are quadratic with respect to the length of the sequences can detect similarities between the query sequence and a subject sequence [8]. One frequently used approach to speed up this prohibitively time consuming operation is to introduce heuristics in the search algorithm. Examples of such heuristic tools include BLAST [1], BLAT [6], and Patternhunter [7]. Among these tools BLAST, the Basic Local Alignment Search Tool, is the most widely used software.

BLASTN, a version for BLAST that searches DNA sequences consists of a three-stage-pipeline:

- Stage 1: *Word Matching*. This stage detects *seeds*. Seeds are short exact matches between the query sequence and a subject sequence;
- Stage 2: *Ungapped Extension*. Each detected seed is extended to the left and to the right allowing mismatches;
- Stage 3: Gapped extension. High score matching segments detected in Stage 2 are further extended by allowing insertions and deletions.

The basic idea underlying BLASTN searching is *filtration*. Filtration assumes that good alignments usually contain short exact matches. Such matches can be quickly computed by using data structures such as hash tables or suffix trees. Identified matches are then used as seeds for further analysis. Unfortunately, these data structures require a significant amount of memory space and therefore usually do not scale well on traditional computer architectures. Since filtration is typically the most time-consuming step (Table 1 shows that filtration is around 85% of the overall runtime of NCBI BLASTN [9]), this approach often results in prohibitive runtimes for large genome sequencing projects.

Table 1. Percentage of time spent in each stage of NCBI BLASTN

Query size	10Kb	100Kb	1Mb
Stage1(word matching)	86.5%	83.3%	85.3%
Stage2(ungapped extension)	13.3%	16.6%	14.65%
Stage3(gapped extension)	0.2%	0.1%	0.05%

One possible solution to the filtration problem is to use a Bloom filter [4], which is a simple space-efficient randomized hashing data structure that has been widely utilized in network packet processing [3,4]. In this paper, we propose an efficient Bloom filter architecture based on field programmable gate arrays (FPGA), applying partitioning, pipelining, and parallelism techniques to accelerate the first stage of BLASTN. FPGAs are suitable candidate architectures for such a design due to their fine-grained configurability and parallel embedded memories. The paper is organized as follows. In Section 2, we introduce the Bloom filter data structure. The conventional Bloom filter architecture for sequence filtration is explained in section 3. Section 4 presents our new parallel partitioned Bloom filter architecture. The performance of our new architecture is evaluated in section 5. Section 6 concludes the paper.

2 Bloom Filter Data Structure

A Bloom filter is a space-efficient probabilistic data structure. It represents a set of given keys in a bit-vector. Insertion and querying of keys are supported using several independent hash functions. Bloom filters gain their space-efficiency by allowing a false positive answer to membership queries. Space savings often outweigh this drawback in applications where a small false positive rate can be tolerated, particularly when space resources are at a premium. Both criteria are certainly met for seed-based genomic sequence database scanning, since:

- Wrongly identified word matches can be efficiently detected in subsequent stages.
- Seed-based scanning tools like BLAST require a significant amount of secondary memory for long query sequences.

In the following, we briefly describe the definition, programming, querying and false positive probability of Bloom filters.

Definition: A Bloom filter is defined by a bit-vector of length m, denoted as $BF[1..m]$. A family of k hash functions $h_i: K \rightarrow A$, $1 \leq i \leq k$, is associated to the Bloom filter, where K is the key space and $A = \{1,...,m\}$ is the address space.

Programming: For a given set I of n keys, $I = \{x_1,...,x_n\}$, $I \subseteq K$, the Bloom filter is *programmed* as follows. The bit vector is initialized with zeros; i.e. $BF[i] := 0$ for all $1 \leq i \leq m$. For each key $x_j \in I$, the k hash values $h_i(x_j)$, $1 \leq i \leq k$, are computed. Subsequently, the bit-vector bits addressed by these k values are set to one; i.e. $BF[h_i(x_j)] := 1$ for all $1 \leq i \leq k$. Note that, if one of these values addressed a bit which is already set to one, that bit is not changed.

Querying: For a given key $x \in K$, the Bloom filter is *queried* for membership in I in a similar way. The k hash values $h_i(x)$, $1 \leq i \leq k$, are computed. If at least one of the k bits $BF[h_i(x)]$, $1 \leq i \leq k$, is zero, then $x \notin I$. Otherwise, x is said to be a member of I with a certain probability. If all k bits are found to be one but $x \notin I$, x is said to be a false positive.

False Positive Probability: The presence of false positives arises from the fact that the k bits in the bit-vector can be set to one by any of the n keys. Note that a Bloom filter can produce false positive but never false negative answers to queries. The false positive probability of a Bloom filter (denoted as *FPP*) is given by [2]:

$$FPP = \left(1 - \left(1 - \frac{1}{m}\right)^{kn}\right)^k \approx \left(1 - e^{-\frac{kn}{m}}\right)^k \qquad (1)$$

Obviously, *FPP* decreases as the bit-vector size m increases, and increases as the number of inserted keys n increases. It can be shown that for a given m and n, the optimal number of hash functions k_{opt} is given by:

$$k_{opt} = \frac{m}{n}\ln 2 \qquad (2)$$

The corresponding false positive probability is then:

$$\left(\frac{1}{2}\right)^{k_{opt}} \approx 0.6185^{\frac{m}{n}} \qquad (3)$$

Hence, in the optimally configured Bloom filter, the false positive rate decreases exponentially with the size of the bit-vector. Furthermore, to maintain a fixed false positive probability, the bit-vector size needs to scale linearly with the inserted key set.

3 Conventional Bloom Filter Architecture for Word Matching

Our system is concerned with accelerating the performance of Stage1 of the BLASTN algorithm. This stage identifies all exactly matching substrings of length w, so called

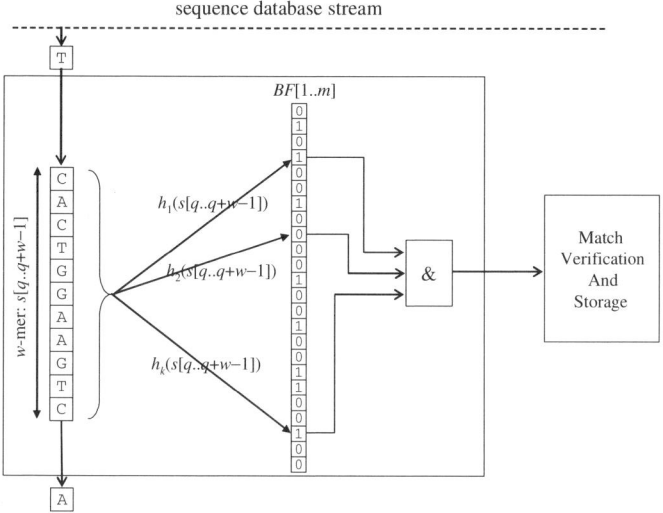

Fig. 1. Conventional design for identifying w-mers in a sequence database stream using a Bloom filter

w-mers, between the query sequence and each sequence in the database. The value of w is chosen by the user as an input parameter. The default value for a nucleotide search with NCBI-BLASTN is $w = 11$.

The conventional design for identification of w-mers using a Bloom filter is shown in Figure 1. As a preprocessing step, the Bloom filer is programmed, which is done by parsing the query sequence into overlapping substrings of length w. For example, suppose $w = 3$ and a short query of `cttgtata`, then the parsed substrings are: `ctt`, `ttg`, `tgt`, `gta`, `tat`, and `ata`. The Bloom filer is programmed using these substrings as the set of keys.

Once the Bloom filter has been programmed it is used to search the sequence database for hits. To do this, the database is parsed in overlapping substrings of length w using the same process as the query. In each step, the w-length window is shifted by one position by reading a new nucleotide letter from the database stream. Each w-mer is queried in the Bloom filter and zero or more exact matches to query hits are identified.

Finally, the position in the query and the position in the database of the matching substrings are stored in the off-chip match verification and storage unit for subsequent processing. This unit verifies if the identified match is an actual match or a false positive match. Conceptually, the position of the w-mer is passed in to the Bloom filer with the w-mer value from the database stream. Practically, this can be efficiently implemented by incrementing a counter each clock cycle. If there is a match then only the position in the stream is passed on to the match verification and storage unit.

In order to accelerate NCBI BLASTN effectively, with this architecture the size of the Bloom filter is crucial. Table 2 shows the required Bloom filter size for FPP values of around 10^{-5} and around 10^{-3}, and varying query lengths. It can be seen that almost 2 Megabits of memory is required for scanning a database with a query sequence of length 100K bases and 16 hash functions.

Another parameter that does not influence the false probability rate but the effectiveness of the Bloom filter is w. Table 3 shows the percentage of hits identified in a database scan for varying values of w and query lengths. It can be seen that for larger query sizes larger values of w are required to filter the database effectively.

Table 2. Bloom filter memory size (in bits) for different parameter combinations

Query size (n)	# of hash functions (k)	Bit length of Bloom filter (m)	False positive probability
1K		23,084	
10K	16	230,832	1.53e-5
100K		2,308,313	
1K		11,542	
10K	8	115,416	2.91e-3
100K		1,154,157	

Table 3. Percentage of hits identified by the first stage of NCBI-BLASTN for scanning the full NT database with varying values of w and random queries of different length

w	9		11		15	
Query length	10k	100k	10k	100k	10k	100k
% hits per nucleotide	22.7%	26.3%	11.3%	22.43%	0.3%	4.5%

4 Parallel Partitioned Bloom Filter Architecture

This section describes our new parallel partitioned Bloom filter architecture and how it can be mapped efficiently onto an FPGA. Our design takes the advantage of the fact that mismatches appear far more frequently than matches in the BLASTN word matching stage. Our design uses three techniques to improve the throughput compared to the conventional Bloom filter architecture:

- *Partitioning*. We first partition the Bloom filter vector into a number of smaller vectors, which are then looked up by independent hash functions.
- *Pipelining*. We further increase the throughput of our design using a new pipelining technique.
- *Local stalling*. We use a local stalling mechanism to guarantee all w-mers are tested by the Bloom filter.

The memory containing the Bloom filter vector in Figure 1 has to support k random lookups every clock cycle. However, embedded memories are usually limited in their

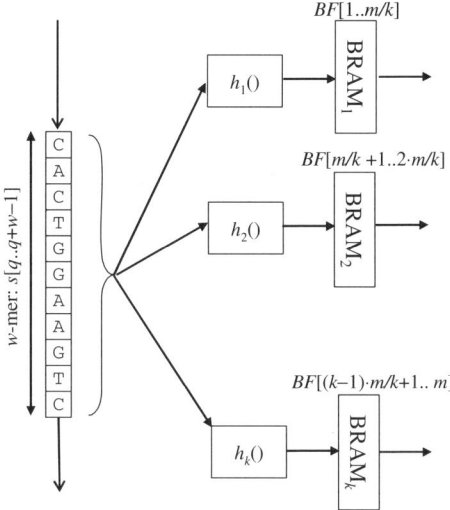

Fig. 2. Partitioned Bloom filter architecture using on-chip Block RAM (BRAM) modules

lookup capacity. Therefore, we partition a Bloom filter of bit-length m into m/k embedded memory blocks (BRAMs) where k is the number of hash functions (see Figure 2). Since each hash function $h_i(\cdot)$ is now restricted to only map into memory block i, $1 \leq i \leq k$, the false positive probability is changed to:

$$FPP_p = \left(1 - \left(1 - \frac{1}{m/k}\right)^n\right)^k \quad (4)$$

For instance, using the parameter combinations shown in Table 3 we get $|FPP_p - FPP| \leq 5.5e\text{-}8$ for $k=16$ and $|FPP_p - FPP| \leq 5.5e\text{-}20$ for $k=8$. Thus, partitioning has a negligible effect on the false positive rate for typical input parameter combinations of a BLASTN search.

Throughput can be further improved by deploying several Bloom filters in parallel. Each of the Bloom filters then looks-up a different w-mer in parallel. The disadvantage of this approach is that the total amount of memory for the Bloom filter vectors is of size $P \cdot m$, where P is the number of Bloom filters, each of length m. In the following we present a space-saving Bloom filter architecture that can support several input w-mers and while keeping a vector of length m.

The architecture uses a single Bloom filter of length m and k hash functions. The memory space of Bloom filter is portioned into k pieces corresponding to the hash functions. The design can support the look-up of up to P w-mers per clock cycle by using P parallel pipelines, where k is a multiple of P.

Our basic building block is a pipelined partitioned Bloom filter with k/P hash functions, denoted as PPBF(k/P), which is shown in Figure 3. Figure 4 shows our parallel Bloom filter architecture consisting of P pipelined partitioned Bloom filters, which are

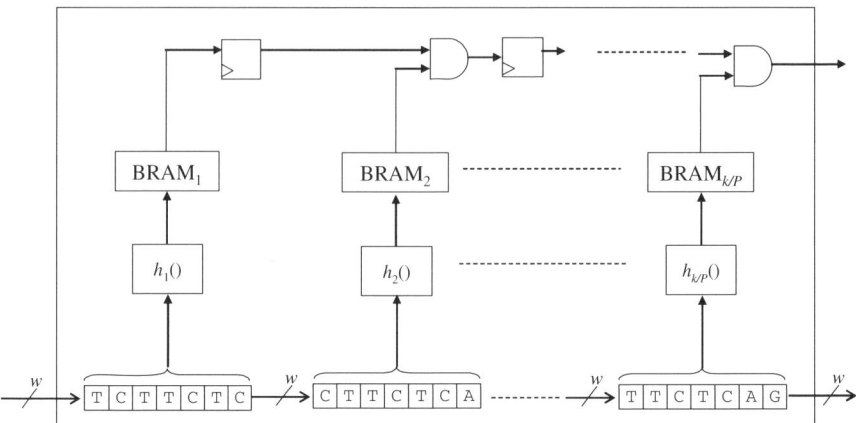

Fig. 3. Pipelined partitioned Bloom filter (PPBF) architecture with k/p hash functions, denoted as PPBF(k/p)

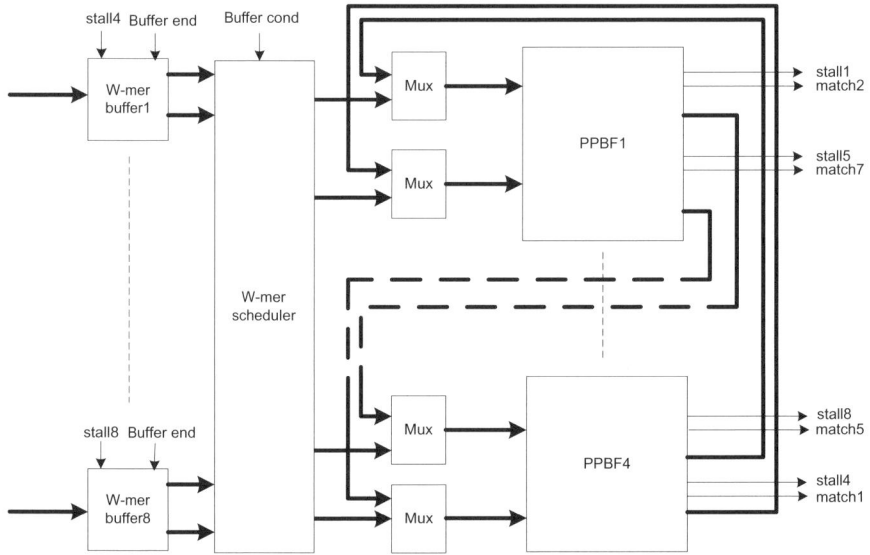

Fig. 4. Parallel Bloom filter architecture consisting of four pipelined partitioned Bloom filter with 4 hash functions

denoted as PPBF$_i$ for $1 \leq i \leq P$ (in our design, the total number of hash functions is 16, the parallel Bloom filter is constructed using 4 PPBFs, each of which has 4 hash functions). Every clock cycle each PPBF$_i$ reads two new input w-mers from pre-generated local w-mer buffers. Note that we implement our 'm-bit' vector using dual-port RAM, which will double the w-mer's processing speed without introducing any further burden on the BRAM consumption.

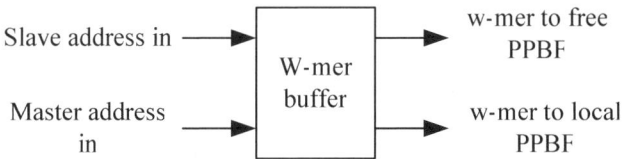

Fig. 5. *w*-mer buffer with master-slave ports

If the output match-bit of PPBF$_i$ equals zero for any $1 \le i \le P$, which indicates that a mismatch is found, then a new *w*-mer is input to next PPBF$_i$. If an output match bit of any PPBF$_i$ equals one, the corresponding *w*-mer is passed to PPBF$_{(i+1)}$ for all $1 \le i \le P-1$. At the same time, a corresponding input *w*-mer from the *w*-mer buffer should be stalled in order to prevent a *w*-mer loss. The match output from PPBF$_p$ is sent to PPBF$_1$ for further testing. A true match is generated if and only if a *w*-mer passes all PPBFs.

The local stalling mechanism is applied to guarantee no *w*-mer loss. However, a processing speed difference can appear among different *w*-mer buffers. Therefore, we have integrated a *w*-mer scheduler as switch logic. The *w*-mer scheduler works according to the following rules:

- if *w*-mer buffer$_i$ is empty, PPBF$_i$ processes data from its nearest *w*-mer buffer
- if only one *w*-mer is non-empty, all PPBFs process data from this buffer
- if all *w*-mer buffers are empty, update all *w*-mer buffers simultaneously.

Buffer cond is a control signal that informs the *w*-mer scheduler about empty buffers.

In our design, a *w*-mer buffer is implemented using dual-port RAM (see Figure 5). The *Master address in* port is used for general *w*-mer read/write operations; the *slave address in* port is enabled only if a nearby *w*-mer buffer is empty, controlled by the *buffer end* signal.

5 Performance Analysis

We have designed a parallel Bloom filter with 16 hash functions, which receives 8 new *w*-mers in parallel each clock cycle using VHDL and targeted it to an EP3SL200F1517C2 device of the Stratix III family. The Quatus II timing analysis tool estimated a highest clock frequency of 151.9 MHz. The total length of the m-bit vector is 2Megabits (see Table 2). Block RAM consumption is about 31% of the total BRAM resource. Logic utilization is about 6%. Our simulation experiments show that, at a clock frequency of 150MHz, the parallel partitioned Bloom filter achieves a theoretical maximum throughput rate of 1.2Gbases/second (zero match condition). The achieved throughput rate depends on the actual match rates of query and subject sequences. Generally, Stage1's match rate is very low for small query sizes. Our current design can support query lengths of up to 100K bases. Table 4 shows that the Stage 1 match rate for queries up to 100K is typically less than 10%. Therefore, our design should be able achieve a throughput rate close to 1.2Gbases/second for query lengths up to 100K. For query lengths greater than 100K bases, we should split the query sequence into several segments of size $\le$ 100K and run the programming and querying process iteratively until all query segments are checked.

A performance comparison between Stage 1 of the NCBI BLASTN software and our design is shown in Table 5. The throughput is measured for queries of different size and

Table 4. Typical match rates p for different pipeline stages[5]

Query size (bases)	Stage1 P_1	Stage2 P_2	Stage3 P_3
10k	0.00858	0.0000550	0.32
25k	0.0205	0.0000619	0.141
50k	0.0411	0.0000189	0.194
100k	0.0841	0.0000174	0.175

Table 5. Performance comparison between software and hardware platforms

Performance comparison between NCBI BLASTN stage1 and PBF				
Query size (base)	10k	25k	50k	100k
NCBI stage1 (Mbase/s)	114	105	78	53.4
PBF (Mbase/s)	1161	1137	1088	988
Speedup	10.18	10.83	13.95	18.5

Table 6. Key features of several Bloom filter implementation

Bloom filter implementations	Key feature in architecture
Bloom filter in Mercury system[5]	4-port m-bit vector
2-stage pipelined Bloom filter[4]	Stage threshold
Partial Bloom filter[3]	Control interface

a subset of the gene bank database. The NCBI software is measured on an Intel(R) Pentium 4 3GHz CPU with 1.00GB RAM. Our Bloom filter performance is measured using a clock frequency of 150MHz.

As mentioned previously, Bloom filers are widely used for membership testing. Previous research [3-5] has presented several application specific structures derived from the conventional architecture of Figure 1 (see Table 6 for an overview). The Mercury system [5] uses a 4-port m-bit vector, which is designed by doubling clock frequency through a clock management circuit. A two-stage pipelined Bloom filter with two groups of hash functions is presented in [4]. The second pipeline stage computes matches from the first stage. The bits in the partial Bloom filter presented in [3] are set or reset when a string is added or deleted through a control interface, which largely increases design's flexibility. However, from a string processing efficiency point of view, all these structures have limitations. Mercury has high throughput rate but much computation is wasted; the 2-stage Bloom filter has higher computational efficiency but the hash functions in Stage 2 are always in an idle state; the partial Bloom filter also has similar efficiency problem as Mercury. In contrast, the partitioned Bloom filter architecture presented in this paper has been designed based on the fact that a matching string is found if and only if all hash values point to programmed bits in the Bloom filter vector. A mismatch is found once it fails in any of the hash queries (obviously the constraints on a matched string are much stronger than a mismatch), which guarantees computational efficiency.

6 Conclusion and Future Work

In this paper, we have presented an FGPA-based Bloom filter architecture to accelerate the word matching stage of BLASTN. It has been optimized by using three techniques: partitioning, pipelining, and parallelism. The performance comparison to the corresponding NCBI BLASTN software implementation for different query sizes shows that our design achieves one order of magnitude speedup with only modest resource utilization.

Our current architecture is the first step towards accelerating DNA sequence filtration speed and efficiency. For example, different combinations of hash functions and partitioned Bloom filter vectors could gain higher throughput rates without introducing any extra burden on BRAM consumption, which is part of our future work. Furthermore, we plan to utilize the FPGA's outstanding performance for parallel data processing and fine-grained pipelining, to design an architecture for Stage 2 of the BLSTN pipeline (ungapped extension) to achieve higher throughput rates. After implementation of the first 2 stages of BLASTN search using FPGA, we will integrate them into the BLASTN software to test the overall performance improvement.

References

1. Altschul, S.F., Madden, T.L., Schaffer, A.A., Zhang, J., Zhang, Z., Miller, W., Lipman, D.J.: Gapped BLAST and PSI-BLAST: a new generation of protein database search programs. Nucleic Acids Res. 25, 3389–3402 (1997)
2. Bloom, B.: Space/Time Trade-Offs in Hash Coding with Allowable Errors. Commun. ACM 13(7), 422–426 (1970)
3. Dharmapurikar, S.: Design and Implementation of a String Matching System for Network Instruction Detection using FPGA-based Bloom Filters. In: Proc. of 12th Annual IEEE symposium on Field Programmable custom Computing Machine (2004)
4. Kaya, I., Kocak, T.: Energy-Efficient Pipelined Bloom Filters for Network Instruction Detection. In: IEEE international conference on communications 2006, vol. 5, pp. 2382–2387 (2006)
5. Karishmamurthy, P., Buhler, J., et al.: Biosequence Similarity Search on the Mercury System. Journal of VLSI Signal Processing Systems 49(1), 101–121
6. Kent, W.J.: BLAT – the BLAST-like alignment tool. Genome Research 12(4), 656–664 (2002)
7. Ma, B., Tromp, J., Li, M.: PatternHunter: faster and more sensitive homology search. Bioinformatics 18, 440–445 (2002)
8. Smith, T.F., Waterman, M.S.: Identification of Common Molecular Subsequences. Journal of Molecular Biology 147, 105–197 (1981)
9. BLAST programs at NCBI, http://www.ncbi.nlm.nih.gov/BLAST/

SoCWire: A Robust and Fault Tolerant Network-on-Chip Approach for a Dynamic Reconfigurable System-on-Chip in FPGAs

Björn Osterloh, Harald Michalik, and Björn Fiethe

IDA TU Braunschweig, Hans-Sommer-Str.66,
D-38106 Braunschweig, Germany
b.osterloh@tu-bs.de, {michalik,fiethe}@ida.ing.tu-bs.de

Abstract. Individual Data Processing Units (DPUs) are commonly used for operational control and specific data processing of scientific space instruments. These instruments have to be suitable for the harsh space environment in terms of e.g. temperature and radiation. Thus they need to be robust and fault tolerant to achieve an adequate reliability. The Configurable System-on-Chip (SoC) solution based on FPGA has successfully demonstrated flexibility and reliability for scientific space applications like the Venus Express mission. Future space missions demand high-performance on board processing because of the discrepancy of extreme high data volume and low downlink channel capacity. Furthermore, in-flight reconfiguration ability and dynamic reconfigurable modules enhances the system with maintenance potential and at run-time adaptive functionality. To achieve these advanced design goals a flexible Network-on-Chip (NoC) is proposed for applications with high reliability, like space missions. The conditions for SRAM-based FPGA in space are outlined. Additionally, we present our newly developed NoC approach, System-on-Chip Wire (SoCWire) and outline its performance and suitability for robust dynamic reconfigurable systems.

Keywords: SoCWire, Network-on-Chip, dynamic reconfigurable system, VMC, Sytem-on-Chip, SRAM-based FPGA.

1 Introduction

The Institute of Computer and Communication Network Engineering (IDA) at the Technical University of Braunschweig develops Data Processing Units (DPUs) for space applications. DPUs are used as interface between spacecraft and several instrument sensor electronics or heads, providing the operational control and specific data processing of scientific space instruments. These systems have to provide sufficient computing power, volume, mass and low power consumption. Furthermore these instruments have to be suitable for the harsh space environment conditions (e.g. temperature, radiation). They need to be robust and fault tolerant to achieve an adequate reliability at moderate unit costs. Different implementation approaches for DPUs exist in traditional designs (i) based on rad-hard discrete components, (ii) Application–Specific integrated Circuits (ASICs) of high quality and (iii) Commercial Off-The-Shelf (COTS) devices. The major disadvantage of these three approaches is reduced design flexibility. A change in a specific data processing algorithm results in major hardware design changes. The Configurable System-on-Chip approach is based on radiation tolerant SRAM-based FPGAs and provides the capability for both flexibility and reliability. The Venus Express Monitoring Camera (VMC) is one example of such a flexible SoC approach [1]. The scientific objective of VMC is to observe the Venus atmosphere with a 1Mpixel detector sub-divided in four optical channels. It is based on a "LEON-2" processor, achieving a computer power of 20 Million Instructions Per Second (MIPS) in our system. Image processing (e.g compression) can be done in software because of the moderate acquisition time and read out data rate of the detector. For future space missions the demand for high performance on-board processing has drastically increased. High resolution detectors with high data rate and data volume need intensive data processing (e.g. image and video compression) on board. In-flight reconfigurability is a significant advantage for maintenance purposes and the capability to update processing modules to improve functionality. Additional, dynamic reconfiguration enhances the system with run-time adaptive functionality. An important requirement for DPUs in space is the qualification of system. The system is qualified on ground by intensive test (e.g. temperature, shock, stress). This qualification has to be guaranteed in space after a module update or during the dynamic reconfiguration of a module. Therefore the modules need to be isolated from the host system logically and physically. To achieve such an enhanced space suitable Dynamic Reconfigurable System-on-Chip (DRSoC) approach a flexible, robust and fault tolerant communication architecture is needed, which provides high data transfer rates and is suitable for dynamic reconfigurable modules as well.

In this paper we will focus on our newly developed Network-on-Chip architecture approach System-on-Chip Wire (SoCWire). The conditions for SRAM-based FPGAs in space will be depicted. We will then present the advantage of a DRSoC and outline its requirements for space and the essential for a Network-on-Chip (NoC). Finally, we will introduce our SoCWire based architecture and outline its performance, which has been measured in a demonstration implementation.

2 SRAM-FPGAs in Space

The space radiation environment is composed of a variety of energetic particles with energies ranging between keV to GeV and beyond. These particles are either trapped by the Earth's magnetic field or passing through the solar system. The damage of semiconductor components through charged particles may be separated into two categories: Total Ionizing Dose (TID) and Single Event Effects (SEE). TID is a cumulative long-term degradation of the device when exposed to ionizing radiation. SEEs are individual events which occur when a single incident ionizing particle deposits enough energy to cause an effect in a device. This effect produces different failure modes, depending of the incident particle and specific device. From their appearance two categories will be more focused (i) the Single Event Latchup (SEL) and (ii) Single Event Upset (SEU). A SEL leads to ignite a parasitic thyristor in the silicon structure which result is that the circuit turns fully on and causes a short across the device until the latter burns up or the power to it is cycled. SEU is a change of state (bit-flip) or transient induced by an ionizing particle. Xilinx provides the XQR Virtex family

FPGAs of large gate counts with required qualification level and radiation tolerance to TID and SEL. Xilinx Virtex FPGAs are SRAM-based and customized by loading configuration data into the internal memory cells. These memory cells (Logic, Routing, BRAM) are sensitive to SEU. A SEU can change the internal logic state, routing and memory contents of BRAM. Therefore the customized logic need to be fault tolerant with dedicated mitigation techniques (Triple Modular Redundancy, TMR, configuration scrubbing) which reduces the SEU rates to an at least tolerable value. The advantage of SRAM-based FPGAs is their capability of reconfiguring the complete or partial system even during operation but they need fault tolerant techniques to achieve a reliable and robust system.

3 Requirements for Future Space Missions

VMC demonstrated a successful and space suitable configurable SoC approach. Science operation has been started in the mid of May 2006. Since then, VMC was switched on for an accumulated time of 6800h, taking more than 103,000 images and is running well. So far only three non-correctable SEUs in the Xilinx FPGAs have been observed, which is in the expected range and shows the suitability of this approach for space applications. For future space mission advanced data processing needs to be done on-board. With high resolution detectors of 5Mpixel the data rate and data volume increases drastically but the average data rate to spacecraft remains at 20...60 kbps. Therefore image and video compression needs to be done on-board in a reliable and robust system. In-flight update of processing modules enhances the system with maintenance potential and performance improvement; an image compression core could be replaced by a sophisticated core to calculate scientific parameters directly on-board. Dynamic partial reconfiguration enhances the system with at run-time adaptive functionality e.g. an image compression core could be replaced by a video compression core on demand, which is an improvement in terms of resource utilization and power. Our framework for in-flight reconfigurability is based on the VMC approach with the additional features of dynamic partial reconfiguration. The FPGA is subdivided into static and Partial Reconfigurable Areas (PR-Areas) which

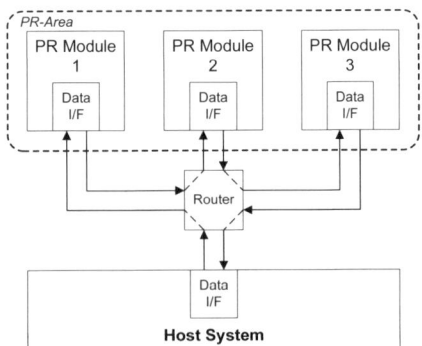

Fig. 1. DPU architecture macro-pipeline system

can be updated during operation. The static area remains unchanged during the whole mission and comprises all critical interfaces (e.g. processor, communication interfaces). This offers the advantage that only the updated module has to be qualified in a delta-qualification step, not the whole system [2]. The model we use for our instrument DPU designs is usually a macro-pipeline system with pre- and post- processing steps in a dedicated structure as depicted in Figure 1. This architecture covers the typical processing chain requirements in classical instruments up to complete payload data handling.

4 Dynamic Partial Reconfiguration in Virtex-4 FPGA

The Xilinx Virtex-4 QPro-V family is available as space suitable radiation tolerant FPGA. In contrast to earlier Virtex families e.g. Virtex-II the internal configuration of the hardware architecture has changed. In previously FPGAs the CLBs (Configurable Logic Block) were surrounded by a ring of IOBs (Input-Output Buffer). The IOBs are now organized in columns. Additionally the FPGA is divided in clock regions, each comprising 16 CLBs. These clock regions have significant influence on the configuration process of the FPGA. Xilinx FPGAs are customized by loading configuration data into the internal configuration memory. The configuration memory is arranged in frames that are tiled about the device. These frames are the smallest addressable segment of the configuration memory space. One frame comprises 16 CLBs and therefore one clock region [3]. This architecture with clock regions and IOB structures has the advantage to overcome the limitation of partial reconfiguration in the Virtex-II architecture. Partial Reconfigurable Modules (PRMs) do not have to occupy the full height of the device and IOBs above the top edge and below the bottom edge of the module are not part of the module resources. Therefore the logic resources left, right, top and bottom of a PRM can be used for the static area. The Virtex-4 family provides now a 32Bit data word width configuration interface (SelectMap) running at 100Mhz which significantly decrease reconfiguration time by a factor of 8 compared to Virtex-II. For communication between modules (static and partial reconfigurable area) Xilinx provides new unidirectional Bus-Macros in the Virtex-4 family which can connect modules horizontal and vertically. These Bus-Macros are suitable for hand shaking techniques and bus standards like AMBA or Wishbone. As mentioned before, classically the instrument DPU architecture is a macro-pipeline system with high data rate point-to-point communication. To realize this architecture in a bus structure, multi master and bus arbitration are needed. Also bus structures are limited in the Xilinx hardware architecture. In a partial reconfigurable system a bus requires wires that distribute signals across the device. The Virtex family provides bidirectional vertical, horizontal long lines that span the full high and width of the device and 3-State buffer horizontal long lines that span the full width of the device. These long lines are limited in resources in the device, 24 bidirectional horizontal, vertical and 4 3-State buffer long lines per column CLB [4]. Furthermore the dynamic partial reconfiguration process does not have an explicit activation. New frames become active as they are written. If bits are identical to the current value, the bits will not momentarily glitch to some other value. If the bits change, those bits could glitch when the frame write is processed. Furthermore some selections (e.g. the input multiplexers on CLBs) have their control bits split over multiple frames and thus do not change atomically. A fault tolerant bus structure with hot-plug ability is necessary to guarantee data integrity. With these limitations a bus structure based system would encounter the following disadvantages:

- An SEU in the PRM bus interface logic could stop the system
- No dedicated Bus-Macros are provided by Xilinx to access long lines which lead to manual time consuming routing.
- Failure tolerant bus structure (high efforts) with hot-plug ability is necessary to guarantee data integrity
- Dynamic reconfiguration of a PRM could block the bus and stop the system
- Limited long lines resources restrict the bus structure in data word width.

Further issues come from the physics of micro technology: long global wires and buses have unpredictable performance, high power consumption and noise phenomenon [5]. With the issues mentioned before we consider instead a networked architecture with a Network-on-Chip (NoC) approach providing:

- Reconfigurable point-to-point communication
- Support of adaptive macro-pipeline
- High speed data rate
- Hot-plug ability to support dynamic reconfigurable modules
- Easy implementation with standard Xilinx Bus-Macros.

In order to achieve these requirements we have developed our own NoC architecture: System-on-Chip Wire (SoCWire).

5 System-on-Chip Wire (SoCWire)

Our approach for the NoC communication architecture, which we have named SoCWire, is based on the ESA SpaceWire interface standard [6]. SpaceWire is a well established standard, providing a layered protocol (physical, signal, character, exchange, packet, network) and proven interface for space applications. It is an asynchronous communication, serial link, bi-directional (full duplex) interface including flow control, error detection and recovery in hardware, hot-plug ability and automatic reconnection after a link disconnection.

5.1 SpaceWire

SpaceWire uses Data Strobe (DS) encoding. DS consists of two signals: Data and Strobe. Data follows the data bit stream whereas Strobe changes state whenever the Data does not change from one bit to the next. The clock can therefore be recovered by a simple XOR function. The performance of the interface depends on skew, jitter (Figure 2) and the implemented technology. Data rates up to 400 Mb/s can be achieved.

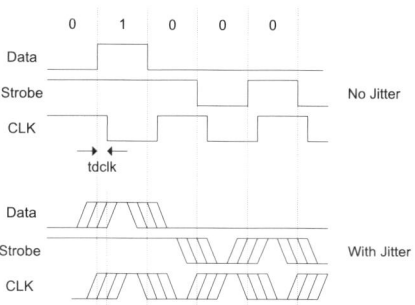

Fig. 2. Data Strobe encoding

5.1.1 Character Level

The SpaceWire character level protocol is based on the IEEE Standard 1355-1995 with additional Time-Code distribution. The character level protocol includes two types of characters (i) data character and (ii) control character. A data character (10bit length) is formed by 1 parity bit, 1 data-control flag and 8 data bits and includes data to be transmitted, as shown in Figure 3. The data-control flag indicates, if the current character is a data (0) or control character (1). Control characters (4-bit length) are used for flow control: normal End of Packet (EOP), Error End of Packet (EEP), Flow Control Token (FCT) and an escape character (ESC) which is used to form higher level control codes (8-14bit length) e.g. NULL (ESC+FCT) and Time-Code (ESC + Data character). The odd parity is assigned to data and control characters to support the detection of transmission errors. The parity bit covers the previous eight bits of a data character or two bits of a control character.

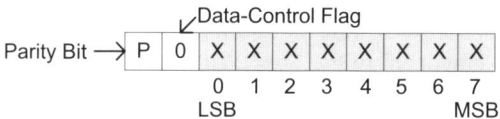

Fig. 3. Data character

5.1.2 Exchange Level

The exchange level is responsible for making a connection across a link and for managing the flow across the link. The exchange level is separated into two types: Link-Characters (L-Char) and Normal-Characters (N-Char). N-Char comprises data character, EOP and EEP and are passed to the network level. L-Char are used in the exchange level and are not passed to the network level. They include FCT and ESC characters and are responsible for link connection and flow control. Link connection is initialized by sending NULL characters from both ends of a link. When the receiver detects NULL character the link is connected, if no NULL characters are received a time out procedure re-initialized the link and restarts the sending of NULL characters. After link connection is established, FCTs are transmitted over the link. FCT signify that one end of the link is ready to receive data, this avoids host receive buffer overflow. SpaceWire can detect and recover from different errors: disconnect error (lost of link connection), parity error, escape error (received character is formed with ESC and is not FCT or Time-Code), credit error (2 bit errors are detected which are not covered by parity) and character sequence error (FCT or N-Char is received and is not expected). These errors initialize a silence error recovery procedure. If an error is detected the link is disabled at one end, which leads to disabling the link also on the other end. The error is passed to the network level by indicating an EEP. The link is then re-connected automatically.

5.1.3 Packet Level

The packet level describes the packet format to support routing of packets over a SpaceWire network. A SpaceWire packet comprises Destination Address + Cargo + EOP/EEP. The destination address contains the destination identifier. The cargo contains the user data. EOP/EEP indicates the packet status. The SpaceWire standard covers all requirements for a fault tolerant and robust network. It comprised recovery from link disconnection, which could occur during the dynamic partial reconfiguration process, and error recovery which makes it suitable for a dynamic reconfigurable system even for the harsh space environment.

5.2 SoCWire CODEC

As mentioned before, SpaceWire is a serial link interface and its performance depends on skew, jitter and the implemented technology. For our NoC approach we are in a complete on-chip environment with up to 6 reconfigurable modules, which can be operated by one switch. The maximum character length in the SpaceWire standard without time code, which is not needed in our NoC, is 10bit (data character). Therefore we have modified the SpaceWire interface to a 10bit parallel data interface. The advantage of this parallel data transfer interface is that we can achieve significantly higher data rates as compared to the SpaceWire standard. Additionally, we have implemented a scalable data word width (8-128bit) to support medium to very high data rates. On the other hand we keep in our implementation the advantageous features of the SpaceWire standard including flow control and hot-plug ability. Also the error detection is still fully supported making it suitable even for an SEU sensitive environment. For a parallel data transfer the flow control characters (FCT, NULL) need to be included in the parallel data transfer. NULL characters are only presented for the initial link connection phase. After initialization phase, every eight data character is followed by one FCT to signal the readiness of the core to receive data. The maximum data rate for a bi-directional (full-duplex) transfer can therefore be calculated by:

$$DRate_{Bi}\left[\frac{Mb}{s}\right] = f_{Core(MHz)} \times DWord\ Width - \frac{f_{Core(MHz)} \times DWord\ Width}{8} \quad (1)$$

For a unidirectional data transfer the flow control characters are processed in parallel and the maximum data rate can be calculated by:

$$DRate_{Uni}\left[\frac{Mb}{s}\right] = f_{Core(MHz)} \times DWord\ Width \quad (2)$$

Table 1 shows data rates for different data word width, unidirectional and bi-directional (full-duplex) data transfer. The SoCWire CODEC has been implemented and tested in a Xilinx Virtex-4 LX60-10. Table 2 shows the occupied area and maximum clock period depend on the data word width.

Table 1. SoCWire CODEC data rates for given core clock frequency

DWord Width	f_{Core} (MHz)	DRate [Mb/s]	
		Unidirect.	Bi-direct.
8	100	800	700
32	100	3200	2800

Table 2. SoCWire CODEC synthesis report

DWord Width	Max. f_{Core} (MHz)	Area	
		LUT	FlipFlops
8	200	297	140
32	180	447	260

Table 1 and Table 2 show that high data rates are achieved at significantly small area cost occupied by the SoCWire CODEC.

5.3 SoCWire Switch

The switch enables the transfer of packets arriving at one link interface to another link interface on the switch, and then sending out from this link. The SoCWire Switch and its protocol are again based on the SpaceWire standard. The SoCWire Switch determines from the destination address where the packet is to be routed to. As mentioned before, our NoC consists of up to 6 reconfigurable modules. Therefore the direct port addressing (packets with a port address are routed directly to one of the output ports) has been implemented. As soon as the destination port of a packet is determined and the port is free, the packet is routed immediately to that output port. The port is marked as busy and can not be accessed until the end of the packet. This is also known as wormhole routing which reduces buffer space and latency. Our SoCWire Switch is a fully scalable design supporting data word width (8-128bit) and 2 to 32 ports. It is a totally symmetrical input and output interface with direct port addressing including header deletion. The SoCWire Switch has been implemented and tested in a Xilinx Virtex-4 LX60-10. Table 3 shows the occupied area and maximum clock period for a 4 port switch dependent on the data word width.

Table 3. SoCWire Switch (4 Ports) synthesis report

DWord Width	Max. f_{Core} (MHz)	Area	
		LUT	FlipFlops
8	190	1736	668
32	170	2540	1169

The SoCWire Switch basically consists of a number of SoCWire CODECs according to the number of ports and additional fully pipelined control machines. The maximum data rate is therefore equivalent to the SoCWire CODEC. With additional SoCWire Switches and path routing the network can be extended.

6 Test and Results

We have implemented four SoCWire CODECs, one in the Host system, three in the PRMs and one SoCWire Switch in a dynamic reconfigurable macro-pipeline system, see Figure 1. The Host system and SoCWire Switch where placed in the static area and the PRMs in the partial reconfigurable area. All SoCWire CODECs where configured with an 8 bit data word width. The implementation of the system with reconfigurable areas could be easily implemented with the standard unidirectional Xilinx Bus-Macros. Figure 4 shows a cut out of the placed and routed SoCWire macro-pipeline system: the PRMs (PRM1, PRM2 and PRM3) and Bus-Macros in a Virtex-4 LX 60. The static area is distributed over the FPGA. The PRMs were configured as packet forwarding modules. We have tested different configuration of packet forwarding e.g. between modules, through the whole macro-pipeline system, under the condition of parallel communication between nodes. The system runs at 100MHz and the maximum data rates of the simulation could be validated to be 800 Mbps. We dynamically reconfigured one PRM in the system.

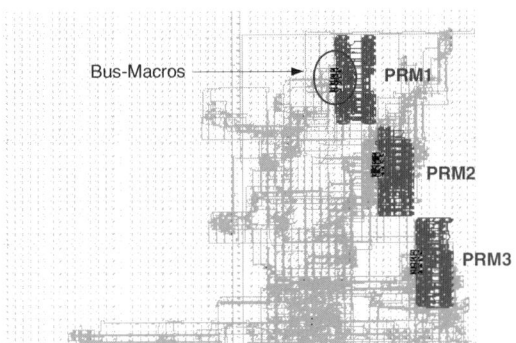

Fig. 4. SoCWire Macro Pipeline System

During the reconfiguration process the communication between the PRM and SoCWire Switch was interrupted, the other PRMs connections were still established. After the reconfiguration process was completed the communication between the two nodes was built up automatically without any further external action (e.g. reset of node or switch). This makes the system ideal for dynamic reconfigurable systems. The Partial Reconfiguration Time (PRT) can be calculated by:

$$PRT[s] = \frac{PRM[Bytes]}{CCLK[Hz] \times SelectMap_{DWordWidth}[Bytes]} \quad (3)$$

The size of one PRM was 37912 Bytes (64 Bytes command + 37848 Bytes data) and therefore the PRT 758µs (SelectMap, 8Bit data word width at 50Mhz). For this test system the area for one PRM was set to utilize 0.6 % of the logic resources

7 Conclusion

Configurable System-on-Chip Data Processing Units based on state-of-the art FPGAs are a proven solution for the harsh space environment. For future space applications the demands for high performance on-board processing increases enormously. Additionally, in-flight reconfigurability and dynamic reconfiguration is a further enhancement to support update of hardware functions on-board even on demand. To meet these requirements an enhanced communication architecture with a NoC approach is needed. In this paper we presented our NoC approach SoCWire. SoCWire meets all requirements for a high speed dynamic reconfigurable architecture. High data rates are achieved with significantly small implementation efforts. Hardware error detection, hot-plug ability and support of adaptive macro-pipeline are provided. SoCWire can be easily implemented with standard Xilinx Bus-Macros in the Virtex family. The high flexibility of the reference design allows the designer to adapt the SoCWire system quickly to any possible basis architecture. Additional SoCWire Switches can be implemented to extend the network. SoCWire and PR-Areas provide guaranteed system qualification (with PRM self-testing features) and therefore is suitable for robust dynamic reconfigurable systems.

References

1. Fiethe, B., Michalik, H., Dierker, C., Osterloh, B., Zhou, G.: Reconfigurable System-on-Chip Data Processing Units for Miniaturized Space Imaging Instruments. In: Proceedings of the conference on Design, automation and test in Europe (DATE), pp. 977–982. ACM, New York (2007)
2. Osterloh, B., Michalik, H., Fiethe, B., Bubenhagen, F.: Enhancements of reconfigurable System-on-Chip Data Processing Units for Space Application. In: Second NASA/ESA Conference on Adaptive Hardware and Systems (AHS 2007), Edinburgh, pp. 258–262 (August 2007)
3. Xilinx, Virtex-II Pro and Virtex-II Pro X Platform FPGAs: Functional Description (September 2005), http://www.xilinx.com
4. Xilinx, Virtex-4 Configuration Guide (October 2007), http://www.xilinx.com
5. Jantsch, A., Tenhunen, H.: Networks on Chip. Kluwer Academic Publishers, USA (2003)
6. ECSS, Space Engineering: SpaceWire–Links, nodes, routers, and networks, ESA-ESTEC, Noordwijk Netherlands, ECSS-E-50-12A (January 2003)

A Light-Weight Approach to Dynamical Runtime Linking Supporting Heterogenous, Parallel, and Reconfigurable Architectures

Rainer Buchty, David Kramer, Mario Kicherer, and Wolfgang Karl

Universität Karlsruhe (TH)
Institut für Technische Informatik, Lehrstuhl für Rechnerarchitektur
76128 Karlsruhe, Germany
{buchty,kramer,kicherer,karl}@ira.uka.de

Abstract. When targeting hardware accelerators and reconfigurable processing units, the question of programmability arises, i.e. how different implementations of individual, configuration-specific functions are provided. Conventionally, this is resolved either at compilation time with a specific hardware environment being targeted, by initialization routines at program start, or decision trees at run-time. Such technique are, however, hardly applicable to dynamically changing architectures. Furthermore, these approaches show conceptual drawbacks such as requiring access to source code and requiring upfront knowledge of future system configurations, as well as overloading the code with reconfiguration-related control routines.

We therefore present a low-overhead technique enabling on-demand resolving of individual functions; this technique can be applied in two different manners; we will discuss the benefits of the individual implementations and show how both approaches can be used to establish code compatibility between different heterogeneous, reconfigurable, and parallel architectures. Further we will show, that both approaches are exposing an insignificant overhead.

1 Introduction and Motivation

With Moore's Law still being valid, further increase in integration density – due to technological limitations – does not lead to faster uniprocessors, but rather multicore processors and significant advances in FPGA technology. This offers the possibility to create heterogeneous architectures comprising a mix of general-purpose and specialized processing units, potentially including dynamically reconfigurable hardware accelerators. A current example are so-called Platform FPGAs [17] which basically combine reconfigurable logic with conventional processor cores, dedicated communication hardware, and additional circuitry such as on-chip memory or hardware multipliers.

Such advances in technology will lead to massively parallel architectures, and, following vendor forecasts, these will likely be heterogeneous, i.e. architectures where the individual cores might show different characteristics. Considering hybrid approaches as e.g. outlined in the context of terascale computing [6] or the AMD Fusion concept [1] it can be therefore safely predicted that future architectures will not only feature heterogeneity but also will employ more and more reconfigurability to enable maximum use of the silicon area. Two academic research platforms illustrate such upcoming architectures: the Molen processor architecture [14] features a fixed processor core enhanced by user-defined commands executed on a reconfigurable hardware infrastructure. The Digital On-demand Computing Organism (DodOrg) [3] is an example of a dynamically reconfigurable system architecture, specifically addressing the aspects of parallel heterogeneous systems. DodOrg comprises an array of individual processing cells, connected using peer-to-peer networking. Each processing cell is reconfigurable in terms of function and connectivity, therefore not only supporting HW-based application acceleration and memory resources, but also required grouping and communication of cooperating processing cells. As demonstrated, future platforms extend the flexibility beyond task/node assignment into the hardware layer, therefore introducing a new class of problems with regard to application programming and execution.

The key problem of such architectures is exploiting their full potential. Here, the application itself must benefit from the architectures' features, e.g. by showing significant program phase behavior and/or requiring use of dedicated application accelerators. This must be taken into account by the application programmer and being supported by the runtime environment. A unified code representation is required, supporting all present computation nodes regardless of node type. Typically, therefore only a potentially accelerable computing routine is present as multiple, node-specific instances. A corresponding representation is used depending on the assigned computing node with the selection logic, i.e. which representation to use, being typically coded into the application itself. Reconfigurable hardware further increases this problem as certain hardware configurations might not be available or foreseeable at program development time.

As part of our effort on programming tools and environment targeting high-performance heterogeneous and reconfigurable computing, we therefore developed a light-weight approach enabling dynamic alteration of function calls at runtime, achieving dynamic adaptation of a running program to changing processing hardware. This addresses the major issue of program development and execution on heterogeneous and reconfigurable platforms: using a runtime layer, performing appropriate function mapping according to the current system configuration and provided node-specific implementations of individual functions, re-enables the programmer to fully concentrate on the application itself, rather than dealing with side effects of heterogeneity or reconfigurability issues.

Different from existing approaches, we implemented such a runtime layer as a light-weight extension to an existing OS runtime system, showing no measurable overhead during typical operation in contrast to heavy-weight virtual machine approaches. As a beneficial side effect, this approach offers a smooth upgrade path from static to dynamic systems is provided, and even mixed execution of adaptable and static application is possible.

The following paper therefore is structured as follows: first, we provide an overview over related work, highlighting differences and benefits of our approach. We will then introduce our concept in detail and discuss potential implementation alternatives, outlining the benefits of the chosen alternative. This is followed by the evaluation of the individual approaches, showing the overall feasibility and integrateability. The paper is concluded with a summary and outlook.

2 Related Work

One example of running applications on a heterogeneous and potentially changing hardware was recently presented by Stanford's Pervasive Parallel Lab (PPL) [11]. Basically extending the Java Virtual Machine approach [9], the PPL concept features a parallel object language to be executed on a common parallel runtime system, mapping this language onto the respective computing nodes using either interpretation or JIT techniques (including binary optimization). This approach requires applications to be rewritten from scratch to fit into the framework and its specific runtime system.

Breaking the border between hard- and software is the focus of IBMs long-term research project Lime [2,12]. Lime uses a uniform programming language and an associated runtime system, enabling that each part of the system may dynamically change between hard- and software. Similarly to the PPL concept, also Lime targets Java applications to be dynamically translated for co-execution on general-purpose processors and reconfigurable logic.

Based on the concept of cache-only memory architectures (COMAs) is the SDVM [5]. COMAs feature a distributed shared memory in which data migrates automatically to the computing nodes where it is needed. The SDVM extends this concept in a way that both, data and instructions, can transparently migrate, enabling automatic data and code migration within an SDVM-equipped parallel system. The $SDVM^R$ [7] furthermore adds so-called configware migration to this concept targeting transparent automatic hardware reconfiguration. Both SDVM incarnations require special program treatment and, moreover, a dedicated runtime layer.

The programming of heterogeneous parallel system is the focus of EXOCHI [16]. EXOCHI consists of the *Exoskeleton Sequencer* EXO and the C/C++-programming environment *C for Heterogeneous Integration* CHI. CHI extends the OpenMP pragma regarding heterogeneity. The code is compiled into a so-called *fat binary*, containing the whole program code for the given heterogeneous system, which then will be mapped to current hardware configuration by the CHI-own runtime system. EXO supports this mapping by managing a heterogeneous system as ISA-based MIMD resources.

A similar approach is presented by the Merge Framework [8]. Merge is based upon the EXO representation used in EXOCHI and, using a runtime system in combination with a library model, aims at complete execution dynamization on heterogeneous systems. Merge uses *map-reduce* as its input language to permit proper use of available parallelism.

Program generation and application execution for heterogeneous architectures consisting of CPUs and GPUs is addressed by several projects. Within the scope of this paper, a most prominent example is the Khronos OpenCL approach featuring program generation for computation offloading to either CPU or GPU [4]. OpenCL defines a programming model supporting data- and thread-parallelism with the according runtime layer dealing with thread management and deploying in GPU-accelerated systems.

From the cited work our approach differs in several ways: it was designed in a most compatible way, requiring ideally no changes on application level. It offers a versatile control interface, enabling the combination with existing programming models, resource and configuration managers, and is therefore applicable to a wide range of heterogeneous and reconfigurable management and programming approaches. It is particularly lightweight, not requiring an additional virtualization or abstraction layer. Instead, it is an extension of the OS's runtime system, making it possible to perform dynamic runtime function resolution, i.e. map individual functions of an application to one of several provided implementation alternatives. Targeting parallel systems, our approach also supports the OpenMP programming model. It therefore provides a smooth upgrade path from conventional to reconfigurable systems.

To address the different viewpoints, the following section contains an introduction to our basic approach and discusses possible implementation methods, their specific properties, and use within an OpenMP environment.

3 Runtime-Reconfigurable Function Calls

Our approach was explicitly designed with easy integrateability into existing systems in mind. Therefore, compatibility and lightweightedness were topmost design criteria. No extra runtime layer shall be required, no dedicated programming language or special binary format mandatory. In contrast to existing approaches, we therefore chose to realize our approach as an extension of the existing OS runtime system. As our implementation example, we chose Linux, but our approach is generally applicable to any Unix- or Unix-like system.

The underlying concept, depicted in Figure 1, consists of an adaptive processing hardware, on which a universal, i.e. configuration-independent, binary is executed which contains the control thread and computing functions to be dynamically mapped to the computing hardware. Depending on the current system configuration this may result in pure software, hardware, or hybrid implementations of the affected functions.

Such function resolution can be achieved by substituting the actual function call by a function pointer with the same name, arguments, and return value which during runtime gets resolved to the desired implementation. This function resolution ideally is individually controllable per thread and offers sufficient security against potentially malicious interference. That way, application code and reconfigurability issues can be strictly separated. A dynamic linker therefore is the central element of this function resolution. It is responsible for resolving configuration-specific functions and mapping them to the desired implementation during runtime, including on-demand retriggering of the dynamic linking process due to hardware changes. This is different to conventional approaches for dynamic runtime linking, where a function resolution takes only place once, or compiler-based decision trees which include the control logic into the application program.

To accomplish this, we introduce two different approaches to runtime reconfigurable function resolution. Our first approach is using so-called proxy functions in which any reconfigurable function is represented by its proxy; during runtime, the proxy is resolved to the desired implementation. The second approach performs dynamic changes within the Global Object Table (GOT) using the ELF binary format's lazy linking technique [13]. Both approaches have different capabilities, benefits, and drawbacks. In the following we will therefore present both implementation alternatives and discuss their individual advantages and disadvantages.

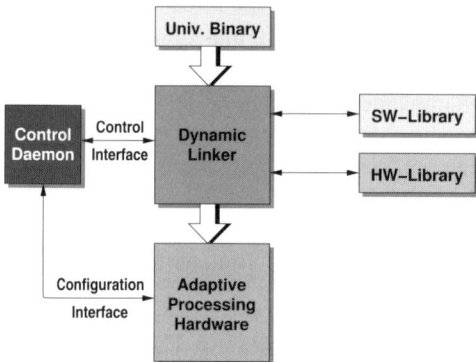

Fig. 1. Application Execution on Dynamically Reconfigurable Systems

Both approaches require steering the dynamic linking process, i.e. control of which functions may be mapped to what implementations without breaking an application's requirements. This is typically the task of a dedicated control daemon which can be considered an additional system service, triggering hardware configurations through a configuration interface and communicating with the linker through a dedicated control interface. Via this interface, specific function implementations may be added, removed, or selected during runtime. For maximal flexibility and interfaceability with a wide variety of control instances, we implemented this control interface using the process file system or *procfs* [10]; *procfs* is a pseudo file-system used to access process information from the kernel and is available on most Unix and Linux environments.

3.1 TSS-Based Dynamic Linking System (DLS)

Our first approach, called DLS (Dynamic Linking System), uses a proxy function concept depicted in Figure 2 implemented by augmenting a task-management kernel structure, the *task-state segment* (TSS) [15][1]. The benefit of this approach is fine-grain control on a per-thread base. In theory, an unlimited amount of function pointer substitutions is possible, even with an overlapping set of functions and libraries.

This approach requires minor changes to the kernel source code, basically to support task-associated management structures for the dynamic functions, as well as modifications within the program source code: using this approach, an application program must declare affected functions as runtime reconfigurable and perform necessary bookkeeping operations. To accomplish this, three dedicated functions are provided by the runtime system which the programmer needs to use to initialize and register required data structures and to provide pointers to function implementations.

This registration process is illustrated by Figure 3 where a function is first defined as runtime reconfigurable and an according management structure dls_struct is

---

[1] Please note that several operating systems, including Linux, do rely on software task switching as opposed to hardware task switching mechanisms provided by some CPUs. The TSS is therefore not bound to a specific hardware-dependent layout such as e.g. the IA32 TSS.

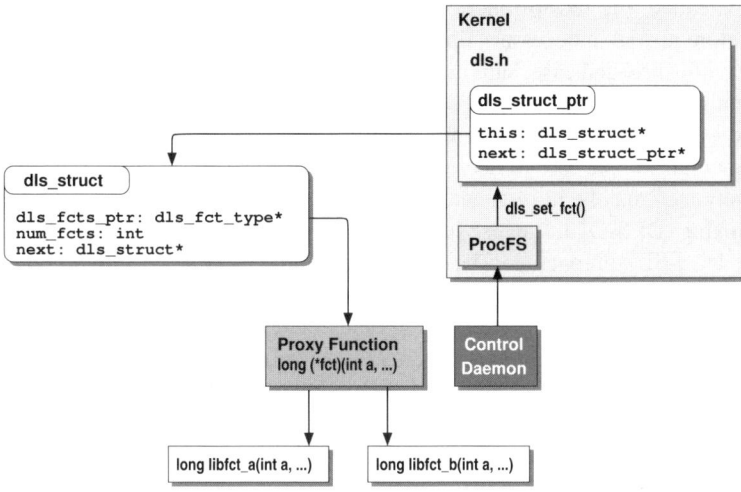

Fig. 2. DLS: TSS-based Proxy System

```
dls_define(testfct, int, char *str, int len);

dls_init(testfct);
dls_add(testfct, "libs/liba.so",testfcta);
dls_add(testfct, "libs/libb.so",testfctb);
```

Fig. 3. Initialization and Registration Example (see text)

provided. In further steps this structure is initialized and registered to the kernel, and individual implementations of this very functions are added.

Upon program execution, the proxy function pointer is then resolved to the currently selected implementation; this selection can be changed on-demand via *procfs* by triggering a dedicated switch logic. If the switch logic receives the command to change a function pointer, it will search for the corresponding dls_struct in the affected thread's linked list and change the function pointer to the desired function to be called. The previous value of this function pointer is stored separately for safe library unloading.

This concept aims at ease of implementation from a programmer's and runtime perspective. However, it does not come free of charge but requires certain kernel modifications: the task management structure task_struct needs to be expanded by a pointer to a linked list of function management structures dls_struct_ptr, which holds a pointer to the corresponding function resolving structure dls_struct. Furthermore, an exit function for freeing dls_struct_ptr is added.

Considering only single-threaded tasks, the unloading of libraries in this approach is safe. One possibility would be the counting of how many function pointers are connected with a library. So every library can be unloaded from address space if its usage counter equals zero. But even forced or speculative unloading of libraries is safe. If a function pointer still has a reference to a function in such a library and this current function is called, the fix-up function gets activated and reloads the library. In worst case therefore just an unnecessary time overhead is created.

In the multi-threaded case, safe unloading can only be performed automatically under certain circumstances. Simple counting of enter and return events is not always sufficient – a thread being inside a function can be destroyed before it returns, so the programmer has to take care of decreasing the counter.

This approach may be implemented in two ways, Static Linking (DLS-SL) and Dynamic Linking (DLS-DL). If every function implementation is known at compile-time, the static DLS-SL approach can be used. Because of the known function addresses, there is no need for an dynamic loader and proper steering functions, therefore reducing the switching overhead. If function implementations should be added or removed dynamically during program execution, the dynamic linking approach DLS-DL must be used. Using this implementation, a dynamic loader and a so-called fix-up function are necessary: the fix-up function uses the dynamic loader to load and unload function implementations and performs function resolution by changing the function pointer to the appropriate function symbol.

Without any switching, both implementation alternatives show a minimal runtime overhead at worst (see Section 4) as also the standard function resolution taking place during execution of dynamically linked functions requires an indirection: the according function is searched in an object table and then executed. The only difference in this approach is the use of a different search function taking place on an own, task-dependent management list. Due to the fix-up function and the dynamic loader, the switching overhead for DLS-DL is about 100% higher compared to DLS-SL.

While function switching is ideally steered from outside for proper separation of program execution and configuration control, the DLS approach is also capable of triggering the switching logic from inside the application, further decreasing the switching overhead as no *procfs* call to the kernel is required.

In our current implementation, dedicated initialization and registering routines are required. We are currently evaluating possibilities to also do this from outside the program code using *procfs* calls.

3.2 GOT-Based Linking System (GLS)

The GLS approach utilizes the lazy-linking technique used in the ELF binary format. The advantage of this approach is its independence of both, compiler and used programming language, as it purely operates on the ELF file format. Also, no source code changes are required, making it ideal for binary-only distributions and approved legacy code where code changes would lead to costly re-approval.

This approach is therefore tied to the ELF format by design. Porting to other file formats with similar features is potentially feasible, though. Compared with DLS, GLS needs just smallest changes to kernel source code: only the support for accessing the virtual memory of other processes needs to be activated. The switching logic itself can be realized as a kernel module which can be loaded at runtime.

Furthermore, this method only allows coarse-grained decisions, i.e. the redirection of function calls are effective for the whole program instance, therefore providing no way to individually adjust functions for different threads like in DLS.

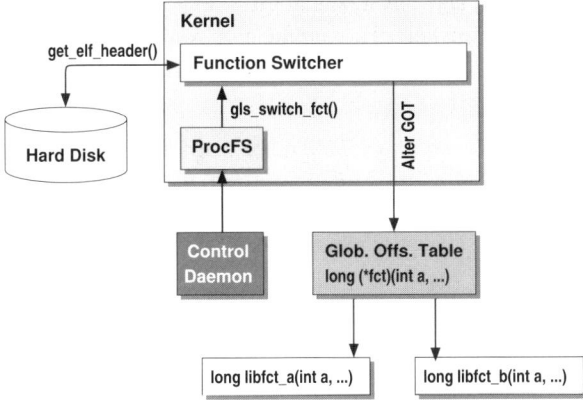

Fig. 4. GLS: GOT-Manipulation

Lazy linking means that a symbol will be resolved when it is first used and not at the beginning of the execution when the libraries are loaded. To use this method, we alter the name of the symbol at runtime and reset according data structures in a way that the next time the symbol is used, the dynamic linker is called and resolves the symbol with the new name. Within ELF files, this is supported by individual sections, of which the following are of special interest: The *.got* section contains the address of the symbol in user space or the associated *.plt* entry pointing towards the procedure look-up table (PLT), which in term contains code that calls the dynamic linker. The *.dynsym* section contains some details about the symbols, e.g. the address of a symbol name. These symbol names are provided by the *.dynstr* section. Finally, the *.rel.plt* section among other information contains the address of the corresponding GOT entry of the symbol.

During runtime, the kernel has to take the following steps: it will first iterate through the *.rel.plt* table and calculate the address of a symbol name based on associated entries in *.dynsym* and *.dynstr*. When a match is found, then the symbol in the *.dynstr* table is changed. For current limitations of our implementation, the new name must not be longer than the existing name. Finally, the entry in *.got* is set to the associated *.plt* entry. This is illustrated by Figure 4.

3.3 Multi-threading Considerations

In order to be suitable for multi- and many-core architectures, the support of the OpenMP programming model is mandatory. DLS is an ideal candidate for use in combination with OpenMP as it supports function redirection on a per-thread base, i.e. allows that each thread can execute a different implementation of the same function. However, in addition to the modifications mentioned in Section 3.1, some further but minor modifications to an application's source code are required: in order to properly identify the individual threads, the function call itself must be extended by the ID of the calling thread so that each thread is provided a private function pointer.

As mentioned above, GLS only allows function redirection on a per-task base, therefore only OpenMP applications with different workloads for each thread, e.g. using the sections-construct, can take advantage of GLS. In this case no additional modifications are necessary, neither to kernel nor application source code.

4 Evaluation

Our approach follows a low-overhead design. In this section we present measurement numbers proving that during normal operation our approach does not implicate any additional overhead. Such does only occur for function switching, where numbers are presented showing how this overhead distributes to the function switching itself and the overhead induced by the control interface.

For our evaluation we used an AMD Opteron 870 system equipped with 2 cores and 2 GB main memory, running Ubuntu Linux with a patched 2.6.20-kernel, providing the required alterations described in Section 3.

Aim of this evaluation is to determine the overhead of our runtime system and how the control interface and function switching contributes to the measured overhead. We therefore explicitly chose a minimal application calling a simple function return a+b; provided by two different libraries. That way, no side effects from configuring hardware accelerators, peripheral communication or function workload interfere with the measurements, exposing the runtime system's overhead for control, function switching, and function resolution. The measurements were conducted as follows: for each configuration, individual batches of 10,000,000 function calls per batch were performed. The batch runtime was measured using the Unix time command and the average runtime was calculated based on the measured times of 20 runs.

4.1 Single-Threaded Execution

Without any switching, the runtime of GLS is identical to normal program execution as depicted in Table 1(a), because no symbol needs to be changed and both binaries are identical. This is confirmed by our measurements. It is also shown that no measurable overhead exists for the DLS-SL and DLS-DL approaches during normal execution without function switching, i.e. with no function resolution occurring.

To measure the theoretical maximum overhead, we used the same test application, but this time we forced a function switch with each function call. It must be noted that this is a pure stress-test example and does in no way reflect ordinary use: typically, function switching will occur at most every few seconds as dictated by the hardware reconfiguration time. Under such conditions, function switching will have no measurable impact to the overall execution time and our approach will show the same performance as the OS's native, unaltered runtime system.

For the stress test, we see an overhead of 1.72 to 3.22 for the individual implementations as shown in Table 1(b). These numbers include both, overhead for function switching and communication through *procfs*. Naturally, DLS-SL shows better performance due to lower overhead compared to the dynamic approaches DLS-DL and GLS. The difference between GLS and DLS-DL results from the dynamic (un-)loading of the libraries after each function call: for GLS, every library function remains in the memory while for DLS-DL the libraries may be evicted from main memory.

The results in Table 1(c) show the overhead purely related to function resolution, excluding communication overhead. The overhead of the DLS-SL approach is therefore, as expected, negligible, ranging in the area of about 1%. The overhead of DLS-DL decreases by approx. 70% from 3.22 (Table 1(b)) to about 2.24, clearly exposing the influence of the external control interface and the pure switching and resolution overhead.

4.2 Multi-threaded Execution (OpenMP)

To measure the overhead for OpenMP applications, we used the same test application, but this time the reconfigurable function was called from inside a parallel OpenMP region. The iterations were equally distributed among each thread. Unless marked otherwise, we measured the overhead running 10 threads, using the DLS-SL approach.

We first determined the general overhead related to thread-dependent function resolution and switching. Tables 2 and 3 basically show the same behavior as in the single-threaded case. Without any switching occurring, the overhead is negligible. The switching overhead in the OpenMP case is in the same range as for the single-threaded case.

To demonstrate that, as expected from the implementation, the overhead of our solution is independent of thread number and number of function alternatives per thread, we tested the influence on runtime of both alternatives. According to the results shown in Table 4 the caused overhead is independent of the number of threads; the deviations in the presented numbers are solely related to OpenMP scheduling overhead and not caused by our implementation. Table 5 proves that the overhead is independent of the number of function implementations and therefore fixed within measuring accuracy.

Table 1. Runtime System Overhead Measurements (see text for interpretation)

(a) w/o Switching

	min	avg.	max	Ovhd.
(1) **native**	21.26s	21.60s	21.91s	–
(2) **GLS**	21.26s	21.60s	21.91s	0
(3) **DLS-DL**	21.08s	21.54s	21.88s	~0
(4) **DLS-SL**	21.06s	21.57s	21.94s	~0

(b) Switching Stress Test (controlled externally)

	min	avg.	max	Ovhd.
(1)	21.26s	21.60s	21.91s	–
(2)	60.86s	63.22s	65.58s	2.93
(3)	66.88s	69.60s	72.41s	3.22
(4)	35.20s	37.20s	39.40s	1.72

(c) Switching Stress Test (in-application)

	min	avg.	max	Ovhd.
(1)	21.26s	21.60s	21.91s	–
(2)	n/a	n/a	n/a	n/a
(3)	47.33s	48.41s	49.35s	2.24
(4)	21.03s	21.85s	22.66s	1.01

Table 2. OpenMP runtimes w/o switching

	min	avg.	max	Ovhd.
w/o	24.09s	24.88s	25.84s	–
DLS-SL	25.88s	26.53s	28.26s	1.06

Table 3. OpenMP Switching Stress Test

	min	avg.	max	Ovhd.
w/o	24.09s	24.88s	25.84s	–
DLS-SL	36.32s	38.36s	41.87s	1.54

Table 4. Thread-related Overhead

#Threads	1	5	10	20
DLS-SL	35.93s	39.38s	38.36s	38.29s

Table 5. Functions-related Overhead

#Functions	2	4	8	16
DLS-SL	37.28s	38.10s	37.46s	37.76s

5 Conclusion and Outlook

Heterogeneous, dynamic systems call for methods reflecting the required dynamics also in software. Conventional techniques such as on-demand compilation or explicit code switches are not sufficient for dynamically changing systems, especially when reconfigurable resources are shared among several individual tasks. In addition, such solutions require source code access for adjusting code generation to a given configuration, which especially in commercial environments is not always the case.

We therefore presented a lightweight and compatible way of supporting dynamic function resolution in an OS's native runtime system. Such support can be implemented in different alternatives with only minimal changes on OS level, eventually supporting dynamic resolution without the need for application source code access. The presented solution complies with the requirements of multi- and manycore architectures supporting existing parallel programming models. We hence presented both implementation alternatives, DLS and GLS, based on the task-state segment (TSS) using so-called proxy functions and the ELF binary format's object table (GOT). The latter does not require any changes on application level and can be easily implemented as a kernel module. By design, it however is tied to the ELF format and does not enable easy per-thread but rather per-instance control. DLS, in term, allows per-thread control but (in the current implementation) requires slight code changes to register and initialize reconfigurable functions. Both approaches require changes at kernel level for enabling reconfigurability and according control interfaces.

We proved the low-overhead claim with a dedicated test case exposing the individual contributions of control interface and function switching to the overall overhead. By design, overhead takes only place when function switching is performed. As expected, any measurable overhead therefore only occurs for synthetic stress tests with constant change of function pointers and no function workload. Hence, for real-world application examples it can be safely assumed that our approach does only produce negligible (if at all measurable) overhead during program execution. We furthermore demonstrated the applicability of our approach to OpenMP, making our approach suitable for both, conventional multitasking and multi-threaded parallel systems.

We are currently refining this runtime system with respect to increased transparency and security aspects especially suiting the needs of multithreaded applications. We recently demonstrated the general usability with a heterogeneous processing case study employing hardware acceleration. As of now, a case study from the field of numerical mathematics is being performed, exhibiting distinct program phases, therefore requiring and benefitting from dynamic function resolution.

References

1. Advanced Micro Devices. AMD Fusion Whitepaper,
   http://www.amd.com/us/MarketingDownloads/
   AMD_fusion_Whitepaper.pdf
2. Hormati, A., Kudlur, M., Bacon, D., Mahlke, S., Rabbah, R.: Optimus: Efficient Realization of Streaming Applications on FPGAs. In: Proceedings of the 2008 International Conference on Compilers, Architecture, and Synthesis for Embedded Systems (CASES) (to appear) (October 2008)

3. Becker, J., Brändle, K., Brinkschulte, U., Henkel, J., Karl, W., Köster, T., Wenz, M., Wörn, H.: Digital On-Demand Computing Organism for Real-Time Systems. In: Karl, W., Becker, J., Grobietsch, K.-E., Hochberger, C., Maehle, E. (eds.) Workshop Proceedings of the 19th International Conference on Architecture of Computing Systems (LNI P81), March 2006, pp. 230–245 (2006)
4. Khronos Group. Khronos OpenCL API Registry (December (2008), http://www.khronos.org/registry/cl/
5. Haase, J., Eschmann, F., Klauer, B., Waldschmidt, K.: The SDVM: A Self Distributing Virtual Machine for computer clusters. In: Müller-Schloer, C., Ungerer, T., Bauer, B. (eds.) ARCS 2004. LNCS, vol. 2981, pp. 9–19. Springer, Heidelberg (2004)
6. Held, J., Bautista, J., Koehl, S.: From a Few Cores to Many: A Tera-scale Computing Research Overview. Research at Intel Whitepaper (2006),
http://download.intel.com/research/platform/terascale/terascale_overview_paper.pdf
7. Hofmann, A., Waldschmidt, K.: SDVM^R: A Scalable Firmware for FPGA-based Multi-Core Systems-on-Chip. In: 9th Workshop on Parallel Systems and Algorithms (PASA 2008), Dresden, Germany, vol. LNI P-124, pp. 59–68. GI e.V. (January 2008)
8. Linderman, M.D., Collins, J.D., Wang, H., Meng, T.H.: Merge: a programming model for heterogeneous multi-core systems. In: ASPLOS XIII: Proceedings of the 13th international conference on Architectural support for programming languages and operating systems, pp. 287–296. ACM, New York (2008)
9. Lindholm, T., Yellin, F.: The Java Virtual Machine Specification. Sun Microsystems, 2nd edn. (1999) ISBN 978-0201432947, http://java.sun.com/docs/books/jvms/
10. Jones, M.T.: Access the Linux kernel using the /proc filesystem. In: IBM developerWorks (2006), http://www.ibm.com/developerworks/library/l-proc.html
11. Olukotun, K., et al.: Towards Pervasive Parallelism. In: Barcelona Multicore Workshop (BMW (June 2008),
http://ppl.stanford.edu/wiki/images/9/93/PPL.pdf
12. Huang, S., Hormati, A., Bacon, D., Rabbah, R.: Liquid Metal: Object-Oriented Programming Across the Hardware/Software Boundary. In: Vitek, J. (ed.) ECOOP 2008. LNCS, vol. 5142, pp. 76–103. Springer, Heidelberg (2008)
13. The Santa Cruz Operation, Inc. System V Application Binary Interface (Edition 4.1) (1997), http://www.caldera.com/developers/devspecs/gabi41.pdf
14. Vassiliadis, S., Wong, S., Cotofana, S.D.: The MOLEN μ-coded Processor. In: Brebner, G., Woods, R. (eds.) FPL 2001. LNCS, vol. 2147, pp. 275–285. Springer, Heidelberg (2001)
15. Shukla, V.: Explore the Linux memory model. In: IBM developerWorks (2006), http://www.ibm.com/developerworks/linux/library/l-memmod/
16. Wang, P.H., Collins, J.D., Chinya, G.N., Jiang, H., Tian, X., Girkar, M., Yang, N.Y., Lueh, G.-Y., Wang, H.: EXOCHI: architecture and programming environment for a heterogeneous multi-core multithreaded system. SIGPLAN Not 42(6), 156–166 (2007)
17. Xilinx, Inc. Virtex^{TM} Family FPGAs (2008), http://www.xilinx.com/products/silicon_solutions/fpgas/virtex/index.htm

Ultra-Fast Downloading of Partial Bitstreams through Ethernet

Pierre Bomel, Jeremie Crenne, Linfeng Ye, Jean-Philippe Diguet,
and Guy Gogniat

Lab-STICC, Université de Bretagne Sud, UEB, CNRS UMR 3192, Lorient, France
{pierre.bomel,jeremie.crenne,linfeng.ye,jean-philippe.diguet,
guy.gogniat}@univ-ubs.fr

Abstract. In this paper we present a partial bitstreams ultra-fast downloading process through a standard Ethernet network. These Virtex-based and partially reconfigurable systems use a specific data-link level protocol to communicate with remote bistreams servers. Targeted applications cover portable communicating low cost equipments, multi-standards software defined radio, automotive embedded electronics, mobile robotics or even spacecrafts where dynamic reconfiguration of FPGAs reduces the components count: hence the price, the weight, the power consumption, etc... These systems require a local network controller and a very small internal memory to support this specific protocol. Measures, based on real implementations, show that our systems can download partial bitstreams with a speed twenty times faster (a sustained rate of 80 Mbits/s over Ethernet 100 Mbit/s) than best known solutions with memory requirements in the range of 10th of KB.

Keywords: partial reconfiguration, FPGA, link layer, bitstream server, ultra-fast downloading, Ethernet.

1 Introduction

Field programmable gate arrays (FPGAs) are now being integrated into applications ranging from handheld devices to space-based applications. These heterogeneous reconfigurable platforms provide a flexible way to build highly reusable systems on demand. Today, runtime partial reconfiguration can potentially reduce the number of devices or the device size, thereby reducing size, weight and power consumption. Systems requiring dynamicaly a subset of their functionnalities can take advantage of this partial reconfigurability because it allows swapping of hardware accelerators "on demand". In this context Xilinx's Virtex FPGA partial reconfiguration can be exploited in different ways, partially or globally, externally (exo-reconfiguration) or internally (endo-reconfiguration).

Virtex's dynamic and partial reconfiguration (PR) requires additional resources to store the numerous partial configuration bitstreams. Researchers exploit in vast majority local FLASH and RAM memories as bitstreams repositories. In the best case Huebner et al. [1] reduce up to 50% of the bitstream memory footprint with the help of a small hardware decompressor. Recently, Haiyun and Shurong [2] proposed a new adaptive LZW compression algorithm demonstrating bitstreams size gains about 43%. Then, we face the migration of silicon square millimeters from FPGAs to memories. Although their low cost, when compared to FPGAs, is in favor of this migration, there are some drawbacks.

1. First, their reuse rate can be extremely low, since these memories could be used just once at reset in the worst case.
2. Second, the balance in terms of global silicon square millimeters, component number reduction, PCB area, static power consumption and MTBF, is negative.
3. Third, for a single function to implement, the space of possible bitstreams can be extremely large and become bigger than local memories. This is particularly true for embedded, high-volume and low-cost systems. There are three combinatorial explosion factors namely:
   (a) the FPGAs types with their numerous devices, families, sizes, packages and speed grades variations,
   (b) the number of possible configurations depending on shape and placement of the IP on the 2D FPGA grid,
   (c) and the natural commercial life of the IP producing regularly new versions and updates.

In this paper we are presenting an evolution of a previous work [3] where we proposed a specific and quite simple protocol for partial reconfiguration over Ethernet. Through a better balanced harware/software partitionning of our hardware architecture and, with no change at protocol level, we have been able to double the sustained speed over a standard 100Mb/s (Mb = Mega bits) Ethernet local Network. The experimental results obtained prove that our systems can reach reconfiguration speeds twenty times faster than today's ones. Moreover their PR software memory footprint is small enough (a few 10th of KB, KB = Kilo Bytes) to be stored in FPGA internal memory hard blocks.

For systems having a reconfiguration latency constraint so strong that (even with a specific protocol) they need shorter downloadings we have also proposed the concept of a hierarchy of bitstreams servers [4]. It allows remote storage of bitstreams on LAN or WAN-shared servers and local storage of bitstreams copies in external RAM. A possible instance of a three level LRU caching strategy permits to cumulate advantages of distant and local storage of bitstreams.

In the following we review in Sect. 2 the previous PR related works via a standard LAN. In Sect. 3 we present our design choices and improvements to double the past downloading speed. In Sect. 4 we describe our experiments and measures about the partial reconfiguration speeds and memory footprints. We make measures with the help of signal processing IPs representative enough of the complexity expected in such embedded systems. Finally, in Sect. 5, we conclude and explain what extensions we intend to short-term focus on.

2 Related Work

The PR community agrees on the fact that, in applicative domains with strong real-time constraints, PR latency is one of the most critical aspects in its implementation. If not brief enough, the PR interest to build efficient systems can be jeopardized. Reconfiguring times will be highly dependent upon the size and organization of the partially reconfigurable regions inside a FPGA. Virtex-2 (V2) has column-wide frames embbeded into partial bitstreams: hence V2's bitstreams are bigger than necessary. Virtex-4s (V4) and Virtex-5s (V5) have relaxed this constraint, they now allow for arbitrarily-shaped regions. They have frames composed of 41 32-bits words. The smallest V4 device, the LX15, has 3740 frames, and the largest V4 device has, the FX140, has 41152 frames. From Xilinx's datasheets, four methods of partial reconfiguration exist and have different maximum downloading speeds:

1. externally (exo-reconfiguration)
   (a) serial configuration port, 1 bit, 100 MHz, 100 Mb/s
   (b) boundary scan port (JTAG), 1 bit, 66 MHz, 66 Mb/s
   (c) SelectMap port, 8 bits parallel, 100 MHz, 800 Mb/s
2. internally (endo-reconfiguration)
   (a) internal configuration port (ICAP), V2, 8 bits parallel, 100 MHz, 800 Mb/s

Of course, peak values are only objectives and ICAP inside V4 and V5 have bigger word accesses formats (16 and 32 bits). Depending on the system designer's ability to build an efficient data pipeline from the bitstream storage (RAM, FLASH, or remote) to the ICAP, the performances will be close (or not) to the peak values. The good questions are "what latency is acceptable" for a given application and "what is its related cost" in term of system cost (added memory/peripherals components). In particular, in the field of partial reconfiguration, to be able to compare contributions, we must identify what is the average size of a partial bitstream and what is its average acceptable reconfiguration latency. Finally, because systems can run at different frequencies, we must also integrate the system frequency in the numbers. Then, we will be able to fairly compare efficiencies of the various proposals. This will be done in the following paragraphs.

Compton and Hauck [5] give a complete and global survey of the whole problematic about reconfigurable computing. Walder and Platzner [6] confirm the need for fast reconfiguration in the field of the "wearable-computing". They conclude that PR latency can be neglected if its effective latency is negligible when compared to the applications computing time. We clearly see here that the "average acceptable latency" is application dependant. Researchers investigate two strategies to reduce the PR latency. These are the systematic reduction of the bitstream files size (offline compression) and the speedup of their downloading (online decompression and optimised protocols). The first strategy relies on off-line tools and methodologies for FPGA design: "Module Based" and "Difference Based" are two design flows from Xilinx [7]. The second strategy is an on-line approach based on embedded network services. In this paper we address the second strategy with dynamic partial endo-reconfiguration and consider the first one as necessary and complementary.

Partial and dynamic reconfiguration of Xilinx's FPGAs goes through the control of a configuration port called ICAP [8] (Internal Configuration Access Port). V2, V4 and V5 contain this port and a set of one or several PPC405 hard core processors. The ICAP port can be interfaced with "hard block" processors (PPC405) as well as synthesizable soft cores (Microblaze, PicoBlaze, etc ...) with more or less engineering work. The ICAP has been wrapped into a HWICAP component which implements around it a standard OPB interface for a cost of 150 slices and a single BRAM. With the last version of EDK (version 10.2) there is now a PLB bus version of this ICAP wrapper. The ICAP reconfiguration peak rate announced by Xilinx is exactly of one byte per clock cycle, it means 100 MB/s (MB = Mega Bytes) for systems running at 100 MHz. Because systems work at different frequencies, we'll express all measures in number of bits transmitted per second and per MHz. The reference ICAP bandwidth of 100 MB/s becomes 8 Mb/(s.MHz). From now, we will use this "figure of merit" (FOM) to compare contributions to the ICAP's peak value. Quantities will be expressed in bits, times in seconds, and frequencies in MHz.

$$FOM = quantity/(time * frequency)$$

Claus et al. [9] consider that, for real-time video applications like driver assistance, the average bitstreams size is about 300 KB. The adaptive nature of the image flow processing implies to dynamically change algorithms without loosing a single image (640x480 pixels, VGA, black and white). Under these conditions, Claus accepts to loose one eighth of the processing time for each image. With a rate of 25 images/s, the processing time is 40 ms, and a maximum of 5 ms can be devoted to endo-reconfiguration. Transmitting 300 KB in 5 ms fixes the speed constraint at 60 MB/s, which is sustainable by the ICAP. The experimental platform is a V2 inside which a PPC405 executes the software (no RTOS specified) managing the PR. Unfortunately they did not provide speed measurements at publication time.

Not strictly dedicated to PR, the XAPP433 [10] application note from Xilinx, describes a system built around a V4 FX12 running at 100 MHz. It contains a synthesized Microblaze processor executing the code of an HTTP server. The HTTP server downloads files via a 100 Mb/s Ethernet LAN. The protocol stack is Dunkel's lwIP [11] and the operating system is Xilinx' XMK. A 64 MB external memory is necessary to store lwIP buffers. The announced downloading rate is 500 KB/s, be 40 Kb/(s.MHz). This rate is 200 times lesser than ICAP's one.

Lagger et al. [12] propose the ROPES (Reconfigurable Object for Pervasive Systems) system, dedicated to the acceleration of cryptographic functions. It is build with a V2 1000 running at 27 MHz. The processor is a synthesized Microblaze executing νClinux's code. It downloads bitstreams via Ethernet with HTTP and FTP protocols on top of a TCP/IP/Ethernet stack. For bitstreams of an average size of 70 KB, PR latencies are about 2380 ms with HTTP, and about 1200 ms with FTP. The reconfiguration speed is about 30 to 60 KB/s, be a maximum of 17 Kb/(s.MHz).

Williams and Bergmann [13] propose νClinux as a universal PR software platform. They have developed a character mode device driver on top of the ICAP. This driver enables to download the content of bitstreams coming from any location because of the full separation between the ICAP access and the file system. Junction between a remote file system and the ICAP is done at the user level by a shell command or a user program. When a remote file system is mounted via NFS the bitstreams located there can be naturally downloaded into the ICAP. The system is built with a V2 and the processor executing νClinux is a synthesized Microblaze. The authors agree that this ease of use has a cost in term of performances and they accept it. No measures are provided. To have an estimation of such performances we made some measures in a similar context and got transfer speeds ranging from 200 KB/s to 400 KB/s, representing a maximum of about 32 Kb/(s.MHz). We agree that νClinux is a universal platform but we want to pinpoint its extremely low bitstream dowloading performance. Certainly extremely usefull for fast development νClinux probably does not provide fast enough downloading facilities to be used in a highly time-constraints environment. We think that further experiments should be done with a real-time "flavor" of Linux and with better written/optimized ICAP drivers.

This first part of the state of the art establishes that "Microblaze + Linux + TCP" is widely accepted. Unfortunately, best downloading speeds are far below the ICAP and network maximum bandwidth. Moreover, memory needs are in the range of megabytes, thus requiring addition of external memories. Such a gap in speed and such a memory footprint for a PR service seem to us really excessive. First, Linux and its TCP/IP stack can't run without an external memory to store the kernel code and the communication protocols buffers. Secondly, the implementation, and probably the nature (specified in the 80s for much slower and unreliable data links) of the protocols, is such that only hundredths of KB/s can be achieved on traditional LANs.

Finally, the authors [3] propose the implementation of a specific data link level protocol over a standard 100 Mb/s local Ethernet dedicated to lightweight and partially reconfigurable systems. This work has been initially implemented on a V2 running at 100 MHz. No specific RTOS is needed (but XMK is sufficient) and a set of interrupt handlers with a background task handle the data pipeline from the remote bitstreams server to the local ICAP. Sustained speed is ranging from 375 to 400 Kb/(s.MHz) for bitstreams of sizes ranging from 50 to 200 KB. This FOM is 10 times greater than the best previous works's FOMs.

Table 1. Identified bistreams sizes and latencies requirements from previous works

	Claus [9]	Lagger [11]	Authors [3]
Bitstream (KB)	300	70	50-200
Latency (ms)	5	1200-2380	10

On top of [3], the authors have build a hierarchy of bitstreams servers [4] to implement an LRU caching strategy for partial bitstreams. This hierarchy, being paid the cost of cache in external memory, allows to reduce the average downloading latency of partial bistreams. Hence, for systems with a known behavour, memory needs can be estimated and allocated to build the necessary cache memory. Based on [3], the worst case downloading speed has a FOM of 375 to 400 Kb/(s.MHz). But, once partial bitstreams are loaded into RAM, their downloading speed from external memory to ICAP is rising up to 4 Mb/(s.MHz), which is ten times faster. The value of the average downloading speed depends, of course, on the cache miss frequency. The smaller it is, the higher the average value is. This value of 4 Mb/(s.MHz) cannot not be considered as a contribution to ultra-fast downloading of partial bitstreams because it does not represent a pure network downloading speed. This a mix between memory accesses and network communications.

3 Contribution

In this section we present our contribution in terms of hardware and software architectures for PR. We present in details the essential points improving the speed and reducing the memory footprint. All ICAP accesses are 8 bits wide.

This contribution does not depend on the FPGA type but rather on the architecture build inside it. Tests show that, at the same frequency of 100 MHz, FOM has similar values (not strictly equals because Ethernet controllers are not the same) on a V2 or V4 implementation. We did not make a test on V5 yet, but this will be done soon. This allows us to place the discussion on the embedded architecture rather than on the latest version of FPGA available on the market. Of course, latests versions of FPGA can bring our systems to higher frequencies but should not change the FOM which is frequency independant.

3.1 Hardware Architecture

The hardware architecture we have first choosen (Fig. 1) relied on a V2 PRO 30 running at 100 MHz on a XUP evaluation board from Xilinx. A PPC405 core executed the PR software. We considered that dynamic IPs communicated with the FPGA environment directly via some pads. Thus, the FPGA was equivalent to a set of reconfigurable components able to switch rapidly from one function to another. Communication with the PPC405 and inter-IPs communication are out of the scope of this article but can be implemented with Xilinx's and Huebner's bus macros [14] and OPB/PLB wrappers for partially reconfigurable IPs as well as with an external crossbar like in the Erlangen Slot Machine of Bobda et al. [15]. We have specified with EDK, XPS and Planahead tools a system which contained a PPC405 surrounded by its minimal devices set for PR. The PPC405 having a Harward architecture, we have added two memories to store the executable code and the data. These are respectively the IOCM (Instruction On Chip Memory) and the DOCM (Data On Chip memory). The PPC405

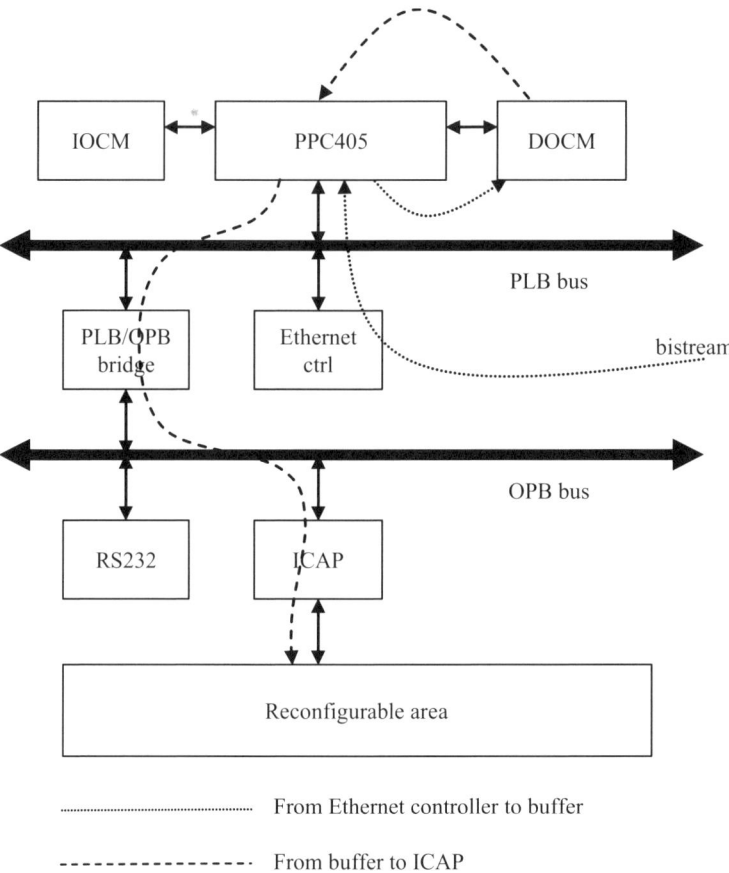

Fig. 1. Arch-1, Bitstreams path from Ethernet to ICAP

communicated with its devices through two buses connected through a bridge. These were the PLB (Processor Local Bus) for the faster devices and the OPB (On Chip Peripheral Bus) for the slower devices. The Ethernet PHY controller was connected to the PLB. The UART serial line, for instrumentation and trace purpose, was connected to the OPB. Finally the ICAP, connected to the OPB, managed the access and the downloading of bitstreams into the reconfigurable areas. The full exo-reconfiguration at reset was done through the external JTAG port while the endo-reconfiguration was dynamically done through the ICAP. This architecture allowed to download partial bistreams with a FOM of 400 Kb/(s.MHz).

Measurements made later showed us that the partitionning between hardware and software was not ideal. The bottleneck coming from software. Actually, more than 90% of the processing time was spend in data transfers from Ethernet controller to circular buffer and from circular buffer to ICAP (Fig. 3).

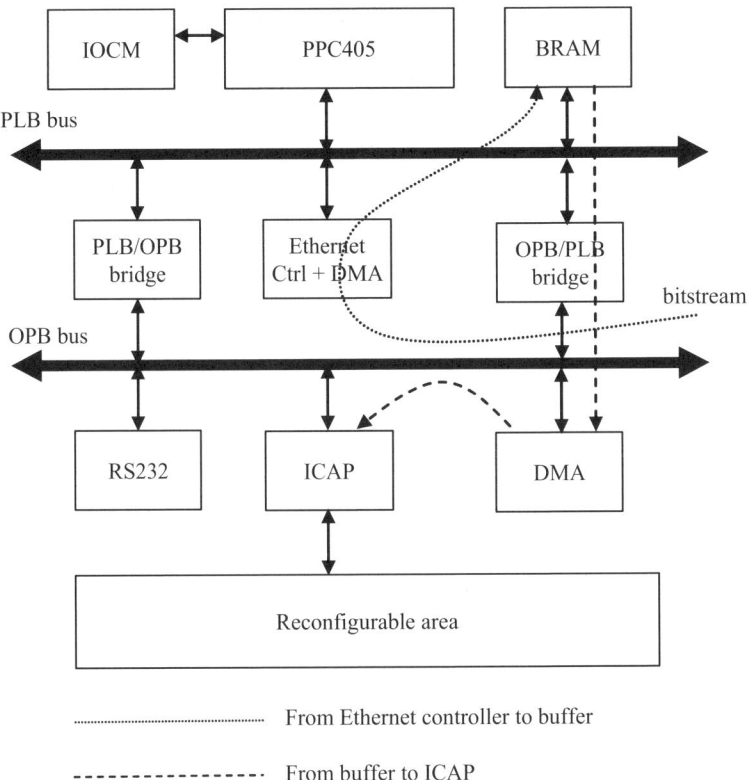

Fig. 2. Arch-2, Bistreams path from Ethernet to ICAP

The second hardware architecture we propose (Fig. 2) relies on a V4 VFX 60 running also at 100 MHz (which simplifies comparisons with first hardware harchitecture) on a ML410 evaluation board from Xilinx. This FPGA has four embbeded 10/100/1000 Mb/s Ethernet MAC controllers, among which only two are used on the ML410 board. Our architecture then uses only one of these two, configured to communicate at 100 Mb/s. Instead of relying on pure software data transfert loops executed by the PPC, we decided to use two DMAs in order to 1) transfer the data from the Ethernet controller to the packets circular buffer and 2) to transfer the data from the circular buffer to the ICAP. The first DMA is easily activated thanks to the configuration of the Ethernet controller IP available in EDK. The second DMA has to be instanciated (223 slices) and managed by the PPC itself when needed. The packets buffer, to be accessible by both DMAs cannot stay in DOCM (private to PPC) and must migrate in BRAMs located either on PLB or OPB bus. Because master accesses must be allowed for both DMA, two bus bridges (PLB/OPB and OPB/PLB bridges) must be added to allow for such data transfers. After testing on V2/XUP and V4/ML410, we obtained similar results: be a FOM about 800 Kb/(s.MHz).

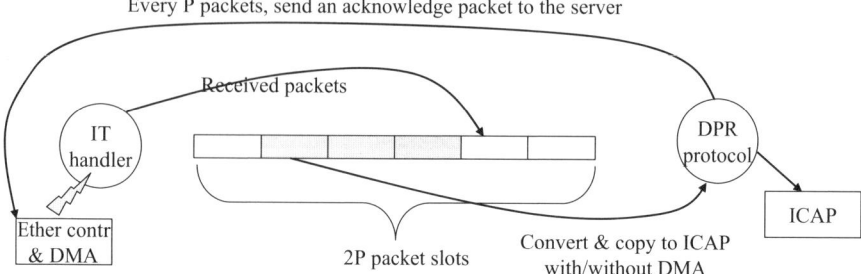

Fig. 3. Producer-consumer packets reception buffer

3.2 Software Architecture

The software architecture (Fig. 3) is based on three modules: the ICAP driver, the Ethernet driver and the PR protocol processing. Main objective is to reduce the number of software layers to cross when bitstreams are flowing from the Ethernet controller to the ICAP port. A time measurement module based on the internal hardware timer of the PPC405 and the access to the serial line via Xilinx's libc are also used and will not be commented as their use is marginal. This software establishes a data pipeline between the remote bitstreams server and the reconfigurable areas in the FPGA. We planned to reach the Ethernet maximum bandwidth of 100 Mb/s and today, with our 800 Kb/(s.MHz) FOM, we have reached a sustained rate of 80 Mb/s.

To uncouple the ICAP downloading from the Ethernet packet reception we have designed in software a producer-consumer paradigm: the producer being the Ethernet controller and the consumer being the ICAP port. A circular buffer is asynchronously fed with Ethernet packets by the Ethernet controller private DMA. Packets reception occurs by bursts: several packets are received without any data flow control feedback. The packet burst length (P) is less than or equal to the half capacity of the packets buffer. Each Ethernet packet has a maximum size of 1518 bytes and has a maximum payload of 1500 bytes of bitstream data. The PR protocol is executed concurrently with the Ethernet interrupt handlers. It analyzes the packets content and transfers the bitstream data from the buffer to the ICAP port via the second DMA programmation. The intermediate buffer sizing is a critical point in terms of performances. The bigger the burst is, the faster the protocol is. The buffer size depends on the available memory at the reconfiguration time and this scare resource can change in time. The protocol has been tailored to dynamicaly adapt its burst sizes to the buffer size, [3] gives its detailed specification.

4 Results

Our measures are based on the repetitive endo-reconfiguration of cryptography IPs like DES and triple DES producing bitstreams file sizes about 60 KB and 200

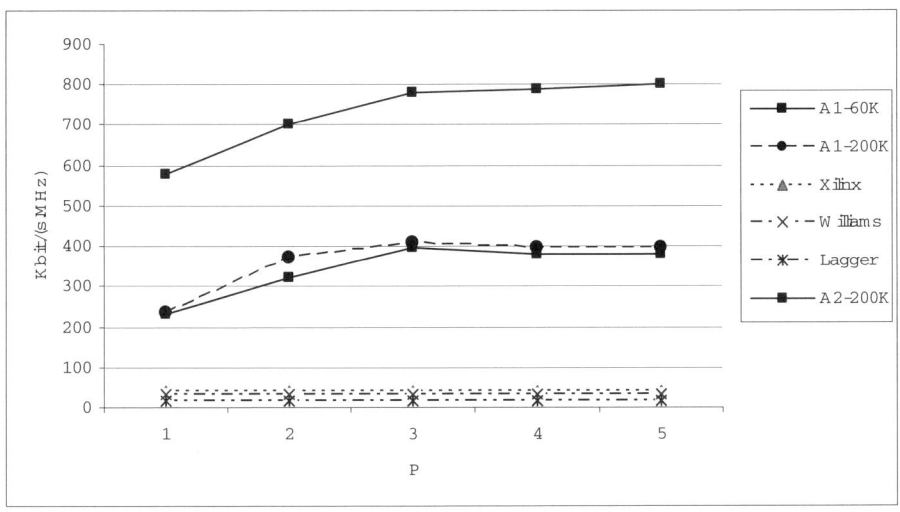

Fig. 4. Endo-reconfiguration speed vs P

KB. Results obtained (Fig. 4) depend also, as we could expect, on the producer-consumer packets buffer size allocated to the PR protocol. So the FOMs depend on P. The curves at the top (plain and dashed curves) represent respectively measured speeds for 60 KB and 200 KB bitstreams for Arch-1 and 200 KB bitstreams for Arch-2. One can establish that, in all cases, when the packets burst has a size greater or equal to three packets (P = 3), maximum speeds of 400 Mb/(s@MHz) (first architecture) and 800 Mb/(s.MHz) (second architecture) are reached and are stabilized. The size of the circular buffer being 2P, it needs room for exactly six packets, be 9 KB ($6 * 1.5KB$) only. Compared to usual buffer pools of hundredths of KB for standard protocol stacks, this is a very small amount of memory to provide a continuous PR service.

Dotted curves at the bottom represent the average speeds reached by Xilinx, Lagger and probably Williams. Our PR protocol exhibits a reconfiguration speed 80 Mb/s closer to our local 100 Mb/s Ethernet LAN limit. The gap between the reconfiguration speed and the ICAP speed is now about one order of magnitude instead of three orders of magnitude as previously. Finally, our PR software fits into 32 KB of data memory and 40 KB of executable code memory.

When compared to related works, the endo-reconfiguration speed we have reached with our ultra-fast downloading is 20 times more efficient and needs less

Table 2. Comparative endo-reconfiguration speeds and memory footprints

	Lagger [11]	Williams [12]	Xilinx [9]	Arch-1 [authors]	Arch-2 [authors]
FOM (Mb/s@MHz)	17	32	40	400	800
Memory (bytes)	$> 1M$	$> 1M$	$> 1M$	$< 100K$	$< 100K$

memory space. Table 2 sums up the respective speeds expressed in Mb/(s.MHz) and memory footprints in bytes.

5 Conclusion and Future Extensions

Our PR platform and experiments show there are still opportunities to improve LAN-level, and probably IP-level, protocols in order to provide an efficient and remote reconfiguration service standard networks. Our implementation exhibits an order of magnitude gain (X 20) in speed when compared to related works.

From here, we target implementations and protocol optimizations for future low-latency, high-bandwidth and network-reconfigurable sets of partially reconfigurable embedded systems. Would another FPGA maker provide a new configuration port, the protocol presented here could be reused "as is". Integration of our specific PR protocol on top of UDP into Dunkel's lwIP stack will be a way to promote its usage as well as the customization of UDP/IP stacks inside a real-time version of Linux or MicroC/OS-II.

Also, a software implementation running on a Microblaze soft core and a full hardware implementation of the PR protocol might be welcome when targeting systems without PPC405 hard cores. Ferivatives will be necessary when PR-based systems will be connected to other LANs like Wifi or CAN. At last, for performance purpose, 1 Gbit/s Ethernet and wider (16 bits and 32 bits) ICAP word accesses should be tested together to raise the FOM.

References

1. Huebner, M., et al.: Real-time Configuration Code Decompression for Dynamic FPGA Self-Reconfiguration. In: Proc. of the 11th Reconfigurable Architectures Workshop (RAW/IPDPS 2004), Santa Fe, New Mexico, USA, April 26-30 (2004)
2. Haiyun, G., Shurong, C.: Partial Reconfiguration Bitstream Compression for Virtex FPGAs. In: Proc. of International Congress on Image and Signal Processing (CISP 2008), Sanya, Hainan, China, May 27-30 (2008)
3. Bomel, P., Gogniat, G., Diguet, J.-P.: A Networked, Lightweight and Partially Reconfigurable Platform. In: Woods, R., Compton, K., Bouganis, C., Diniz, P.C. (eds.) ARC 2008. LNCS, vol. 4943, pp. 318–323. Springer, Heidelberg (2008)
4. Bomel, P., Gogniat, G., Diguet, J.-P., Crenne, J.: Bitstreams Repository Hierarchy for FPGA Partially Reconfigurable Systems. In: Proc. of 7th Intl. Symposium on Parallel and Distributed Computing (ISPDC 2008), Krakow, Poland, July 1-5 (2008)
5. Compton, K., Hauck, S.: Reconfigurable Computing: A Survey of Systems and Software. ACM Computing Surveys 34(2), 171–210 (2002)
6. Walder, H., Platzner, M.: Online Scheduling for Block-partitioned Reconfigurable Devices. In: Proc. of Design, Automation and Test in Europe Conference and Exposition (DATE 2003), Munich, Germany, March 3-7 2003. IEEE Computer Society, Los Alamitos (2003)
7. Xilinx XAPP290. Two Flows for Partial Reconfiguration: Module Based or Difference Based (September 2004)

8. Blodget, B., McMillan, S., Lysaght, P.: A lightweight approach for embedded reconfiguration of fpgas. In: Proc. of Design, Automation and Test in Europe Conference and Exposition (DATE 2003), Munich, Germany, March 3-7, 2003. IEEE Computer Society, Los Alamitos (2003)
9. Claus, C., Zeppenfeld, J., Muller, F., Stechele, W.: Using Partial-Run-Time Reconfigurable Hardware to accelerate Video Processing in Driver Assistance System. In: Proc. of Design, Automation and Test in Europe Conference and Exposition (DATE 2007), Nice, France, April 20-24 (2007)
10. Xilinx, XAPP433. Web Server design using MicroBlaze Soft Processor (October 2006)
11. Adam Dunkels. lwIP. Computer and Networks Architectures (CNA), Swedish Institute of Computer Science, http://www.sics.se/~adam/lwip/
12. Lagger, A., Upegui, A., Sanchez, E.: Self-Reconfigurable Pervasive Platform For Cryptographic Application. In: Proc. of the 16th Intl. Conference on Field Programmable Logic and Applications (FPL 2006), Madrid, SPAIN, August 28-30 (2006)
13. Williams, J., Bergmann, N.: Embedded Linux as a platform for dynamically self-reconfiguring systems-on-chip. In: Proc. of the Intl. Conference on Engineering of Reconfigurable Systems and Algorithms (ERSA 2004), Las Vegas, Nevada, USA, June 21-24 (2004)
14. Huebner, M., Becker, T., Becker, J.: Real-Time LUT-based Network Topologies for Dynamic and Partial FPGA Self-Reconfiguration. In: Proc. of the 17th Symposium on Integrated Circuits and Systems design (SBCCI 2004), Ipojuca, Brazil, September 7-11 (2004)
15. Bobda, C., Majer, M., Ahmadinia, A., Haller, T., Linarth, A., Teich, J.: The Erlangen Slot Machine: Increasing Flexibility in FPGA-Based Reconfigurable Platforms. Journal of VLSI Signal Processing Systems 47(1), 15–31 (2007)

SCOPE - Sensor Mote Configuration and Operation Enhancement

Harun Özturgut[1,*], Christian Scholz[1], Thomas Wieland[1], and Christoph Niedermeier[2]

[1] University of Applied Sciences Coburg
Friedrich-Streib-Str. 2, 96450 Coburg, Germany
harun.oezturgut@coburg.de, {scholz,wieland}@hs-coburg.de
[2] Siemens AG, CT SE 2
Otto-Hahn-Ring 6, 80200 München, Germany
christoph.niedermeier@siemens.com

Abstract. Wireless sensor networks are difficult to manage and control due to their large geographical distribution and the lack of visual feedback. Tasks of configuration, debugging, monitoring and role assignment are only possible with access to the running application.

With SCOPE we developed a generic management framework for such networks. It can be integrated in every TinyOS application to monitor and adjust application values such as configuration variables, sensor readings or other data. To be most flexible a generic approach was taken to read and set variables by Remote Instance Calls. SCOPE is a demon application running on every mote and sending the desired data to a Java application on a PC with network access. This enables the system administrator to manage and control every single node by adjusting these values.

This paper describes the architecture and use of the SCOPE framework as well as compares it with other non-commercial state-of-the-art system management frameworks for wireless sensor networks.

1 Introduction

Wireless sensor networks consist of sensor nodes, called motes, sending their data to each other or a base station to perform certain calculations. After the deployment of the sensor nodes, tasks and requirements may change. Errors, failures or other problems may occur, which also have to be handled. Because of the large geographical distribution, it is hard to collect every single mote making adjustments. Therefore easy to use concepts for node management are required.

A possible solution to adjust configurations is the update of the complete program on the mote. This approach is already discussed widely, but is only necessary if the complete application needs to be updated, for example because of corrupt software or a complete change in requirements. On the other hand it

---

* Current affiliation: Stadt Coburg, Markt 1, 96450 Coburg, Germany.

might be enough to only adjust the preferences of a mote. In this case a complete update of the software or even partial updates would not be acceptable. Too much energy would be lost by distributing the new software in the network, which is bad for small electronic devices with no static power supply. To avoid this waste of energy the focus lies on the possibility to customize already deployed motes by only changing some configuration values. Thereby nearly every requirement can be met with regard to managing and controling a wireless sensor network.

The ease of use, dynamic customization of the mote application, management of large amounts of motes and the ability to manage different applications at a time were the constraints for this framework. Moreover, *TinyOS* [3] and *nesC* [2] as programming language were used to programme the motes, because of the worldwide acceptance and the large community of developers. The requirements concerning the system management of a node in a wireless sensor network can be defined as:

- *Configuration management*
  Design, extension and modification of the configuration of motes, which are already deployed. Hence a possibility is required to customize the motes on demand.
- *Roll back functionality*
  The configuration of a mote should be resetable into a well defined initial state.
- *Distribution of tasks*
  Different tasks should be allocated to motes during run-time. For example changing from senor reading mode to sleep mode.
- *Power management*
  The power consumption of a mote should be monitorable to use the most important resource (energy) in the most efficient way. As most energy is lost while communication, it is a special target to give the administrator control of the radio interface.
- *Over the air provisioning*
  The running application on a mote should be updatable. As mentioned earlier a partial update of a software would be desirable, where only the needed components are exchanged. Software distribution, update and update continuation ability are also requirements belong to this requirement.

In this paper we want to introduce a new framework for system management and control of wireless sensor networks called SCOPE (Sensor mote Configuration and OPeration Enhancement), which serves these requirements. The last requirement is not part of this work, because it is discussed in numerous other works. These are well known and provide a good opportunity to serve this requirement. One example would be *Deluge*[5,6].

The following section gives an overview of existing approaches of system management. After that the architecture and design of SCOPE is described in more detail. Section 4 gives an insight into the real use and integration of the framework. The next chapter evaluates the framwork and compares it with other methods of application adjustment. Finally we want to draw a conclusion about SCOPE and look out on future work.

2 Related Work

There are some operating systems for wireless sensor networks, such as *Mantis OS*[1] and *SOS*[4], which already are able to dynamically insert or alter modules into motes. *Mantis OS* even provides built-in functions which are similar to the abilities provided by this framework. In *TinyOS* there is still a lack of this functionality. Here are only some approaches of system management for wireless sensor networks which are discussed exemplarily. *Deluge* and *Nucleus* [10] are both rather specific approaches. With *Deluge* only the software can be updated and *Nucleus* only provides read access to certain values of a mote. However, *PyTOS* [11] provides similar possibilities to interact with a mote, but it has a completely different philosophy: the mote application has to be integrated in *PyTOS* and not vice versa.

With *Deluge* a reliable reprogramming system is available for wireless sensor networks running on *TinyOS*. New software images can be distributed and installed over the air. For dissemination of the images more than one source node can be used. Here the algorithm of *Trickle* [8] is used, which is designed to distributed new code in wireless sensor networks. *Deluge* is an extension to it, to allow bigger blocks of code to be propagated.

In *Nucleus* a network management system is the collection of the information of the used mote application. For this purpose the administrator gets the *TinyOS* components and *Java* tools for monitoring and debugging. These components can be easily integrated into an application by the developer to monitor the data of a mote. There are three different types of data queries: "attribute queries", "RAM queries" and "log events".

PyTOS is an environment based on *Python*, where mote applications can be imported. Thereby information about variables and functions can be extracted to enable the use of Remote Procedure Calls (RPC) in wireless sensor networks. To convert a function into a RPC it has to be declared with *@rpc()* in the application. The update on PC side is automatically done, when the *nesC* code changes.

Table 1. Comparison of different approaches

Requirements	Functions	Deluge	Nucleus	PyTOS	SCOPE
configuration management	setting values/variables	+	-	+++	+++
roll back functionality	reading values/variables	-	+++	+++	+++
distribution of tasks	application messages	-	-	-	+++
power management	radio configuration	+	-	+	++
over the air provisioning	-	+++	-	-	-

Legend: +++ : fully supported, ++ : supported, + : partly or inefficiently supported, - : not supported.

Deluge is a pure application for re-programming the mote application. This makes a certain degree of system management possible, but in a quite inefficient way. On the other hand *Nucleus* provides the ability to monitor application data, but not to control a mote. *PyTOS* is a system that mostly serves the requirements of a wireless sensor network system management, but it is not easy to use and to integrate in existing applications. Our system management system SCOPE has some advantages, which these applications do not have: It provides a complete, easy to use infrastructure to communicate with any mote in the network. So the developer can concentrate on his application and he does not need any other knowledge to use this framework. SCOPE also enables the user to call instances remotely in comparison to *PyTOS*. In table 1 the approaches are compared by requirements and the resulting functionalities.

3 Architecture

3.1 Components

SCOPE consists of three parts of software outlining a distributed system. They can be divided by the underlying platform in a mote part and a PC part. There are two components of software running on the mote: the actual application and the SCOPE demon. The application is developed by the user of the system management by integrating the demon. As *TinyOS* is not multi-threaded, the demon is included as interfaces to the main application, which are explained in section 4.2.

Figure 1 describes the architecture of these components and their possible interactions. A middleware is not necessarily needed, but can also be integrated into the system management environment.

On PC side the administrator can control the wireless sensor network with a management application. It communicates with the demon on the motes which is waiting for instructions. Otherwise the demon can use the management application to alarm the administrator, e.g. about temperature exceedings or other asynchronous events.

There are of course more parts that are needed for this framework. One is a gateway which is directly linked to the PC and provides access to the wireless senor network. Communication between the management application and the

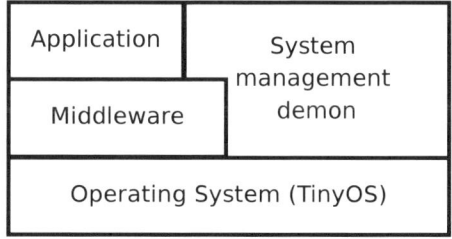

Fig. 1. Mote software architecture

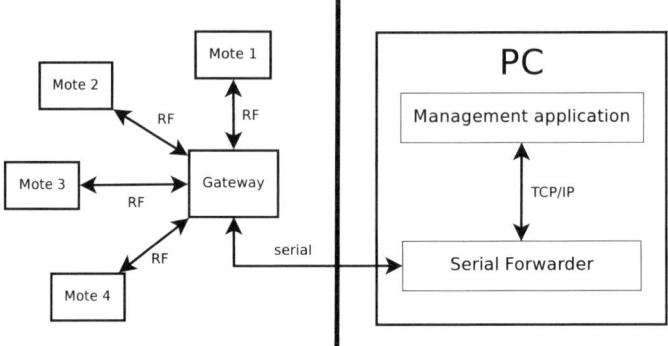

Fig. 2. Network communication

gateway is done by a *TinyOS* tool, called *SerialForwarder*, which is included in the *TinyOS* environment. This tool provides a TCP/IP connection to the wireless sensor network, shown in figure 2.

3.2 Functionality

The key task of the demon application is to wait for incoming instructions over the radio interface. On reception the type of address is checked, whether it is a broadcast message or a message for itself. Since the functionality of the demon can be integrated into the application as needed, a validity check is made to ensure the support of the incoming instruction. Only after that the instruction is processed.

There are two types of instructions: configuration and information instructions. With the first type configuration variables can be set to realize task distribution, configurations, rollback functionality, etc. Information instructions are only able to request data values and configuration variables.

When an instruction is about to be processed, the main application on the mote is interrupted by this event. With the trigger of thes event the application gets all data needed to process the instruction. The returned value of the event indicates, if processing was successful or not. Besides requested information can be returned, too. These values are transmitted back to the gateway and forwarded to the system management application on the PC.

While an instruction is processed, additional requests may reach the mote. These are stored in the queue of the scheduler for a later execution.

3.3 Message Protocols

In this subsection the two protocols are described, which were developed for the communication of SCOPE. The instruction message protocol allows the transmission of instructions to the motes. The mote message protocol in contrast was developed for the responses of the motes to these requests. That means there are

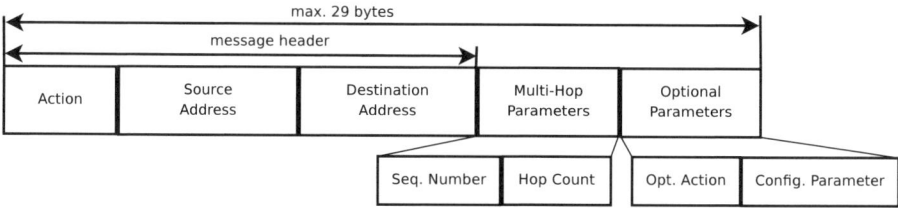

Fig. 3. Instruction message protocol

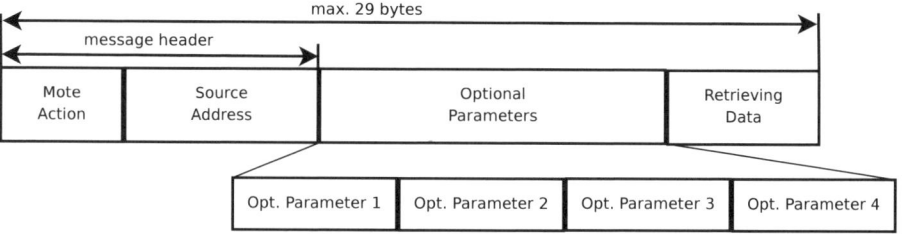

Fig. 4. Mote message protocol

two protocols depending on the direction of the communication, exactly fitted to the needs of the according message. Both protocols are embedded into the Active Message Protocol used by *TinyOS* to be most flexible with underlying routing algorithms. On the other hand the payload shrinks to only 29 Bytes. According to the used active message protocol, the message is always send as broadcast to the motes and then filtered by the header elements of the SCOPE internal protocol headers.

The instruction message protocol shown in figure 3 starts with the action field. The actions are predefined and can be extended by the developer. All actions a mote can perform - depending on the degree of integration into its main application - are queried and shown on the PC side in the management application. Then the header continues with the source and destination address fields. The multi-hop parameters are used in multi-hop networks only. These are followed by two optional parameters which are used for additional information needed by some actions or the new configuration value to be set.

In figure 4 the mote message protocol is described. The mote action field indicates which instruction is replied. Followed by address of the source mote. Depending on the replied action the layout of the message varies:

- transmission of status messages of the application of a certain mote. It is also used for sending configuration identifiers
- transmission of a requested certain value
- transmission of a requested data array

This variation is built up by the different use of the four optional parameter fields and the retrieving data field.

4 Implementation

This section outlines the realized functionality and the actual implementation on mote and PC side.

4.1 Key Features

The SCOPE management application is able to list and show every mote in range, which is prepared with the SCOPE demon. The range of the basestation is varying by the used routing algorithms. Depending on the use it can only be a small star network with only the directly neighbored nodes or even a mesh network with nodes in range over some hops. Mote discovery has to be initiated by the system administrator with the PC application. To avoid collisions all motes wait a calculated amount of time depending on their address before replying to the discovery request. The reply message includes what actions the mote is able to perform.

After the discovery the motes can be selected in the management application and only the supported instructions are listed. Additionally the PC application is now able to receive alert messages from the mote which are displayed immediately. The administrator is able to get and set configuration and data values from the main application running on the motes by using a graphical front-end on th PC.

4.2 Mote Side

Within the remote instance call model the demon provides four interfaces to be integrated within the mote application:

- *MDemonI*
  This is the main interface and always has to be integrated. It holds all the logic to send and receive data and handle the incoming action request from the radio interface as well as from the main application.
- *ConfigI*
  This is an optional generic interface to allow write access to configuration variables of the application (e.g. timer periods, sensor selection, etc.).
- *DataI*
  This is an optional generic interface providing read access to data values (e.g. sensor readings, computations, etc.). In contrast to the configuration varibles these data types can not be written by the demon.
- *DataArrayI*
  This is also an optional generic interface for reading data array types like strings (e.g. application name, variable names, etc.)

To use the functionality of SCOPE these interfaces have to be wired to the corresponding values in the main application. Of course this includes the integration of their events into the module code. A simple configuration would look like this:

SCOPE - Sensor Mote Configuration and Operation Enhancement

```
...
component MDemonC;
...
testM.MDemonI -> MDemonC;
testM.TaskControlConfig -> MDemonC.ConfigI[0];
testM.SampleData -> MDemonC.DataI[0];
testM.SenseControlDataArray -> MDemonC.DataArrayI[0];
...
```

This code shows the wiring of three data types: one configuration variable, one data value and one data array to the SCOPE demon. The instances of the interfaces can have other identifiers in the application module code. Here for example the instance of DataI is called "SampleData".

In the module file these interfaces have to be added to the module block:

```
...
uses interface MDemonI;
uses interface ConfigI as TaskControlConfig;
uses interface DataI as SampleData;
uses interface DataArrayI as SenseControlDataArray;
...
```

Further on all events of the SCOPE demon have to be implemented. For setting the name of the mote application, the following event has to be adjusted:

```
event AppInter MDemonI.getApplicationName()...
```

Because the demon has to know how many variables it has to control the following three events also have to be implemented for these three data types:

```
event uint8_t MDemonI.getConfigSize()...
event uint8_t MDemonI.getRetrieveDataSize()...
event uint8_t MDemonI.getRetrieveDataArraySize()...
```

Additionally the demon has to know what functionalities should be provided, this is done by the four events below:

```
event result_t MDemonI.isAppMsgSupported()...
event result_t MDemonI.isConfigSupported()...
event result_t MDemonI.isRetrieveDataSupported()...
event result_t MDemonI.isRetrieveDataArraySupported()...
```

For the ConfigI instances there are two events that have to be implemented: one for getting the identifier of the variable and one for setting the value. With the last event the user is enabled to set any declared variable of the application.

```
event AppInter TaskControlConfig.getConfigVariable()...
event result_t TaskControlConfig.setConfigVariable(uint32_t value)...
```

The DataI instance provides three events for accessing the data value. One for getting the identifier of the variable and two for reading the value depending on the data type. To implement these events the user only needs to specify the returned variables.

```
event AppInter SampleData.getRetrieveData()...
event uint32_t SampleData.getRetrieveDataValue()...
event char* SampleData.getRetrieveDataString()..
```

Two events are necessary for the DataArrayI instance, where the identifier of the array can be read and the array itself:

```
event AppInter SenseControlDataArray.getRetrieveData()...
event DataValueInter SenseControlDataArray.getRetrieveDataValues()...
```

This only should be a brief introduction into the implementation of an application under SCOPE surveillance, but it shows how easy it is to use. With this mechanism every variable of an application can be monitored or set.

4.3 PC Side

The management application of SCOPE is written in *Java*. The whole package includes the structure of the *TinyOS* java tools to get access to the *SerialForwarder*. The SCOPE classes can be divided into three categories: classes for interaction, helper classes and the main class. Classes for interaction are the counterparts to the interaction structures on motes side. Every structure has a corresponding class with the same active message type. This correlation is shown in table 2.

The receiving classes need to be registered to the *SerialForwarder* to be able to listen to the network. Another tool from the *TinyOS* environment helps to convert the *nesC* message types into interaction classes. These generated classes provide access to the message elements, return the offset of a message element, set message elements, etc. The tool is called *"Message Interface Generator"* and works with a make file. It reads out the information of the SCOPE header files including the message types and variables and generates classes for each message type.

The helper classes are needed to build up the table with the information of the motes and solve some other layout problems.

Table 2. Correlation between classes and structures of interaction

Receiving classes	Mote message structures
MoteMsg	MoteMsg
DataMoteMsg	DataMoteMsg
SingleDataMoteMsg	SingleDataMoteMsg
sending classes	**instruction message structures**
InstructionMsg	InstructionMsg
ConfigInstructionMsg	ConfigInstructionMsg

MMain is the main class and has to implement all necessary interfaces like MassgeListener, ActionListener and ItemListener for receiving mote messages and management instructions. With the methods of this class it is easy to integrate into other applications and frameworks.

The frontend of the SCOPE application is a Swing based graphical user interface which enables the administrator to control the network by only a few clicks. Motes are displayed in a table with all necessary information at a glance. Single motes and actions can be selected on another tab to get control even on the smallest parts of the network.

5 Evaluation

For evaluation we take one of the most simple programs in *TinyOS*: the Blink aplication. The application does nothing else than setting one Led to blink every 500 miliseconds. We made some modifications to the original code to abstract the blinking LED:

```
...
  event result_t Timer.fired() {
    if(toggle==1)
      call Leds.set(led);
    else
      call Leds.set(0);
    toggle = -toggle;
    return SUCCESS;
  }
...
```

To change the blinking LED only the `led` value has to be manipulated. But as the code has changed it hast to be recompiled and sent again to the mote. The implemented application results in an binary image of 2630 Bytes. This amount is needed when directly transferred to the mote via the programmer. That means the administrator has to collect all motes and reprogram them by a direct connection. Although the flashing process only takes less than 10 seconds, the time for collection and redeployment can take days.

More comfortable is a way to provide the new image over the air. We take Deluge as representative of such bootloaders. Integration of Deluge takes two lines code wich link the other sources needed. With Deluge the image is extended to nearly 20 kByte. Additionally metadata, crc checksums and extra data for dissemination inflate the image again with 20% of data. Although in this case the time to collect and flash every single mote by hand is not existend. The complete 24 kByte of data have to be transmitted through the whole network from one node to another. Depending on the network size and routing algorithm the time to disseminate the image increases and the transmission costs rise. With increasing complexity and size of the application the percentage of Deluge is increasing as well, because more packages have to be sent.

With SCOPE integrated into the application the source code is 36 lines of code longer, because the MdemonI interface has to be linked as well as one ConfigI for accessing the led variable. With these additions the image size increases to nearly 15 kBytes. With increasing complexity of the application the part of SCOPE stays the same. Changing the light of the LED costs only one message of 35 Bytes (excluding other network traffic for identifying the node). Surely this method is not applicable for an application where unpredictable changes have to be made. In this case Deluge is still the only fall back strategy to avoid reprogramming every node by hand. But with predictable changes this framework decreases the time and energy costs of adjustments immensly.

6 Conclusion

This work points out the way of an easy to use and simple to integrate system management framework for *TinyOS* based wireless sensor networks. Although it is not able to initiate complete updates of a mote software itself, it is possible to switch a task, adjust or reset the main application and monitor every used variable. Asynchronous triggered events in the network are also forwarded to the management application to be displayed to the administrator.

The framework is fully implemented and tested on TelosB motes from Crossbow Inc. [9,7] and Microsoft Windows as well as Linux PCs. Current work is a port of the mote application to *TinyOS 2.x* and the extension of the PC side to web service access. Grouping of nodes and mass configuration are also a desired target for ongoing work.

Another feature would be the integration of a re-programming system such a Deluge and a more autonomous control of the system for a degree of self-management and control. This might be done either decentralized by adjusting the SCOPE demon code or by adding more logic to the PC application.

Acknowledgements

We want to thank the team of CT SE 2 for their technical and financial support and the *TinyOS* community for some good hints.

References

1. Bhatti, S., Carlson, J., Dai, H., Deng, J., Rose, J., Sheth, A., Shucker, B., Gruenwald, C., Torgerson, A., Han, R.: MANTIS OS: An embedded multithreaded operating system for wireless micro sensor platforms. ACM/Kluwer Mobile Networks and Applications (MONET), Special Issue on Wireless Sensor Networks 10(4), 563–579 (2005)
2. Gay, D., Levis, P., Culler, D., Brewer, E.: nesC 1.1 Language Reference Manual, 03 (2003)

3. Gay, D., Levis, P., von Behren, R., Welsh, M., Brewer, E., Culler, D.: The nesc language: A holistic approach to networked embedded systems. In: PLDI 2003: Proceedings of the ACM SIGPLAN 2003 conference on Programming language design and implementation, pp. 1–11. ACM Press, New York (2003)
4. Han, C., Rengaswamy, K., Shea, R., Kohler, E., Srivastava, M.: SOS: A dynamic operating system for sensor networks. In: Proceedings of the Third International Conference on Mobile Systems, Applications, and Services (Mobisys 2005), Seattle, Washington (June 2005)
5. Hui, J.W.: Deluge 2.0 - TinyOS Network Programming, 05 (2005)
6. Hui, J.W., Culler, D.: The dynamic behavior of a data dissemination protocol for network programming at scale. In: SenSys 2004: Proceedings of the 2nd international conference on Embedded networked sensor systems, pp. 81–94. ACM, New York (2004)
7. C. Inc. TelosB Datasheet. Crossbow Inc., SanJose, California
8. Levis, P., Patel, N., Culler, D., Shenker, S.: Trickle: a self-regulating algorithm for code propagation and maintenance in wireless sensor networks. In: NSDI 2004: Proceedings of the 1st conference on Symposium on Networked Systems Design and Implementation, p. 2. USENIX Association, Berkeley (2004)
9. Polastre, J., Szewczyk, R., Culler, D.: Telos: enabling ultra-low power wireless research. In: IPSN 2005: Proceedings of the 4th international symposium on Information processing in sensor networks, p. 48. IEEE Press, Piscataway (2005)
10. Tolle, G.: Nucleus Manual. Computer Science Department, University of California, Berkeley, 08 (2005)
11. Whitehouse, K.: Pytos Development Environment, 01 (2006)

Generated Horizontal and Vertical Data Parallel GCA Machines for the N-Body Force Calculation

Johannes Jendrsczok, Rolf Hoffmann, and Thomas Lenck

Technische Universität Darmstadt, Hochschulstr. 10, 64289 Darmstadt, Germany
{jendrsczok,hoffmann}@ra.informatik.tu-darmstadt.de

Abstract. The *GCA model* (Global Cellular Automata) is a massively parallel computation model which is a generalization of the Cellular Automata model. A GCA cell contains data and link information. Using the link information each cell has dynamic read access to any global cell in the field. The data and link information is updated in every generation. The GCA model is applicable and efficient for a large range of parallel algorithms (sorting, vector reduction, graph algorithms, matrix computations etc.). In order to describe algorithms for the GCA model the experimental language GCAL was developed. GCAL programs can be transformed automatically into a data parallel architecture (DPA). The paper presents for the N-body problem how the force calculation between the masses can be described in GCAL and synthesized into a data parallel architecture. At first the GCAL description of the application is transformed into a Verilog description which is inserted into a Verilog template describing the general DPA. Then the whole Verilog code is used as input for an FPGA synthesizing tool which generates the application-specific DPA. Two different DPAs are generated, a "*horizontal*" and a "*vertical*" DPA. The horizontal DPA uses 17 floating-point operators in each deep pipeline. In contrast the "vertical" DPA uses only one floating-point operation at a time out of a set of 6 floating-point operators. Both architectures are compared to resource consumption, time per cell operation and cost (logic elements * execution time). It turned out that the horizontal DPA is approximately 15 times more cost efficient than the vertical DPA.

1 Introduction

The GCA (Global Cellular Automaton) model [1,2] is a generalization of the classical CA (Cellular Automaton) model [3,4]. In the CA model the cells are arranged in a fixed grid with fixed connections to their local neighbors. Each cell computes its next state by the application of a local rule depending on its own state and the states of its neighbors. The data accesses to the neighbors' states are read-only and therefore no write conflicts can occur. The rule can be applied to all cells in parallel and therefore the model is inherently massively parallel. The GCA model is not restricted to the local communication because any cell can be a neighbor. Furthermore the links to the global neighbors are not static; they can be changed by the local rule from generation to generation. Thereby the range of parallel applications for the GCA model is much wider than that for the CA model. Typical applications for the GCA model are – besides all CA applications – graph algorithms, hypercube algorithms, logic simulation, numerical algorithms, communication networks, neural networks, games, and graphics. Generally speaking the GCA model allows describing all kinds of applications with global data access and local processing.

The GCA can be easily supported by hardware because of the inherent massively parallelism due to the model. Three principle hardware architectures are available for an implementation: (1) *Fully Parallel Architecture*. All the cells, the computational logic, and the dynamic global connections are directly implemented in hardware. The execution time is minimized but the number of cells is directly limited by the hardware resources [5,6]. (2) *Data Parallel Architecture*. N pipelines are used to process the N cell rules in parallel, comparable to the execution of vector instructions [7]. Each pipeline uses a primary memory section (with $1/N$ of the whole address space) and a secondary memory (with whole address space). This architecture can be used for a very large amount of cells and is easily scalable in the number N of pipelines. (3) *Multiprocessor Architecture*. A programmable tightly coupled multiprocessor system [8] is used, in which the communication and computation is program controlled. This architecture is more flexible than the data parallel architecture but it is not clear how the same performance as for the data parallel architecture can be achieved using the same amount of hardware.

The N-body problem is a well-studied problem and special hardware was developed for it (e.g. with ASICs [9] or GPUs [10]). Multi-pipeline approaches were already investigated in a number of publications. For example multi-pipelines were used to support application-specific processors [11], discrete fourier transformations in real-time [12] and medical imaging [13]. Our architectures differ from these approaches in the way how the pipelines are interwoven with a complex memory organization supporting the GCA model.

The paper is organized as follows: In the following paragraph the GCA model is briefly reviewed. In Sec. 2 the multi-pipeline data parallel architecture is explained in which application-specific ("adapted") operators can be embedded. Then the N-body force calculation is described in GCAL in two versions (horizontal, vertical) (Sec. 3). Then they are synthesized to application-specific machines, which are evaluated and compared (Sec. 4). In our contribution we show: (1) how high-performant application-specific data parallel architectures can be generated automatically from high level descriptions and (2) that a "horizontal" implementation is much more efficient than a "vertical" implementation.

The GCA model. A GCA consists of an array of processing cells. Each cell contains a data field d and one or more pointer (link information) fields p. A cell k dynamically establishes a link to some other cell (the *global neighbor cell*). We call the GCA model *one-handed* if only one neighbor can be addressed, *two-handed* if two neighbors can be addressed and so on. We will restrict the following considerations to the one-handed model because most applications can be described with one pointer only or mapped to this form. The local information

(d, p) and the global information (d^*, p^*) are input of the functions e and g which compute the next data and the next pointer respectively. All cells are updated in parallel in a synchronous way. The functions e and g may further depend on the *space index* k of the cell and central control information. Typical central control information is the generation counter t, an additional operation code, address offsets or general parameters. An optional function h is used to compute the effective address $p_{\it eff}$ of the global cell in the current generation.

2 Data Parallel Architecture (DPA)

The data parallel architecture [7] is highly parametrized and is targeted to configurable FPGAs. This machine was implemented for dedicated applications on an Altera FPGA using Verilog and the Quartus synthesis tools. Furthermore a simulator was implemented in Java in order to test the design for functional correctness. The main advantage of this machine is its scalability without changing the machine code due to the inherent parallelism of the GCA model.

Each GCA cell of the DPA consists of an integrated information field d which can be split into a data field d_d and a pointer field d_p. The data field can again be split into a number of sub-data fields. The type and bit size of each field can be configured. A certain number of cells are grouped into a so called *cell object*. Cell objects can be interpreted as matrices or vectors of cells. The destination object contains all cells which shall be modified. The source object contains all global neighbor cells. The destination object may also serve as source object. Several objects can be used in an application, e. g., for solving linear equations (Jacobi iteration [7]) or graph algorithms (Hirschberg [5]). All cells of the destination object can be computed in parallel using the synchronous parallel updating principle. In practice the parallelism is restricted by the resources available on the chip (embedded memories, computing logic, routing logic, etc.).

Parallel Structure and Organization. The machine consists of: an instruction memory *IM*, an object table memory *OM*, and P execution pipelines containing the cell memories R, S and the result memories R', S'.

The instruction memory *IM* holds special GCA instructions (defined later) which are interpreted by the controller. The attributes of the objects are stored in the object table memory. The source and destination objects are stored in the memories of the pipelines. A typical GCA instruction changes all the cells of a destination object and uses the global cells located in a source object: Destination Object ← f(Destination Object, Source Object).

After fetching and decoding of an instruction the attributes (start address, rows, columns) about the source and destination objects are read from the object table memory *OM*. The elements of each object are distributed columnwise onto the different memory banks. The processing hardware consists of P pipelines working in parallel. Cell i is processed by the pipeline (i mod P). The pipeline uses several memories R and S in order to implement the GCA principle: (1) access of cell, (2) use or compute effective address and (3) access global cell.

Thus the memory R is used to read the cell contents d and the memory S is used to read the cell contents d^* of the global cell. In order to read in parallel the cell contents and the global neighbor cell contents within two different pipeline stages the data memory is replicated.

In order to implement the synchronous updating scheme, two pairs (R, R') and (S, S') with alternative memories are used. Thereby the old values of the cells are always available during the calculation of the current generation and cannot be overwritten in between. For each written object a write flag is set which tells the hardware whether the object has to be read next either from the memory R or from R', and from S or S'. By this technique only the cells which belong to the destination object are updated and no superfluous write or copy operations are necessary. Thereby it can happen that the source object and the destination object are located in different memories. The calculation of the new cell contents is performed using five pipeline stages:

1. The cell contents d (divisible into data and pointer information) is read from the primary cell memory R (or R', depending on the object's write flag).
2. The effective address p_{eff} (buffered in ea) pointing to the global cell is computed by the use of d (or a part of it), the current cell index k, the logical indices (i, j) of the object's elements if considered as matrix, the operator code OP_{ea} and the descriptor of the source object form the object memory.
3. The global neighbor cell is read from the cell memory S (or S') using p_{eff}.
4. The next cell contents d' is computed applying the operator OP_{nd} for the next data part of d_d and OP_{np} for the next pointer part of d_p. Depending on the complexity of the operators more than five pipeline stages can be used.
5. The next cell contents is saved in the buffer memories R' (or R) and S' (or S).

Instruction set. The rule instruction executes for each cell in the destination object the selected operations. The source and the destination object may be identical. Several RULEs adapted to the application can be used. Note that the RULE instructions are complex instructions (comparable to vector instructions of conventional computers) iterating over all cells of the destination object and using the global cells located in the source object. Destination and source object may be identical. A cell operation is defined by the adapted operators OP_{ea}, OP_{nd}, and OP_{np} according to the functions h, e, g of the model. OP_{ea} computes the effective address of the global cell, OP_{nd} computes the next data field, and OP_{np} computes the next pointer field. *Adapted operators* are functions which are adapted to the particular application in mind and which are inserted into the synthesis process. They are either selected from a library of logic modules (defined by Verilog code), or have to be implemented in Verilog for a specific application, or they are extracted and compiled from the language GCAL. GCAL [14] is an experimental high level language which was developed in order to describe, simulate, and synthesize GCA algorithms.

Design flow. An application-specific DPA can automatically be generated by a framework implemented in Java by the following design flow:

1. (*Programming*) Description of the application in the language GCAL.
2. (*Rule Extraction*) The GCAL program description is transformed by the GCA compiler into an abstract syntax tree (AST). The GCA compiler is constructed by the compiler generator SableCC based on the GCAL grammar in BNF. The AST is traversed using depth first traversal and the visited nodes are executed according to the visitor pattern of the compiler generator. During this traversal the nodes are composed into the necessary operators (OP_{ea}, OP_{nd} and OP_{np}) and the corresponding Verilog code. Pipeline register are automatically inserted. Output: Application specific RULEs.
3. (*Binding*) The RULEs are inserted into the highly parameterized DPA generator. The DPA generator generates Verilog code for the data parallel architecture. Output: Application-specific DPA described in Verilog.
4. (*Synthesizing*) The Verilog description is synthesized for the target FPGA using Altera Quartus II.
5. (*Analyzing*) The results of the synthesis process and from additional simulations are verified and evaluated.
6. (*Executing*) The synthesized DPA can be loaded into a prototyping platform and executed.

3 Application: N-Body Problem

The force calculation as part of the N-body problem was chosen as an example in order to show how an application-specific DPA can be generated. The total force F_i on the own body i (the cell i) is the sum of the partial forces F_{ij} induced by the other bodies (global cells j). A partial force is proportional to the mass m_i of the own body and the mass m_j of the other body divided by the square of the distance. In order to compute the next position the acceleration has to be computed. The acceleration is the force divided by the mass of the own cell. Therefore the own mass can be eliminated from the formula because it appears in the numerator and in the denominator. The acceleration vector $\vec{a_i} = (a_x, a_y, a_z)_i$ is given by

$$\vec{a_i} = G \left(\sum_{j \neq i} \frac{m_j}{|r|^3} \vec{r} \right), r = \sqrt{(x_j - x_i)^2 + (y_j - y_i)^2 + (z_j - z_i)^2} \qquad (1)$$

The force calculation is first described in the language GCAL. The GCAL programs may differ in the number of operators used in combination. Two programs and implementations are compared: (1) *Horizontal* approach and (2) *Vertical* approach. "Horizontal" means that all operators needed for the application are rolled out according to the data/operation flow (chaining of operators). Pipeline register are used between the operators and inside the operators. "Vertical" means that only one operator out of a set can be chosen in one generation. The horizontal approach allows computing with a very high degree of parallelism and deep pipelines whereas the vertical approach allows computing with a minimum of resources (one active floating-point operation only). The horizontal GCA program is given in Listing 1.1.

```
program // horizontal
    cellstructure = m, x, y, z, ax, ay, az; // mass, position, acceleration
    neighborhood = neighbor;
    celltype cell = float,float,float,float,float,float,float; // 7 * 32 bit
    cell C[256];
    parameter N = 256; // number of bodies

    for index = 1 to N−1 do // generation counter specifying another body
        foreach C[i] with // for each cell i=0...99 in C
            neighbor = &C[(i + index) % N] // use neighbor j with distance = 1,2, ...
        do
            deltaX = neighbor.x − x;
            deltaY = neighbor.y − y;
            deltaZ = neighbor.z − z;
            rq = deltaX * deltaX + deltaY * deltaY + deltaZ * deltaZ;
            r = sqrt(rq);
            temp = neighbor.m / (r * rq);
            ax <= ax + temp * deltaX; // <= synchronous update
            ay <= ay + temp * deltaY; // accumulating
            az <= az + temp * deltaZ;
        endforeach
    endfor
endprogram
```

Listing 1.1. Horizontal GCAL program for the N-body force calculation. Each cell of the cell vector stores seven floating-point numbers (7·32 bit). The influence of another body on the acceleration is computed in one generation.

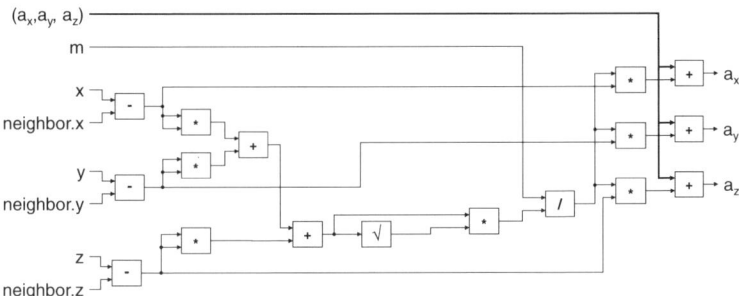

Fig. 1. Horizontal DPA: Next data operator OP_{nd} computing the local partial acceleration (a_x, a_y, a_z) induced by the global neighbor body. This operator is realized by a pipeline of 9 sections with 17 floating-point operations (IP cores from Altera) extracted from the horizontal GCAL program. The floating-point operations are internally also pipelined (−: 14, *: 11, +: 14, $\sqrt{x}$: 28, /: 33 stages). The whole number of pipeline stages is $14 + 11 + 14 + 14 + 28 + 11 + 33 + 11 + 14 = 150$. Resources for one partial acceleration computation: Logic elements: 9,551 ALUTs; Register: 9,847.

A cell is structured into the data fields mass m, coordinates (x, y, z), and acceleration (a_x, a_y, a_z). All attributes are of type float. The cell field $C[256]$ defines the target and the source object. Note that in the first generation (for $index = 1$) the partial influence on the acceleration induced by the first right neighbor is computed (potentially in parallel "foreach" cell in the cell object). In the second generation the influence of the second right neighbor is added, and so on. It is not necessary to define a pointer field in the cell, although this would be possible. (In this case the pointer can be switched one position further

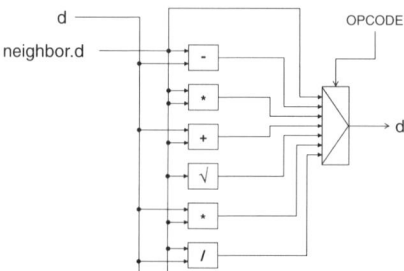

Fig. 2. Vertical DPA: One out of seven simple next data operations OP_{nd} are used to compute sequentially the accelerations. The floating-point operators are internally pipelined ($-$: 14, $*$: 11, $+$: 14, $\sqrt{x}$: 28, $/$: 33 stages). Resources for one partial acceleration computation: Logic elements: 5,741 ALUTs; Register: 5,399.

to the right in each step). In the given implementation the effective address is computed by adding the generation counter index to the cell index i. While the horizontal program needs only one generation per iteration the vertical program (Listing 1.2) needs 22 sub-generations. In each sub-generation one of the operators out of $+, -, *, /, \sqrt{x}$ is chosen. Therefore the vertical program uses only one out of 7 operators (Fig. 2) instead of 17 (Fig. 1) which are needed in the horizontal program.

```
program // vertical
    cellstructure = d;
    neighborhood = neighbor;
    celltype cell = float; // 32 bit
    parameter N = 256;
    central index;
    cell X[N]; cell Y[N]; cell Z[N]; cell M[N]; cell Ax[N]; cell Ay[N]; cell Az[N];
    cell T1[N]; cell T2[N];cell T3[N]; cell D1[N]; cell D2[N]; cell D3[N]; // temporaries

    for index = 1 to N-1 do
        // calculation of deltaX, deltaY, deltaZ, start of the 22 sub-generations
        foreach D1[i] with neighbor=&X[i] do d <= neighbor.d endforeach; // D1 <- X
        foreach D1[i] with neighbor=&X[(i+index)%N] do d <= d - neighbor.d
            endforeach;
        foreach D2[i] with neighbor=&Y[i] do d <= neighbor.d endforeach; // D2 <- Y
        foreach D2[i] with neighbor=&Y[(i+index)%N] do d <= d - neighbor.d
            endforeach;
        foreach D3[i] with neighbor=&Z[i] do d <= d - neighbor.d endforeach; // D3 <-
            Z
        foreach D3[i] with neighbor=&Z[(i+index)%N] do d <= neighbor.d endforeach;

        // delta squared
        foreach T1[i] with neighbor=&D1[i] do d <= neighbor.d * neighbor.d endforeach;
        foreach T2[i] with neighbor=&D2[i] do d <= neighbor.d * neighbor.d endforeach;
        foreach T3[i] with neighbor=&D3[i] do d <= neighbor.d * neighbor.d endforeach;

        // calculation of +,+,sqrt,*
        foreach T2[i] with neighbor=&T1[i] do d <= d + neighbor.d endforeach;
        foreach T3[i] with neighbor=&T2[i] do d <= d + neighbor.d endforeach;
        foreach T2[i] with neighbor=&T3[i] do d <= sqrt(neighbor.d) endforeach;
        foreach T3[i] with neighbor=&T2[i] do d <= d * neighbor.d endforeach;

        // division by mass
        foreach T3[i] with neighbor=&M[i] do d <= neighbor.d / d endforeach;
```

```
                // calculation of vector a
                foreach T1[i] with neighbor=&T3[i] do d <= neighbor.d endforeach;  // T1 <- T3
                foreach T2[i] with neighbor=&T3[i] do d <= neighbor.d endforeach;  // T2 <- T3
                foreach T1[i] with neighbor=&D1[i] do d <= d * neighbor.d endforeach;
                foreach T2[i] with neighbor=&D2[i] do d <= d * neighbor.d endforeach;
                foreach T3[i] with neighbor=&D3[i] do d <= d * neighbor.d endforeach;

                // result: sum a
                foreach Ax[i] with neighbor=&T1[i] do d <= d + neighbor.d endforeach;
                foreach Ay[i] with neighbor=&T2[i] do d <= d + neighbor.d endforeach;
                foreach Az[i] with neighbor=&T3[i] do d <= d + neighbor.d endforeach
            endfor
        endprogram
```

Listing 1.2. Vertical GCAL program for the N-body force calculation. The cell components are stored in seven separate sub-cell vectors. In addition six temporary vectors are used. Updating of the acceleration is performed sequentially in 12 sub-generations.

4 Generated DPAs with Adapted Operators

Both application-specific DPAs were synthesized for an Altera Stratix II FPGA (EP2S180 with 143,520 ALUTs, 9,383,040 memory bits) with different number of pipelines P. The adapted operators for this application were extracted automatically from the GCAL programs and were integrated in the instruction set of the machine:

Horizontal: Adapted operators of the RULE instruction.

OPC	OP_{ea}	OP_{nd}
0	neighbor = &SRC[(i + index)% N]	deltaX = neighbor.x - x; deltaY = neighbor.y - y; deltaZ = neighbor.z - z; rq = deltaX * deltaX + deltaY * deltaY + deltaZ * deltaZ; r = sqrt(rq); temp = neighbor.m / (r * rq); ax <= ax + temp * deltaX; ay <= ay + temp * deltaX; az <= az + temp * deltaZ;

Vertical: Adapted operators of the RULE instruction.

OPC	OP_{ea}	OP_{nd}
0	neighbor = &SRC[(i + index) % N]	d <= neighbor.d
1	neighbor = &SRC[i]	d <= neighbor.d - d
2		d <= neighbor.d * neighbor.d
3		d <= d + neighbor.d
4		d <= $\sqrt{neighbor.d}$
5		d <= d * neighbor.d
6		d <= neighbor.d / d

Horizontal DPA. The operator OP_{nd} extracted from the horizontal program corresponds to the arithmetic pipeline shown in Fig. 1. The results of the synthesis (Table 1) show that the reached pipeline clock rates are decreasing moderately with the number of pipelines (Fig. 4(a)). The number of ALUTs and the number of memory bits are increasing almost linear with the number of pipelines (Fig. 3(b), 3(a)).

After the latency of the pipelines, P results are produced in every clock cycle. The time for one GCA cell operation (t_{cop}, time per cell operation) is approximately T/P (with T = clock period) if the number of cells is much higher

Table 1. Horizontal DPA: Hardware resources and values depending on the number of pipelines P for $N = 256$ cells (224 bit each) on a Stratix II FPGA (EP2S180)

P	ALUTs	Reg.	Memory	Clk. Rate	t_{cop}	Speedup	Cost
1	10,313 (7%)	10,147	179,617 (2%) bits	55.42 MHz	18.0ns	1	186,088
2	20,620 (14%)	23,333	374,360 (4%) bits	54.00 MHz	9.3ns	1.9	190,926
4	40,841 (28%)	50,689	632,766 (7%) bits	48.33 MHz	5.1ns	3.4	211,261
8	79,344 (55%)	76,807	1,032,192 (11%) bits	43.66 MHz	2.9ns	6.3	227,164

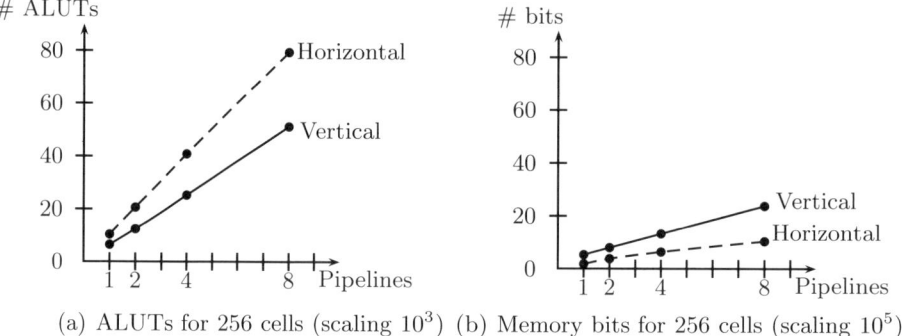

(a) ALUTs for 256 cells (scaling 10^3) (b) Memory bits for 256 cells (scaling 10^5)

Fig. 3. Resources

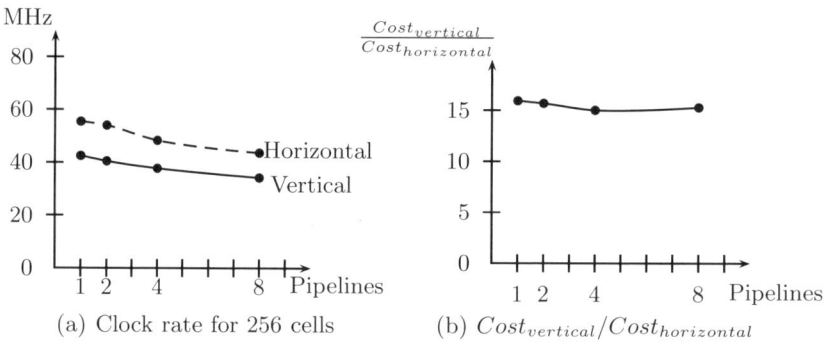

(a) Clock rate for 256 cells (b) $Cost_{vertical}/Cost_{horizontal}$

Fig. 4. Speed and Cost

than the pipeline length. The floating-point performance reaches 5.94 GFlops for $P = 8$. This is comparable to other highly optimized FPGA implementations for the force calculation of the N-body problem, e.g., [15] with 6.5 GFlops, although the here presented implementation was generated automatically from a program to a configurable GCA architecture. Note that the floating-point operations are 32 bit wide and include complex operations like square root and division.

Vertical DPA. In order to compare the results with a pipeline which can only process one operation at a time, the application was also described vertically in

Table 2. Vertical DPA: Hardware resources and values depending on the number of pipelines P for 4096 sub-cells (32 bit each) for $N = 256$ on a Stratix II FPGA (EP2S180). (address width of the memory $adr\_width = \lceil \log_2(N \cdot \#Variables) \rceil$, $\#Variables = 13 \Rightarrow 2^{adr\_width} = 4096$).

P	ALUTs	Reg.	Memory	Clk. Rate	t_{cop}	Speedup	Cost
1	6,396 (4%)	5,734	527,150 (6%) bits	42.53 MHz	517.3ns	1	2,966,095
2	12,365 (9%)	11,027	791,300 (8%) bits	40.51 MHz	271.5.3ns	1.9	2,994,248
4	25,246 (18%)	21,793	1,319,504 (14%) bits	37.78 MHz	145.6ns	3.6	3,172,618
8	51,157 (36%)	43,269	2,375,872 (25%) bits	34.27 MHz	80.2ns	6.4	3,472,126

GCAL (Listing 1.2). In principle each of the 17 operators shown in Fig. 1 are computed sequentially by sub-generations. Altogether 22 sub-generations are needed to execute one *"for index"* iteration. The arithmetic pipeline becomes simpler because it has only to supply alternatively the operators $+, -, *, /, \sqrt{x}$. Although the resources (Table 2) are reduced compared to the horizontal DPA the clock rate is lower because of the additional multiplexers who are needed to implement the alternative data paths. The memory resources are about two times higher than for the horizontal case mainly due to the temporary variables.

Comparison. In order to compare the two architectures a cost function was defined: $cost = t_{cop} \cdot (number\ of\ ALUTs)$.

The time per cell operation t_{cop} is the time to compute a new "horizontal" cell state of the application. In the horizontal case $t_{cop} = T/P$ and in the vertical case $t_{cop} = (T/P) \cdot (sub\text{-}generations)$. We will not take into account the performance loss due to the latency of the pipelines and assume that in a practical application the number of cells is much larger than the length of the pipelines.

The number of ALUTs in the cost function represents the amount of logic elements which mainly reflect the resources for the floating-point operators, the register (part of the ALUTs) and partly the routing.

The memory resources were not reflected in the cost function because they depend significantly on the problem size. But it should be noted that the vertical DPA needs more memory because of the additional temporary variables (Fig. 3(b)).

Comparing the cost it turned out that the vertical DPA is around 15 times more expensive than the horizontal DPA, relatively independent of the number of pipelines. There are three reasons: (1) the clock-frequency of the horizontal DPA is higher, (2) in the horizontal DPA 17 floating-point operators are active whereas in the vertical DPA only one (or none in case of transport) is active, and (3) in the vertical DPA additional sub-generations are necessary to transport the subcells to the locations where they can be used for further computations.

5 Conclusion

The used data parallel GCA machine architecture DPA is highly scalable due to the inherent parallelism of the model. The number of processing pipelines, the data structure of a cell and the hardware supported operators can be configured. Each pipeline has an associated primary memory bank and an associated secondary global memory. The most important instruction is the RULE instruction which computes the new contents for each cell in the destination object. The adapted operators can automatically be extracted from a high level description (GCAL) of an application. In order to demonstrate the automatic generation of the hardware the force calculation of the N-body problem was described horizontally and vertically in GCAL. The GCAL descriptions were transformed into the adapted operators defining the application-specific RULE instructions. The whole application-specific machines were synthesized with up to eight pipelines for an Altera Stratix II FPGA (EP2S180) using the Quartus II synthesis tools. The generated "horizontal" DPA with 8 pipelines reaches a floating-point performance of 5.94 GFlops, disregarding the latency of the pipelines. Each pipeline contains 17 floating-point operators $(+, -, *, /, \sqrt{x})$ forming a deep pipeline with 150 stages. In order to reduce the floating-point operators the pipeline was also implemented "vertically" with only one active floating-point operation (out of a set of 7 operations) per pipeline. When comparing the vertical against the horizontal DPA (for the amount of 256 cells, 8 pipelines) the results are: (1) the consumed ALUTs are $\approx 35\%$ lower, (2) the reached clock frequency is $\approx 22\%$ lower (due to the multiplexers selecting the actual floating-point operator) and (3) the cost (ALUTs * computation time) is ≈ 15 times higher. Therefore the horizontal approach should be favored for similar applications with a complex rule which should be directly mapped into a deep pipeline. Further research is in progress to develop also a programmable multiprocessor architecture supporting the GCA model and to build a compiler translating GCAL programs onto it.

Acknowledgement

The authors like to express their thanks to the "Deutsche Forschungsgemeinschaft" for funding the project "Massively Parallel Systems for GCA".

References

1. Hoffmann, R., Völkmann, K.P., Waldschmidt, S.: Global Cellular Automata GCA: An Universal Extension of the CA Model. In: Worsch, T. (ed.) ACRI 2000 Conference (2000)
2. Hoffmann, R., Völkmann, K.P., Waldschmidt, S., Heenes, W.: GCA: Global Cellular Automata. A Flexible Parallel Model. In: Malyshkin, V.E. (ed.) PaCT 2001. LNCS, vol. 2127, pp. 66–73. Springer, Heidelberg (2001)
3. von Neumann, J.: Theory of Self-Reproducing Automata. University of Illinois Press, Urbana and London (1966)
4. Zuse, K.: Rechnender Raum. Schriften zur Datenverarbeitung. Schriften zur Datenverarbeitung. Vieweg & Sohn, Braunschweig (1969)
5. Jendrsczok, J., Hoffmann, R., Keller, J.: Implementing Hirschberg's PRAM-Algorithm for Connected Components on a Global Cellular Automaton. International Journal of Foundations of Computer Science (2008) (accepted for publication)

6. Heenes, W., Hoffmann, R., Kanthak, S.: FPGA Implementations of the Massively Parallel GCA Model. In: International Parallel & Distributed Processing Symposium (IPDPS), Workshop on Massively Parallel Processing (WMPP) (2005)
7. Jendrsczok, J., Ediger, P., Hoffmann, R.: A Scalable Configurable Architecture for the Massively Parallel GCA Model. In: International Parallel & Distributed Processing Symposium (IPDPS), Workshop on Advances in Parallel and Distributed Computational Models (APDCM) (2008)
8. Heenes, W., Hoffmann, R., Jendrsczok, J.: A multiprocessor architecture for the massively parallel model GCA. In: International Parallel and Distributed Processing Symposium (IPDPS), Workshop on System Management Tools for Large-Scale Parallel Systems (SMTPS) (2006)
9. Makino, J., Ito, T., Ebisuzaki, T., Sugimoto, D.: GRAPE: a special-purpose computer for N-body problems. In: Proceedings of the International Conference on Application Specific Array Processors (1990)
10. Nyland, L., Harris, M., Prins, J.: Fast N-Body Simulation with CUDA. In: Nguyen, H. (ed.) GPU Gems 3. Addison Wesley Professional, Reading (2007)
11. Radhakrishnan, S., Guo, H., Parameswaran, S.: Customization of application specific heterogeneous multi-pipeline processors. In: DATE 2006: Proceedings of the conference on Design, automation and test in Europe, Leuven, Belgium, Belgium, European Design and Automation Association, vol. 3001, pp. 746–751 (2006)
12. Petrovsky, A.A., Shkredov, S.L.: Multi-Pipeline Implementations of Real-Time Vector DFT. In: DSD 2004: Proceedings of the Digital System Design, EUROMICRO Systems on (DSD 2004), pp. 326–333. IEEE Computer Society, Los Alamitos (2004)
13. Li, J., Papachristou, C., Shekhar, R.: An FPGA-based computing platform for real-time 3D medical imaging and its application to cone-beam CT reconstruction. Journal of Imaging Science and Technology, 237–245 (2005)
14. Jendrsczok, J., Ediger, P., Hoffmann, R.: Language and Machine Support for the Massively Parallel GCA Model. Technical Report RA-1-2007, Technische Universität Darmstadt, FB Informatik (2007)
15. Lienhart, G., Kugel, A., Männer, R.: Using floating-point arithmetic on fpgas to accelerate scientific n-body simulations. In: FCCM 2002: Proceedings of the 10th Annual IEEE Symposium on Field-Programmable Custom Computing Machines, p. 182. IEEE Computer Society, Washington (2002)

Hybrid Resource Discovery Mechanism in Ad Hoc Grid Using Structured Overlay

Tariq Abdullah[1], Luc Onana Alima[2], Vassiliy Sokolov[1],
David Calomme[2], and Koen Bertels[1]

[1] Computer Engineering Laboratory, EEMCS, Delft University of Technology,
Mekelweg 4, 2624 CD, Delft, The Netherlands
{m.t.abdullah,v.sokolov,k.l.m.bertels}@tudelft.nl
[2] Distributed Systems Laboratory, University of Mons, Belgium
{luc.onana,david.calomme}@umh.ac.be

Abstract. Resource management has been an area of research in ad hoc grids for many years. Recently, different research projects have focused resource management in centralized, decentralized or in a hybrid manner. In this paper, we discuss a micro economic based, hybrid resource discovery mechanism. The proposed mechanism focuses on the extension of a structured overlay network to manage the (dis)appearance of matchmakers in the grid and to route the messages to the appropriate matchmaker in the ad hoc grid. The mechanism is based on the emergent behavior of the participating nodes and adapts with respect to changes in the ad hoc grid environment. Experiments are executed on PlanetLab to test the scalability and robustness of the proposed mechanism. Simulation results show that our mechanism performs better than previously proposed mechanisms.

1 Introduction

Ad hoc grid (also called Public Resource Computing [1], Desktop Grid Computing [2], or Volunteer Computing) has autonomous, geographically distributed, and heterogeneous nodes with intermittent participation. The intermittent participation of nodes results in varying workload of the resource manager. Furthermore, different underlying network infrastructures and varying access/use policies of the nodes increase the administrative complexity of the resource management system in the ad hoc grid.

There exist different resource discovery techniques for ad hoc grid. Centralized approaches are efficient and consume less time to find a resource. But these approaches have a single point of failure and are not scalable. In contrast to centralized approaches, peer to peer (P2P) approaches are scalable and depict low management complexity. Whereas, the P2P approaches are less efficient and can have time and network overhead while finding a resource. P2P and centralised systems are often considered to be mutually exclusive and reside on both ends of an infrastructural spectrum. We consider them to be part of a continuum where the system should be capable of restructuring itself in either of these states, or any intermediate state between those two extremes.

This paper is an extension of the work presented in [3], where, we proposed a resource management mechanism that enabled the ad hoc grid to self-organize according to the workload of the resource manager (referred to as *matchmaker* hereafter). The mechanism is based on the emergent behavior of the participating nodes and adapts itself with respect to the changes in the ad hoc grid environment. In [3], we assumed the availability of a structured overlay network to handle node join/leave, de(segmentation) of ad hoc grid, message routing among matchmakers, node to matchmaker message exchange and matchmaker to node message exchange. Furthermore, a node belonged to only one matchmaker and there was no mechanism to find a new responsible matchmaker in the event of a matchmaker failure. We now address some of the open issues reported there.

This paper focuses on some of the open issues mentioned above. The main contributions of the paper are as follows. The proposed extension defines the algorithms for node joining, for finding a responsible matchmaker by a joining/existing node, for ad hoc grid segmentation (by promoting nodes as matchmakers), and for ad hoc grid desegmentation (by demoting matchmakers as normal nodes). Experiments are executed, on PlanetLab [4], to verify that the proposed extension enables ad hoc grid to self-organize according to the workload of the resource manager. The proposed extension makes our hybrid resource discovery mechanism, for ad hoc grid, dynamic and flexible.

The rest of the paper is organized as follows. An overview of the related work and necessary background knowledge to understand the proposed model is in section 2. Section 3 describes the proposed extension of the structured overlay network. Section 4 explains the experimental setup and discusses the results. Section 5 concludes the paper and describes our future work.

2 Related Work and Background Knowledge

In literature, we find different solutions for load balancing in distributed systems. Mercury [5] used node leave/rejoin for load balancing. The overloaded node leaves and then joins the ring as a neighbor of a lightly loaded node. Node leave/rejoin introduces message overhead. Cai et al. [6] used customized hashing function. The customized hashing functions required a prior knowledge of the attributes value distribution. Mastroianni et al. [7] used unstructured P2P networks to construct a super-peer model for resource discovery in grids and used experience based query forwarding. Attribute encoding of static or dynamic computational resource information for resource discovery in DHT based overlay networks is also studied in [8]. The majority of the encoded attributes may be mapped to a small set of nodes in the overlay network, therefore attribute encoding may result in a load imbalance condition. Padmanabhan et al. [9] proposed a self-organized grouping method that formed and maintained autonomous *resource groups*. These resource groups are formed according to some pre-specified resource characteristics and each group contained a set of similar resources. The main drawback of their work is that there is no load balancing mechanism among the groups formed. Butt et al. [10] implemented a P2P based Condor flocking to share resources in different Condor pools. They did not consider the dynamic introduction/removal of Condor pools or the workload condition of a Condor pool manager.

The above discussed approaches used different ways to distribute the workload of one matchmaker among multiple matchmakers. These include node leave/rejoin [5], customized hash functions [6], super peer model on top of unstructured networks [7], or attribute encoding [8]. All these approaches attempt to balance the workload of the resource manager/ matchmaker by sharing the workload, they may end up with an inappropriate infrastructure for the given state of the grid.

2.1 Continuous Double Auction Based Resource Allocation

Our ad hoc grid consists of autonomous, dynamic, volatile and loosely connected nodes that can join, leave or change their roles whenever needed. Each node is composed of three agents: *Consumer*, *Producer* and *Matchmaker*. Structure of these agents is depicted in Figure 1. The *Resource/Task Manager* module of the producer/consumer agent prepares *asks/bids*. The resource offers are called *asks* and the resource requests are called *bids*. An *ask* is defined by attributes like resource quantity, Time To Live (TTL) and resource price in this paper. A *bid* is represented by resource quantity, job execution time, bid price and Time To Live (TTL) in this paper.

The matchmaker uses Continuous Double Auction (CDA) to perform resource allocation in its *MatchMake* module. The matchmaker agent continuously receives *asks/bids* from producer/consumer agents and stores the received asks/bids in the offer/request repositories, maintained by the *Repository Manager* module. The matchmaker finds the matches between the producers and consumers by matching offers (starting with lowest ask price and moving up) with requests (starting with highest bid price and moving down). The matchmaker matches a compatible ask/bid pair immediately. A compatible ask/bid is a resource offer/request pair where resource request (*bid*) constraints are satisfied by the matching resource offer (*ask*). The received ask/bid remains in the offer/request repositories of the matchmaker till the expiry of its Time To Live (TTL). The *Segmenter Module* performs segmentation and desegmentation by promoting and demoting the matchmakers. All consumer/producer to matchmaker and vice verse communication is done through the *communication* module of the respective consumer/producer or matchmaker agent. The communication module uses underlying structured overlay network for communication between the consumer/producer or matchmaker agent.

The *Job Manager Module* of consumer/producer agents is responsible to execute the consumer jobs and return the computation results to the consumer, after receiving a matchmaking notification from the matchmaker. The producer/consumer does not have a system wide (global) knowledge and are not aware of the other's ask/bid prices. The

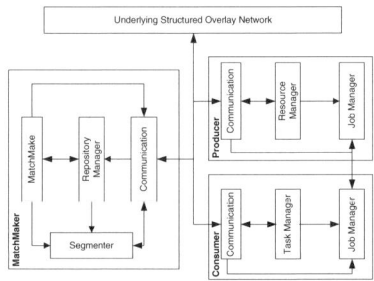

Fig. 1. System Architecture

producer/consumer use a dynamic history based pricing function to calculate the ask/bid price for each offered/requested resource [3].

2.2 Transaction Cost (TCost) Threshold Determination

The matchmaker attaches a transaction cost (TCost) to each offer/request, which reflects the workload of the matchmaker. The node submitting a request/offer is supposed to pay this TCost to the matchmaker. Every node is given an initial budget which can be used to this purpose. Formula for calculating TCost, discussion of TCost upper and lower thresholds for promoting normal nodes as matchmaker and demoting underloaded matchmaker nodes as normal nodes are described in our previous paper [3].

3 Proposed Algorithm

There can be N nodes in our experiments. Each node can play the role of a consumer, producer or a matchmaker. A *producer node* offers its available resources (such as CPU, memory, disk space or bandwidth). A *consumer node* requests for the desired resources to execute its job. The node playing the role of a mediator between the consumer and the producer nodes are named as resource allocators or *matchmaker*s in this work. The matchmaker receives offers and bids of resources from the nodes in the ad hoc grid, which are then matched by the matchmaker. Each node is assigned a unique node identifier (nodeID). As the proposed algorithm is an extension of a structured P2P overlay network, principally any structured P2P overlay network, can be used to implement the proposed algorithm. We used Pastry [11] to implement the proposed extension. As the Pastry identifier space can have $2^{128} - 1$ unique identifiers, the maximum number of nodes (N) in our ad hoc grid can also be $2^{128} - 1$. There can be a maximum of M matchmakers out of N nodes.

The whole identifier space is divided into zones. Each zone has a responsible matchmaker. Each joining consumer/producer/matchmaker node is provided with M, N and the *zone number* to which the node belongs to. It is ensured that each consumer/producer node is under the responsibility of a matchmaker. When a matchmaker becomes overloaded then it promotes its predecessor matchmaker node to perform matchmaking. The consumer/producer nodes under the responsibility of overloaded matchmaker are now under the responsibility of the predecessor matchmaker. In case, the predecessor matchmaker is already performing matchmaking (i.e active) then the excess workload is forwarded to the successor matchmaker of the overloaded matchmaker. The algorithm for matchmaker promotion is explained in Section 3.1.

Conversely, when a matchmaker is underloaded then it demotes itself and informs its predecessor and successor matchmakers about the change in its matchmaking status. The successor matchmaker of the demoted matchmaker becomes the responsible matchmaker for consumer/producer nodes that were previously under the responsibility of the demoted matchmaker. After demoting itself, the demoted matchmaker will forward the request/offer messages to its successor matchmaker node. The demoted matchmaker also informs the consumer/producer node, under its responsibility, about the change of its matchmaking status and about their new matchmaker. The matchmaker demotion (desegmentation) algorithm is explained in Section 3.2.

A consumer/producer node finds its responsible matchmaker node with the provided information, after joining the ad hoc grid. In case there is only one matchmaker in the ad hoc grid then it becomes responsible matchmaker for all the consumer/producer nodes. The consumer/producer node can submit request/offer to the matchmaker node after finding the responsible matchmaker node. Each matchmaker node maintains matchmaking status information (active/inactive) about its predecessor and successor matchmaker nodes. The matchmaker does so by exchanging matchmaking status information with its successor and predecessor nodes. The algorithms for node joining and matchmaker discovery are explained in Section 3.3 and 3.4 respectively.

3.1 Matchmaker Promotion: Segmentation

This algorithm is executed by an overloaded matchmakers in the ad hoc grid. An overloaded matchmaker (say M_i is matchmaker for zone i) promotes its predecessor matchmaker node (say M_{i-1}).

The newly promoted matchmaker (M_{i-1}) changes its matchmaking status to active, as depicted in Figure 2a and Figure 2b. The matchmaker (M_{i-1}) updates its predecessor matchmaker (M_{i-2}) about the change in its matchmaking status. The matchmaker (M_{i-1}) is now ready to perform matchmaking for the consumer/producer nodes belonging to zone $i-1$.

The consumer/producer nodes belonging to zone $i-1$ are still unaware of the change of their new matchmaker in their zone. We applied "correction on use" policy to update the consumer/producer nodes belonging to zone $i-1$. The matchmaker M_i, after promoting its predecessor (M_{i-1}) as active, will process the currently received request/offer message from nodes belonging to zone $i-1$ and will update the respective node, in zone $i-1$, about their new matchmaker (M_{i-1}). The consumer/producer nodes in zone $i-1$ change their responsible matchmaker to M_{i-1} from M_i and send the request/offer messages to their new matchmaker (M_{i-1}). This process is graphically illustrated in Figure 2c.

If the predecessor matchmaker (M_{i-1}), of matchmaker M_i, is already active then the overloaded matchmaker node (M_i) will forward its excess workload to its successor matchmaker (M_{i+1}). The matchmaker promotion algorithm is listed in Algorithm 1.

As stated before, there can be N nodes (consumer/producer/matchmaker) in the ad hoc grid and there can be a maximum of M matchmakers ($M < N$), out of N nodes. The

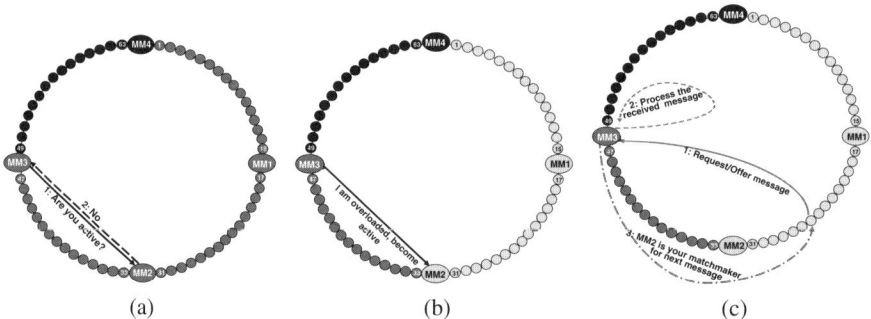

Fig. 2. Promote a Matchmaker

Algorithm 1 Promote Matchmaker

1: IF(M_i is overloaded) THEN
2:   M_i Query M_{i-1} matchmaking status
3: IF(M_{i-1} *matchmaking status is false*) THEN
4:   M_i change M_{i-1} matchmaking status to TRUE
5:   M_{i-1} update its changed matchmaking status to M_{i-2}
6:   M_i update matchmaker change to consumer/producer nodes in zone $i-1$
7: ELSE
8:   M_i Forwarded excess workload to M_{i+1}
9: END IF
10: END IF

ad hoc grid is thus divided into maximum of $(N/M) - 1$ zones. This zone information is only effective when there is an active matchmaker in that zone. If the matchmaker for a zone i does not exist or is inactive then the consumer/producer nodes, continue looking for an active matchmaker in the successor zones of zone i (refer Section 3.4 for details). The number of effective zones increases with the promotion of matchmakers and decreases with the demotion of matchmakers, explained in Section 3.2. In this way, the matchmaker promotion results in the segmentation of the ad hoc grid and the matchmaker demotion results in desegmentation of ad hoc grid.

3.2 Matchmaker Demotion: Desegmentation

This algorithm is executed by an underloaded matchmaker in the ad hoc grid. An underloaded matchmaker (say M_i is matchmaker for zone i) demotes itself by changing its matchmaking status. The demoted matchmaker updates its predecessor matchmaker node (M_{i-1}) and successor matchmaker node (M_{i+1}) about the change in its matchmaking status, as depicted in Figure 3a and Figure 3b.

The "correction on use" policy is also applied to update the consumer/producer nodes in zone i about the change of their responsible matchmaker. The matchmaker node M_i, after demoting itself, will forward the currently received request/offer messages, from nodes in zone i, to its successor matchmaker node (M_{i+1}). The matchmaker M_i also sends a message to the respective consumer/producer node, about the change of

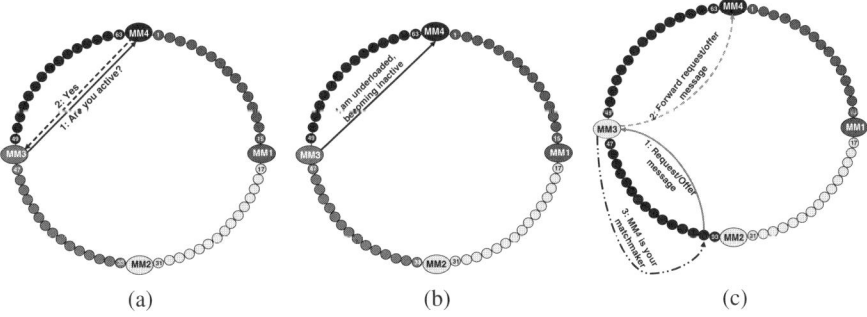

Fig. 3. Demote a Matchmaker

Algorithm 2 Demote Matchmaker

1: IF (M_i is underloaded) THEN
2:   M_i change its matchmaking status to FALSE
3:   M_i update its changed matchmaking status to M_{i-1}
4:   M_i update its changed matchmaking status to M_{+1}
5:   Notify consumer/producer nodes about change of matchmaker
6: END IF

Algorithm 3 Node Join Algorithm

1: Node join the ad hoc grid into zone i
2: IF ($Joining\,node\,is\,Consumer/Producer$) THEN
3:   CALL $Find - Responsible - Matchmaker$
4: ELSE IF ($Joining\,node\,is\,Matchmaker$) THEN
5:   Query predecessor node's matchmaking status
6:   Query successor node's matchmaking status
7:   END IF
8: END IF

matchmaker from M_i to M_{i+1}. The consumer/producer nodes in zone i change their responsible matchmaker to M_{i+1} from M_i and send the request/offer messages to their new matchmaker (M_{+1}). This process is graphically illustrated in Figure 3c. The matchmaker demotion algorithm is listed in Algorithm 2.

3.3 Node Joining Algorithm

Each joining consumer/producer/matchmaker node is provided with M, N and the zone number to which the node belongs to. We used Pastry node join protocol [11] for node joining in our ad hoc grid. After joining the ad hoc grid, the consumer/producer and matchmaker node performs different set of actions.

The consumer/producer node discovers its responsible matchmaker node with the provided information (refer Section 3.4). It can send the resource request/offer messages after discovering the responsible matchmaker.

A matchmaker node maintains matchmaking status information (active/inactive) about its predecessor and successor matchmaker nodes. When a matchmaker node joins the ad hoc grid then it exchanges predecessor/successor matchmaking status information. The algorithm for joining the ad hoc grid is listed in Algorithm 3.

3.4 Matchmaker Discovery

As stated before, there can be N nodes (consumer/producer/matchmaker) in the ad hoc grid and there can be M matchmakers, out of N nodes. (N being the maximum number of nodes and M being the maximum number of matchmakers in ad hoc grid). The first node of each zone is considered the matchmaker for the previous zone. In this way each consumer/producer node is under the responsibility of a matchmaker.

The "Matchmaker Discovery" algorithm is executed by the joining consumer/producer node for discovering its responsible matchmaker node. If the matchmaker

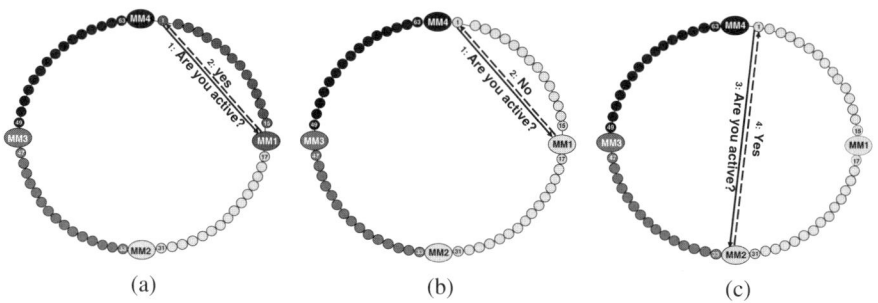

Fig. 4. Discovering a Responsible Matchmaker

Algorithm 4 Discovering Responsible Matchmaker

1: Consumer/producer node join the ad hoc grid into zone i
2: IF (M_i is active) THEN
3:   set M_i as responsible matchmaker
4: ELSE
5:   set $I = i + 1$
6:   set $counter = 1$
7:   WHILE ($counter < M$)
8:     Query $Matchmaker_I$
9:     IF ($MatchMaker_I$ is active) THEN
10:       set $MatchMaker_I$ as responsible matchmaker
11:       BREAK
12:     END IF
13:     $I = I + 1$
14:     $counter = counter + 1$
15:   END WHILE
16: END IF

(say M_i) for zone i is active then the joining consumer/producer node sets this matchmaker (M_i) as its responsible matchmaker (refer Figure 4a). The consumer/producer node will send all its resource requests/offers messages to this matchmaker.

If the matchmaker for a zone does not exist (say matchmaker M_i for zone i does not exist), then the consumer/producer node checks for the successor matchmaker (M_{i+1}) of M_i. The consumer/producer node continues searching for an active matchmaker node, until it finds one (refer Figure 4b and Figure 4c). It is important to mention that the algorithm for finding a responsible matchmaker by a newly joining node does not cover matchmaker node failure. The matchmaker failure handling will be in our future work. The algorithm for finding the responsible matchmaker by a newly joining node is listed in Algorithm 4.

4 Experimental Setup and Results

The purpose of the experiments is to validate the proposed algorithm and to assess how it allows self organization. To this purpose, the proposed extension is implemented on

Pastry [11] and is tested on PlanetLab [4]. Pastry[11] is a completely decentralized, scalable and self-organizing structured overlay network with respect to node join/leave or departure and overlay network maintenance. Although we used Pastry in this work, it can be replaced with any other structured P2P overlay network.

The message routing process in Pastry is briefly described as follows. When a node receives a message from another node, it first checks whether the destination nodeID falls within its leaf set or not. If the destination nodeID exists in its leaf set, then the message is directly forwarded to the destination node, otherwise the routing table of the node that received the current message is used and the message is forwarded to the node that shares a common prefix with the destination node ID by at least one digit. The routing performance of Pastry is scalable and the maximum expected number of routing steps is $\log_{2^b} N$ [11], where b is a Pastry configuration parameter with $b = 4$ as the default value and N is the total number of nodes in the Pastry ring. We refer to [11] for Pastry details.

PlanetLab is an open, geographically distributed computing environment/test-bed. PlanetLab makes it possible to demonstrate the scalability and robustness of a proposed mechanisms given real network traffic, generated from real users while considering the inherent unpredictability of the Internet. It [4] currently includes more than 893 machines, spanning 461 sites and 40 countries. Over 600 research projects, called *service*, are currently running on the PlanetLab. Each project runs in its own network of virtual machines, called *slice*. A slice isolates projects from each other. Moreover there is no centralized control over resources in PlanetLab. Data represented in the paper is extracted after $1/4^{th}$ of the experiment time has elapsed.

The matchmaker's throughput is determined in terms of its matchmaking efficiency, Transaction Cost (TCost) and the response time. The matchmaking efficiency is calculated in terms of request/offer utilization. The request utilization is calculated as

$$\left(\sum MatchedRequest / \sum Request\right) * 100$$

and the offer utilization is calculated as

$$\left(\sum MatchedOffer / \sum Offer\right) * 100$$

The Transaction Cost (TCost) calculation and TCost upper and lower threshold determination is discussed in Section 2.2. The matchmaker response time is the time interval between receiving a request/offer message by the matchmaker and the time instance when matchmaker has processed a request/offer message.

The experiments are executed with varying numbers of the participating nodes. The number of the nodes is varied from 15-650 and the number of matchmakers is varied from 1-5. The workload is managed in such a way that the maximum number of matchmakers are needed and then gradually decreased to provoke the demotion of matchmakers to normal nodes again. The Job execution time, job deadline and required/offered resource amount are randomly generated from a predefined range. Quantity of requested/offered computational resource is varied for each request/offer message. The TTL of a request/offer message is fixed to 10000 milliseconds, reflecting the delays observed in PlanetLab.

4.1 Experimental Results

In this section, we first present the experimental results with one matchmaker. Later, we present experimental results with multiple matchmakers to show the effect of dynamic promotion and demotion of matchmaker(s). The effect of promotion (segmentation of ad hoc grid) and demotion (desegmentation of ad hoc grid) of matchmaker(s), in ad hoc grid, on Transaction Cost (TCost), matchmaker response time and consumer/producer utilization are compared with the ad hoc grid having only one matchmaker.

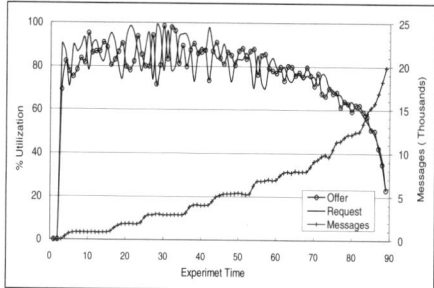 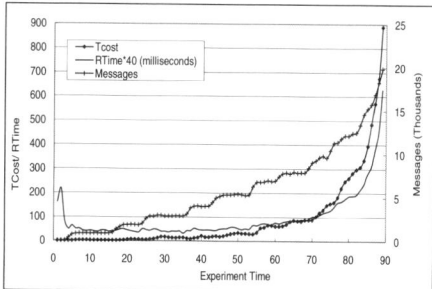

(a). Request/Offer Utilization of One Matchmaker with increasing workload

(b). TCost and Response Time of One Matchmaker with increasing workload

Fig. 5. Ad Hoc Grid with One Matchmaker

Figure 5a depicts the effect of request/offer utilization with increasing workload of one matchmaker. *Request*, represents the consumer utilization and *offer* represents the producer utilization in Figure 5a. Whereas, Figure 5b depicts the effect of the consumer/producer TCost and response time variation with increasing workload of one matchmaker.

Figure 5a and 5b indicate that the TCost and the response time increase with increasing workload and consumer/producer utilization decreases with the increasing workload of one matchmaker. The increasing trend of TCost and response time, and decreasing trend of the consumer/producer utilization represent that the matchmaker is overloaded and is unable to maintain its matchmaking capacity. It also implies that the consumer/producer have to pay a higher TCost for availing the matchmaking service. The matchmaker needs additional matchmakers, at the point, when its matchmaking efficiency starts to decrease. This is the point, where our mechanism becomes useful.

Figure 6 depicts the TCost and Response Time variation in presence of multiple adaptive matchmakers. The TCost value keeps on increasing with increasing matchmaker workload. A new matchmaker is introduced when the first matchmaker reached its TCost threshold value. When a new matchmaker is introduced, the TCost value decreases. The opposite is observed when a matchmaker is removed. Evidently, the TCost also increases/decreases temporarily reflecting changes in the workload of the overall grid. Overall and compared with the TCost evolution with a single matchmaker and increasing workload (Refer Figure 5b), the TCost remains relatively stable and does

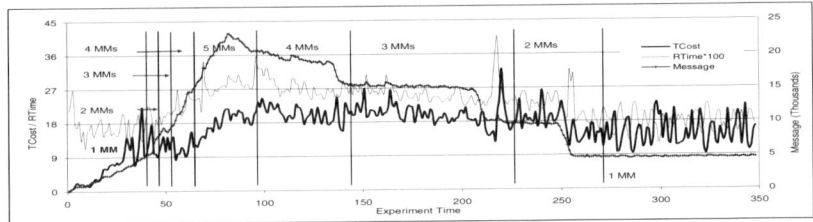

Fig. 6. TCost and Response Time with Multiple Adaptive Matchmakers

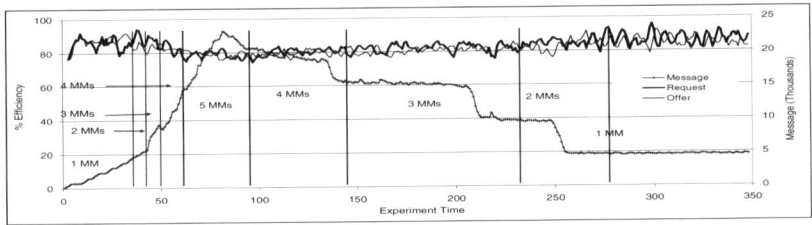

Fig. 7. Matchmaking Efficiency with Multiple Adaptive Matchmakers

not increase (Refer Figure 6). Instead of going up with an increasing workload, the increase of the number of matchmakers has a stabilizing effect on the response time. This is exactly what was expected.

Figure 7 depicts the matchmaking efficiency with multiple adaptive matchmakers. The matchmaking efficiency remains 80% with increasing workload of the matchmaker. Whereas, in case of one matchmaker, matchmaking efficiency showed a continuous decreasing trend with increasing workload (Refer Figure 5a).

In conclusion, we can observe from the above experiments that the capability of the ad hoc grid to instantiate multiple matchmakers has a stabilizing effect on the TCost and response time without affecting negatively the offers/request utilization. This way, we guarantee that the transaction cost and response time become invariant to the scale on which the grid is operating. These conclusions also confirm that the proposed algorithms for joining ad hoc grid, finding responsible matchmaker, promoting a matchmaker, demoting a matchmaker and message routing on P2P overlay network work as expected.

5 Conclusions

A dynamic, self-organizing mechanism, for a dynamic ad hoc grid infrastructure was proposed in this paper. The proposed mechanism focuses on the extension of a structured overlay network to manage the (dis)appearance of matchmakers in the grid and to route the messages to the appropriate matchmaker in the ad hoc grid. The mechanism dynamically segmented the ad hoc grid into multiple segments and merged the ad hoc grid segments according to the workload in the ad hoc grid. The matchmaking efficiency and capacity of the ad hoc grid was sustained, in spite of the increasing workload, by applying the proposed mechanism. All experiments were executed on PlanetLab providing a realistic platform for testing the proposed mechanisms. Our future research will focus on the failure handling of the matchmaker node. We will also look into a different QoS issues for the proposed mechanism.

References

1. Anderson, D.P.: BOINC: A system for public-resource computing and storage. In: 5th IEEE/ACM International Workshop on Grid Computing (2004)
2. Chien, A., Calder, B., Elbert, S., Bhatia, K.: Entropia: Architecture and performance of an enterprise desktop grid system. JPDC 63(5), 597–610 (2003)
3. Abdullah, T., Sokolov, V., Pourebrahimi, B., Bertels, K.: Self-organizing dynamic ad hoc grids. In: 2nd IEEE International Conference on Self-Adaptive and Self-Organizing Systems Workshops (October 2008)
4. PlanetLab Online, https://www.planet-lab.org/
5. Bharambe, A.R., Agrawal, M., Seshan, S.: Mercury: supporting scalable multi-attribute range queries. In: The ACM SIGCOMM Conference (2004)
6. Cai, M., Frank, M., Chen, J., Szekely, P.: MAAN: A multi-attribute addressable network for grid information services. Journal of Grid Computing 2(1), 3–14 (2004)
7. Mastroianni, C., Talia, D., Verta, O.: A super-peer model for building resource discovery services in grids: Design and simulation analysis. In: European Grid Conference (2005)
8. Gupta, R., Sekhri, V., Somani, A.K.: Compup2p: An architecture for internet computing using peer-to-peer networks. IEEE Transactions on Parallel and Distributed Systems 17(11), 1306–1320 (2006)
9. Padmanabhan, A., Wang, S., Ghosh, S., Briggs, R.: A self-organized grouping (SOG) method for efficient grid resource discovery. In: 6th IEEE/ACM International Workshop on Grid Computing, pp. 312–317 (2005)
10. Butt, A.R., Zhang, R., Hu, Y.C.: A self-organizing flock of condors. JPDC 66(1), 145–161 (2006)
11. Rowstron, A., Druschel, P.: Pastry: Scalable, decentralized object location, and routing for large-scale peer-to-peer systems. In: Guerraoui, R. (ed.) Middleware 2001. LNCS, vol. 2218, p. 329. Springer, Heidelberg (2001)

Marketplace-Oriented Behavior in Semantic Multi-Criteria Decision Making Autonomous Systems

Ghadi Mahmoudi, Christian Müller-Schloer, and Jörg Hähner

Institute of Systems Engineering – System and Computer Architecture, Appelstraße 4,
30167 Hannover, Germany
{mahmoudi,cms,haehner}@sra.uni-hannover.de

Abstract. Autonomy in Organic Computing systems is supposed to ensure well-functioning engineering systems. Our approach called Semantic Multi-Criteria Decision Making (SeMCDM) brings the decision making process of autonomous units close to the intention of human designers. This paper studies the integration of marketplace-oriented behavior into SeMCDM. It defines distributed and centralized market scenarios, suggests evaluation metrics with consideration of resource-restricted applications, extracts related characteristics of the application environment and presents simulation results. The paper concludes with recommendations about the adequate market scenario in relation to the application environment.

1 Introduction

In parallel to the increasing deployment of computerized solutions in engineering systems, the complexity of whole systems reaches new records. The interconnection of distributed systems, which have to work together to fulfill the designers' expectations, represents a real technical challenge. Delivering a brilliant example, automotive systems show the limits of the traditional way towards a "well-functioning design". Beside the design time difficulties, more dangerous problems arise at runtime. Technicians in repair and assembly shops have usually restricted possibilities to identify the source of a failure, in particular in the electrical system. Self-organizing systems, as suggested in the research field of "Organic Computing" [1], benefit from the autonomy of system components. Through their cooperative behavior, the system components are expected to (re)configure themselves to face dangerous situations. To facilitate technical systems with autonomy, different design solutions have been proposed. In [2] and [3] the marketplace-oriented behavior provides an upper behavior schema for the autonomous system components (called also units), where a system configuration results from the exchange of "offers" and "enquiries". In our previous work in [3], the role of semantic matching between offers and enquiries, as well as the need for a decision making mechanism has been underlined. Our approach has the name of "Semantic Multi-Criteria Decision Making" (SeMCDM). A new design question evolved from the integration of marketplace-oriented behavior and SeMCDM concepts: Actions like sending offers or enquiries, the semantic matching process and the multi-criteria decision making can be allocated to offering units, to enquiring units or to a central instance.

The actions' allocation builds the core of this paper. Systematic design conditions have been considered and concrete orders of actions on the marketplace, also called "market scenarios", evolved as a result. This paper defines also different evaluation metrics and applies them to the simulated market scenarios. To bring the simulation results close to real applications, characteristics of the application environment have been considered. The complexity of the environment is not only reflected by the number of the autonomous units, but also by the diversity of their types. This paper puts recommendations to the hands of self-organizing systems' engineers.

Section 2 summarizes the related work. Section 3 presents the principles of SeMCDM with special concentration on the deployment of marketplace-oriented behavior in SeMCDM. Market scenarios are defined in section 4. The simulation of market scenarios, the evaluation metrics and the results are subject of section 5. Design recommendations are presented in section 6. The paper concludes and motivates future work in section 7.

2 Related Work

EvoArch [2] introduced marketplace-oriented behavior as a means to reach self-organization in automotive engineering systems. The main ideas behind EvoArch can be described as follows: An automobile consists of intelligent autonomous units. They have properties and aims. Autonomous units can be active or passive. Active units look for partners to enhance their own functionality, while passive units offer their own capabilities purposing to be accepted as partners. After the selection of a specific partner a contract has to be concluded to build a functioning (automotive) system. EvoArch presented the marketplace-oriented behavior only as a general idea.

Different approaches tried to combine economical mechanisms to (autonomous) information systems. In its approach about distributed self-organizing application layer networks, the CATNET project [5] adopted the economic paradigm of Catallaxy. The Catallaxy paradigm, which goes back to Friedrich August von Hayek, is seen in [6] as a coordination mechanism for information systems consisting of autonomous network elements. It is based on negotiation and price signaling. The whole project can be subsumed under the resource allocation approaches. It finds its application on the top of large Grids and P2P computer networks. CATNET presented a simulation-based comparison between the distributed Catallaxy approach and a centralized solution. Two (although correlated) points distinguish the Catallaxy paradigm from the marketplace scenarios presented in this paper: The Catallaxy paradigm depends on the concept of prices, and it implies negotiations between the autonomous network elements.

In the area of service oriented grid computing, [7] describes various economic models and pricing strategies. Similar to the Catallaxy paradigm, all of these models share the concept of service prices and the need for negotiation. This difference to SeMCDM market scenarios finds its root in the nature of the proposed applications: By allocating homogeneous resources (computer systems: PCs, storage systems, databases etc.) to software programs, the emphasis is not put on "What are these resources?" but on how to allocate them in order to optimize the performance. EvoArch and SeMCDM address the heterogeneity (diversity) of autonomous units, treating the main question of: "Which resource meets the looked-for requirements?", i.e. the matching problem. [8] registers additional principal differences between competitive economically motivated agents (in the research area of information economy) and autonomous agents for the purpose of autonomic computing [9], which may behave in a competitive or cooperative way.

DySCAS [12], another project in the area of autonomous systems, is supposed to adopt the solution of "policy based computing". A policy is a set of rules. Its advantage is that it can be detached from the implementation mechanism. The marketplace-oriented behavior can be understood as a meta-policy for the autonomous units. The commitment to marketplace-oriented behavior seems to imply a kind of restriction, but it has the advantage of being application independent.

3 Semantic Multi-Criteria Decision Making (SeMCDM)

3.1 Principles of SeMCDM

Semantic Multi-Criteria Decision Making (SeMCDM) is a further developed version of our previous work described in [3]. It addresses the design questions of organic computing and its employment in real applications like automotive systems. SeMCDM considers system components as autonomous units, which try to (re)configure the whole system through marketplace-oriented behavior: the exchange of offers and enquiries (consisting of multiple features). The offering units are referred to as passive units, while the enquiring units are referred to as active units. An active unit has at least one looked-for component, and thus one enquiry. The matching process between enquiries and offers is the key for successful self-organization. SeMCDM suggests that autonomous individuals would be only able to build a "suitable order" if they are supplied with "suitable knowledge". A common view to the world between the designer and the autonomous units, as well as between the autonomous units themselves, is a prerequisite for a solution. In analogy to solutions known from the area of Semantic Web [4], SeMCDM represents the knowledge of autonomous units on the base of an ontology, which builds an important bridge between the designer(s) and the autonomous unit(s). The autonomous units would be able to interact using semantically well-defined terms. Interaction models, like the market place arena would benefit from the "semantic matching" between the offers and the enquiries on the market place.

SeMCDM addresses a further problem in relation to multi-dimensional descriptions of both offers and enquiries (through multiple features). While semantic matching presents a solution for matching pairs of features (one feature of the offer and one feature of the enquiry), the evaluation of the whole offer, with all of its features, moves the matching problem to a higher level of complexity. Methods of "Multi-Criteria Decision Making" are used by SeMCDM to support the autonomous units with selection mechanisms. This way, SeMCDM takes advantage of different approaches: autonomous systems, marketplace-oriented behavior, semantic matching and decision making mechanisms.

The matching of one offer feature to one enquiry feature should take the semantic meaning of both features (power, noise, type of signal processing technology) and the semantic meaning of their values (numeric and non-numeric) into account. In SeMCDM, a match occurs when the offer's feature is semantically equal to the enquiry feature, and the offered value has a utility value greater than 0 in relation to the utility function of the enquiry feature. To enable semantic matching in general, SeMCDM deploys an inference engine (Jena [11]). The matching capabilities of the inference engine have been extended to support the matching between utility functions (utility check). This takes place by adding rules and Built-ins (Jena Built-ins are Java programs, which can be accessed by rules).

For more flexibility in the description (and subsequently in the autonomy), the SeMCDM description schema of looked-for components distinguishes between "features to be unconditionally fulfilled" and "features to be preferably fulfilled". Accordingly, the SeMCDM matching process can be divided into two steps:

i. The first matching step proves the adequacy of an offer for an enquiry, i.e. it addresses the features to be unconditionally fulfilled and their utility check. The relation between these features is characterized by a kind of parallelism in the sense of the logical relation "AND".

ii. The second matching step evaluates the offer with relation to the features to be preferably fulfilled, calculates its utility values on these features and aggregates them to one evaluation value. On the base of the offers' evaluations the best offer can be then selected. The second matching step is strongly related to multi-criteria decision making, and therefore it will be called MCDM step. To evaluate the whole offer, SeMCDM defines a special aggregation function of the form (a mixture of weighted sum and weighted product of offers' utilities on related features):

$$v(a) = \prod_{j=1}^{k} u_j(a)^{w_j} [1 + \sum_{i=1}^{n} u_i(a).w_i] \qquad (1)$$

Where a is the considered offer (or alternative); $v(a)$ is the evaluation of offer a; k is the number of features to be unconditionally fulfilled; w_j is the weight of the feature j to be unconditionally fulfilled; $u_j(a)$ is the utility value of offer a on the feature j to be unconditionally fulfilled; n is the number of features to be preferably fulfilled; $u_i(a)$ is the utility value of offer a on the feature i to be preferably fulfilled; w_i is the weight of the feature i to be preferably fulfilled.

3.2 Conditions for the Allocation of the Matching Steps on Autonomous Units

By its very nature, a passive unit is interested only in enquiries and in its own offer. A passive unit is not aware of offers coming from other passive units. For this reason, the allocation of the second matching step (or at least the decision making) to passive units has to be avoided.

SeMCDM scenarios are characterized by the facts that the first matching step is automatically triggered when an enquiry meets an offer and that each enquiry stays available on the marketplace for a predefined time period, i.e. the enquiry has an expiration time (with the exception of the second scenario in its "B" version). SeMCDM adopts a reservation mechanism to avoid negotiations between active units about offers and between passive units about enquiries.

4 Market Scenarios

Table 1 shows the types of the market scenarios with their initiator, the type of messages exchanged between the units and the responsible unit for each matching step.

Table 1. Possible market scenarios with their specifications

	Scenario 1	Scenario 2 (in two versions "2A" and "2B")	Scenario 3
Initiator	Active units	Passive units	Active and passive units
Type of messages	Enquiries	Offers	Enquiries and offers
First matching step	Passive units	Active units	Central
Second matching step	Active units	Active units	Central

According to the type of exchanged messages on the marketplace the market scenarios can be categorized to enquiry-oriented scenarios (scenario 1) and offer-oriented scenarios (scenario 2), while scenario 3 relies on a combination of offers and enquiries.

To exchange offers or enquiries, a communication platform has to gather all autonomous units. In the suggested scenarios below, the existence of a central common memory for communication purposes between the autonomous units is assumed (it can be replaced by a broadcasting mechanism). Even though this central common memory is called "broker", scenarios are still distributed scenarios, unless some matching activities are performed in a central way by the broker itself.

A complete flow through the sequence diagram is called a "cycle". Because of concurrence between the autonomous units more than one cycle can be necessary to find a suitable offer for all looked-for components.

4.1 Market Scenario 1

In this enquiry-oriented scenario, the active units send their enquiries (one for every looked-for component) to the broker, and wait for suitable offers. Every free passive unit reads an enquiry (randomly selected by the broker), checks the matching relation between its own features and the features to be unconditionally fulfilled in the enquiry (first matching step). When a suitable match can be proved for all these features, the passive unit sends an offer, addressed at the specific enquiry. Every passive unit may send only one offer addressed to one enquiry. The broker stores the offers addressed to each enquiry, until the enquiry expires. At this time point, the broker sends the offers to the enquiring active unit and deletes the enquiry. The active unit performs the second matching step and chooses the best available offer. The active units then conclude a contract with the passive unit of the best offer. All other offers will be deleted and all other passive units are free again. In this scenario, multiple offers can be directed to one enquiry, while other enquiries will not receive any offers. Also when suitable offers are available, the active units will generally need more than one cycle in order to detect them.

4.2 Market Scenario 2A

In an offer-oriented scenario, the start point of the marketplace activities is the passive unit, which tries to find a partner, by putting its own features as an offer in the central broker. Each active unit can read an offer (randomly selected by the central broker) and decides about its suitability as one of the looked-for components (first matching step). In the positive case, the active unit tries to reserve the offer (the offer might be already reserved for another active unit). When the enquiry expires, the active unit calls its reserved offers from the broker, and performs the second matching step to choose the best available offer and to make a contract with the corresponding owner (passive unit). All other offers will then be released, and a new cycle can be started.

4.3 Market Scenario 2B

Version "A" of scenario 2 has the disadvantage of reserving more than one offer for one active unit, waiting for the time-out of the enquiry and the end of the second matching step. This prevents other active units from making use of these offers in the same cycle. Version "B" of scenario 2 tries to avoid this disadvantage by performing the second matching step directly after the first matching step, when the offer is proved to be acceptable. This way, only one offer will be reserved for the active unit, i.e. the one with the best evaluation, while other acceptable offers will be released "online".

4.4 Market Scenario 3

This mixed scenario relies more on a central broker, in order to perform the matching steps. In this case the autonomous units only have to send their enquiries or offers to the broker, which will find the best offer for each enquiry. All offers will be matched against all requests (first matching step). Upon time-out the offers' list of each enquiry will be processed by the broker (second matching step). As soon as the best offer has been selected, it will be reserved for the specific active units and it will be deleted from the offers' list of other enquiries. The broker tells the active units about the best available offer for each of their enquiries. Contracts are then concluded directly between the active and passive units.

5 Simulation of the Market Scenarios

The aim of the simulation is to assess the performance of the suggested market scenarios in different settings of the application environment. For this purpose, a specific model of the market scenarios has been developed in Java, so that every unit has the form of a thread, in addition to a broker thread. The fairness between the autonomous units is guaranteed through the equal sleep time of the threads and the random selection of offers/enquiries by the central broker.

5.1 Settings of the Application Environment

To cover the variety of application environments, different settings of units' number and types have been simulated: Single I, Single II, Multi I and Multi II. In Single I application environments all passive units are of the same type but differ in their sub-types. Every active unit looks for one component. The looked-for components share the same type with the passive units. Looked-for components are of different sub-types. Single II is similar to Single I, with two differences: i. Every active unit looks for five components of the same type, ii. Looked-for components of one active unit have different sub-types. In Multi I application environments there are 5 types of passive units and of looked-for components. Passive units of the same type have different sub-types. Every active unit is looking for 5 components. Looked for components of one active unit are of different types. Looked-for components of the same type (in different active units) have different sub-types. Multi II is similar to Multi I with the only difference that the application environment combines 15 types of passive units and of looked-for components.

Table 2. Simulation settings

	# of Types	# of passive units	# of passive units per type	# of components	# of components per type (# of sub-types)	# of components per active unit	# of active units
Single I	1	15/ 30/ 60	15/30/60	30	30	1	30
Single II	1	15/ 30/ 60	15/30/60	30	30	5	6
Multi I	5	15/ 30/ 60	3 / 6 /12	30	6	5	6
Multi II	15	15/ 30/ 60	1 / 2 / 4	30	2	5	6

Through all tests the number of looked-for components is fixed to 30, while the number of passive units took one of three values: 15, 30 or 60. Table 2 summarizes all simulation settings.

For each pair (enquiry, offer), the computing load of the semantic matching is set to 50 ms, and for the MCDM process to 25 ms. Similar execution times have been measured on a prototype of SeMCDM. SeMCDM prototype is a Java application, which uses the Jena inference engine with SeMCDM matching rules. Passive units have been described with the help of 6 features, while enquires combined 5 features (3 features to be unconditionally fulfilled and 2 features to be preferably fulfilled). The features have been specified with different kinds of utility functions. The execution time of the matching steps are not to be confused with the preparation time (forward chaining) of the ontology models, which may last several seconds (4 - 5 s). The experiment has been performed on an AMD Athlon (tm) 64 Processor 3200+, with 1 GB RAM and Microsoft Windows XP operating system. Throughout all experiments, the inferred ontology models (in Ontology Web Language OWL [13]) have the size of 3183 RDF statements (Resource Description Framework [14]) for the passive units and 3133 for the active units.

However, the performance of the market scenarios is affected by the concurrent matching on several units, whereas the absolute execution times play no real role.

The expiration time of the enquiry has the value of 20 s for all distributed scenarios, with cycle time of 30 s. The third scenario has exceptional values, because of the high number of matching attempts: an expiration time of enquiry of 120 s with a cycle time of 200 s.

5.2 Evaluation Metrics of the Market Scenarios

The simulation delivers evaluations of the market scenarios according to the following evaluation metrics:

- **Success rate and time to first solution:** A "solution" is a possible configuration of the application system. A configuration consists of a set of contracts between autonomous units. A first solution is reached when at least one suitable offer for every looked-for component has been found. This leads to the definition of the "success rate" as "the ratio of found components to the total number of looked-for components". A success rate has the maximal value of 1, which means that all looked-for components have got passive units assigned. In the simulation settings with only 15 passive units available, the maximum value of the success rate is limited to 0.5 (there are always 30 looked-for components). In other settings the maximum value of 1 can be reached. The time to the first solution can therefore be evaluated as the number of the needed cycles to reach the first solution.
- **Number of matching attempts:** Scenarios differ in the number of matching attempts carried out to reach the first solution. In the results' diagrams the total numbers of matching attempts are depicted for every scenario. The total number of matching attempts is the sum of matching attempts in all cycles.
- **Quality of solution:** An optimal solution is that, where every looked-for component meets its corresponding optimal offer. The quality of solution is defined as the "distance" between the achieved solution and the optimal solution. To get a numeric impression of the quality of solution for each pair (enquiry, selected offer) the following formula has been used (subtypes are integer numbers), while the average value for all pairs represents the quality of found solution:

    Quality (enquiry, selected offer) =
    1 − (subtype of enquiry − subtype of offer) / total number of subtypes

5.3 Simulation Results of the Market Scenarios

For purposes of better comparability the result diagrams show only the settings of 30 and 60 passive units, where a maximal success rate of 1 is expected. The effect of environment on the results can be seen clearly be considering the extreme settings: Single I and Multi II.

5.3.1 Success Rate and Time to First Solution
Fig. 1 shows the success rates of all scenarios in relation to the time.

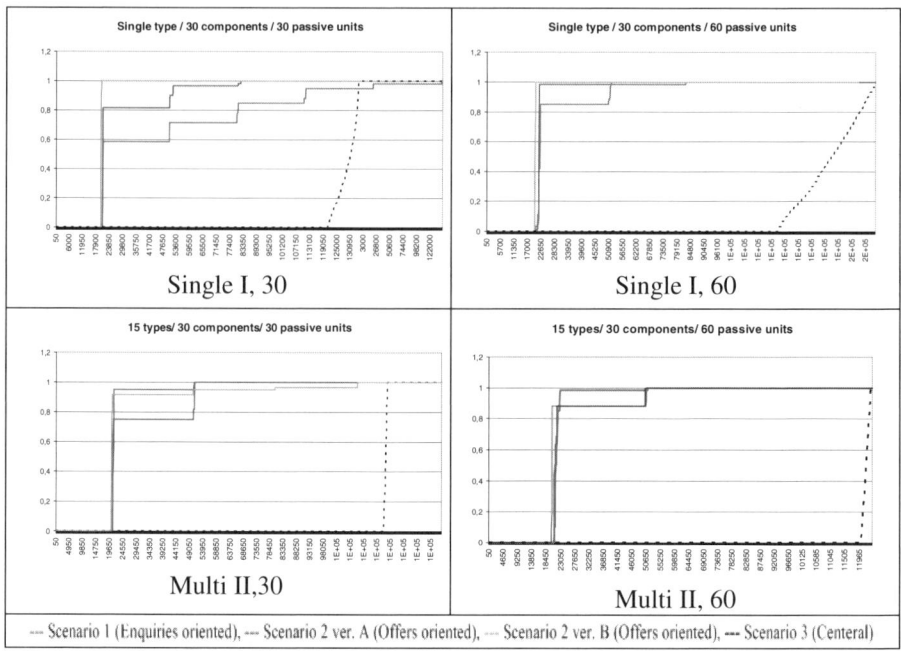

Fig. 1. Success rate and time to first solution

5.3.1.1 Single I, 30. According to scenario 1 more than one offer can be reserved for one enquiry and other enquiries have to wait for a following cycle to get an offer (30 passive units face exactly 30 looked-for components). Single I, 30 represents a worst-case for scenario 1 because all looked-for components and all passive units are of the same type.

The best scenario for Single I, 30 is scenario 2B, which reaches the first solution within the first cycle. In comparison to 2B, scenario 2A delivers a moderate performance (time to first solution of 3 cycles). This difference can be traced back to the fact that scenario 2B avoids the reservation of multiple offers for one enquiry.

According to scenario 3, contracts can be concluded only after achieving both matching steps for all possible pairs (offer, enquiry). This explains the late rise of the success rate values in comparison to other scenarios. The success rate line of scenario 3 is not linearly increasing. This is due to the decreasing number of available offers for each enquiry along with the number of already processed enquiries.

5.3.1.2 Single I, 60. Single I, 60 is a friendly environment in comparison to Single I, 30 because of the high number of available passive units. Therefore, all distributed scenarios show shorter times to the first solution. Only scenario 3 requires a longer time to find the first solution in its second matching step. This indicates that a high number of candidates can be a real problem for the centralized matching.

5.3.1.3 Multi II, 30. In contrast to its bad performance in single I, 30, scenario 1 reaches the first solution in only 2 cycles. Calling back the fact that Multi II, 30 represents a heterogeneous unfriendly environment, it is obvious that scenario 1 benefits from the distribution of the search processes (the first matching step) on a high number of passive units. The rarity of the looked-for components hides the disadvantage of scenario 1 (i.e. the offer reservation problem).

Scenarios 2A and 2B show a weakness in the heterogeneous environment (both distribute the difficult search process on 6 active units). Scenario 2A shares principally the same difficulties with scenario 2B, but it can reach the first solution in two cycles (scenario 2B reserves offers for both matching steps while scenario 2A reserves them only for the first matching step). The second matching step in scenario 3 shows a steeply ascending line (small number of alternatives).

5.3.1.4 Multi II, 60. In scenario 1, 60 passive autonomous units complete the first matching step in parallel. Due to the higher number of passive units, the success rate in the first cycle reaches a better value (near to 1) in comparison to its value in Multi II, 30, and two cycles are sufficient to reach the first solution. In spite of additional passive units, in comparison to Multi II, 30, two cycles are required anyway to reach the first solution by scenario 1.

Even scenarios 2A and 2B deliver better results, but only because of the higher number of available offers, where the reservation time plays only a limited role. The fact that more alternatives are subject to comparison in the second matching step can be seen from the less steeply ascending line of scenario 3.

5.3.2 Number of Matching Attempts

In the central scenario (scenario 3) all possible matching attempts are to be attended, and therefore this scenario is selected to serve as a reference for all other scenarios in all settings. In scenario 3 the central broker achieves (30 * 30 =) 900 matching attempts in settings Single I, 30 and Multi II, 30. In Single I, 60 and Multi II, 60 the number of matching attempts in the central broker reaches the value of (30 * 60 =) 1800. Fig. 2 shows the number of matching attempts of all scenarios as a percentage fraction of matching attempts in scenario 3.

5.3.2.1 Single I, 30. In relation to scenario 1, the passive units perform the first matching step 60 times (6,6%). In the first cycle 30 matching attempts are made by all 30 passive units in parallel. No additional attempts are required, nor possible, in the same cycle because all attempts return positive results (passive units and looked-for components are all of the same type in single I, 30). The other 30 matching attempts are then performed in several additional cycles (see Fig. 1 of the success rate).

The active units have to try the matching 108 time (12%) before reaching the first solution, when adopting scenario 2A. To read an offer from the broker without reservation (through the first matching step) means that the same offer can be a subject of matching in more than one active unit at the same time. This concurrence situation

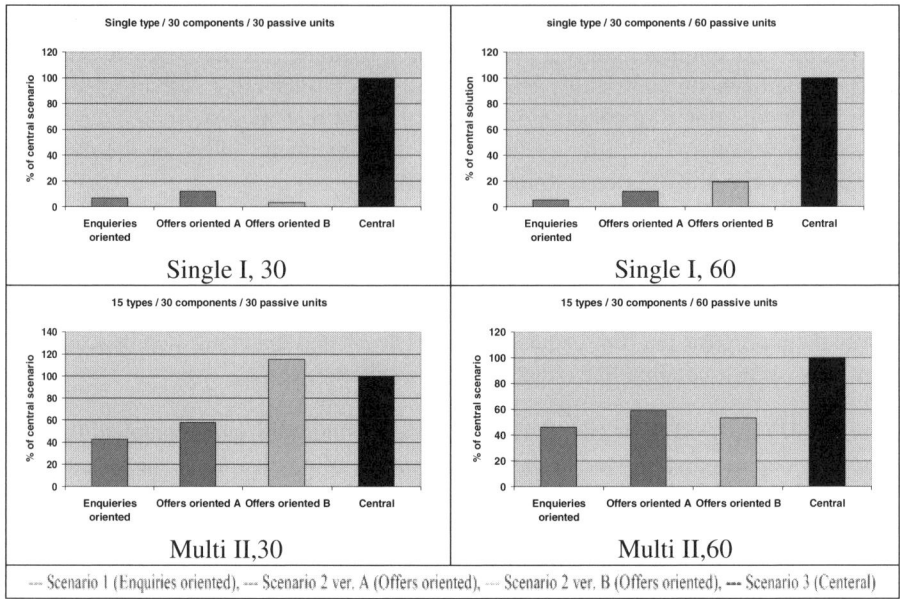

Fig. 2. Number of matching attempts

explains that in the first cycle 94,5 matching attempts have been carried out in scenario 2A (the number of matching attempts exceeds the number of available offers, although all offers are acceptable offers in this setting). Concurrence situations are discovered and solved in the same cycle according to scenario 2A, and in different cycles according to scenario 1. The amount of effort in each scenario is reflected in the achieved success rates shown in Fig. 1.

Scenario 2B is designed to avoid the drawback found in scenario 2A, i.e. the reservation of multiple (acceptable) offers within a cycle. So it is able to get by with 30 matching attempts (3,3%) within only one cycle.

5.3.2.2 Single I, 60. In scenario 1, more passive units (60) attempt to find suitable enquiries, and therefore 60 matching attempts are carried out in the first cycle. In total 93 attempts (5,2% of possible matching attempts) are required to reach the first solution in the third cycle. The number of carried out matching attempts in scenario 2A is directly related to the number of available passive units (a comparison between single I, 30 and single I, 60).

Scenario 2B finds the first solution in only one cycle, but at a price of 345 matching attempts (19,2% of possible matching attempts). In scenario 2A, the offer reservation makes additional matching attempts only in a following cycle possible. In scenario 2B, free offers are always available (in single I, 60 setting), because each active units reserves only one offer.

5.3.2.3 Multi II, 30. The rarity of the looked-for components is the main reason for higher numbers of matching attempts by all distributed scenarios. For scenario 1, 385 attempts (42,7%) have been achieved in two cycles (only 2 attempts in the second cycle), i.e. in order to find suitable offers for the last few enquiries, an enormous number of matching attempts has to be carried out. Keeping in mind that passive units try to find only one suitable enquiry and that there is actually a suitable offer for each looked-for component (according to the selected settings) one discovers that there is a drawback distributing the enquiries on the passive units. The distribution is performed by the broker in a random way. So the search is not as perfect as it could be, if the broker tried to choose enquiries with no available offers at first. An important indicator for this drawback can be found in the second cycle where the number of enquiries is much smaller, and the random selection is not any more a real problem. A similar problem can be expected also by other distributed scenarios, but it cannot be shown as clearly as in scenario 1, because other scenarios try making additional matching attempts.

A dramatic worsening can be observed especially in scenario 2B, which reaches the first solution after 1035 matching attempts (115% of possible matching attempts). This high number of matching attempts has to be explained in correlation with the success rate diagram (Fig. 1), which shows how scenario 2B needs multiple cycles to reach the first solution (because of the too long reservation time of rare offers).

5.3.2.4 Multi II, 60. Scenarios 1 and 2A show similar results to those achieved in the Multi II, 30 setting. This reappoints the relation between the number of available offers (passive units) and the number of required matching attempts in both scenarios. Scenario 2B indicates the relative ability to deal with heterogeneous environments, when the looked-for components are not as rare as in Multi II, 30.

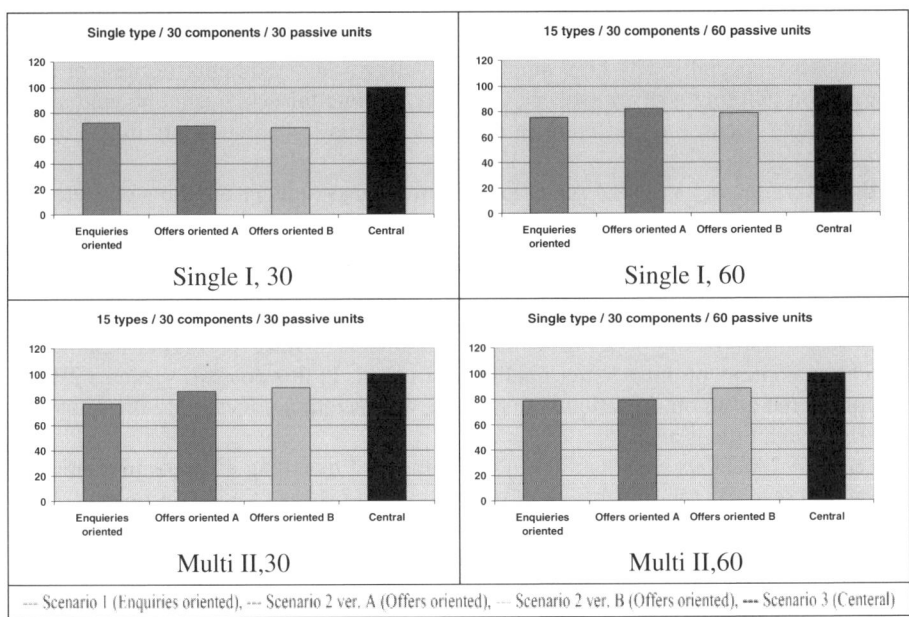

Fig. 3. Quality of solution

5.3.3 Quality of Solution

Fig. 3 shows the quality of solution found by the marketing scenarios. The central solution proves its excellent ability of discovering the optimal solution, independent of the simulation settings. This goes back to the fact, that the central scenario verifies actually all possible pairs (enquiry, offer). Therefore, whenever an optimal offer is available, it can be found and assigned to the enquiry.

All distributed scenarios show in general similar results, but there is almost always a correlation between the number of performed matching attempts and the achieved quality of solution (see Fig. 2). This applies especially for settings Single I,60 and Multi II,60, where the real decision making takes place between multiple alternatives (Settings Single I,30 and Multi II,30 don't give enough margin for the decision making process).

6 Recommendations

In heterogeneous environments (as expected in real applications) it is recommended to use an enquiry-oriented scenario because of its short time to first solution. For a balanced and parallel computing it is strongly recommended to use scenario 1 when a high number of passive units (although of restricted computing capabilities) are available (only small numbers of matching attempts are required in scenario 1).

In contrast to broadcasting mechanisms, a smart broker can enhance the performance of all distributed scenarios by selecting offers (or enquiries) with no suitable enquiries (or offers) at first. Such enhancement leads not only to shorter times to first solution, but also to smaller numbers of required matching attempts and smaller computing loads (especially on small passive units as in enquiry-oriented scenarios).

Adopting offer-oriented scenarios promises high performance in homogeneous environments (especially with high numbers of active units) and better fairness of offer distribution (without a smart broker), although absolute fairness cannot be guaranteed (for example because of different numbers of looked-for components in the active units).

However, enquiry-oriented scenarios require always smaller numbers of matching attempts in comparison to offer-oriented scenarios. Moreover, real application environments are expected to contain more passive units than active units, where enquiry-oriented scenarios deliver better performance.

Pushing towards a "one step matching" is not always a good idea. Scenario 2B faces real difficulties by looking for rare components. However, higher numbers of matching attempts promise better quality of solution. In this context, scenario 2B can be considered as an optimization scenario (the optimization affects only the subtypes) where enough time is available.

Scenario 2A shows high stability of the number of matching attempts in relation to the central scenario (pre-estimation of computing load is easy for the designer).

Scenario 3 is a typical central scenario, because it promises to deliver the optimal results (quality of solution) at the price of centralized heavy-weight computation. In addition to scalability problems with higher numbers of autonomous units, the centralized solution entails the danger of total system breakdown because of a failure in the central computing unit.

7 Conclusions and Future Work

The adoption of a marketplace-oriented behavior in organic computing architectures, like SeMCDM, is not a trivial process. Different market scenarios have been defined by allocating activities on available autonomous units. Reasonable market scenarios have been classified according to the types of exchanged messages. To prove the adequacy of these scenarios in different application environments, a prototype of market scenarios has been developed. Three evaluation metrics of the market scenarios have been defined: success rate and time to first solution, number of matching attempts and quality of solution. A centralized scenario serves as a comparison reference for the defined scenarios. The application environment has been specified by different characterization factors like: the number of available units, the diversity of unit types and additional timing restrictions (computational load). Simulation results proved the effect of the application environment on the performance of market scenarios. The discussion of the simulation results led to recommendations on the most suitable market scenario in different application environments.

The delay time of messages (offers and enquiries) is only considered indirectly in the form of thread sleep time. To study the effect of the communication platform in future work, it is planned to simulate it as a separate variable. Additionally, autonomous units can dynamically change the market scenario in run time.

References

[1] Müller-Schloer, C.: Organic Computing - On the feasibility of controlled emergence. In: International Conference on Hardware/Software Codesign and System Synthesis 2004, CODES + ISSS 2004, September 8-10, pp. 2–5 (2004)
[2] Hoffmann, P., Leboch, S., Daimler Chrysler, A.G.: Evolutionäre Elektronikarchitektur für Kraftfahrzeuge. In: Information Technology, vol. 47, p. 4. Oldenbourg Verlag (2005)
[3] Mahmoudi, G., Müller-Schloer, C.: Towards Ontology-Based Embedded Services. In: Yang, L.T., Jin, H., Ma, J., Ungerer, T. (eds.) ATC 2006. LNCS, vol. 4158, pp. 100–112. Springer, Heidelberg (2006)
[4] Berners-Lee, T., Hendler, J., Lassila, O.: The Semantic Web: A new form of Web content that is meaningful to computers will unleash a revolution of new possibilities. Scientific American (May 2001)
[5] Eymann, T., et al.: Self-organizing Resource Allocation for Autonomic Networks. In: DEXA Workshops, pp. 656–660. IEEE computer society, Los Alamitos (2003)
[6] Eymann, T., et al.: The Catallaxy as a new paradigm for the design of information systems. In: Proceedings of The World Computer Congress 2000 of the International Federation for Information Processing (2000)
[7] Buyya, R., Abramson, D., Giddy, J.: A Case for Economy Grid Architecture for Service Oriented Grid Computing. In: Proceedings of the 10th Heterogeneous Computing Workshop HCW (2001)
[8] Kephart, J.: Software agents and the information economy – again and emergent phenomena. In: A presentation on the workshop of Agent Based Modeling and Simulation, Institute for Mathematics and its Applications, University of Minnesota (2003), http://www.ima.umn.edu/talks/workshops/11-3-6.2003/

[9] Kephart, J., Chess, D.: The vision of autonomic computing. In: Computer Magazine, pp. 41–50. IEEE, Los Alamitos (2003)
[10] Eiselt, H.A., Sandblom, C.-L.: Decision Analysis, Location Models, and Scheduling Problems. Springer, Heidelberg (2004); with contributions by: Blazewicz, J., Church, R. L., Drexl, A., Finke, G., ReVelle, C.S.
[11] Hewlett-Packard Development Company, L.P., Jena Semantic Web Toolkit (2008), http://www.hpl.hp.com/semweb/tools.htm#jena
[12] DySCAS, Dynamically Self-Configuring Automotive systems: Existing technologies. specific targeted research project (2007), http://www.dyscas.org/doc/DySCAS_D1.1A.pdf
[13] Deborah, L.: McGuinness and Frank van Harmelen. W3C recommendation, OWL Web Ontology Language Overview (February 2004), http://www.w3.org/TR/owl-features/
[14] World Wide Web, Resource Description Framework (RDF), W3C 2004 (2004), http://www.w3.org/RDF/

Self-organized Parallel Cooperation for Solving Optimization Problems

Sanaz Mostaghim and Hartmut Schmeck

Institute AIFB
Karlsruhe Institute of Technology
76128 Karlsruhe, Germany
{sanaz.mostaghim,hartmut.schmeck}@kit.edu

Abstract. This paper is about using a set of self-organized computing resources to perform multi-objective optimization. In the proposed approach, the computing resources are presented as a unified resource to the user where in traditional parallel optimization paradigms the user has to assign tasks to the resources, collect the best available solutions and deal with failing resources. In this approach called self-organized parallel cooperation model, the user has to specify the preferences and only give the objective functions to the system. The self-organized computing resources deliver the obtained solutions after a certain time to the user. In such a system, fast resources must continue the optimization as long as the overall computing time is not over. However as the solutions of a multi-objective problem depend on each other (via the domination relation) adding a waiting time to the fast processors would affect the quality of the solutions. This has been studied on a scenario of 100 heterogeneous computing resources in the presence of failures in the system.

1 Introduction

Due to the steady progress in technology and the fact that the number of computing resources is increasing, today parallel computing on computer grids or multi-core systems can significantly reduce the computation time for highly complex modeling, simulation, and optimization problems. In this paper, we study multi-objective optimization algorithms on a set of heterogeneous computing resources. The solution of multi-objective optimization problems is usually a set of solutions represented as an optimal front i.e., none of these solutions can be improved in one objective without getting worse with respect to some other objective.

It is logical to solve optimization problems with very expensive function evaluations on a parallel environment. For solving such problems, population-based methods such as Evolutionary Algorithms (EA) have shown to be good candidates as they are inherently parallel by design [11]. Some difficulties arise, though, when we solve multi-objective problems [16,4,9,17,2,6].

Solving such problems using a set of computing resources is achieved by dividing the task (finding the set of non-dominated solutions) between the computers. This idea has already been studied e.g., in [4,9]. The task partitioning can be successfully done, when there is a priori knowledge about the number of resources and their properties. If one of the resources fails, its related part has to be re-assigned. The other issue is the assumption of communication between the processors like in [4].

As in the other papers, we partition the optimization task between the available processors meaning every computing resource is responsible for generating one part of the optimal front so that in a collective way all of them obtain a good approximation of the true Pareto-optimal solutions. Here we design the algorithm to be independent of the number of resources. The resources act as computing agents, which look for a partition to optimize and try to avoid overlaps. If one of them fails working, other resources which are done with their own tasks, take care of the missing partition.

Besides this, we allow the cooperative aspect in the heterogeneous system such that the computing resources indirectly exchange the best found solutions. In this way, the computing resources are represented as a unified resource to the user, who gives the objectives to the system and receives the optimal solutions in the end whereas in the traditional parallel systems, the user has to assign the tasks and permanently monitors the system.

Another aspect here is the fact that in a heterogeneous system we must make use of all of the resources from very slow to very fast ones. In a non-parallel case all of the population members are available in each evaluation step. However in our new approach, the solutions of the fast resources build a disconnected front and continue the optimization where the slow resources must still finish their tasks. Indeed, this issue affects the results. If the fast processors wait for the slow ones, the results are changed as the solutions of a multi-objective problem depend on each other by the domination relation. This aspect is being studied on a test scenario of 100 heterogeneous resources where we add some waiting time to the fast processors and study the quality of the obtained solutions. Furthermore, we add some failures to the system and observe the quality of solutions in such unreliable environments.

This paper is structured as follows. The next section is assigned to the parallelization paradigms, basics in multi-objective optimization, and the model of self-contained parallel cooperation in optimization. In Section 3, we explain the new approach called self-organized parallel cooperation and study different aspects in parallelization of multi-objective algorithms. Section 4 is dedicated to experiments and the last section concludes the paper.

2 Parallel Computing

Distributed and parallel computing are about using several computing resources in parallel in order to solve time-intensive problems in a low computation time. Ideally, these computing resources are represented as one unified resource to the user who defines the task to be run in parallel [1]. A typical task can be a simulation with different input parameters or an optimization algorithm which can be run in parallel. In such a computing environment we deal with a set of heterogeneous resources. There are very fast and very slow computing resources, some computing resources may fail working, or get overloaded. Also, we assume that there is a limitation on the communication capability between the resources.

In optimization, different parallel models have been proposed in the literature [16]. They follow three major hierarchical models such as: (1) Self-contained parallel cooperation (2) Problem independent intra-algorithm parallelization and (3) Problem dependent intra-algorithm parallelization. The last two models do not alter the behavior of the algorithms and therefore are generally used to speedup the search.

The group of Self-Contained Parallel Cooperation algorithms also known as the *Island model* is used for parallel systems with very limited communication. In the island model, every processor runs an independent optimization using a separate (sub)population. We study this family of the parallel models throughout this paper.

2.1 Multi-objective Optimization

A multi-objective optimization problem is of the form

$$\text{minimize} \quad \boldsymbol{f} = (f_1(\boldsymbol{x}), f_2(\boldsymbol{x}), \cdots, f_m(\boldsymbol{x})) \quad (1)$$

subject to $\boldsymbol{x} \in S$, involving $m (\geq 2)$ conflicting objective functions $f_i : \Re^n \rightarrow \Re$ that we want to optimize simultaneously. The parameters $\boldsymbol{x} = (x_1, x_2, \cdots, x_n)^T$ belong to the feasible region $S \subset \Re^n$.

We denote the image of the feasible region by $Z \subset \Re^m$ and call it a feasible objective region. The elements of Z are called objective vectors and they consist of objective (function) values $\boldsymbol{f}(\boldsymbol{x}) = (f_1(\boldsymbol{x}), f_2(\boldsymbol{x}), \cdots, f_m(\boldsymbol{x}))$. A parameter vector $\boldsymbol{x}_1 \in S$ is said to *dominate* a parameter vector $\boldsymbol{x}_2 \in S$, iff (a) $\boldsymbol{x}_1$ is not worse than $\boldsymbol{x}_2$ in all objectives and (b) $\boldsymbol{x}_1$ is strictly better than $\boldsymbol{x}_2$ in at least one objective.

$\boldsymbol{x}_1 \in S$ is called *Pareto-optimal* if there does not exist another $\boldsymbol{x}_2 \in S$ that dominates it. Finally, an objective vector is called Pareto-optimal if the corresponding decision vector is Pareto-optimal. The main goal of multi-objective optimization algorithms is to approximate the set of Pareto-optimal solutions by a set of well-distributed solutions.

The importance of distributed computing is even greater for multi-objective than for single objective optimization. In case of having many objective functions, the number of solutions needed to represent the multi-dimensional Pareto-front is large and therefore we require a large population size to perform a good exploration in the parameter space.

2.2 Self-contained Parallel Cooperation

The model of self-contained parallel cooperation, also known as the island model, is quite adequate for solving multi-objective problems in parallel [16]. This model is used, if there is a limitation in the communication between the processors. Here, we can parallelize the EA so that every processor runs an independent optimization with the goal of covering only one part of the Pareto-front. The optimized regions are collected by a master resource and build the approximated Pareto-front. Figure 1 shows an example of an ideal partitioning of the Pareto-front into several partitions and assigning different parts as tasks to k processors. Every resource contains an EA and has to optimize the solutions in the allocated region. A problem in this approach is, though, that it is not clear initially how to achieve a well-balanced distribution of the workload, since the solutions are not necessarily spread evenly over the Pareto-front.

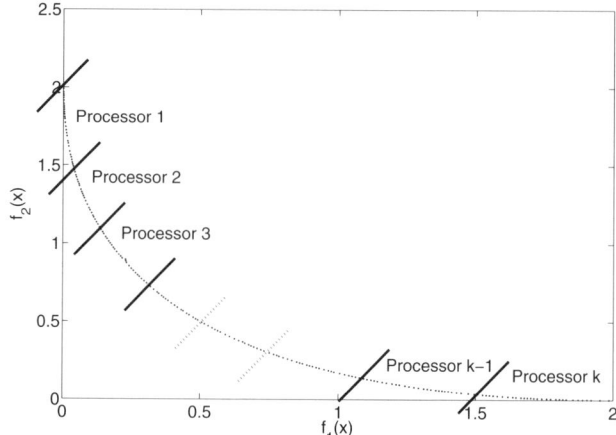

Fig. 1. An example of partitioning the objective space into sub-regions. The sub-regions are assigned to the k available resources.

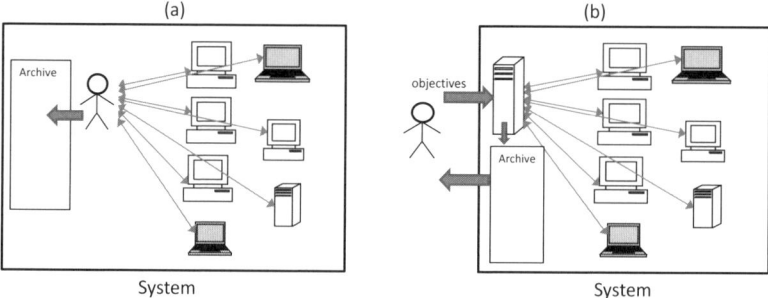

Fig. 2. (a) Traditional self-contained parallel cooperation model of optimization. The user is integrated into the system. (b) The self-organized parallel cooperation model, where the computing resources are represented as an unified resources to the user.

This kind of optimization has been studied as a category of Self-Contained Parallel Cooperation [4,9], where the user is aware of the exact number of available processors and divides the population of solutions into a fixed number of subpopulations. In such an approach, the user has to define the tasks of each processor, gather the obtained solutions from the resources, and build the global archive in which the non-dominated solutions are stored. Figure 2 (a) illustrates the system which optimizes the objective functions. The user is involved in the optimization process; in case that a processor fails working, the user manually reassigns the tasks.

3 Self-organized Parallel Cooperation

Based on the idea of self-contained parallel cooperation, we design a new model containing a set of self-organized resources. This so called self-organized parallel cooperation is intended to change the system of computing resources into a unified resource to the user. Figure 2 (b) shows the main concept. The system contains the cooperating computing resources which are represented as a unified resources to the user. In contrast to the traditional parallel models, the user is not involved in the assignment of tasks to processors and is not aware of the number of resources and their corresponding properties such as speed. In such a system, the user defines the tasks (the objectives) and obtains the optimal solutions after a certain time.

Generally, designing an algorithm for parallel implementation requires the following steps [7]: (1) Task partitioning which allocates independent tasks to multiple recourses (2) Task scheduling and assignment (3) Task synchronization which is about exchanging the information from the processors in order to ensure correct progress. These three aspects are considered in the self-organized model as follows:

- *Task partitioning*: The computing resources must find the most proper partition of the objective space to optimize. In traditional methods [4,9], the space has been divided into a fixed number of sub-regions for a fixed number of resources. The resources consider their own sub-region as the feasible region and the solutions that are not in this region are considered to be infeasible. In this way, they force their populations to reside in the corresponding sub-region. In the self-organized parallel cooperation, this is completely different: The resources always look for the least populated part of the approximated front and start optimization in throes areas (this part will be studied in the next section).
- *Task scheduling*: All of the resources from very fast to the slow ones have to collaborate to perform the optimization task. Also, in case of failures in one or more computing resources, the other resources take care of the failing subtasks.
- *Task synchronization*: There must be an indirect way of communication between the resources to ensure correct progress. The computing resources have to collect their results, remove the overlaps, and report the currently best solutions to the user.

In the following, we consider K heterogeneous computing resources which perform a multi-objective optimization algorithm for a specific range of parameters and a set of given objective functions. The resources may contain different algorithms and deliver a set of non-dominated solutions after a certain time $T_i, \forall i = 1, 2, \cdots, K$. We assume that the computing resources can communicate with a main master node in which we keep a global repository (called Archive) for storing the non-dominated solutions.

3.1 Task Partitioning

Depending on the optimization goals and the user preferences, every processor selects a sub-region of the objective or parameter space for optimization. For instance, the user preferences could be (a) a set of well-distributed solutions in the objective space or (b) a set of solutions with very good convergence to one predefined point or an area in the objective space or (c) both.

In the self-organized parallel cooperation model, the resources find the sub-regions based on the so far obtained solutions. For this purpose, as soon as a processor updates the global archive, it must evaluate the so far obtained non-dominated solutions in the archive. The evaluation of the archive members can be done by using a metric to observe the quality of the so far obtained solutions with respect to the user preferences. The following example clarifies this idea.

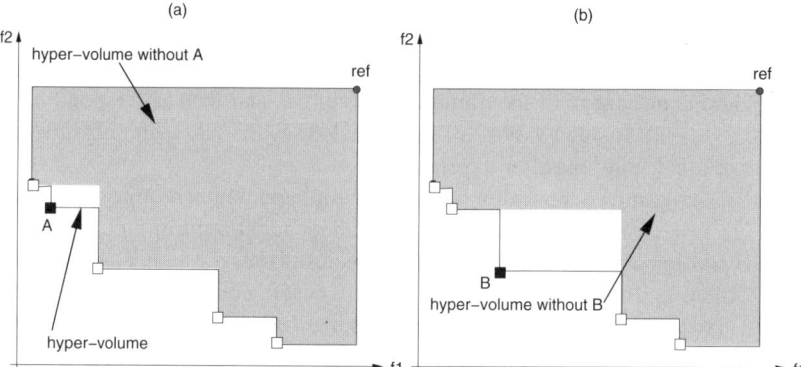

Fig. 3. Marginal Hypervolume Measure. The area between the non-dominated solutions and a predefined point called ref is shown by the solid line. The area without A in (a) is smaller than the area without B in (b) indicating the importance of B.

Example. Consider that a good distribution of solutions along the non-dominated front is the goal of the user. The resources must find the large gaps in the front and concentrate on finding some optimal solutions in those regions. For this purpose one proper metric is the marginal hypervolume measure. The hypervolume is the area dominated by all solutions stored in the archive [18]. The marginal hypervolume of a solution is the area dominated by the solution that is not dominated by any other solution. Figure 3 illustrates this. Solution A has a smaller contribution to the whole hypervolume value than solution B. Therefore, solution B would be selected first. So the processor looking for a good sub-space can select the area around B to explore more in the next optimization run. B is called to be a reference point. In general as a reference point, the solution from the archive is selected which has not been selected before and which has the largest marginal hypervolume. In order to avoid that several computing resources select the same point, only if all archive solutions have been used as reference points, they are allowed to be re-used.

After selecting a proper reference point, the computing resource starts the optimization in that direction. The directed optimization can be performed in several ways such as by **reference based method** or **reference direction approach** in the context of non-evolutionary approaches [12] or by using the preference based multi-objective evolutionary approaches such as in [3]. We propose to use the multi-objective particle swarm optimization [14,5,15]. By giving the reference point as a global guide, the particles are drawn toward the reference point and hence the optimization concentrates around the desired area.

3.2 Task Scheduling

As soon as a resource finds the reference point, it starts the optimization. The scheduling is therefore straight forward. Algorithm 1 shows the routine performed in each of the resources. In the case that the entire system can be used for a certain time $T_{total}(\geq T_i)$, $(i = 1, 2, \cdots, K)$ fast resources might be able to perform several optimization tasks

Algorithm 1. Task of resource i

repeat
    Find a task partition
    Perform the optimization
    Send update to main archive
until $(T_i \leq T_{total})$

depending on their computation power. In this algorithm, whenever a processor is done with the optimization, the obtained results are integrated into the (global) archive in which only non-dominated solutions are kept.

3.3 Task Synchronization

The indirect communication between the resources is indeed achieved via the archive. Every computing resource must select a task to optimize and continue the optimization as long as the total computation time is not over.

3.4 Comments

Note that the above approach reduces the waiting time of the traditional self-contained parallel cooperation model in which the fast resources do not wait for the slow ones. Indeed, saving computation time is a desirable fact, but note that the solutions of a multi-objective problem depend on each other. This means that if the fast processors wait for the slow ones, the quality of solutions might get better. This will be studied in the experiments (Section 4). In this approach, any desirable interaction between a decision maker and the system can be easily implemented. Also the communication overhead between the resources is reduced to the communication between the resources and a master node managing the archive which could be viewed as some type of blackboard system. Except for the master node, failures are automatically compensated, because other processors will draw their attention to a region that has not been worked on. Obviously, though, a failure of the master node would require a restart of the optimization process.

4 Experiments

The major goal of the experiments is to evaluate the quality of the solutions when running the system for a certain time and adding failures to the resources. The system is also analyzed by adding waiting time to the fast resources to wait for a certain percentage of the slow ones. The experiments are performed on a simulation environment containing 100 resources with 5 different computation speeds. The simulation is based on the real scenario in a typical Grid. Figure 4 illustrates 5 different kinds of available resources. There are 3, 3, 20, 43, and 31 number of type 1 (very fast), type 2, type 3, type 4, and type 5 (very slow) resources, respectively.

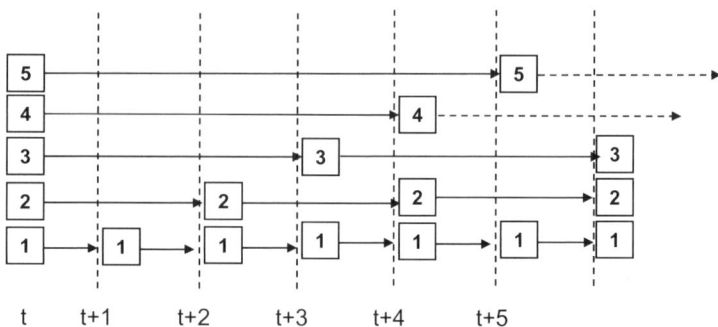

Fig. 4. Five different resources are illustrated in terms of speed. The resource type 1 is five times faster than the resource type 5. Resource types are shown in the Boxes.

The test function selected from [10,8] contains 10 parameters and 2 objectives:

$$f_1(x) = 1 - exp(-\sum_{i=1}^{n}(x_i - \frac{1}{\sqrt{n}})^2)$$

$$f_2(x) = 1 - exp(-\sum_{i=1}^{n}(x_i + \frac{1}{\sqrt{n}})^2)$$

where $x_i \in [-4, 4]$ and $n = 10$. The quality of the solutions is computed by the hypervolume metric [18] averaged over 20 runs.

The first experiments are intended to analyze the behavior of the system when adding waiting time to the processors. Therefore, the following parameter setting is proposed. Every resource contains a multi-objective particle swarm optimization from [14] with one particle running for one generation. The total time T_{total} is set to be 120. Meaning the fast resources are able to evaluate 120 particles. The given user goals besides the objective functions are to achieve a good convergence and spread of solutions. For this, we employ the idea of using marginal hypervolume presented in the example in Section 3.1.

The main archive stored in the master node is set to be empty at the beginning (first run). The selected parameter settings indicate that the first runs of the 100 resources include only a random sampling of the search space until the fast processors finish the evaluations and update the archive. As soon as the archive is updated, the preference of the user can be considered.

Figure 5 shows the quality of the archive members over time. Different plots illustrate the quality if the done resources which wait for j other resources to finish and update the archive ($j = 0, 10, 20, 30, 40, 50$).

We observe that if the resources do not wait the results are worse than if they wait for at least 10 to 20 percent of the resources. This is an expectable result as in multi-objective optimization the results depend on each other through the dominance relation. If the resources wait for (in this case) up to 20 percent, they achieve a better quality than if they do not wait. In fact, in every step of optimization it is better to have enough

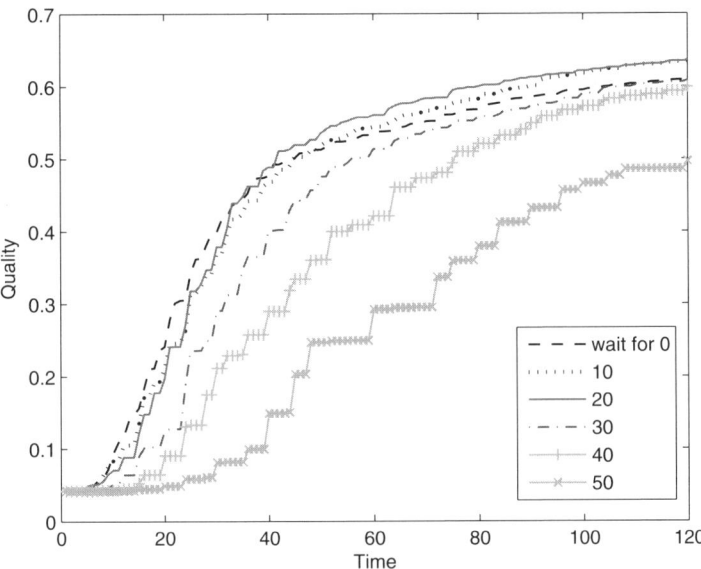

Fig. 5. The quality of the obtained solutions over time. The plots show the quality if the computing resources wait for at least 0, 10, 20, 30, 40 and 50 other computing resources to continue the optimization. A long waiting time indicates the worst quality, whereas waiting time for less than 20 percent is shown to increase the quality.

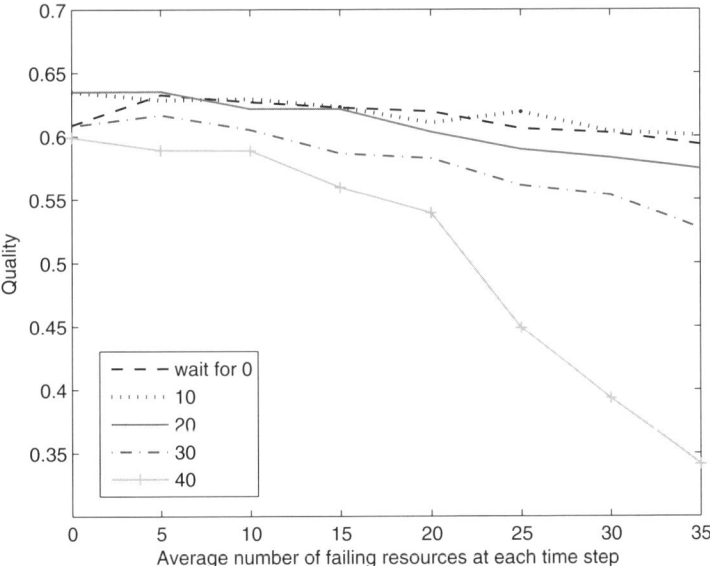

Fig. 6. The quality after the total time of 120 for different failure rates. The different plots indicate the waiting time for the resources.

evaluations to find more dominated and non-dominated solutions. Hence the waiting time has the advantage of having more solutions. This leads to a better direction in the optimization than not waiting. However, waiting for a large number of other resources means that the fast processor stay for a long time in idle mode which is on the other hand not desirable when having a fixed time for the entire optimization process (like in the Grid).

The next experiments are dedicated to failures in the system. Here we also analyze the waiting time. The failures are simulated by randomly removing some number of resources from the system. Figure 6 shows the quality of the archive members for different failure rates. The failure rates change from 0 to 35 percent. The result of having zero failure rate is the same as the results in Figure 5. Here we observe if we increase the failure rate, the best results are obtained by zero waiting time. This indicates that in unreliable systems, the fast resources have to make use of the available computing time and do not wait for the slow resources, where in a reliable environment waiting for up to 20 percent of the slower resources leads to a better quality of the results.

5 Conclusions

In this paper, we propose a new parallel paradigm, called self-organized parallel cooperation, for solving multi-objective optimization problems using a set of heterogeneous computing resources. Apart from gaining computation time through the parallelization, the quality of the solutions can be improved by the new approach. The computing resources (computing agents) run optimization algorithms to solve different parts of the approximated front in the way that they observe the so far obtained quality of solutions over time and select a sub space to optimize.

This approach has been studied on a scenario containing 100 computing resources with 5 different speeds. The scenario is depicted from a real grid environment with different failure percentage of computing resources. Furthermore, we analyze the quality of solutions, when keeping the fast processors to wait for the slow ones for a certain time. The experiments illustrate that when dealing with reliable environments, i.e., here no failure rates, the best solutions are obtained when the fast processors wait for the slow ones. However in unreliable environments, where some resources randomly fail during the run time, waiting does not result in the best quality.

In future, we will study interactive optimization methods in which the user changes the preferences during the optimization. Also, we will investigate different failure models as studied in this paper and study several other aspects in unreliable environments.

References

1. Abramson, D., Lewis, A., Peachy, T.: Nimrod/o: A tool for automatic design optimization. In: The 4th International Conference on Algorithms and Architectures for Parallel Processing (ICA3PP 2000) (2000)
2. Alba, E., Tomassini, M.: Parallelism and evolutionary algorithms. IEEE Transactions on Evolutionary Computation 6(5), 443–461 (2002)
3. Branke, J., Deb, K., Miettinen, K., Slowinski, R.: Multiobjective Optimization Interactive and Evolutionary Approaches. Springer, Heidelberg (2008)

4. Branke, J., Schmeck, H., Deb, K., Reddy, M.: Parallelizing Multi-Objective Evolutionary Algorithms: Cone Separation. In: IEEE Congress on Evolutionary Computation, pp. 1952–1957 (2004)
5. Bui, L.T., Abbass, H.A., Essam, D.: Local models - an approach to distributed multiobjective optimization. Journal of Computational Optimization and Applications (2007)
6. Cantu-Paz, E.: Efficient and Accurate Parallel Genetic Algorithms. Kluwer, Dordrecht (2000)
7. Censor, Y., Zenios, S.A.: Parallel Optimization: Theory, Algorithms, and Applications. Oxford University Press, Oxford (1997)
8. Coello Coello, C.A., Van Veldhuizen, D.A., Lamont, G.B.: Evolutionary Algorithms for Solving Multi-Objective Problems. Kluwer Academic Publishers, Dordrecht (2002)
9. Deb, K., Zope, P., Jain, S.: Distributed computing of pareto-optimal solutions with evolutionary algorithms. In: Fonseca, C.M., Fleming, P.J., Zitzler, E., Deb, K., Thiele, L. (eds.) EMO 2003. LNCS, vol. 2632, pp. 534–549. Springer, Heidelberg (2003)
10. Fonseca, C.M., Fleming, P.J.: On the Performance Assessment and Comparison of Stochastic Multiobjective Optimizers. In: Ebeling, W., Rechenberg, I., Voigt, H.-M., Schwefel, H.-P. (eds.) PPSN 1996. LNCS, vol. 1141, pp. 584–593. Springer, Heidelberg (1996)
11. Goldberg, D.E.: Genetic Algorithms in Search, Optimization and Machine Learning. Addison-Wesley Publishing Company, Inc, Reading (1989)
12. Miettinen, K.M.: Nonlinear Multiobjective Optimization. Kluwer Academic Publishers, Dordrecht (1999)
13. Mostaghim, S., Branke, J., Schmeck, H.: Multi-objective particle swarm optimization on computer grids. In: The Genetic and Evolutionary Computation Conference, vol. 1, pp. 869–875 (2007)
14. Mostaghim, S., Teich, J.: Strategies for finding good local guides in multi-objective particle swarm optimization. In: IEEE Swarm Intelligence Symposium, pp. 26–33 (2003)
15. Reyes-Sierra, M., Coello Coello, C.A.: Multi-objective particle swarm optimizers: A survey of the state-of-the-art. International Journal of Computational Intelligence Research 2(3), 287–308 (2006)
16. Talbi, E.-G., Mostaghim, S., Okabe, T., Ichibushi, H., Rudolph, G., Coello Coello, C.: Parallel Approaches for Multiobjective Optimization, pp. 349–372. Springer, Heidelberg (2008)
17. Van Veldhuizen, D.A., Zydallis, J.B., Lamont, G.B.: Considerations in engineering parallel multiobjective evolutionary algorithms. IEEE Transactions on Evolutionary Computation 7(2), 144–173 (2003)
18. Zitzler, E.: Evolutionary Algorithms for Multiobjective Optimization: Methods and Applications. Shaker (1999)

Improving Memory Subsystem Performance Using ViVA: Virtual Vector Architecture

Joseph Gebis[1,2], Leonid Oliker[1,2], John Shalf[1], Samuel Williams[1,2], and Katherine Yelick[1,2]

[1] CRD/NERSC, Lawrence Berkeley National Laboratory Berkeley, CA 94720
[2] CS Division, University of California at Berkeley, Berkeley, CA 94720
{JGebis,LOliker,JShalf,SWWilliams,KAYelick}@lbl.gov

Abstract. The disparity between microprocessor clock frequencies and memory latency is a primary reason why many demanding applications run well below peak achievable performance. Software controlled scratchpad memories, such as the Cell local store, attempt to ameliorate this discrepancy by enabling precise control over memory movement; however, scratchpad technology confronts the programmer and compiler with an unfamiliar and difficult programming model. In this work, we present the Virtual Vector Architecture (ViVA), which combines the memory semantics of vector computers with a software-controlled scratchpad memory in order to provide a more effective and practical approach to latency hiding. ViVA requires minimal changes to the core design and could thus be easily integrated with conventional processor cores. To validate our approach, we implemented ViVA on the Mambo cycle-accurate full system simulator, which was carefully calibrated to match the performance on our underlying PowerPC Apple G5 architecture. Results show that ViVA is able to deliver significant performance benefits over scalar techniques for a variety of memory access patterns as well as two important memory-bound compact kernels, corner turn and sparse matrix-vector multiplication — achieving 2x–13x improvement compared the scalar version. Overall, our preliminary ViVA exploration points to a promising approach for improving application performance on leading microprocessors with minimal design and complexity costs, in a power efficient manner.

1 Introduction

As we enter the era of billion transistor chips, computer architects face significant challenges in effectively harnessing the large amount of computational potential available in modern CMOS technology. Although there has been enormous growth in microprocessor clock frequencies over the past decade, memory latency and latency hiding techniques have not improved commensurately. The increasing gap between processor and memory speeds is a well-known problem in computer architecture, with peak processor performance improving at a rate of 55% per year, while DRAM latencies and bandwidths improve at only 6% and 30% respectively [13]. To mask memory latencies, current high-end computers now demand up to 25 times the number of overlapped operations required of supercomputers 30 years ago. This "memory wall" is a primary reason why high-end applications cannot saturate the system's available memory bandwidth, resulting in delivered performance that is far below peak capability of the system.

Numerous techniques have been devised to hide memory latency, including out-of-order superscalar instruction processing, speculative execution, hardware multithreading, and stream prefetching engines; nevertheless, these approaches significantly increase core complexity and power requirements [12,9] (the "power wall") while offering only modest performance benefits. This is particularly true of irregularly-structured and data-intensive codes, which exhibit poor temporal locality and receive little benefit from the automatically managed caches of conventional microarchitectures. Furthermore, a significant fraction of scientific codes are characterized by predictable data parallelism that could be exploited at compile time with properly structured program semantics; superscalar processors can often exploit this parallelism, but their generality leads to high costs in chip area and power, which in turn limit the degree of parallelism. This benefit is as important for multicore chips as it is for chips in the area of exponential clock frequency scaling.

Two effective approaches to hiding memory latency are vector architectures [5] and software controlled memories [8]. These techniques are able to exploit regularity in data access patterns far more effectively than existing prefetching methods using minimal hardware complexity. However, vector core designs are costly due to the limited market and limited applicability, while software controlled memories require radical restructuring of code and the programming model, and are currently incompatible with conventional cache hierarchies.

In this work we extend the Virtual Vector Architecture (ViVA[1]), which combines these two concepts to achieve a more effective and practical approach to latency hiding. ViVA offers the hardware simplicity of software controlled memory hardware implementations, with familiar vector semantics that are amenable to existing vectorizing compiler technology. Additionally, our approach can coexist with conventional cache hierarchies and requires minimal changes to the processor core, allowing it to be easily integrated with modern microprocessor designs, in a power-efficient fashion.

Overall results, measured by a series of microbenchmarks as well as two compact numerical kernels, show that ViVA offers superior performance compared to a microprocessor using conventional hardware and software prefetch strategies. ViVA thus offers a promising, cost-effective approach for improving latency tolerance of future scalar processor chip designs, while employing a familiar programming paradigm that is amenable to existing compiler technology.

2 ViVA Architecture and Implementation

In this section we present the ViVA programming model and design philosophy. As shown in Figure 1, ViVA adds a software-controlled memory buffer to traditional microprocessors. The new buffer logically sits between the L2 cache and the microprocessor core, in parallel with the L1 cache. Block transfer operations move data between DRAM and the ViVA buffer, and scalar operations move individual elements between the ViVA buffer and existing scalar registers in the microprocessor core. Extensive details of the ViVA infrastructure are provided in a recent PhD thesis [6].

---

[1] The ViVA acronym was developed with IBM during the BluePlanet collaboration [4].

Programming Model. The block transfers, between DRAM and the ViVA buffer, are performed with new instructions that have vector memory semantics: unit-stride, strided, and indexed (gather/ scatter) are all supported. In order to fully take advantage of the benefits of ViVA, and maximize the amount of concurrency available to the memory system, most programs should use ViVA in a double-buffered approach whenever possible. A thorough exploration of techniques is given in [6].

The basic ViVA programming model is conceptually simple:

```
do_vector_loads;
for(all_vector_elements) {
   transfer_element_to_scalar_reg;
   operate_on_element;
   transfer_element_to_buffer;
}
do_vector_stores;
```

A major advantage of the ViVA approach is that it can leverage vector compiler technology with only minor modifications, since the new ViVA instructions have vector memory semantics. The compiler can generate regular vector code, with one straightforward exception: the arithmetic vector operations have to be replaced with a scalar loop that iterates over a vector's worth of elements. Since vector compilers are a mature, well-understood technology, real applications could benefit from ViVA immediately.

VIVA Buffer Hardware Details. Our approach allows the ViVA buffer to act as a set of vector registers, but without the associated datapaths that accompany registers in full vector computers. This reflects one of the main goals of ViVA: efficient memory transfer at low cost. Since there are no datapaths associated with the ViVA buffer, no arithmetic operations can be directly performed on elements stored within the buffer. In order to perform arithmetic operations, elements must first be transferred to existing scalar (integer or floating-point) registers.

As with most vector register files, the ViVA register length is not fixed in the ISA. Instead, control registers are used for hardware to describe the lengths of the registers to software. This allows a single binary executable to run on different hardware implementations. Thus, a low-cost ViVA design may have shorter hardware register lengths, while a higher-performance version may have longer registers. In our experiments, we study hardware registers lengths that vary from sixteen 64-bit words through 256 words, with most experiments using 64 words (typical of many traditional vector computers). Thus the ViVA buffer would require total storage of 16KB, approximately the same modest chip area as L1 data cache of the PowerPC G5 (used in the experiments of Section 4).

The ViVA buffer is logically positioned between the core and the L2 cache. In the system we model, no additional ports are added to the L2 cache. Instead, the cache arbiter is modified slightly to add ViVA requests to the collection of other types of requests that it prioritizes and presents to the L2 cache: demand and prefetch requests for both the L1 data and instruction caches. Figure 1(b) and (c) show the operation request and data flow for loads and stores performed with traditional scalar accesses, as well as with ViVA accesses; thin arrows correspond to requests alone (that don't need to transfer data), while thick arrows correspond to actual data flow. This flow diagram

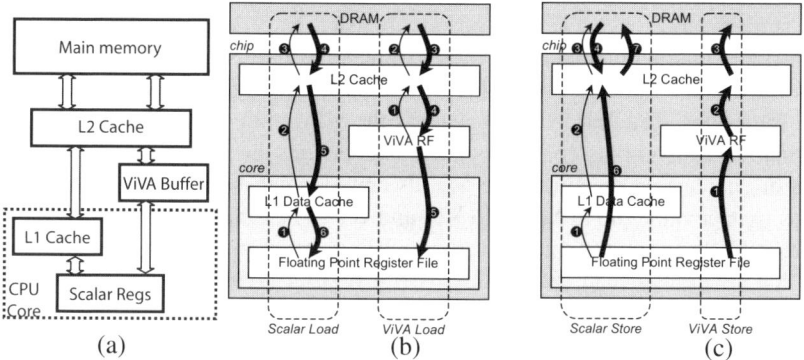

Fig. 1. ViVA overview showing (a) existing memory hierarchy with ViVA buffer, and data flow between DRAM and registers with and without ViVA for (b) loads and (c) stores. Requests without associated data are shown with thin arrows, and data transfer is shown with thick arrows.

clearly shows ViVA's potential to reduce memory traffic and requests compared with the default scalar processor.

In many ways, the ViVA buffer acts as a vector register file and is logically split into registers, which are used to identify the target or source for transfers. As a result, no coherence mechanisms are required in the buffer. An element loaded into the ViVA buffer will not be updated by scalar stores, much as an element that has been loaded into a scalar register will not be updated by scalar stores. Once values are stored from the ViVA buffer into the L2 cache, regular memory consistency models apply. No consistency orderings are guaranteed between ViVA and scalar stores; memory fences are required to enforce a particular order.

Because the ViVA buffer is treated as a vector register file, the lack of automatic coherence between values in the buffer and memory values is not problematic. Vector compiler technology can manage the coherence in the same manner as with traditional vector machines. In some cases, scalar and vector memory operations in the same program can be mixed without requiring the use of memory fences. As long as no single memory location is written by one type of operation (e.g., a non-ViVA scalar store) and then read by the other type (e.g., a vector load), a memory fence is not needed. This memory model tends to work well for vectorizable applications.

The out-of-order handling of the ViVA buffer works similarly to the handling of scalar out-of-order registers, with a few small differences. As with scalar registers, a number of extra physical registers are used in the system — in ViVA's case, that means that the physical buffer is larger than the visible state. The system keeps track of both committed state, as well as current state; in the case of an exception, the processor can recover the committed state and begin re-processing from there.

New Instructions and Control Registers. The second major component to ViVA is a small set of new instructions that are added to the processor's ISA. The first class of new instructions performs vector memory transfers between DRAM and the ViVA buffer; the second class performs scalar transfers between the ViVA buffer and scalar registers. The third and final class of new instructions contains only two operations: one that stores a value from a general-purpose register to a ViVA control register, and a complementary instruction that reads values from control registers.

ViVA has a small number of control registers: two that control the lengths of vectors, and one for strides. The first length register is the maximum vector length (MVL) — this is a hardwired read-only control register, that contains the physical length of vector registers on the current machine. The MVL's complement is the vector length (VL). Programs write a value (up to MVL) to VL, and vector instructions are only processed to that length. By writing a smaller value to VL, a program can run instructions on vectors that are shorter than the physical vector registers. The stride register sets the distance between consecutive elements for strided memory operations.

3 Experimental Platform

The ViVA simulator is based on Mambo, a cycle-accurate full-system simulator developed and used by IBM [3]. We modified the original version of Mambo to allow us to model various configurations of ViVA. Approximately two years of graduate student effort was required to modify the simulator, and to test the ViVA extensions. A detailed description of the process is presented in [6].

The Mambo simulator used for our experiment was designed to model PowerPC systems, and it was carefully calibrated to simulate our Apple G5 hardware platform. This architecture contains a 2.7 GHz IBM PowerPC 970FX CPU, PC-32000 DDR memory with 6.4 GB/s of memory bandwidth, 5.4 GB/s of North Bridge bandwidth (each direction), and a load-to-use latency of approximately 156 ns. The overall structure of the modeled system is generally similar to platforms that include Intel or AMD processors; while the specific details may differ, the general out-of-order processing, memory configuration, and operation closely resemble our evaluated platform. Thus, we expect many of the insights gained in this study to be applicable to broad range of modern microprocessor technologies.

In order to calibrate the simulator, we compared the performance of the real and simulated systems running a variety of existing and targetted custom benchmarks. The first calibration benchmark uses a variety of arithmetic operations within small loops, including: fixed- and floating-point operations, adds and multiplies, independent (to test maximum throughput) and dependent (to test ALU latency) operations. Next, we examined memory system latency at various levels using a version of the lat_mem_rd code from the LMbench [11] benchmark suite. The benchmark creates a linked list of pointers in an array of a particular size, and then measures the average time it takes to read each element. Finally, we calibrate the memory bandwidth using a benchmark that streams data out of arrays, which are sized to fit within the various levels of the memory hierarchy. Figure 2(a–c) shows simulated performance compared with the G5 hardware for the arithmetic, latency, and bandwidth calibration benchmarks respectively. Observe that in general all configurations closely match the actual hardware performance, giving us high confidence in our simulation results.

ViVA Programming. In a full system implementation, ViVA would be programmed much as vector computers are programmed today: a vector compiler would vectorize the

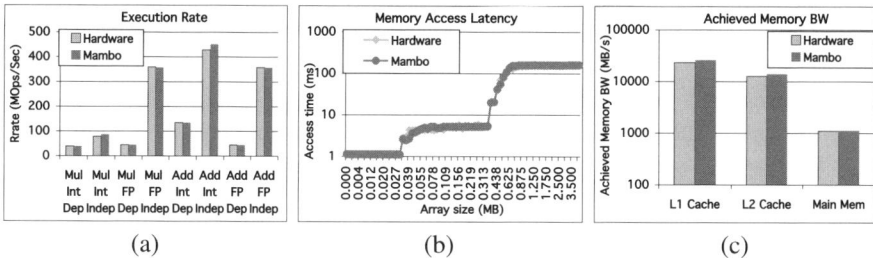

Fig. 2. Calibration results comparing G5 hardware and Mambo for (a) various arithmetic operations, (b) memory latency times for pointer-chasing and (c) achieved memory bandwidth for varying array sizes

loops and structure the code appropriately (using stripmining, etc). The ViVA compiler would require the additional straightforward step (included as the last part of a vector compilation phase) of adding a scalar loop, to replace traditional vector arithmetic instructions.

Since this effort focuses on ViVA's proof of concept, we use assembly language programming as the first step for conducting our experiments. Individual functions are written in assembly, and then called from the main C code. Note that no special assembly optimizations were used — in general, the code is a direct translation of the kernel into assembly, with the ViVA buffers being used in a double-buffered approach (values loaded into half of the registers, while the other half were used for calculations).

4 Performance Evaluation

We now examine performance results using ViVA within the Mambo simulator against the conventional hardware, using several microbenchmarks and two frequently used compact kernels. ViVA's target applications include memory-intensive programs that are common in traditional scientific computing. Such applications are also becoming increasingly important as drivers of desktop and handheld systems, in the form of recognition, synthesis, and other media processing programs. Because the simulator models a complete system, its slowdown prohibits the full execution of large applications in a timely manner, but the benchmark codes we use exercise the memory system in a manner that mirrors that of our target workload.

4.1 Microbenchmarks

In this section, we examine four memory microbenchmarks that provide insights into performance of numerous applications. We start with the unit-stride stream triad benchmark, which takes one dense vector, scales it by a constant, adds it with a second, and stores to a third, executing the loop with the body: $z[i] = x[i] \times factor + y[i]$. The parallelism expressed to the memory subsystem is equal to the array size. Since accesses are in unit stride, all data within each cache line are used. The next experiment explores strided memory accesses. The code is the same as the unit-stride benchmark, except that it only operates on elements spaced apart a constant displacement (called the stride). Once again, the memory level parallelism is as large as the number of elements accessed.

We then examine the microbenchmark: $z[i] = values[index[i]]$, which loops over indexed accesses. The indices point to random locations within the value array, where some values may be retrieved more than once, and some may not be retrieved at all. The cache is cleared before each run, and the index array is streamed through exactly once. Finally, we investigate a microbenchmark that mimics the memory access patterns for blocking optimizations, used in such computations as dense matrices, structured grids, and FFTs. This fourth kernel performs a *stanza triad*, where a given length stanza is accessed in a unit-stride fashion, followed by a jump to another memory address. Note that memory operations within and across stanzas are independent.

Unit-Stride Performance Results. Figure 3(a) presents the unit-stride triad benchmark, showing performance of a straightforward scalar implementation, an optimized scalar implementation, and ViVA with a variety of MVLs. Observe that for a small MVL=16, performance is comparable to the scalar rate. This highlights that, unlike traditional vector platforms, we do not see significant penalties for small vector length accesses. Additionally, as MVL increases we see significant performance benefits — more than 1.8x at MVL=256.

It may seem counterintuitive that the ViVA approach can outperform the scalar core for long unit-stride accesses, as the G5's hardware prefetcher is designed to optimize memory access patterns of this kind. However, the G5 prefetcher works on physical memory addresses, which limits its ability to fetch across page boundaries. Thus, between page boundaries prefetching must ramp up streaming accesses before it can reach a steady state. ViVA, on the other hand, does not have these constraints, allowing it to request address across numerous pages. Additionally, a traditional hardware prefetcher accesses a fixed number of lines ahead, a decision that could not possibly account for the ultimate microprocessor's clock speed, memory type, etc. Finally, a hardware prefetcher in steady state is limited to prefetching lines from DRAM one at a time as the program submits new demand requests, to avoid cache pollution. However, the ViVA approach can submit multiple line requests at once, as it is known a priori that all of the requested values are actually needed.

Finally, ViVA has another advantage for the case of storing a full cache line at once. Typically, stores to lines that are not present in the L2 cache are required to first be filled. ViVA is able to express full cache line writes directly to the processor, thus not requiring a memory fetch for the fill. In principle a processor can perform the same optimization for scalar stores, but the cache organization makes this unlikely for most cases. Special instructions do exist on some architectures to avoid a cache fill, such as the PowerPC *dcbz* instruction that zeros an entire cache line. However, these result in relatively small performance improvements, as can be seen in the optimized scalar behavior of Figure 3(a), which includes the use of the *dcbz* instructions, as well as software prefetching, manual unrolling, and a variety of compiler flags.

Strided Performance Results. Figure 3(b) shows the speedup of ViVA compared to a default scalar version for varying strides; attempts to optimize the scalar code using *dcbz*, software prefetching, manual unrolling, and compiler flags did not improve

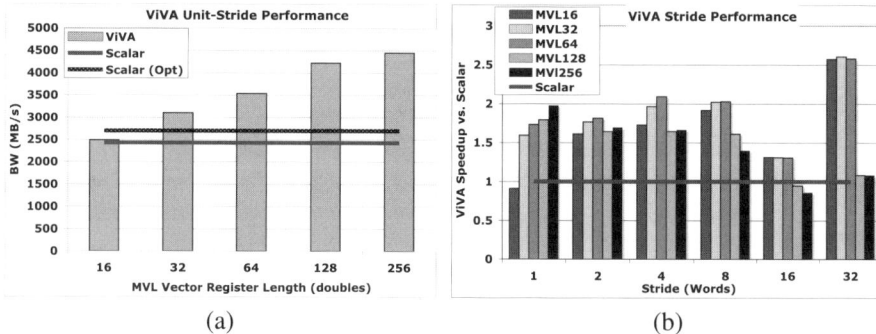

Fig. 3. Scalar vs. ViVA (a) bandwidth of unit-stride, for varying MVLs and optimized scalar code (*dcbz*, software prefetching, manual unrolling) and (b) speedup relative to scalar for varying strides and ViVA MVL (optimization of the scalar strided version did not improve performance)

performance. Observe that in almost every case, ViVA is able to deliver a significant improvement over the scalar implementations, attaining a 2.5x improvement for stride=32.

The results for longer MVLs shows the effects of two opposing trends. Longer MVLs allow more concurrency to be expressed to the memory subsystem, thereby increasing the memory bandwidth potential. However, long MVLs also increase the range of memory addresses touched by a single instruction, especially for operations with long strides. Thus, long MVLs can actually reduce performance, while consuming more register real estate and power. Due to these considerations we choose an MVL of 64 doubles as a "sweetspot" of these tradeoffs, and conduct the remainder of our experiments with this parameter.

Indexed Performance Results. Figure 4(a) shows the scalar and ViVA bandwidth rate of the indexed microbenchmark for varying array sizes; attempts to optimize the scalar version did not improve performance. At the smallest array size of 1 KB (doubles) ViVA shows only a slight advantage compared with the default hardware. Both implementations improve in performance as the array size grows, but ViVA shows a clear advantage, achieving up to 4.3x speedup at 512KB arrays. In the scalar case, unit-stride data streams (for both stores, and loads of indices) become longer with larger arrays, allowing the hardware prefetcher to ramp up to its full potential – however, the hardware prefetcher is not able to provide any benefit for value elements. For ViVA, larger array sizes correspond to more available parallelism presented to the memory subsystem, for all loads and stores. As the array sizes become much larger than the cache there is a high probability that fetched cache lines will evict subsequently required data, resulting in reduced performance. Additionally, as the total data size becomes much larger than the amount of memory covered by the TLB, more page translation overhead is required.

Stanza Triad Performance Results. Figure 4(b) presents the bandwidths of varying stanza lengths for the G5 scalar processor (default and optimized) and ViVA (default and optimized). For both scalar lines, performance continues to improve with increasing stanza lengths as the prefetcher ramps up and becomes fully engaged. The

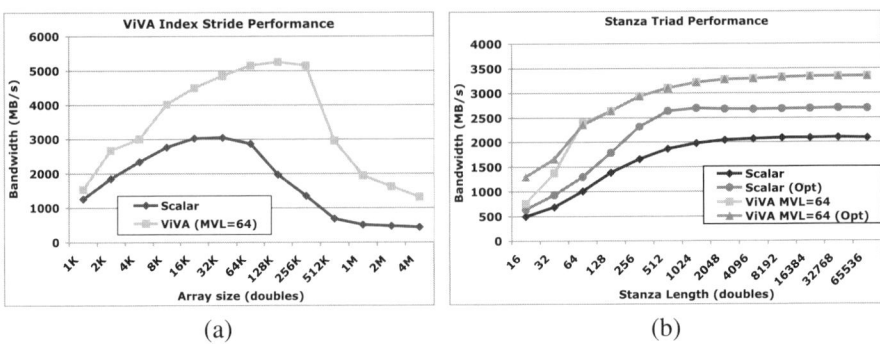

Fig. 4. Performance comparison of scalar versus ViVA for (a) indexed microbenchmark (optimizing the scalar indexed version did not improve performance) and (b) stanza triad where "ViVA (Opt)" uses indexed accesses to transfer multiple short stanzas with a single vector instruction

hardware prefetcher reaches its steady-state behavior after five consecutive cache lines are accessed, equal to 80 doubles. Performance continues to improve past stanzas of 80 doubles because various overheads (such as prefetch ramp-up, TLB misses and page translation) are amortized over the full length of the stream.

Figure 4(b) also shows that the ViVA implementation achieves better performance for all stanza lengths. At short stanzas, the vector benefits are limited since each instruction expresses less parallelism to the memory system. As stanza lengths increase so does the amount of parallelism expressed by a single ViVA instruction. As with scalar stanza triad, bandwidth continues to increase, as page translation costs are amortized over the number of elements accessed in the page.

4.2 Compact Kernel: Corner Turn

Having explored ViVA's microbenchmark behavior, we now examine the behavior of two compact kernels. The corner turn (CT) operation is frequently used in signal and image processing applications that operate on multi-dimensional data in multiple stages. An example where this is required is certain filtering operations followed by a beamforming computations [10]. CT's pseudocode is simply:

   for(i = 0 to row_length) {   for(j = 0 to col_length) {   out[j][i] = in[i][j]; } }

The idea behind this data-intensive kernel is to preserve data locality in the dimension being operated on by performing a matrix transpose, thus creating enormous pressure on the memory subsystem. This kernel depends on two memory access patterns — unit-stride and strided accesses — both of which were highlighted in our previous microbenchmarks. For larger sizes, the unit-stride reads can benefit from spatial locality and hardware prefetching, but the strided accesses will likely be in different cache lines and memory pages.

Figure 5(a) presents relative performance of the default and unrolled scalar codes as well as the ViVA version. The unrolled scalar implementation sees an improvement of approximately 4x and 6x for the small and large arrays (respectively). This speedup

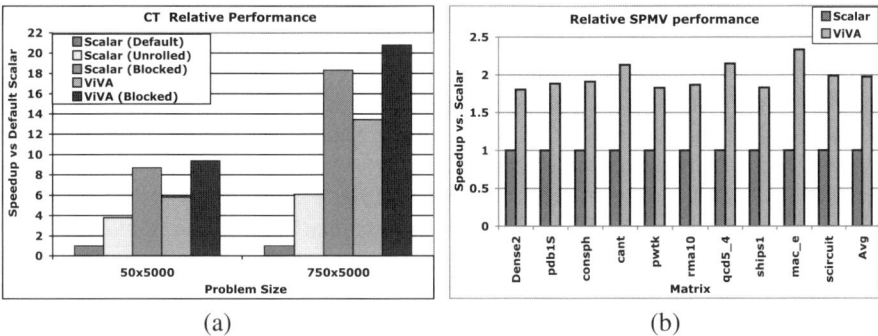

Fig. 5. Speedup over default scalar version for (a) CT for two (out of cache) problem sizes, showing unrolled scalar and ViVA performance and (b) SPMV for a variety of matrix structures

is seen because (after the initial fetch) strided loads access the same page (and potentially the same cache line). The ViVA results show even more impressive performance, achieving a 5x and 13x improvement for the small and large arrays. The ViVA strided accesses get the same benefit from page and cache-line reuse as the unrolled scalar implementation, however, overall delivered bandwidth is higher because ViVA is able to express more parallelism to the L2 cache. The relative advantage of ViVA compared to the unrolled scalar code, is consistent with the trends of the unit-stride and strided microbenchmarks (Figure 3).

Performance of CT using cache blocking, with and without ViVA, is also shown in Figure 5(a). Note that blocking is an algorithmic transformation that is normally not performed by a compiler, but instead requires hand optimization. Results show that (as expected) the blocked scalar version significantly outperforms the default CT. However, the blocked ViVA implementation delivers an additional performance improvements compared to the blocked scalar code (8% and 14% for the small and large test case). This demonstrates that ViVA can provide a performance boost either as a stand-alone approach or in conjunction with traditional algorithmic optimization techniques.

4.3 Compact Kernel: Sparse Matrix Vector Multiplication

We now examine the more complex memory access patterns associated with SpMV, an important kernel that dominates the performance of diverse applications in scientific and engineering computing, economic modeling and information retrieval. The sparse matrix structure is primarily filled with zero valued elements, which neither need to be stored nor computed on. As a result, significant instructions and meta-data are required to correctly index the vector per floating point operation [14]; thus, conventional implementations have historically delivered less than 10% of machine peak on single-core cache-based microprocessor systems [15]. Extensive research has been conducted to improve performance of this kernel, including code and data structure transformations and sophisticated auto-tuning libraries [15]. The standard scalar implementation utilizes the compressed sparse row (CSR) format. CSR stores nonzeros by encoding their values and columns, and an indexed operation is used to access the source vector. Additionally, an array is created to specify the first and last nonzero for each row.

The ViVA implementation follows the segmented scan algorithm [2], which stripmines the matrix into vectors that may straddle multiple rows. For each of these vectors of nonzeros, ViVA uses unit-stride loads for the values and column indices, and an indexed load to access the source vector. Once the data is in the ViVA registers, it processes nonzeros using regular scalar FPU operations. Finally, at the end of a row, the sum is stored using scalar accesses. These two phases can be double buffered by loading a group of vectors while processing a previous group.

To evaluate SPMV performance, we examine a variety of matrix structures and nonzero patterns from actual physical simulations [15]. Figure 5(b) presents the ViVA speedup compared with the scalar version for each studied matrix. Results show that ViVA delivers an average of 2x performance (right-most values) compared with the scalar code. Although raw performance drops for poorly structured matrices with large vectors — which have trouble exploiting L2 temporal locality — ViVA consistently outperforms the scalar version for a wide variety of underlying matrix structures.

5 Related Work

A number of strategies have been employed to balance Little's Law — which states that the number of outstanding memory requests in progress must match the product of the memory latency and the available memory bandwidth [1] — by increasing the number of concurrent requests presented to the memory subsystem. Different approaches (detailed in [6]) explored in high-performance computing, microprocessors, and embedded computers [7], include software prefetching, hardware (stream) prefetching, out-of-order instruction processing, multithreaded and multicore processors, vector architectures, and software controlled memories. Nonetheless, the "memory wall" problem generally continues to be exacerbated between successive microprocessor generations.

We summarize leading approaches in Table 1, which compares a variety of hardware and software techniques to hiding memory latency (using the U.S. A–F grading system).

Table 1. Qualitative comparison of DRAM latency hiding techniques using the A-F grading system

	Effectiveness			integration complexity[1]	compiler		user programmability
	unit	strided	indexed		complexity	maturity	
Out-of-order	D	D	D	D	D	n/a	A
HW Prefetch	A	B	F	B	A	n/a	A
SW Prefetch	B	C	D	A	B	C	D
Multithreaded	B	B	B	C	D[2]	D	C
DMA/Local Store	A	B	B	B	D	F	D
Vector	A	A	B	C	D	B	B
ViVA	A	A	B	B	D	B[3]	B

[1] Integration complexity compared versus unithreaded, in-order core.
[2] For auto-parallelization.
[3] Leveraging existing vector compilers.

In the first three columns we note whether the technique is effective in hiding DRAM latency for the specified memory access pattern. We also qualitatively note the VLSI design effort required to implement such a solution — ViVA being a memory external to the core requires relatively little work.

Perhaps one of the most important metrics for techniques which require software changes is the compiler technology: in terms of both the compiler complexity as well as the current maturity of this compilers technology. Vectorizing compilers, which ViVA leverages, are decades old, and well established technology. The maturity of many other compilation techniques is relatively poor. Finally we note the programmability, under an ideal programming model, for each techniques. For example, multithreading works well on multithreaded or parallelized codes; similarly, programmers are productive on Vector and ViVA architectures when implementing data parallel codes. Clearly, when compared to other techniques over a multidimensional analysis, ViVA provides a very attractive solution to hiding memory latency.

6 Summary and Conclusions

In this work we present ViVA, which incorporates the minimum set of hardware features required to see the benefits of vectorization without dramatically increasing the complexity of existing processor design or programmability. The ViVA infrastructure can exist within conventional cache hierarchies while employing familiar vector semantics that can take advantage of existing vectorizing compiler technology; resulting in memory accesses that are simpler and more power-efficient than the scalar approach.

ViVA has several important advantages over prefetching for tolerating memory latency. It allows programs to explicitly describe their memory access patterns, avoiding the need for power-hungry and error-prone stream detection hardware. A single ViVA instructions expresses many memory accesses, increasing the parallelism that can be presented to the memory systems. The use of a software-controlled memory buffer is a simple, efficient way to allow many memory accesses to proceed concurrently. Additionally, no coherence mechanism is needed for the ViVA buffer, since elements loaded into a scratchpad memory do not maintain automatic coherence with memory elements.

To validate our approach, we implemented ViVA on the Mambo cycle-accurate full system simulator, which was carefully calibrated to match the performance on our underlying G5 architecture. Results show that ViVA is able to deliver significant performance benefits over scalar techniques for a variety of memory access patterns as well as two important memory-bound compact kernels, CT and SpMV —- achieving 2x–13x improvement compared to the scalar version. Overall, our preliminary ViVA exploration points to a promising approach for improving application performance on leading microprocessors with minimal design and complexity costs, in a power efficient manner.

In future work, we plan to consider a broader array of application kernels, while studying additional extensions of the ViVA architecture that relax the strict semantics of vectorization. We also plan to further compare ViVA to related technologies such as DMA transfers. Additionally, ViVA could be extended to support more complex latency-bound load patterns such as pointer-chasing that are common in database and data mining applications. Finally, we plan to investigate the integration of ViVA to help organize memory access patterns for chip multiprocessors.

Acknowledgments

All authors from LBNL were supported by the Office of Advanced Scientific Computing Research in the DOE Office of Science under contract number DE-AC02-05CH11231.

References

1. Bailey, D.: Little's law and high performance computing. In RNR Technical Report (1997)
2. Blelloch, G.E., Heroux, M., Zagha, M.: Segmented Operations for Sparse Matrix Computation on Vector Multiprocessors. Technical Report CMU-CS-93-173 (August 1993)
3. Bohrer, P., Peterson, J., Ozahy, M., Rajamony, R., Gheith, A., Rockhold, R., Lefurgy, C., Shafi, H., Nakra, T., Simpson, R., Speight, E., Sudeep, K., Hensbergen, E.V., Zhang, L.: Mambo: a full system simulator for the PowerPC architecture. ACM SIGMETRICS Performance Evaluation Review 31(4), 8–12 (2004)
4. Creating science-driven computer architecture:a new path to scientific leadership, http://www.nersc.gov/news/reports/blueplanet.php
5. Espasa, R., Valero, M., Smith, J.E.: Vector architectures: past, present and future. In: Proceedings of the 12th international Conference on Supercomputing (1998)
6. Gebis, J.: Low-complexity Vector Microprocessor Extensions. PhD thesis, University of California, Berkeley, CA, USA (May 2008)
7. Grun, P., Nicolau, A., Dutt, N.: Memory Architecture Exploration for Programmable Embedded Systems. Kluwer Academic Publishers, Norwell (2002)
8. Gschwind, M.: Chip multiprocessing and the cell broadband engine. In: Proceedings of 3rd Conference on Computing Frontiers, New York, NY, USA, pp. 1–8 (2006)
9. Guo, Y., Chheda, S., Koren, I., Krishna, C.M., Moritz, C.A.: Energy characterization of hardware-based data prefetching. In: ICCD 2004: Proceedings of the IEEE International Conference on Computer Design, Washington, DC, USA, pp. 518–523. IEEE Computer Society, Los Alamitos (2004)
10. HPEC Challenge Benchmark Suite, http://www.ll.mit.edu/HPECchallenge
11. McVoy, L.W., Staelin, C.: lmbench: Portable tools for performance analysis. In: USENIX Annual Technical Conference, pp. 279–294 (1996)
12. Natarajan, K., Hanson, H., Keckler, S.W., Moore, C.R., Burger, D.: Microprocessor pipeline energy analysis. pp. 282–287 (August 2003)
13. Patterson, D.A.: Latency lags bandwith. Commun. ACM 47(10), 71–75 (2004)
14. Temam, O., Jalby, W.: Characterizing sparse algorithms on caches. In: Proc. Supercomputing (1992)
15. Vuduc, R., Demmel, J.W., Yelick, K.A.: OSKI: A library of automatically tuned sparse matrix kernels. In: Proc. SciDAC 2005, Journal of Physics (2005)

An Enhanced DMA Controller in SIMD Processors for Video Applications

Guillermo Payá-Vayá[1], Javier Martín-Langerwerf[1], Sören Moch[2], and Peter Pirsch[1]

[1] Institute of Microelectronic Systems, Leibniz Universität Hannover
Appelstr.4, 30167 Hannover, Germany
{guipava,jamarlan,pirsch}@ims.uni-hannover.de
[2] videantis GmbH
Schneiderberg 32, 30167 Hannover, Germany
soeren.moch@videantis.de

Abstract. Although current SIMD processor architectures can improve the processing performance by exploiting the data level parallelism inherent in video applications, an important performance penalty appears when processing data that is not formatted in an amenable way, e.g. unaligned memory access. This paper presents an enhanced DMA controller that performs block-based data transfers and a realignment when accessing a word in an external memory that is not aligned with the natural data memory/bus width boundary. Moreover, the enhanced DMA controller performs a signal extension while accessing data outside a specific region, e.g. a video frame, decreasing the total amount of processing cycles required for a typical video application. Performance improvements of up to 25% can be achieved when running a highly time consuming video encoding task (motion estimation) on a generic VLIW architecture with the enhanced DMA controller compared to a basic block-transfer DMA controller.

1 Introduction

Nowadays, continuous improvements in current image and video applications, e.g. JPEG2000, MPEG-4, or H.264, are pushing the limits of existing media processors. Given the existing high degree of inherent parallelism in this kind of applications, it is appropriate to include Single Instruction Multiple Data (SIMD) units, that split traditional wide scalar data paths into multiple narrow data paths which perform the same operation on each packed element [1,2]. These structures significantly improve the processor performance when running multimedia applications where the same operations are often performed over a lager number of elements.

Although current SIMD implementations can potentially increase the performance of media processors, there are some limitations related to memory architectures. An important performance penalty appears when current SIMD implementations process data that is not formatted in an amenable way [3]. For

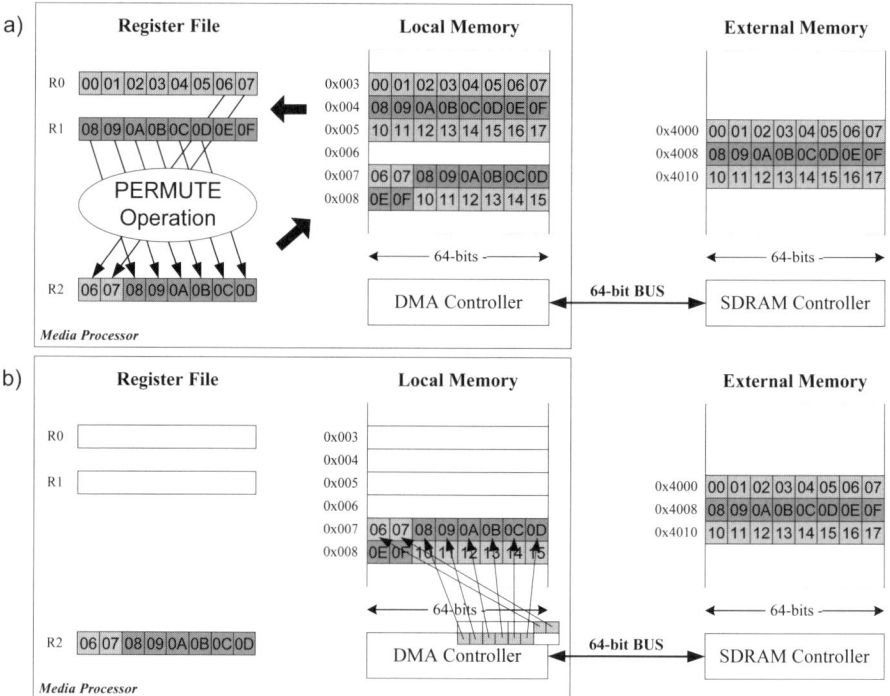

Fig. 1. Alignment process required when accessing the external memory (address 0x4006) for reading two consecutive 64-bit words: a) using an special instruction, e.g. permute [1], and b) using an enhanced DMA controller that performs the realignment process internally. In this example, the media processor uses a big-endian format and works internally with 8-bit subwords.

example, an unaligned or misaligned memory access is performed when accessing a word in the external memory that is not aligned with the natural data width boundary, e.g., a 64-bit (eight-byte) data packet that starts at a byte address of 0x4006 is not aligned to a 64-bit boundary. In this case, a realignment process should be performed by reading two consecutive words and rearranging the data. Figure 1 shows two ways to perform the alignment process in a system based on a media processor that includes a local memory and a direct memory access (DMA) controller.

Some architectures implement special instructions or include expensive specific hardware to support unaligned memory accesses. In any case, the programmer is always forced to take care of the alignment in software. This extra code introduces a computational overhead. Moreover, not only this alignment is required in video applications, also some boundary policies. For example, the H.264 decoder implements motion compensation in which motion vectors are allowed to point outside the decode area of a reference frame.

Unaligned transfers are specified in current bus protocols, e.g. AXI [4] and OCP [5], where it is possible that the first byte to access in a burst is not aligned with the natural width of the bus. In any case, these bus protocols specify that the slaves will not transfer the bytes located before or after the unaligned access, so no realignment is done.

In this paper, we analyze a new way to perform the required alignment and padding process in video applications by using an enhanced DMA controller, which:

- Performs *block-based data transfers* in background between the local memories, located in the media processor, and any peripheral connected to the system bus, while the media processor is executing other tasks.
- Performs a *data realignment process*, if required, when accessing peripheral devices (see Figure 1), e.g. external memories.
- Performs some *boundary policies* when accessing data that is outside of a frame, e.g. signal extension.
- Implements a simple mechanism to *configure several transfers at once*, without waiting for the end of each transfer before configuring the next one.

The enhanced functionality of the DMA controller will decrease the total number of processing cycles, the instruction memory size, and eventually the local memory size required for a typical multimedia task. This paper is organized as follows. Section 2 summarizes actual rearrangement mechanisms implemented in current media processors. A novel enhanced DMA controller specially designed for video applications is described in Section 3. Then, in Section 4, an evaluation of the proposed DMA controller is done by using a highly time consuming task, motion estimation. Finally, this paper is concluded in Section 5.

2 Related Work

Most of the current SIMD architectures that implement some kind of realignment process present some limitations that do not allow an efficient processing. Different strategies to perform the realignment process are:

- *Use of special sequences of instructions* to do the data rearrangement in software, e.g. a load instruction followed by a shift operation performed in multiples of bytes or a shuffle operation [6] allowing greater flexibility. One example is the Altivec extension [7]. This strategy requires several cycles for each memory access implying the use of the processing core and eventually large local memories to store the unaligned data.
- *Special load/store mechanisms* [3] that transparently perform the unaligned memory accesses reading from two consecutive words, e.g. in INTEL SSEx extensions [8], Trimedia TM3270 [9], or TMS320C64x/C64x+ Texas Instruments DSP [10]. These architectures support unaligned access to local memories (or caches), but the unaligned data has to be stored previously in these memories requiring extra space. Moreover, an extra read port in each local

memory is required to perform the realignment process in one cycle, significantly increasing the hardware cost.
- *Dedicated hardware resources*, e.g. a data alignment buffer that provides single-cycle throughput on a series of consecutive misaligned memory accesses and is specially useful in FIR algorithms [11].

Another possibility is to include an enhanced DMA controller inside the media processors to perform the realignment process. This new concept will decrease the computational overhead required by video applications to perform this realignment, and allows other simple processing tasks like signal extension to be done inside the DMA controller.

3 An Enhanced DMA Controller

The main motivations of enhancing a DMA controller can be seen by studying the data transfer characteristics of common video application tasks. Then, considering these characteristics, different enhancements (profiles) [12] of the proposed DMA controller are explained in detail.

3.1 Video Data Transfer Characteristics

In video applications, algorithms can be divided into two different classes [13]: pixel-based and block-based algorithms. Block-based algorithms are commonly used in video coding standards, i.e., MPEG-4, AVC/H.264, and VC-1. These algorithms split a frame into blocks of pixels, usually 16x16, 8x8, or 4x4 pixels blocks, and perform the processing in a block-by-block fashion. Some video coding tasks are motion compensation, motion estimation, integer transform, quantization, and deblocking filter.

An SIMD architecture can compute several subwords in parallel in one operation [1], taking profit on the parallel processing characteristics of block-based algorithms. But for a higher processing performance, the data must be correctly aligned inside the local memory reducing the time required for the data formatting process. Usually this data is located in the external memory and is accessed via DMA controller.

In block-based algorithm implementations, the transfer between external memories and local memories is characterized by:

- **Block-based transfers.** A complete frame is stored line-by-line in an external memory. A block-based transfer should only access the data belonging to the block, avoiding unnecessary data transfers.
- **Unaligned access.** The block position could be not aligned with the natural data width boundary of memory or bus system. For example, motion estimation and motion compensation algorithms perform unpredictable unaligned memory accesses.
- **Frame boundary policies.** Some boundary policies are used when accessing data out of the frame. For example, in H.264 video coding standard [14]

(MC and ME tasks), an out-of-frame read access leads to replication of the nearest boundary pixels of the frame. The input data is therefore obtained with padding.

3.2 Enhanced DMA Controller Implementation

Taking the mentioned video transfer characteristics into account, a new enhanced DMA controller is proposed. This controller is part of a media processor and in charge of performing transfers between external memories and local memories. The proposed DMA controller provides an easily extensible modular structure divided into four different submodules (see Figure 2):

- **Configuration register bank.** The media processor programs one (or more) transfer(s) by writing to the configuration register bank.
- **DMA control unit.** By using the information provided by the configuration registers, the DMA control unit leads the bus master unit by indicating the transfer type, the direction and the start address of the current transfer.
- **BUS master unit.** This unit performs read and write transfers over the on-chip bus using the information provided by the DMA control unit. This is the only unit whose implementation depends on the used bus protocol. The used bus master unit conforms to the 64-bit AMBA AHB specification [15]. By substituting this unit, the DMA unit can be connected to other buses, e.g., AXI [4] or OCP [5], to investigate the hereby resulting performance differences.

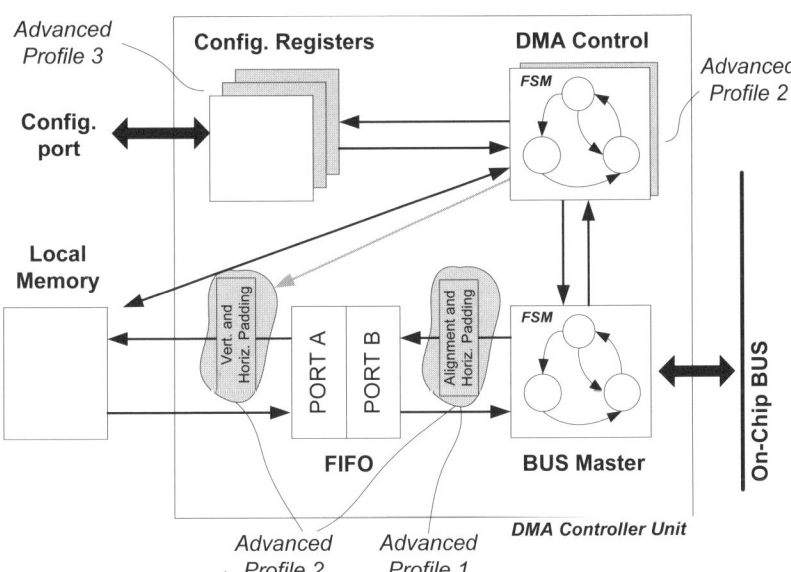

Fig. 2. Block diagram of the proposed enhanced DMA controller. The gray areas indicate the required modifications to implement the advanced profiles.

- **FIFO.** An internal memory is used for buffering the data between the local memory and bus master, which allows to work with different frequencies and a higher flexibility when accessing the local memories.

Figure 2 shows a block diagram of the proposed DMA controller. Different advanced profiles are available by adding new logic or modifying the existing one (gray boxes in the figure). In Section 4, a performance and hardware cost evaluation of the different profiles is presented. The selection of the appropriate DMA profile for a specific processor depends on the application field.

DMA Basic Profile (BP): Block-based transfers

The basic profile (BP) performs block-based transfers by programming the basic profile configuration registers (see Table 1). In [16], an exhaustive explanation about one-dimensional and two-dimensional DMA controllers is given. The developed DMA controller works basically with a 2D-to-1D scheme, performing block-based access to external memories and storing/reading data sequentially to/from the local memory.

DMA Advanced Profile 1 (AP1): Alignment process

Usually, the alignment process is done by the media processor itself. This would be the case when using a BP DMA to access data. This data realignment can also be performed by the DMA controller on-the-fly with low hardware cost. Figure 3 shows a simple scheme that implements this realignment process inside the enhanced DMA controller by reading two consecutive 64-bit words and shifting left (packing) the loaded data into an aligned 64-bit word. The last three bits of the word address are used to guide the shift operation.

DMA Advanced Profile 2 (AP2): Boundary extension

In the AP2 profile, two new parameters (configuration registers) are used to indicate to the DMA controller when the block to be transfered is outside the frame,

Table 1. Basic Profile and Advanced Profile 2 configuration registers

Parameter	Description
dma_bp_transfer_cfg	Transfer configuration, e.g. external memory read or write.
dma_bp_local_addr	Local memory base address (64-bit word address).
dma_bp_ext_addr	External memory base address (8-bit word address).
dma_bp_block_width	Block width in 64-bit words.
dma_bp_block_height	Block height in number of lines.
dma_bp_block_stride	Number of 64-bit words per frame line.
dma_ap2_xedge	Number of 64-bit word outside the frame. A positive value indicates that the outside words are in the left side. And a negative value indicates the right side.
dma_ap2_yedge	Number of lines outside the frame. A positive value indicates that the outside lines are in the top. And a negative value indicates the bottom.

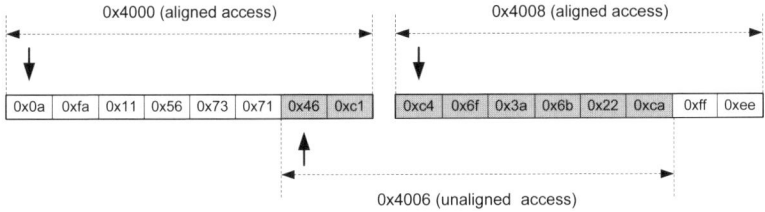

Fig. 3. Alignment process required to access to the external word 0x4006

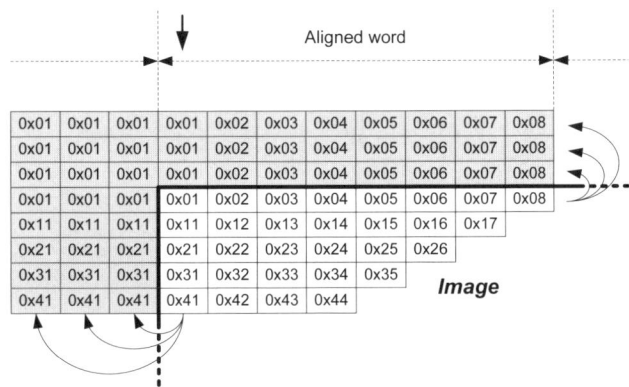

Fig. 4. Boundary extension in the corner of a reference frame

and also, which part of the block is outside. These parameters (dma_ap2_xedge and dma_ap2_yedge) are defined in Table 1. Figure 4 depicts an example of boundary extension as required by a typical video coding standard. Two kinds of padding processes can be differentiated:

- **Horizontal padding.** The horizontal padding process is performed by a set of multiplexers controlled by signal X_EDGE_SIGN (indicates left or right side padding), then a left shifter is used to obtain the aligned word (see Figure 5.a). In case of accessing several words outside the frame (left or right side), only the words inside the frame are read from the external memory, the padding process for the first or last word is performed and all words are written to the FIFO. The full padded words are generated between the FIFO (port A) and the local memory (see Figure 5.b). These padding words are stored in the local memory as many times as indicated by dma_ap2_xedge.
- **Vertical padding.** Vertical padding means replicating the top or bottom lines of a block. Each word of the top or bottom line to be replicated is written dma_ap2_yedge times in the local memory (using PORT A) before accessing the next word of the FIFO. During this replication, the subsequent local memory addresses are computed by adding a $dma\_bp\_block\_width$ offset.

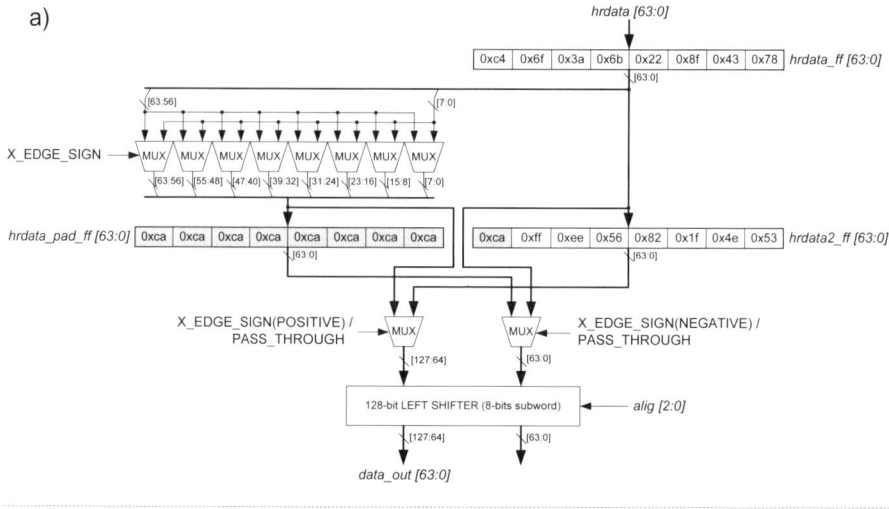

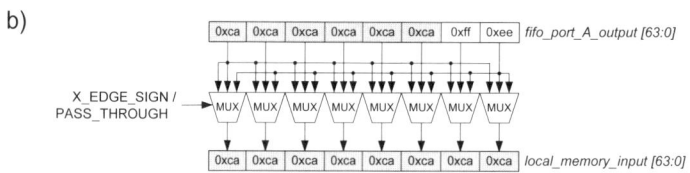

Fig. 5. Example of two processing structures; a) performs alignment and horizontal padding before storing the data in the FIFO (port B), and b) performs a complete subword extension (horizontal padding) in case of requiring several words that are left from the reference frame.

The goal of this extension is to force the DMA controller to perform only the necessary transfers between the bus master and the external memory. This can eventually lead to a lower total execution time (see results in section 4.1).

DMA Advanced Profile 3 (AP3): Queue of transfers

In this profile, a queue scheme is implemented by replicating the whole configuration register set (see Table 1). Several independent transfers can be programmed at any time without requiring to wait for the end of a previous transfer. A detailed explanation about the enhancements provided by this profile is out of the focus of this paper.

4 Evaluation

In order to show the advantages of the proposed enhanced DMA controller, an environment based on a generic VLIW processor that includes the enhanced DMA controller with different profiles is used for a highly time consuming video coding task (motion estimation).

4.1 Design Space Exploration Environment

In order to explore and optimize a VLIW processor for a specific group of applications [17], a generic VLIW processor is desirable, in which virtually all characteristics can be changed. In this work, a generic VLIW architecture [18] is used together with the different profiles of the enhanced DMA controller to obtain different performance measures.

A motion estimation algorithm based on a 3-D Recursive Search (3DRS) block matching method [19] is also used to compare the performance of the DMA profiles while using the same generic VLIW processor configuration. We have chosen this algorithm because of the high number of unaligned block-transfers required.

The 3DRS algorithm starts generating a list of motion vector candidates for each block of data or macroblock (MB) from the motion vector of the surrounding blocks. Then, block matching is performed, using a sum-of-absolute differences (SAD) cost function. The implemented version performs up to 9 comparisons (block matching) per MB and provides a half-pixel accuracy [20].

In order to obtain more realistic performance measures, an external access delay parameter is used. This parameter characterizes the delay cycles required by an external memory controller to access non-consecutive words.

4.2 Performance Measures

Motion estimation eventually requires alignment and/or padding every time a block of data is transfered from the external memory. In a media processor with a BP DMA, these two tasks are executed in the processor in a single code-block, whereas with an AP2 DMA the tasks are performed by the DMA while transferring the data. Using an AP1 DMA requires rewriting the code segment for alignment and padding to assign each part to the DMA and to the processor, respectively. For simplicity, only the best (AP2) and the worst (BP) case regarding achievable performance have been analyzed using the environment explained before and the same input sequence. A comparison of the average number of cycles per MB for the different profiles for different external access delays is shown in Figure 6 and Table 2.

For any delay, the DMA advanced profile (AP2) presents a lower number of cycles per MB than the basic profile (BP). This reduction is due to the effective computational load reduction in the VLIW. In the AP2 profile, the alignment and padding process is performed by the DMA controller while the VLIW processor executes other computing tasks.

However, the performance improvement decreases with increasing access delay, since in this context no computational load can be saved. This is because the VLIW processor has to wait for the end of the slow block-transfers in order to perform the block matching process, whether alignment and padding is done or not. In any case, AP2 requires fewer cycles because few transfers are employed for those blocks that are partially outside the reference frames.

Finally, it should be noticed that AP2 requires less application code, herewith saving valuable instruction memory (see Table 2).

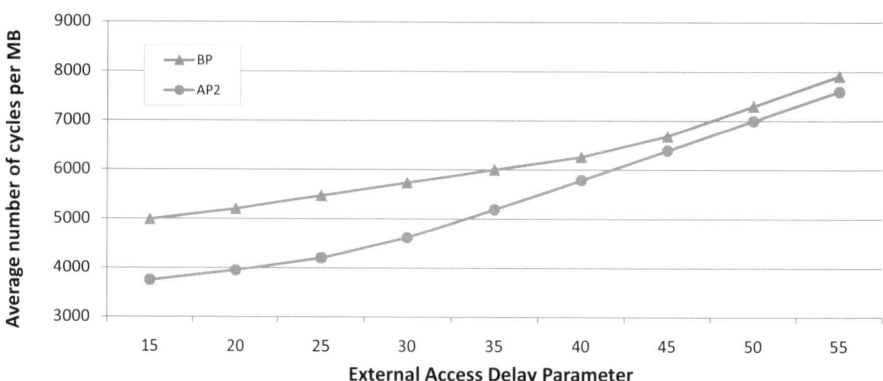

Fig. 6. Performance comparison between the best (AP2) and the worst (BP) case

Table 2. Synthesis results vs. performance measures. The different measures are normalized with the BP measures.

Profile	Estimated area in μm^2	App. Instruction code size in 64-bit words	Number of cycles per MB Delay 15	Delay 30
BP	83899 (1.00)	457 (1.00)	4988 (1.00)	5732 (1.00)
AP1	86634 (1.03)	-	-	-
AP2	106456 (1.27)	398 (0.87)	3746 (0.75)	4621 (0.81)

4.3 Synthesis Results

The proposed enhanced DMA controller has been implemented in VHDL [21] and verified using the described DSE environment. In Table 2, the estimated silicon area for the different DMA profiles is shown. These ASIC synthesis were obtained by Synopsys Design Compiler [22] and a 130nm general purpose TSMC standard cell library [23]. All the designs are synthesized for a 3.0 ns clock period.

A direct hardware cost comparison between the different profiles shows that the alignment and the padding schemes require 3% and 24% more area than a BP implementation, respectively. A fair comparison is only done when the complete processor estimated area is considered. The used media processor corresponds to a dual issue generic VLIW processor [18] with six functional units. The estimated area for this configuration is between 3 and 4 mm^2 depending on the size of the employed memories. In this case, the increase in area between the implementation of a BP and AP2 represents less than 1% of the total processor area.

5 Conclusions

In this paper an enhanced DMA controller specially designed for video processors is described. Different enhancements are explained in detail and a complete evaluation using a specific video application task and a reference video processor is done. The results show that a performance improvement up to 25% can be achieved when using the proposed enhanced DMA controller, without significantly increasing the total estimated area of our reference VLIW processor.

Acknowlegments

The authors thank I. Vivancos San Nicolás and F. Reino Gómez for developing the DMA simulation environment and verifying the different profiles of the DMA HDL code.

References

1. Lee, R.: Subword parallelism with MAX-2. Micro. IEEE 16(4), 51–59 (1996)
2. Slingerland, N., Smith, A.: Measuring the Performance of Multimedia Instruction Sets. IEEE Transactions on Computers 51(11), 1317–1332 (2002)
3. Alvarez, M., Salami, E., Ramirez, A., Valero, M.: Performance Impact of Unaligned Memory Operations in SIMD Extensions for Video Codec Applications. In: Proc. IEEE International Symposium on Performance Analysis of Systems & Software ISPASS 2007, pp. 62–71 (2007)
4. ARM Limited: AMBA AXI Protocol Specification, v1.0. (2004)
5. OCP-IP Association: Open Core Protocol Specifications, Release 1.0. (2001)
6. Lee, R.: Subword Permutation Instructions for TwoDimensional Multimedia Processing in MicroSIMD Architectures. In: Proc. IEEE International Conference on Application-Specific Systems, Architectures, and Processors, July 2000, pp. 3–14 (2000)
7. Diefendorff, K., Dubey, P., Hochsprung, R., Scale, H.: AltiVec extension to PowerPC accelerates media processing. IEEE Micro 20(2), 85–95 (2000)
8. Boggs, D., Baktha, A., et al.: The Microarchitecture of the Intel Pentium 4 Processor on 90nm Technology. Intel Technology Journal 8(1), 7–23 (2004)
9. van de Waerdt, J.W., Vassiliadis, S., Das, S., Mirolo, S., Yen, C., Zhong, B., Basto, C., van Itegem, J.P., Amirtharaj, D., Kalra, K., Rodriguez, P., van Antwerpen, H.: The TM3270 Media-processor. In: Proc. 38th Annual IEEE/ACM International Symposium on MICRO-38 Microarchitecture, p. 12 (2005)
10. Texas Instruments: TMS320C64x/C64x+ DSP CPU and Instruction Set Reference Guide. SPRU732C edn. (August 2006)
11. Fridman, J.: Data Alignment for Sub-word Parallelism in DSP. In: Proc. IEEE Workshop on Signal Processing Systems SiPS 1999, pp. 251–260 (1999)
12. Reino-Gomez, F.: Design Space Exploration of an Advanced Direct Memory Access Unit for a Generic VLIW Processor. Master's thesis, Institute of Microelectronic Systems, Leibniz Universitaet Hannover (July 2008)
13. Beric, A.: Video Post Processing Architectures. PhD thesis, Technische Universiteit Eindhoven (2008)
14. ISO/IEC 14496-10: Coding of Audiovisual Objects - Part 10: Advanced Video Coding (2003)
15. ARM Limited: AMBA Specification, v2.0 (1999)
16. Katz, D., Gentile, R.: Embedded Media Processing. Elsevier, Amsterdam (2006)

17. Payá-Vayá, G., Martín-Langerwerf, J., Pirsch, P.: RAPANUI: Rapid Prototyping for Media Processor Architecture Exploration, pp. 32–40. Springer, Heidelberg (2005)
18. Payá-Vayá, G., Martín-Langerwerf, J., Pirsch, P.: Design Space Exploration of Media Processors: A Generic VLIW Architecture and a Parameterized Scheduler. In: Lukowicz, P., Thiele, L., Tröster, G. (eds.) ARCS 2007. LNCS, vol. 4415, pp. 254–267. Springer, Heidelberg (2007)
19. de Haan, G., Biezen, P., Huijgen, H., Ojo, O.: True-motion estimation with 3-D recursive search block matching. IEEE Transactions on Circuits and Systems for Video Technology 3(5), 368–379, 388 (1993)
20. de Haan, G., Biezen, P.: Sub-pixel Motion Estimation with 3-D Recursive Search Block-maching. Signal Processing: Image Communication 6, 229–239 (1994)
21. Vivancos-SanNicolas, I.: VDHL-Implementation and Verification of an Advanced Direct Memory Access Unit for a Generic VLIW Processor. Master's thesis, Institute of Microelectronic Systems, Leibniz Universitaet Hannover (July 2008)
22. Synopsys: Design Compiler User Guide. Synopsys. version Z-2007.03 edn. (2007)
23. Taiwan Semiconductor Manufacturing Company Limited (TSMC): TSMC 0.13um Core Library Databook. Release 2.1 edn. (October 2004)

Cache Controller Design on Ultra Low Leakage Embedded Processors

Zhao Lei[1], Hui Xu[1], Naomi Seki[1], Saito Yoshiki[1], Yohei Hasegawa[1], Kimiyoshi Usami[2], and Hideharu Amano[1]

[1] Keio University, Japan
[2] Shibaura Institute of Technology, Japan
geyser@am.ics.keio.ac.jp

Abstract. A leakage-efficient cache controller design targeted on ultra low power embedded processors is proposed. The key insight is that a large circuits subset is accessed only when cache misses happen. By utilizing the fine-grained run-time power gating technique, such a subset can be dynamically powered-off as a power gated domain. Two simple but effective sleeping control policies are proposed to assure the leakage reduction effect; and to eliminate the impact of wake-up process, a latency cancellation mechanism is also proposed. Evaluation results show, in 90nm CMOS technology, 69% and 64% of leakage power can be reduced for instruction cache controller and data cache controller without performance degradation.

1 Introduction

Leakage power has emerged as a limiting factor in modern processor design. As the feature size shrinks, leakage power exhibits an exponential-increasing characteristic, and is expected to become the dominant source of power consumption[1]. The leakage problem is more critical in the field of embedded applications, such as cell phones and mobile game engines, because the leakage energy continuously dissipates even when the system is in the idle state.

Leakage energy optimization for processor has been the target of much recent efforts. In paper[2][3], effective leakage control mechanisms had been proposed on cache memories, which constitute a major portion of a processor's transistor budget; and paper[4] demonstrated the potential to reduce leakage by power-gating execution units in a fine granularity.

In our prototype Geyser-0[5], a low leakage, MIPS R3000 based processor is designed and implemented with 90nm ASPLA's CMOS technology. To explore the leakage reduction to the maximum extent, the arithmetic logic unit is divided into four different functiton units: a common arithmetic and logic unit, a shifter, a multiplier and a divider. These function units combined with an exception-handle coprocessor CP0 can be put into a low leakage mode dynamically by run-time power gating technique. Power evaluation shows the leakage power can be reduced up to 47% percent.

Geyser-0 also includes a "Bridge Unit", which includes a 16-entry TLB unit, a Memory Management Unit (MMU), a 64Bytes×64 instruction cache and a 64Byte×64 data cache. At this version, the Bridge Unit is not power-optimized. During the process of power analysis, we found the leakage power of cache controller is surprisingly high: the cache controllers take up 11.4% and 19.2% of the leakage consumption when compared to the cache memories of instruction cache and data cache respectively. When traditional leakage power reduction techniques are applied to the cache memories, the ratio for cache controller will further increase. This unexpected high leakage dissipation of cache controller may come from two aspects: on one hand, cache controllers are usually on the critical path of a processor, so the synthesis result is usually in favor of speed and not economical in terms of area; on the other hand, the cache controller itself is increasingly becoming complex so as to support some operating system assisted "cache instructions"[6] other than only memory accessing and temporally data store. Furthermore, unlike cache memories and TLB, the leakage consumption of cache controller has not been noticed and researched yet, and it may becomes a "short-slab" in the leakage efficient processor design.

Fortunately, a large portion of cache controller is not accessed frequently. Here, we propose an approach to apply the fine-grained Run-Time Power Gating (RTPG) technique to the cache controller design. Leakage reduction effect can be achieved by dynamically putting the unused components into a sleep mode based on the analysis of accessing pattern and break even time. The evaluation result shows the leakage power dissipation can be reduced up to 69% for instruction cache controller and 64% for data cache controller at 100°C, and zero performance penalties can be achieved by latency concealing mechanism.

The remainder of this paper is organized as follows. After an overview of the fine-grained power gating technique in Section 2, the power domain partition method and break-even time analysis will be discussed in Section 3; in Section 4, dynamic sleeping control policies will be proposed for both instruction cache controller and data cache controller; the evaluation results will be shown in Section 5, and Section 6 is for conclusion.

2 Fine-Grained Run-Time Power Gating

Power gating is a well-known technique to reduce leakage current. Between logic components and the real ground, a Virtual Ground (VGND) line is formed by inserting a high Vth power switch. While the power switch is turned off, the VGND line is charged up to the voltage nearby Vdd, the sub-threshold leakage is cut off, and the entire power domain which is connected with the power switch is turned into a sleep mode; when the power switch is turn on, parasitic capacitance on the VGND line is discharged and the power domain is turned back into the active mode. We define the wake-up time as the restoring time from the sleep mode to the active mode. Although this technique has a benefit that the target domain can be designed with the common design method, the wake-up time is

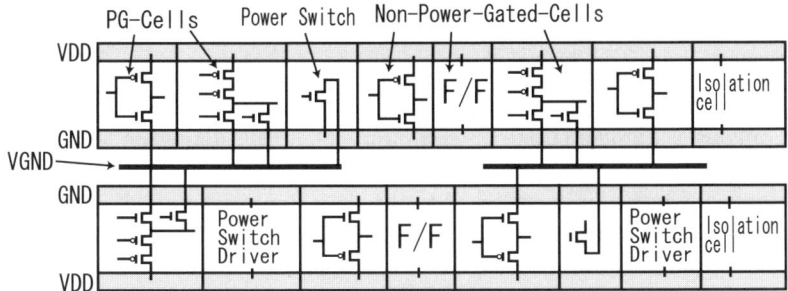

Fig. 1. A VGND architecture for a fine-grained RTPG

the order of micro seconds. Such a long wake-up time prohibits it being used for on-demand leakage reduction applications, like cache controller.

Fine-grained run-time power gating[8], which is a technique to minimize leakage power during the operation by powering on and off circuit components in a finer temporal/spatial granularity, is used in this paper. Unlike the conventional method, the entire power domain is partitioned into smaller local domains. VGND line and the power switch are shared only within the local domain. We can optimize the power switch size in a fine granularity with a set of cells each of which has its own VGND lines (PG-cell). By properly partitioning local domains and fine-tuning the power switch size, the wake-up time can be reduced to a few nano-seconds.

As shown in Fig.1, since existing ground rail in the PG-cells is used as the real ground, non-power-gated cells such as flip-flops, clock buffers, repeaters, isolation cells and power-switch drivers can coexist with the power gated cells in the same row. This allows us to utilize the conventional timing-driven P&R and clock tree synthesis when power gated cells and non-power-gated cells coexist in a target domain.

The design methodology for fine-grained RTPG had been established[7]. At first, we follow conventional standard cell placement flow and then swap the cell with the same-sized PG-cell. PG-cell is connected to a VGND pin instead of the real ground rail. After inserting properly sized power switches and power switch drivers, signal wires and local VGND lines are routed.

Although fined-grain RTPG can reduce leakage current effectively, it is not a non-overhead technique. The state transfer between the sleep mode and the active mode consumes extra dynamic power for power switches, isolation cells and buffers in sleep signal wires. Even in the sleeping mode, leakage current decreases with time but still continues to flow until the capacitance on the VGND and output nodes of logic gates are charged up. The Break-Even Time (BET), which means the time point when the aggregated leakage energy savings equal to the energy overheads due to the power domain state transfer, is a crucial parameter to assure the overall power saving effect. We will illustrate the BET analysis flow in the next section.

3 Power Domain Partition and BET Analysis

To apply the fine-grained RTPG technique into cache controller design, we must divide the common design into different power domains. The Normal domain (NM domain) is implemented by common design methodology with standard cells, and it is always in an active mode. In contrast, the Power Gated domain (PG domain), which can be switched to the sleep mode when in idle state, follows the design methodology mentioned in Section 2.

Power domain partition has a determined effect on the BET and the final leakage reduction result. Since the RTPG is not a non-overhead technique, the partition method needs to be well investigated. Two basic rules should be obeyed to assure the final leakage saving effect: 1) because the leakage power is a function of the number of transistors, better leakage saving efficiency can be achieved by choosing a certain size PG-domain; 2) the chosen PG domain should have a high probability of long sleeping time, so as to compensate for the extra energy caused by power switches, isolation cells and sleep signal buffers.

3.1 Power Domain Partition

Cache controllers are typical finite state machine (FSM) circuits, and only a set of circuits are used each clock cycle. To maintain the right FSM state transition, the state flip-flops must be in the active mode, regardless of their working states. This means that our fine-grained RTPG can only be employed by combinational circuits. Paper[8] proposed a RTPG FSM design flow by taking advantage of the clock gating enable signals. But in that paper, BET analysis is based on an analytical model, and it is hard to be implemented in on-demand applications. Here, we do the power domain partition based on the analysis of the accessing pattern of cache controllers.

The working states of cache controller can be divided into three types: the Processor Access Requirement Operations (PARO); the Next-level Memory Hierarchy Access Operations (NMHAO); and the Operating System Related Operations (OSRO). The PARO answers for all operations related with the processor-cache interface, such as cache memory access, hit/miss detection and cache state update. This part shares the highest access frequency, but just consumes a small fraction of the semiconductor area. The NMHAO controls all next-level memory hierarchy accessing operations. It often takes up a much larger size than PARO, but only be accessed when cache misses happen. The OSRO only happens when operating system gives out explicit signals.

Fig.2 shows our power domain partition result. All logic circuits related to PARO are treated as an NM domain due to it's high accessing frequency and small area; on the other hand, the PG domain includes all logic components realizing functions of NMHAO. Because this part is used only when cache misses happen, it stands a good chance to stay in sleep mode for a long period. Usually the function of OSRA can be implemented by reusing the corresponding parts of PARO and NMHAO, so here we do not treat it as individual domain. Even by fine-grained RTPG, the impact of wake-up time still can not be omitted (about

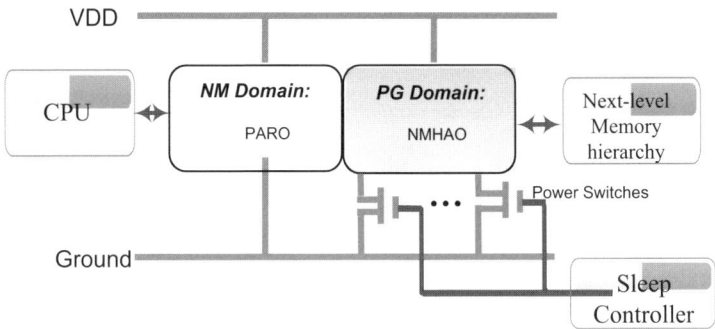

Fig. 2. Power Domain Partition

5ns here). When working at 200Hz, the waking up process of PG domain will lead one clock cycle stall. To conceal the latency penalty of waking up when misses happen, the first state after the cache-miss is overlapped by PARO and NMHAO, hence zero performance penalties can be achieved.

3.2 BET Analysis

To evaluate the BET of PG domains, a real design of fine-grained RTPG is needed, since the number of power switches is dependent on the target domain. The entire flow for fine-grained RTPG design is illustrated as follows.

First, the PG domain is designed with Verilog-HDL and synthesized by Synopsys's Design Compiler as an individual module. Then, the standard cell is replaced with same size PG cells, and power switches are inserted between VGND of cells and real ground by hand. Isolation cells are also inserted at all output ports in order to prevent path-through current when power is shut off, and a port for sleep signal wire must be prepared and connected to every power switch. At present, we couldn't prepare PG-cells for all standard cells in the library due to the limited designing time. This degrades the variety of cell-selection and will enlarge the area. Next, we process placement and routing by Synopsys's Astro. With Sequence Design's tool called CoolPower, the number of sleep power switches is optimized so as to make the time for waking-up as short as possible. Then the energy dissipation for PG domain (E_{PG}) can be analyzed by the extracted RC from post-layout data. By changing the sleep cycles, we can get E_{PG} at different sleeping period. We also evaluate the energy dissipation of a non-power-gated counterparts (E_{NPG}). The ratio E_{PG}/E_{NPG} is plotted against sleeping time in Fig.3 and Fig.4 for the PG domain of Instruction Cache Controller (ICC) and Data Cache Controller (DCC), respectively. The time point at which the ratio equals 1 is the BET. We do such a evaluation at three temperatures: $25°C, 65°C$ and $100°C$.

Two facts need to be further explained. First, the BET reduces with increasing the temperature. This is because sub-threshold leakage increases with the temperature, and the fine-grained RPTG is more efficient in high temperature.

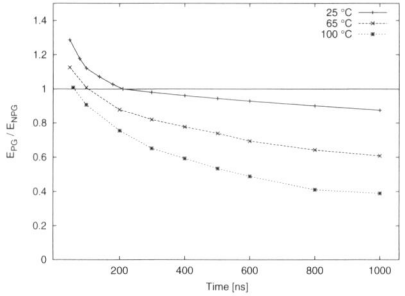
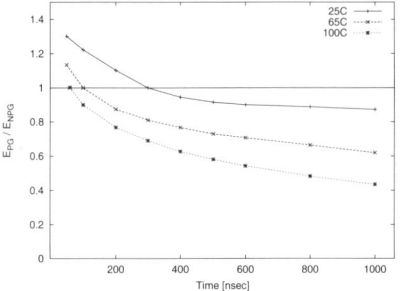

Fig. 3. BET of ICC   **Fig. 4.** BET of DCC

Another fact is that the BET has no direct relationship with the area of PG domain, although in our case the BET of ICC is less than that of DCC which occupies a larger area. The BET is determined by the number and size of power switches. The extra energy dissipation introduce by isolation cells and enable signal buffers also affects the result. Thus the BET analysis for each domain must base on the circuit level simulation, and the simple mathematical model is difficult to apply. The clock cycles of break-even time of each module is summarized in Table.1

Table 1. Break-Even Time for PG domains

Temperature	Break-Even Time [cycles]	
°C	ICC PG domain	DCC PGdomain
25	42	60
65	18	20
100	12	12

4 Dynamic Sleeping Control Policy

Ideally, the PG domain should be switched into the sleep mode when known its idle state will last longer than BET. But this kind of oracle prediction mechanism does not exist in a real design. Sleeping control policies, which decide when to shut down the PG domain, has a decisive effect on leakage saving.

If a sleep event lasts less than its BET, the energy will be increased by power gating instead of being saved. We refer such a case as a Fault Power-Off Event (FPOE). On the contrary, we call the sleep event whose sleeping time is longer than BET as a Safety Power-Off Event (SPOE). The energy reduction result of a PG domain (E_{PG_reduc}) can be expressed by following expression:

$$E_{PG\_reduc} = E_{L\_NPG} - E_{L\_SPOE} - E_{L\_FPOE} - E_{OvC}$$

Where the E_{L_NPG} is the leakage energy dissipated when the PG domain is always kept in the active mode; E_{L_SPOE} and E_{L_FPOE} are the leakage energy caused by SPOEs and FPOEs; and E_{OvC} is the extra energy introduced by the sleeping control logic, which includes both dynamic energy and leakage energy. Here, we conclude a simple guideline for the sleeping control policy design: 1) the SPOEs should be recognized as much as possible, the longer a sleep event stays in the sleep mode, the better leakage reduction effects can be achieved; 2) the E_{L_FPOE} poses a negative effect on energy saving, sleeping control policies should be capable of filtering out such cases; 3) the circuits engaged by sleeping control policies introduce extra energy dissipation, so simple policies share a high priority.

Based on the design guideline, three different policies are proposed in this section:

Fundamental policy: The most straight-forward sleeping control policy is to turn PG domain into the sleep mode automatically as soon as the cache controller exits the cache miss handle process. It will be kept in such a mode until the next cache miss is detected. This fundamental policy shares the merit of no needing to add extra logic circuits, but taking a risk of degrading the leakage saving by FPOEs.

Time-based policy: An alternative to the fundamental policy is to put PG domain into the sleep mode only if a pre-set number of cycles (threshold) has elapsed since its last accesses. Such a time-based policy can effectively reduce the number of FPOEs at the cost of missing further opportunities to turn PG domain into the sleep mode during the idle times that are shorter than threshold. The fundamental policy can also be treated as special case of time-based policy when choosing 0 as the threshold.

Double-checked policy: The double-checked policy comes from the observation that the behavior of previous cache misses can be used to predict the timing slot between current miss and the next. A two-bit shifter is employed to record the behavior of last 2 sleep events, if the sleep event is a SPOE, the corresponding bit in shifter will be set to 1; otherwise it will be set to 0. The PG domain can only be powered-off when both the two bits is 1. This policy can relieve the sleeping time deterioration caused by time-based policy to some extent, but the number of FPOEs may increase.

Here, the efficiency of proposed policies are checked by 4 benchmark programs, Fig.5 shows the number of FOPEs at different threshold by the time-based policy, the results are obtained by clock cycle level simulation based on a 8K 2-way set-associative instruction cache. As the threshold increases, the number of FPOEs decreases dramatically. When choosing 1000ns as the threshold, this policy can avoid most of the FPOEs. Fig.6 compares the ratio of the sleeping time to the running time between the fundamental policy and a 1000ns-threshold time-based policy, from which we can see the sleeping ratio degradation is almost negligible. This is because in our test, the cache misses mainly come from compulsory misses and conflict misses[9], and the time slot between sequential groups of cache misses is often a long period.

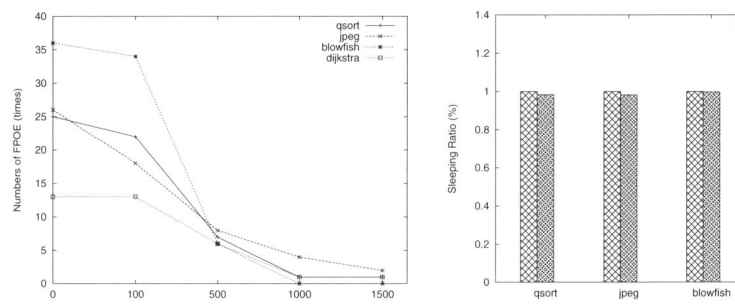

Fig. 5. Number of FPOEs for ICC

Fig. 6. Sleeping Time Ratio of ICC

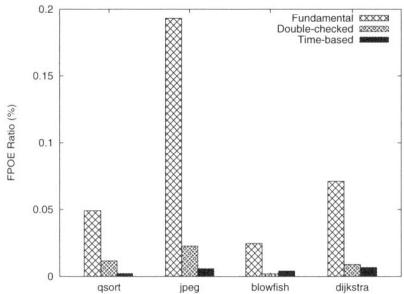

Fig. 7. FPOE Ratio of ICC

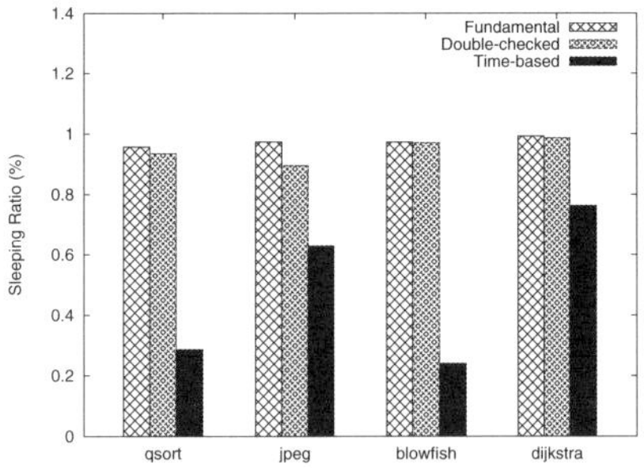

Fig. 8. Sleeping Time Ratio of DCC

Unlike instruction cache, the distribution of data cache misses is more like a uniform distribution and it is difficult to choose a suitable threshold for all applications. Fig.7 shows the ratio of the number of FPOEs to the number of cache misses by three different sleeping control policies for a 8K 2-way set-associative data cache, and Fig.8 compares their sleeping ratio. The 4000ns threshold time-based policy can achieve the best FPOE-reduction effect, but degrades the sleeping ratio significantly. On the other hand, the double-checked policy has an insignificant impact on sleeping ratio, and can keep the number of FPOEs in an acceptable range.

The leakage power is sensitive to the temperature, as mentioned in section 3, the BET tends to become short when the chip becomes hot. Because both the time-based policy and double-checked policy have a counter to calculate the pre-set threshold, if thermal sensors can give an explicit signal to cache controllers, these pre-set threshold can be adjusted to achieve a better leakage reduction effect.

5 Evaluation Results

5.1 Power Analysis Method

Based on the design flow presented in section 2, an 8K 2-way set-associative instruction cache controller with the time-based policy (1000ns threshold) and an 8K 2-way set-associative data cache controller with the double-checked policy are designed with 90nm CMOS technology. We also created their non-power-gated counterparts to do the comparison. In this section, we illustrate the power analysis method for our fine-grained RTPG design. To simplify the evaluation process, here, we assume that no extra power will be introduced by sleeping control policies.

The power consumption in the active mode is evaluated with a standard method. That is, the switching probability is measured with post-layout simulation, and the SAIF file is generated. Synopsys's PowerCompiler is used to compute the power consumption with post-layout netlist.

Unlike the active mode, the power consumption in the sleep mode is complicated since the leakage power dissipated in a sleep event changes with the length of the sleeping time. We analyze the leakage current using transistor level simulations while changing the sleeping time. The sleeping cycles at every sleep event are captured by running an RTL simulation. We recode both the sleeping cycles and the leakage energy caused by this event into a look-up-table, for example, if a N-clock cycles sleep event happens, the sleeping cycles N and the corresponding power consumption Lws_N will be recorded as pairs. After getting the leakage power of the non-power-gated counterpart (Lwa) with the stand method, the average leakage power Lw in a PG domain can be computed with the following expression:

$$Lw = \sum_i (Lws_i * \frac{M_i * i}{T}) + Lwa * (1 - \frac{\sum_i (M_i * i)}{T})$$

Where, it is assumed that i cycles sleeps occur $M(i)$ times in the program whose total number of execution clock cycles is T.

By using the RTL model of Geyser-0[5],a MIPS R3000 CPU, clock-level simulations can be executed. Here, we use 4 benchmark programs for the power analysis, three of them are from MiBench[10]: Quick Sort from mathematics package, Dijkstra from the network package and Blowfish from the security package. As an example of media processing JPEG encoder program is also used.

5.2 Leakage Reduction Efficiency

Fig.9 shows the leakage consumption of both ICC and DCC @65°C. For comparison, the leakage power of their non-power-gated counterparts are also shown. At 65°C, 61% and 50% leakage power can be reduced for ICC and DCC respectively.

Fig 10 and Fig.11 show leakage power of ICC and DCC normalized to their non-power-gated counterpart at 25°C, 65°C, and 100°C. As the temperature increases, the leakage reduction effect can be improved greatly. When working at 100°C, the leakage power of ICC and DCC can be reduced up to 69% and 64% respectively. The overall leakage reduction of ICC is better than DCC due to their different access patterns. Although the area of DCC is much larger than ICC, the short-time-lasting sleep events degrade the final leakage saving.

However, in 90nm process, the leakage power is still not dominant in the total power consumption. In Geyser-0, the normal core consumes 439 μW leakage

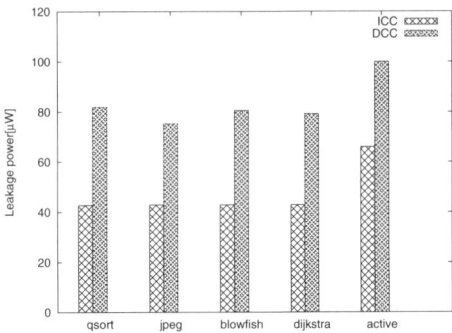

Fig. 9. Leakage comparison @ 65°C

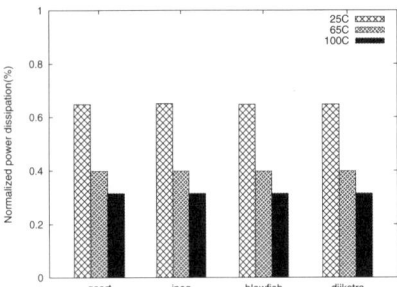

Fig. 10. Normalized power dissipation of ICC

Fig. 11. Normalized power dissipation of DCC

power, while the dynamic power is around 2.8 mW. The proposed design will play a more important role as feature sizes scaled below 45nm. Moreover, the proposed policies can be used to generate the sleep signal to shut down the memory management unit, and with data-retention leakage reduction technique, this signal can also be employed to control the leakage of second level cache. These will belong to the future work.

5.3 Area Overhead

Table.2 shows the area overhead caused by the fine-grained RTPG technique.

Table 2. Area Overhead of PG Domain

PG domain	Non-PG[μm^2]	PG[μm^2]	Overhead[%]
ICache	6773.70	7346.55	8.5
DCache	11768.55	12914.25	9.7

The area overhead of PG domain compared with their non-power-gated counterpart is mainly caused by sleep transistors and isolation cells. As mentioned in Section 3, the incomplete set of PG-cells will result an extra area overhead. In the table, the non-power-gated counterparts are designed with the same limited cell library as PG domain, thus the difference comes from substantial overhead of the fine-grained RTPG, that is, the sleep transistors, and isolation cells. The numbers of inserted sleep transistors are optimized by Cool Power. When the target domain area is larger, more sleep transistors are required for optimization, and vice versa, thus the area overhead ratio for sleep transistors tends to be almost the same. The overhead difference comes from isolation cells. DCC has 14 more bits in terms of output port, so it shares a larger area overhead than ICC.

6 Conclusions

In this paper, we proposed an approach to apply the run-time power gating technique into cache controller design. After partitioning a cache controller into different power domains, leakage saving can be achieved by putting the power gated domain into a low power mode on the fly. We also propose two simple but effective sleeping control policies for both instruction cache controller and data cache controller, based on their accessing pattern. Evaluation results show at 100°C, more than 60% of leakage power can be reduced for both instruction cache controller and data cache controller at a reasonable area penalty.

Acknowledgments

The authors would like to thank VLSI Design and Education Center (VDEC), Synopsys, Cadence, Sequence Design, STARC, and Japan Science and Technology Agency (JST) CREST for their support.

References

1. ITRS: AInt'l Technology Roadmap for Semiconductor (2001),
   http://public.itrs.net
2. Kaxiras, S., Hu, Z., Martonosi, M.: Cache decay: exploiting generational behavior to reduce cache leakage power. In: Proceedings of the 28th annual international symposium on Computer architecture (2001)
3. Kim, N.S., Flautner, K., Blaauw, D., Mudge, T.: Circuit and microarchitectural techniques for reducing cache leakage power. IEEE Transactions on Very Large Scale Integration(VLSI) Systems 12 (2004)
4. Hu, Z., Buyuktosunoglu, A., Srinivasan, V., Zyuban, V., Jacobson, H., Bose, P.: Microarchitectural techniques for power gating of execution units. In: Proceedings of the 2004 international symposium on Low power electronics and design (2004)
5. Seki, N., Lei, Z., Kei, J., Ikebuchi, D., Kojima, Y., Hasegawa, Y., Amano, H., Kashima, T., Takeda, S., Shirai, T., Nakata, M., Usami, K., Sunata, T., Kanai, J., Namiki, M., Kondo, M., Nakamura, H.: A Fine Grain Dynamic Sleep Control Scheme in MIPS R3000. In: Proceedings of IEEE International Conference on Computer Design 2008 (2008)

6. Sweetman, D.: See MIPS Run. Morgan Kaufmann, San Francisco (2006)
7. Usami, K., Shirai, T., Hashida, T., Masuda, H., Takeda, S., Nakata, M., Seki, M., Amano, H., Namiki, M., Imai, M., Kondo, M., Nakamura, H.: Design and Implementation of Fine-grain Power Gating with Ground Bounce Suppression. In: IEEE International Conference on VLSI design 2009 (to appear) (2009)
8. Usami, K., Ohkubo, N.: A Design Approach for Fine-grained Run-Time Power Gating using Locally Extracted Sleep Signals. In: IEEE International Conference on Computer Design 2006 (2006)
9. Hennessy, J.L., Patterson, D.A.: Computer Architecture: A Quantitative Approach, 4th edn. Morgan Kaufmann, San Francisco (2003)
10. Guthaus, M.R., Ringenberg, J.S., Ernst, D., Austin, M.T., Mudge, T., Brown, B.R.: MiBench: A free, commercially representative embedded benchmark suite. In: 2001 IEEE International Workshop on Workload Characterization (2001)

Autonomous DVFS on Supply Islands for Energy-Constrained NoC Communication

Liang Guang[1], Ethiopia Nigussie[1], Lauri Koskinen[2], and Hannu Tenhunen[1]

[1] Department of Information Technology, University of Turku, Turku, Finland
{liagua,ethnig,hatenhu}@utu.fi
[2] Electronic Circuit Design Laboratory, Helsinki University of Technology, Helsinki, Finland
lkoskine@ecdl.tkk.fi

Abstract. An autonomous-DVFS-enabled supply island architecture on network-on-chip platforms is proposed. This architecture exploits the temporal and spatial network traffic variations in minimizing the communication energy while constraining the latency and supply management overhead. Each island is equipped with autonomous DVFS mechanism, which traces the local and nearby network conditions. In quantitative simulations with various types of representative traffic patterns, this approach achieves greater energy efficiency than two other low-energy architectures (typically 10% - 27% lower energy). With autonomous supply management on a proper granularity as demonstrated in this study, the communication energy can be minimized in a scalable manner for many-core NoCs.

1 Introduction

Power consumption has become the most urgent design issue for VLSI system [1,2] under constant technology scaling and higher computing capacity. The manycore system with NoC (Network-on-chip) communication infrastructure has been widely adopted as a promising platform for future multi-billion-transistor chips. Communication power is a major contributor among all consumption sources [3] owing to the switching activities on the link, in the switches, as well as the leakage power in the buffers. For instance, [4] quoted that, for Alpha 21364 processor with distributed memory, the integrated routers and link circuitry consume 23W out of total 125W chip power.

The traffics on NoC channels vary temporally and spatially as a result of manycore parallel processing. For energy constrained network applications [5], a wide range of efforts have been made towards energy minimization under QoS (quality-of-service) requirements, with average packet latency as one of the essential metrics for best-effort service. DVFS (dynamic voltage and frequency scaling), an effective supply minimization techniques, has long been proposed with many implementation variations [6,7,4]. Lowest voltage and frequency are provided to drive the communication so that the performance just meets the requirement. The biggest design issue in realizing any DVFS-enabled system is the overhead for voltage regulators [8,9]. Considering the hardware overhead involved in adaptive supply scaling, voltage islands have been suggested to utilize the traffic spatial variation with minimal implementation penalty [10,11,12,13,14]. The whole system is partitioned into several parts (islands) each with pre-assigned voltage and frequency supplies. However, static supply assignment is not able to accommodate the temporal traffic variations. We observe that the combination of conventional DVFS with supply island partitioning provides the desirable tradeoff between communication energy efficiency and implementation overhead.

This paper presents the design and evaluation of an autonomous-DVFS-enabled supply island architecture on NoC platform. The voltage and frequency of each island are adjusted by the local DVFS monitor based on its *regional network load*, which considers the network condition in the local island and its adjacent neighbors. The supply will be scaled adaptively to keep the network running at a reasonable load, so that the communication energy can be minimized while the average latency of every region is still constrained. The communication is simulated on our transport-level simulator. Communication energy as well as latency and area overhead are analyzed by using widely-acclaimed Orion [15] and Cadence simulators. We compared the energy consumption of the proposed architecture with other energy-efficient architectures: centralized DVFS and conventional voltage-island with pre-determined supply values. From simulations of a wide range of representative synthetic traffic patterns, we observed that autonomous-DVFS-enabled supply island architecture is most capable of reducing the communication energy consumption, especially for traffics with distinctive temporal and spatial variations. With popular performance/energy-aware mapping and configuration techniques [16], applications may very likely have such communication patterns.

2 Related Work

An early work proposing DVFS applied to NoC links is proposed in [4]. It suggests using link and buffer utilization ratio as an effective indicator of network load and accordingly scaling the network supply. As link usage is directly related to buffer utilization, [6] proposed using switch load as the network burden indicator and scaling the supply accordingly. Naturally, the scaling threshold is dependent on switching and routing techniques, which is configured in the design phase before runtime. Dynamic supply scaling considering the scheduling of both processing elements and network communication was suggested by [7]. At the moment, we separate the design of communication structure to address more general traffic patterns. The analysis of autonomous DVFS on supply islands will be applied to the whole system in future work. The overhead of DVFS techniques, especially caused by DC-DC converters has been reported in several previous works [17,8,9].

Considering the overhead of runtime supply management, the concept voltage island architecture has been proposed [10,18], focusing on minimizing power consumption with fixed supply assignment based on application pattern available at design time [12,19].

To enable system-level communication overhead modeling, we used Orion simulator [15] given specific target technology (65nm) for the modeling of routers. In order to get more accurate result, inter-router wires are simulated in Cadence Spectre.

3 DVFS on Supply Island: An Architectural View

The system view of the DVFS-enabled voltage island architecture is illustrated in Fig. 1. Local network conditions in each island are adaptively adjusted by a small DVFS monitor, which collects the network information on separate but narrow links from each of the switches in the island. The island voltage is the output of a voltage regulator (DC-DC converter), and the frequency is determined by one PLL. The configurations of the voltage regulator and PLL are set by the DVFS monitor from a discrete number of voltage and frequency pairs. Between the islands, FIFOs are needed to interface different frequency domains.

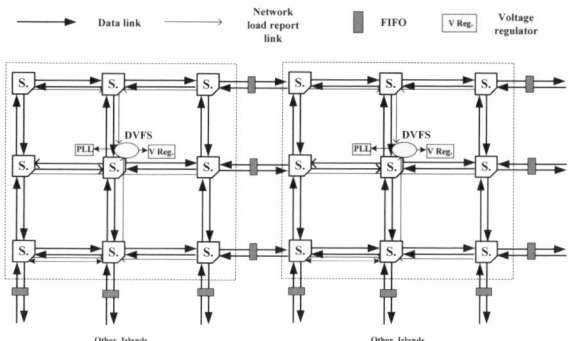

Fig. 1. Illustration of Autonomous DVFS on Supply-islands for NoC

The DVFS-enabled supply island architecture is a scalable design approach, providing an desirable tradeoff between adaptivity and overhead. The conventional voltage scaling is now applied on the granularity of an island, thus alleviating the area and energy overhead. Compared to the chip-wide unified supply scaling (centralized DVFS), it is more capable of exploiting spatial traffic variations. Compared to conventional supply island architectures with pre-assigned voltage/frequency values, it can better exploit the temporal variation of the traffic. This design approach can be applied to in networks with any flow control methods.

Proper supply scaling can be determined in various ways. The most straightforward manner is to trace the run-time packet latency directly. But this manner includes adding a timestamp every hop a packet takes, which lengthens the packet and incurs the arbitration overhead. Another way as in [4] traces both the link utilization and switch buffer utilization ratio and adjusts the frequency while they are heavily burdened or rarely used. [6] suggests the close relationship between switch buffer load and the average latency (Fig. 2), which leads to a simple DVFS algorithm (Algorithm 1). In Algorithm1, the voltage and frequency of each island is adjusted based on its *regional networkload*, which is the average of the local loads and its adjacent neighbors' loads. T_upper and T_lower are the upper and lower network load thresholds for scaling up and down the supplies respectively. The network load is defined as the buffer occupancy ratio in the target region (for the bufferless hot-potato routed networks, we can count the occupancy ratio of input and output registers in the switch). The choice of T_upper and T_lower are network and application dependent.

Algorithm 1. Autonomous DVFS on each supply island based on *regional networkload*

Data: current_voltage, current_frequency, local_load, north_neighbor_load, south_neighbor_load, west_neighbor_load, east_neighbor_load
Result: next_voltage, next_frequency
initialization;
foreach *Island i* **do**
  Regional_networkload = average(local_load, north_neighbor_load, south_neighbor_load, west_neighbor_load, east_neighbor_load) ;
  if *Regional_networkload $\geq T\_upper$* **then**
    next_voltage = Upper(current_voltage);
    next_frequency=Upper(current_frequency);
  else
    if *Regional_networkload $\leq T\_lower$* **then**
      next_frequency=Lower(current_frequency);
      next_voltage = Lower(current_voltage);
    else
      next_frequency= current_frequency;
      next_voltage=current_voltage;
    end
  end
end

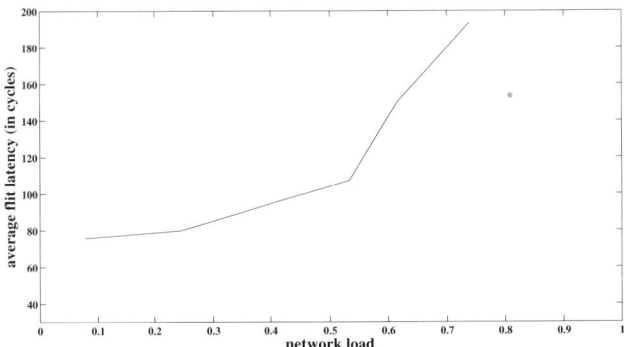

Fig. 2. Dependence of Average Latency on Network Load (on a 15*15 network)

4 Simulation Platform, Energy Modeling and Traffic Patterns

4.1 Network Structure Elaboration

We simulated a 15*15 mesh network in 65nm technology. Without application-specific mapping, the network is separated regularly into 25 islands each with 9 nodes of the mesh. The switches are connected with two uni-directional 64-bit 1mm-long wires. The packet is routed with a minimal-path fully-adaptive deadlock-free routing method in which packets are routed on 4 disjointed virtual networks [20]. We assume simple single-flit store-and-forward switching, and each direction has two-flit(each as 64-bit wide) input buffers for each virtual network. The crossbar uses the pipelined structure with three stages (route, traversal and output [21]). It is important to note that the use of autonomous DVFS-enabled supply island architecture is not limited by such network configuration.

4.2 Energy Modeling

The voltage and frequency scaling are calculated following the alpha-power model (Equ. 1) [22].

$$f \propto K * \frac{(V_{DD} - V_{th})^\alpha}{V_{DD}} \quad (1)$$

f is the switching frequency. K is a fitting parameter. α is the velocity saturation index dependent on the technology. Before transistor-level implementation is available, we assume the base voltage and frequency are (0.6 V, 600MHz) (consistent with [9]). Based on Equ. 1, the following pairs of voltage and frequency are used: (1.3V, 1.2GHz), (0.75V, 0.8G), (0.6V, 0.6G). The switch energy and area overhead are obtained from Orion simulator [15] specifying the switching voltage and frequency, as well as the switch structure. The link energy and overhead are simulated with Cadence as the transistor-level repeater insertion and driver sizing influence the results greatly in sub-100nm technology. The wire parameters used in the simulation are: wire length, 1mm; width, 210nm; spacing, 210nm; repeater interval, 0.25mm; repeater size, 10x[1]; driver size, 12x.

The energy consumed by DVS operation(DC-DC conversion) follows Equ. 2 [23]. C is the decoupling capacitance of the power-supply regulator; μ is the conversion efficiency; V_{dd1} and V_{dd2} are the voltages before and after the switching. C is set as 40nf [9], and the conversion efficiency is set as 80% [2].

$$Energy_{overhead} = C * (1 - \mu) * |V_{dd2}^2 - V_{dd1}^2| \quad (2)$$

---

[1] Relative to a minimal inverter size.
[2] The efficiency is dependent on the output voltage and the regulator's activity factor. 80% is an average figure reported in [9].

4.3 Representative Traffic Patterns

We categorize the experimental traffics based on three features: the injection temporal rate from a single processing element, the injection rate difference between processing elements, and the communication destination pattern.

In terms of injection temporal rates from each processing element, we consider temporally linearly changing and b-model traffics. Temporal linearly changing traffic is a generalized pattern for traffics with modest variations. It assumes a linear change of injection rate from the processing element with time. B-model traffic was originally proposed in [24] and is considered effective in modeling bursty and self-similar traffic [25]. In b-model, a parameter b is used to model the burstiness of the injection. Fig. 3 illustrates a b-model traffic with b as 0.3 and aggregation level 4 (which means the whole period is divided into 16 time periods; details referred to [24]).

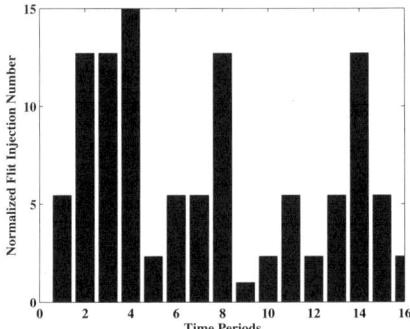

Fig. 3. B-model traffic used in the simulation

Based on the injection intensity pattern of the processing elements, we consider uniform and hotspot injection patterns. Uniform pattern assumes all the processing elements have similar injection rate. Hotspot injection pattern chooses a few processing elements with higher injection rate than others.

In terms of packet destination distribution, we consider locality and hotspot traffic. Locality traffic [25] makes a reasonable assumption that the closer destinations have higher probability: $Prob(d) = \frac{1}{A(D)*2^d}$ (A(D) is normalizing factor that makes sure the probabilities sum up to 1 . $A(D) = \sum_{d=1}^{D}(1/2^d)$. D is the maximum distance in the network). Locality traffic is likely when the resource mapping algorithm assigns commonly-communicating processors as adjacent neighbors. Hotspot traffic [25] models the situation that some nodes are popular communication destinations. The location of hotspots are application specific and may likely be determined at design time.

A type of synthetic traffic is a specific combination of the three features. Table 1 summarizes six types of synthetic traffics used in the simulation[3]. Experimental hotspot regions are illustrated in Fig. 4.

Table 1. Synthetic traffic patterns for simulation

traffic type	temporal feature	injection intensity pattern	destination pattern
1	linear	uniform	hotspot
2	linear	hotspot	locality
3	linear	hotspot	hotspot
4	bmodel	uniform	hotspot
5	bmodel	hotspot	locality
6	bmodel	hotspot	hotspot

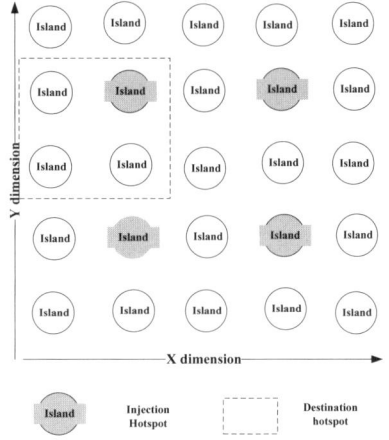

Fig. 4. Experimental Hotspot Regions

For temporally linear changing traffics, the injection rate (of one processing element) of locality traffics increases from 7.68Gbps (120M flit/s) to 15.36Gbps (240M flit/s) in $0.833\mu s$, and the injection rate of other traffics (non-locality traffics can accommodate fewer number of inputs as the average hop count is larger) increases from 4.6Gbps (72M flit/s) to 11.52Gbps (180M flit/s) with the same changing speed. Injection hotspots have constant injection rate, 15.36Gbps for locality traffics and 11.52Gbps for non-locality traffics. For temporally b-model traffics, b is set as 0.3 and the aggregation level is 4. In case of hotspot destination traffics, the percentage of flits addressed to the hotspots is set as 50%.

---

[3] Two other types of synthetic traffics have little spatial variation, which precludes the necessity of voltage-island-based approaches.

5 Energy Minimization and Latency/Area Overhead

We compare the energy efficiency, latency and area overhead of the proposed autonomous DVFS on supply-island architecture with two other energy-efficient architectures: centralized DVFS and conventional supply island architecture with pre-set supply values.

Our architecture follows Algorithm 1. For Centralized DVFS, the supply is scaled based on the networkload of the mostly burdened region where the longest latency may likely to occur. Conventional supply island approach, based on design-time traffic profiling, assigns proper supply values to each island. We emulate the static profiling process by specifying the supply values given the variation details of the traffics. The lower scaling threshold T_lower is set as 0.2 (when the network latency tends to flat off with the decrease of network load as in Fig. 2). The higher scaling threshold T_upper is set as 0.4 (in the middle of the range where the latency steadily increases with higher load as in Fig. 2). The setting of these figures are dependent on the actual communication requirement.

Two small energy contributors are omitted in the simulation at the architectural level. The PLL runs with very small power compared to a NoC system ([26] reports a 65nm CMOS digital PLL runs on 8mW/GHz at 1.2V while a 80-core 65nm NoC [27] consumes 97W at 4.27GHz). The overhead of FIFOs depend on the choice of FIFO sizes. For example, in the 15*15 network with 25 islands, given each uni-directional link between two islands has 2-flit FIFO, the energy consumption of FIFO is less than 4.6% of the energy consumption of the switches [4]. With larger sized islands which may be used for thousand-core NoC systems, the energy share of FIFOs is even lower.

5.1 Energy Minimization

The average per-flit energy consumption of the three architectures is summarized in Table 2. *DVFS Isl.* is short for autonomous-DVFS-enabled supply island architecture. *Cen. DVFS* is short for centralized DVFS. *Isl.* is short for conventional supply island architecture.

We can observe from Table 2 that autonomous-DVFS-enabled supply island architecture is more energy efficient than the two other architectures for all the studied spatially and temporally varying traffics. For traffics with more distinctive variations (Traffic type 2 and 5 which have strong locality features upon temporal variations), the proposed architecture has much better energy efficiency than its counterparts. Understandably the voltage scaling will incur an amount of energy overhead especially for bursty traffics (Type 4-6 with temporally b-model injection rate variation).

---

[4] The number of buffers in FIFOs is only 10.67% of numbers of buffers in switches. And the buffers in switch accounts on average 43.35% of switch energy (based on Orion estimation).

Table 2. Per-flit Energy Consumption of Three Architectures with 6 Traffic Patterns

Traffic Type as in Table 1	Architecture	Communication Energy (pJ)	Scaling Energy (pJ)	Total Average Energy (pJ)	Percentage
1	DVFS Isl.	344.17	13.78	358.95	80.90%
	Cen. DVFS	470.99	0.66	471.65	106.29%
	Isl.	443.72	0	443.72	1
2	DVFS Isl.	267.80	11.77	279.57	78.12%
	Cen. DVFS	340.98	0.73	341.71	95.48%
	Isl.	357.87	0	357.87	1
3	DVFS Isl.	289.72	10.29	300.01	79.36%
	Cen. DVFS	385.50	1.08	386.58	101.98%
	Isl.	378.02	0	378.02	1
4	DVFS Isl.	430.50	20.93	451.43	96.21%
	Cen. DVFS	470.51	0.67	471.18	100.41%
	Isl.	469.23	0	469.23	1
5	DVFS Isl.	280.66	22.57	303.23	73.20%
	Cen. DVFS	354.32	2.50	356.82	86.13%
	Isl.	414.26	0	414.26	1
6	DVFS Isl.	360.72	19.08	379.80	90.18%
	Cen. DVFS	447.75	0.83	448.58	106.52%
	Isl.	421.14	0	421.14	1

5.2 Latency Penalty

To offer a fair latency comparison for island-based approaches, Table 3 summarizes the worst-case latencies of the six traffic patterns with the three architectures. For locality destination traffics, we compared the maximum regional latency (average latency of flits arrived in an island (or region for centralized DVFS with no island partition)). For hotspot destination traffics, we compared the maximum regional latency of the hotspot islands.

We can observe from Table 3 that even the worst-case regional latencies are constrained properly in the proposed architecture. This feature provides

Table 3. Worst-case Latencies (in (ns)) of Experimental Traffics with Different Architectures

Traffic type Indexed as Table 1	Auto. DVFS Supply-island	Centralized DVFS	Conventional Supply-island
1	71.2958	49.6417	37.8708
2	76.0875	66.6333	62.2792
3	57.7208	52.3292	39.9083
4	74.9333	72.1208	54.5625
5	61.1542	55.7042	41.2125
6	80.4250	56.1083	62.6625

predictability to the network distributed configuration and management as the latency will not soar with low-energy gains. Thus it can be applied to a wide range of applications [5].

5.3 Area Overhead Comparison

The area of a switch is estimated by Orion. The wiring area (including drivers, repeaters, wires and receivers) is obtained from Cadence. We assume the network load collecting wires are 4-bit wide (so the resolution is 1/16). The area of one PLL is set as $0.05mm^2$ [26], and the area of one DC-DC converter is set as $0.375mm^2$ (scaled from [17]). Table 4 summarizes the network component areas of the three architectures for a 15*15 network and the percentage of a chip size of present technology($275mm^2$ [27]).

Table 4. Area Overhead Estimation of the three Architectures (in mm^2)

	Switches	Wiring	DC converters and PLLs	Total	Percentage
DVFS-enabled Supply island	12.88	23.35	10.63	46.86	17.04%
centralized DVFS	12.88	23.35	0.38	36.61	13.31%
conventional Supply island	12.88	22.63	0	35.51	12.91%

6 Conclusion and Future Work

This paper presents an autonomous-DVFS-enabled supply-island-based architecture for NoC platforms. This approach fully exploits the temporal and spatial variations for on-chip communication in the minimization of energy consumption while constraining the worst-case latencies properly. With transport-level network simulator and energy inputs from widely-used Orion and Cadence tools, we performed a wide range of simulations on the proposed architecture and two other low-energy architectures. The simulations with six representative synthetic traffic patterns demonstrate the greater energy efficiency of the presented architecture (typically 10%-27% lower energy), at a reasonable latency and area overhead.

The proposed low-energy architecture can be widely used for many applications running on many-core NoC systems when low energy comes at a high priority. This work demonstrates the potential of adaptive power management with a granularity tradeoff, which is a scalable solution with the increase of network sizes. Low-level implementation will be addressed in future work, for instance the analysis on the energy saving potential of clock-tree with the proposed architecture.

---

[5] Some ultra-low-energy approaches have significant latency influence such as sub-threshold logic [28], thus may not be suitable for many common application scenarios.

References

1. Asanovic, K., Bodik, R., Catanzaro, B.C., Gebis, J.J., Husbands, P., Keutzer, K., Patterson, D.A., Plishker, W.L., Shalf, J., Williams, S.W., Yelick, K.A.: The landscape of parallel computing research: A view from berkeley. Technical Report UCB/EECS-2006-183, EECS, Uni. of California, Berkeley (December 2006)
2. Rabaey, J.M.: Scaling the power wall: Revisiting the low-power design rules. In: Keynote speech at SoC 2007 Symposium, Tampere (November 2007)
3. Dally, W.: Computer architecture is all about interconnect. In: HPCA (International Symposium on High Performance Computer Architecture) Panel (February 2002)
4. Shang, L., Peh, L.S., Jha, N.: Dynamic voltage scaling with links for power optimization of interconnection networks. In: Proc. Ninth International Symposium on High-Performance Computer Architecture HPCA-9 2003, pp. 91–102 (2003)
5. Yuan Tian, E., Ekici, F.O.: Energy-constrained task mapping and scheduling in wireless sensor networks. In: IEEE International Conference on Mobile Adhoc and Sensor Systems Conference, p. 218 (2005)
6. Liang, G., Jantsch, A.: Adaptive power management for the on-chip communication network. In: Proc. 9th EUROMICRO Conference on Digital System Design: Architectures, Methods and Tools DSD 2006, pp. 649–656 (2006)
7. Luo, J., Jha, N.K., Peh, L.S.: Simultaneous dynamic voltage scaling of processors and communication links in real-time distributed embedded systems. IEEE transactions on VLSI systems 15(4), 427–437 (2007)
8. Hazucha, P., Schrom, G., Hahn, J., Bloechel, B., Hack, P., Dermer, G., Narendra, S., Gardner, D., Karnik, T., De, V., Borkar, S.: A 233-mhz 80%-87% efficient four-phase dc-dc converter utilizing air-core inductors on package. IEEE Journal of Solid-State Circuits 40(4), 838–845 (2005)
9. Kim, W., Gupta, M.S., Wei, G.Y., Brooks, D.: System level analysis of fast, per-core dvfs using on-chip switching regulators. In: International symposium on high-performance computer architecture (February 2008)
10. Leung, L.F., Tsui, C.Y.: Energy-aware synthesis of networks-on-chip implemented with voltage islands. In: Proc. 44th ACM/IEEE Design Automation Conference DAC 2007, pp. 128–131 (2007)
11. Hu, J., Shin, Y., Dhanwada, N., Marculescu, R.: Architecting voltage islands in core-based system-on-a-chip designs. In: ISLPED 2004: Proceedings of the 2004 international symposium on Low power electronics and design, pp. 180–185. ACM, New York (2004)
12. Wu, H., Liu, I.M., Wong, M., Wang, Y.: Post-placement voltage island generation under performance requirement. In: Proc. ICCAD 2005, IEEE/ACM International Conference on Computer-Aided Design, pp. 309–316 (2005)
13. Ogras, U., Marculescu, R., Choudhary, P., Marculescu, D.: Voltage-frequency island partitioning for gals-based networks-on-chip. In: Proc. 44th ACM/IEEE Design Automation Conference DAC 2007, pp. 110–115 (2007)
14. Lackey, D., Zuchowski, P., Bednar, T., Stout, D., Gould, S., Cohn, J.: Managing power and performance for system-on-chip designs using voltage islands. In: Proc. IEEE/ACM International Conference on Computer Aided Design ICCAD 2002, pp. 195–202 (2002)
15. Wang, H.S., Zhu, X., Peh, L.S., Malik, S.: Orion: a power-performance simulator for interconnection networks. In: Proc. 35th Annual IEEE/ACM International Symposium on (MICRO-35) Microarchitecture, pp. 294–305 (2002)

16. Hu, J., Marculescu, R.: Energy and performance-aware mapping for regular noc architectures. IEEE Transactions on COMPUTER-AIDED DESIGN of Integrated Circuits and Systems 24(4), 551–562 (2005)
17. Wibben, J., Harjani, R.: A high efficiency dc-dc converter using 2nh on-chip inductors. In: Proc. IEEE Symposium on VLSI Circuits, pp. 22–23 (2007)
18. Ogras, U.Y., Marculescu, R., Choudhary, P., Marculescu, D.: Voltage-frequency island partitioning for gals-based networks-on-chip. In: DAC 2007: Proceedings of the 44th annual conference on Design automation, pp. 110–115. ACM, New York (2007)
19. Sengupta, D., Saleh, R.: Application-driven floorplan-aware voltage island design. In: Proc. 45th ACM/IEEE Design Automation Conference DAC 2008, pp. 155–160 (2008)
20. Jesshope, C., Miller, P., Yantchev, J.: High performance communications in processor networks. In: Proc. 16th Annual International Symposium on Computer Architecture, 28 May – 1 June, 1989, pp. 150–157 (1989)
21. Wang, H.: A detailed architectural-level power model for router buffers, crossbars and arbiters. Technical report, Department of Electrical Engineering, Princeton University (2004)
22. Sakurai, T., Newton, A.: Alpha-power law mosfet model and its applications to cmos inverter delay and other formulas. IEEE Journal of solid-state circuits 25(2), 584–594 (1990)
23. Stratakos, A.J.: High-efficiency low-voltage DC-DC conversion for portable applications. PhD thesis, University of California, Berkeley (1998)
24. Wang, M., Madhyastha, T., Chan, N.H., Papadimitriou, S., Faloutsos, C.: Data mining meets performance evaluation: fast algorithms for modeling bursty traffic. In: Proc. 18th International Conference on Data Engineering, pp. 507–516 (2002)
25. Lu, Z., Jantsch, A., Salminen, E., Grecu, C.: Network-on-chip benchmarking specification part 2: Microbenchmark specification version 1.0. Technical report, OCP International Partnership Association, Inc. (May 2008)
26. Tierno, J., Rylyakov, A., Friedman, D.: A wide power supply range, wide tuning range, all static cmos all digital pll in 65 nm soi. IEEE Journal of Solid-State Circuits 43(1), 42–51 (2008)
27. Vangal, S., Howard, J., Ruhl, G., Dighe, S., Wilson, H., Tschanz, J., Finan, D., Singh, A., Jacob, T., Jain, S., Erraguntla, V., Roberts, C., Hoskote, Y., Borkar, N., Borkar, S.: An 80-tile sub-100-w teraflops processor in 65-nm cmos. IEEE Journal of Solid-State Circuits 43(1), 29–41 (2008)
28. Wang, A., Chandrakasan, A.: A 180mv fft processor using subthreshold circuit techniques. In: Proc. Digest of Technical Papers Solid-State Circuits Conference ISSCC, IEEE International, vol. 1, pp. 292–529 (2004)

Energy Management System as an Embedded Service: Saving Energy Consumption of ICT

Francisco Maciá-Pérez, Diego Marcos-Jorquera, and Virgilio Gilart-Iglesias

Computer Science Department, University of Alicante
Carretera San Vicente s/n, Alicante, Spain
{pmacia,dmarcos,vgilart}@dtic.ua.es

Abstract. In this paper we present a service approach based on the use of embedded network devices for the energy management of Information and Communication Technology (ICT) infrastructures. The service is completely compatible with other strategies in order to achieve an efficient management for saving energy. These devices are very small, with low consumption and specially designed to operate with minimum maintenance, and also they are presented under Services Oriented Architecture open standards, more specifically, as Web Services. In addition, these embedded services can work individually or in collaboration with other ICT enterprise services, either through conventional systems or by means of other embedded devices. To validate the proposal we have implemented a prototype and we have designed a test scenario based in the ICT replicated infrastructure in order to support web applications of the Polytechnic University College at the University of Alicante.

Keywords: Saving energy, embedded devices, SOA, network management.

1 Introduction

The importance of Information and Communication Technologies (ICT) in all areas of human activity in today's world is an indisputable fact. In the last years, there has been an exponential increase of the use of these technologies within the society, from its professional use in enterprises and organizations to its personal use in playful and everyday activities at home. In addition, the new ICT paradigms evolution together with the growing use of Internet have caused the apparition of new business models that require complex systems in order to support them, available 24 hours per day 7 days per week, with better quality of service, etc.

However, this growing use of ICT technologies together with the requirements of emerging business models is converting these technologies in one of the main responsible of the worldwide energy consumption increase. In this way, [1] determines that the emission rate of CO_2 originated from the ICT consumption is the 2% and predict that this energy consumption will grow in an exponential way in the next years if solutions are not adopted.

In fact, one part of this consumption is due to an inefficient use of the ICT technologies. According to the study described in [2], a great number of the ICT managers know the necessary measures that they have to realize in order to obtain a energy saving produced by the use of ICT in their organizations, however, usually this measures are not applied if they do not mean an economic benefit for the business. One of the main reasons of the inadequate energy consumption of ICT listed in the study is the lack of awareness of the users in relation to this energetic problem that involve an incorrect use of the ICT infrastructures. Some examples of this uses are to leave power on Personal Computers (PC's), printers, servers or network devices when is not necessary.

There is the paradox that one of the solutions with more repercussion nowadays in order to optimize the energy consumption of the ICT is the use of the same ICT. This approach is one of the main proposals of the European Union [3] that pretend to promote an efficient use of the energy consumption through the use of the Information and Communications Technologies.

In consonance with this approach, our proposal consists of providing embedded IT management services in physical network devices (generally, small sized devices with simple services and low energy consumption), so that, in order to deploy those services, it is enough to select the specific device providing the service, and connecting it to the communications network. The device itself will obtain the minimum information required to activate the initial set up and, once this has been completed, execute the management tasks with minimal human intervention.

Obviously, from a functional point of view the services offered by these devices are totally compatible with the traditional network services and therefore their integration and interoperability are ensured.

By way of illustration and with the aim of arguing the motivating of the proposal, we suggest a specific management service that we named Energy Management System (EMS): a service for the ICT systems monitoring and consumption control of these same systems doing that the ICT resources will be available only when they are necessaries (in a proactive or scheduled way). Thus it will be possible to avoid processing and consumption during the downtimes. The goal of this service is to reduce and to optimize the energy consumption of the ICT infrastructures.

The basic function of the service will be to indicate to the embedded EMS device (eEMS) which equipment and which service or services of those equipments we wish to check in order to reduce the energy consumption. These actions will be done according to system global load or of the requirements defined by the user or system administrator.

In the following sections we provide a review of the current state of the art of the technologies involved; a description of the EMS service, hardware and software structure of the device in which it is embedded; the specification of the application protocol and its implementation as Web Service embedded in a specific network device and the test scenario in order to validate the proposal; and, finally, the conclusions on the research and the current lines of work.

2 Background

The majority of the proposals in order to reduce the ICT energetic consumption are focused on getting better design of the devices architectures. In [4] different design techniques of ICT devices architectures are described with the aim of reducing the energetic consumption of these devices. In this way the Green Grid [5] is focused on the best practices and management approaches for lowering data centers energy consumption. The Department of Energy of USA released the Server Energy Measurement Protocol [6] that establishes a procedure for attaching an energy usage measurement to existing performance measurements for servers.

Another approach [7] very used nowadays to reduce the ICT energetic consumption is the virtualization. This proposal is originated from the hypothesis that the majority of the servers in the data centers are working to the 20% of its capability. The use of virtualization systems such as VMWare enables to execute virtual machines inside an only server, making good use of its processing capability.

However, in complex ICT environments with high availability requirements (replication, load balancing and clusterization), the proposals described previously are not enough to reduce the energetic consumption because the system management is not contemplated in a global way.

The use of embedded devices in order to provide services in a distributed environment is other of the solutions that allow decreasing the ICT infrastructures energetic consumption. In this sense, many of these devices include the Power over Ethernet (PoE) technology. This technology allows providing energy to the devices through of Ethernet wire [8].

On the other hand, there are many proposals in order to monitor and control the energy consumption trough of ICT tools and applications. In [9] several of these tools are described. These tools use emergent technologies such as Internet and distributed systems to control and to supervise energy consumption. This kind of tools is oriented to inspect the general energetic consumption in the buildings, and although they could be used to control the ICT specific consumption, these tools and applications do not include features of proactive management, autonomy and inattention to optimize the consumption. In these cases, the person that manage the application is who once analyzed the information obtained has to take the decision and to execute it himself in order to optimize the consumption. In addition, these tools have to be executed in PC's, servers or more complex systems, and therefore, add an increase of the energetic consumption.

The use of network management systems can help to automate the maintenance activities, allowing an efficient use of the network resources, and to be used to reduce the energy consumption. The first open standards which attempted to address problems of ICT management in a global manner were SNMP and CMIP [10], proposed by the IETF (Internet Engineering Task Force); both protocols being principally oriented towards network monitoring and control. The main inconvenience of these administration models was their dependence on the platform.

The use of multi-agent systems for computer network management provides a series of characteristics which favour automation and self reliance in maintenance processes [11] [12]. The creation of projects such as AgentLink III, the first Coordinated Action on based on Agents financed by the 6th European Commission Framework Programme, is a clear indicator of the considerable degree of interest in research into software agents.

In areas where automated handling of information and those where several devices are involved, such as industrial processes or domotics, there has been a trend in the development of autonomous management towards architectures designed for services for embedded systems [13] [14]. This final framework includes monitoring systems developed by third parties but residing with the client, who is responsible for their control and management. Along these lines we find proposals such as NAGIOS [15], MON [16], MUNIN/MONIT [17, 18] or nPULSE [19] generic monitoring systems for network services for linux, with Web interface, highly configurable and based on open code which monitors the availability of network services and applications. The disadvantage of these proposals is based on the complexity of their installation and configuration in environments without qualified system administrators, in addition to the complex systems and infrastructures required for their implementation.

The approach described in this research work is presented as a solution that bring together the advantages of the current network management systems oriented to the control of ICT energetic consumption together with the use of embedded devices that minimize the consumption of these management systems.

3 Energy Management Service

The main goal of the EMS is to manage the power on or power off of a set of elements in a communications network in terms of a planning or in a proactive manner, analyzing the status of the system that is managed.

The eEMS is the version of the management service that has been implemented in Web Service, and it has been embedded in a network device (known as eEMS Device) designed for this purpose (see fig. 1). This device is small in size, with low consumption, robust, transparent to existing ICT infrastructures and with minimum maintenance required from the system administrators.

The system administrator informs the eEMS device, by means of its *interface agents*, which of the network components require a power management. The eEMS device has sufficient knowledge of each device to carry out this task. This knowledge is included in *management agents* displaced to the device for this purpose. The *management agents* implement specific protocols for power on devices, as the Wake on LAN (WoL) standard, or for power off, as the shutdown in SNMP. In some cases, to take the decision to power off or power on a device, they utilize a set of *monitoring agents* that analyze applications, services or network traffic. In this way, if the device receives a request for manage a set of devices, it will request the adequate *monitoring agents* and *management agents* in a self sufficient manner in order to carry out this work. The *management and monitoring agents* are enough flexible to adapt to the possible different scenarios.

Thus, the eEMS device represents the core of the system. Figure 1 shows a diagram of the main elements and actors involved in the service, together with the existing relation between them. We may synthesise these as: eEMS Device, Network Components, Discovery Service, EMS Center, EMS Clients, a set of Software Agents and the EMS application protocol (EMSP). These elements shall subsequently be described in greater detail.

The **eEMS device**, as has been seen, is the cornerstone of the energy management service. It is designed in order to act as a proxy between the Wide Area Network (WAN) and Local Area Network (LAN) to which it provides support. This device provides a container in which different agents and applications ensure that the service can be executed.

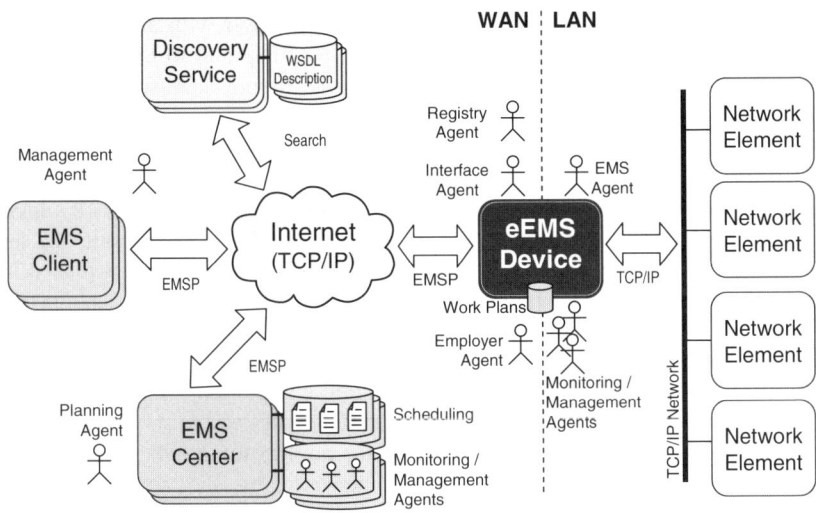

Fig. 1. Organization of functional elements of the EMS service

In the proposal implementation, the device interface with the system administrators and with other management devices or management equipments is provided by agents acting as embedded Web Services (see *interface agent* in figure 1). From a functional point of view, this is the reason why an eEMS device can be to taken into account, simply, as if it were a Web Service. In this way, an eEMS device is responsible for collecting the management request from the WAN. These requests are based on EMSP protocol and encapsulated in SOAP (Simple Object Access Protocol) messages when they are sent to the Web Service Interface.

The **Network Components** are the goal of the network monitoring service and comprise all those devices connected to the TCP/IP network. This include PC's, servers, printers, routers and, in general, any device susceptive to power on or power off in a remote manner.

The **Discovery Service** comprises a standard Universal Description, Discovery and Integration (UDDI) registration service. It is responsible for maintaining the pages describing the EMS services in Web Service Description Language (WSDL) format, as well as facilitating that information to the clients wishing to access the service.

EMS Centers usually act as automated control panels for the eEMS devices distributed through Internet. This control is implemented through the *planning agents* who carry out, execute and verify all the previously established tasks on the eEMS devices. EMS Centres are also responsible for managing the repository of *monitoring and management agents* with the know-how of each device management. Although in large installations it is recommended that management and scheduling services are included, the existence of an EMS centre is not essential. Likewise, although each EMS centre can manage around a thousand eEMS devices, it is possible to use the number of EMS centers considered appropriate, and it is possible to create one hierarchy with these elements.

EMS Clients, through the *EMS agents*, provide the user with access to the EMS Centre (in order to manage work plans or query log files) and to the eEMS Devices (in order to manage particular devices). These clients are not necessary for the normal operating system; however, they avoid physical movements of the system administration staff.

Software agents. System functionality has been defined as a distributed application based on software agents, because this approach intrinsically includes aspects such as: communications, synchronization, updates, etc. Among the agents that have been defined in the system, the most important are the agents placed in the eEMS device, and as a result, they comprise the system core. Of these last agents, the *interface agents* are of prime importance as they allow the device to provide its functionality to external elements (see section).

The **EMS protocol (EMSP)** is a request-response application level protocol using SOAP messages. This protocol is used by the different system components in order to communicate between each other. In fact, as the application has been designed as a set of software agents, the protocol will be used by the software agents to communicate with each other (see section 5).

4 Software Agents

The software agents do not constitute a conventional multi-agent system because a generic context has not been defined for them, they do not use standard agent communication languages and they do not work collaborating to achieve a general target which is used by the agents to take its decisions. In fact, the set of software agents implement part of the functionality of a distributed application which has been designed to provide a network service; in this case, the monitoring service. The reason why agent approach is used lies in its simplicity to design distributed applications and to take into account aspects such as communication, mobility or software updates.

Each eEMS device comprises a set of agents that implement its interface with the system administrators or with others system elements (EMS clients or EMS centers). In order to guarantee the system's compatibility with a large range of technologies, several interface agents have been implemented. In this way, the *interface agent* provides a matching interface with Web Services-based applications. The *interface agent* can identify commands based on *EMSP protocol* and, from these commands, schedule the eEMS device work plan. *EMS agents*, *management agents* and *monitoring agents* are another type of agent placed in the eEMS device and designed to perform the energy management service. The first type of agents ensures execution of the scheduling, delegating the specific monitoring task to a *monitoring agent* and the specific management task to a *management agent*. In addition to these core agents, other agents are included in each eEMS device in order to perform auxiliary tasks. Thus, the *register agents* undertake to check the monitoring service in a Discovery Service; and the *employer agents* are responsible for locating the *management agents* or *monitoring agents* required by the eEMS device to carry out its task. These agents are mobile agents that, initially, can reside in an agent farm located in an EMS Centre.

Table 1. Main instructions of the EMS protocol

CMD	ACTION	ARG	FUNCTION
SET	MODE		Reports the current operation mode.
		PASSIVE [port]	Sets the passive mode and, optionally, the listening port number.
		ACTIVE <ip> [:port]	Sets the active mode, specifying the NSM center's IP address and port number
	RUN		Reports the current NSM service state.
		<STARTS	STOP>	Starts or stops the NSM service.
GET	SCHDL		Returns the list of scheduled tasks in the device.
	STATUS	[<host>[:port] [<service>]]	Returns the status of a specific service or a set of services.
PUT	SCHDL	<schdl-table>	Adds a task or a set of tasks to the scheduling.
MANAGEMENT	ON	<monitor _agent> <management_agent>	Establishes a management rule for the system, establishing the monitor agent and the management agent that will be utilized.
	OFF	<monitor _agent> <management_agent>	Cancel a management rule.
ALERT			Send an alert

Besides the agents located in each eEMS device, the distributed application is completed by other auxiliary agents located outside the device which, while not being crucial to the service, serve to make it more functional. As a result, the *client agents* reside in an EMS Client and are responsible for providing an appropriate interface for the administrators so that they can access the EMS Centre or an eEMS Device from any node connected to Internet. The *planning agents* reside in the EMS Centers and undertake the planning management of eEMS Devices.

5 EMS Protocol

The system agents, implemented in our prototype, communicate with each other by means of messages containing instructions capable of interpreting and executing. These instructions, together with their syntax and its pertinent response, come defined by the EMS Protocol or EMSP. When the agents specifically behave as Web Services, these commands will be incrusted inside the request and response SOAP messages. Web Services has been selected like communication protocol because it is an interoperable specification and that it permits to decouple totally the distinct actors of the system.

The EMS Protocol (EMSP) is a request-response application level protocol which gathers all monitoring service functionality through a set of instructions. The protocol has been defined as a request-response text-based application protocol. This enables it be easily adapted to different models, such as client-server (over basic protocols like HTTP, SMTP or telnet) and SOA (over protocols like SOAP).

The sequence diagram in figure 2 shows the basic service operation and the communication between the system software agents. The diagram comprises two blocks and is executed constantly in parallel mode. In the first block the device *interface agents* are on standby for requests (from a *Planning Agent* or directly from a *Client Agent*). When the interface agents receive a monitoring request, they add the task to the Work Plan database of the eEMS device. The second diagram block corresponds to the execution of the programmed tasks. In this case the *EMS Agent* is constantly checking the Work Plan database and selecting the suitable *Monitoring Agent* and the *Management Agent* to carry out the requested tasks.

Although it is not shown in this diagram, there is also a third block which concerns the contracting of the *Monitoring Agents*. When there is not a *Monitoring or Management Agent* able to deal with the service requested, the *EMS Agent* and the

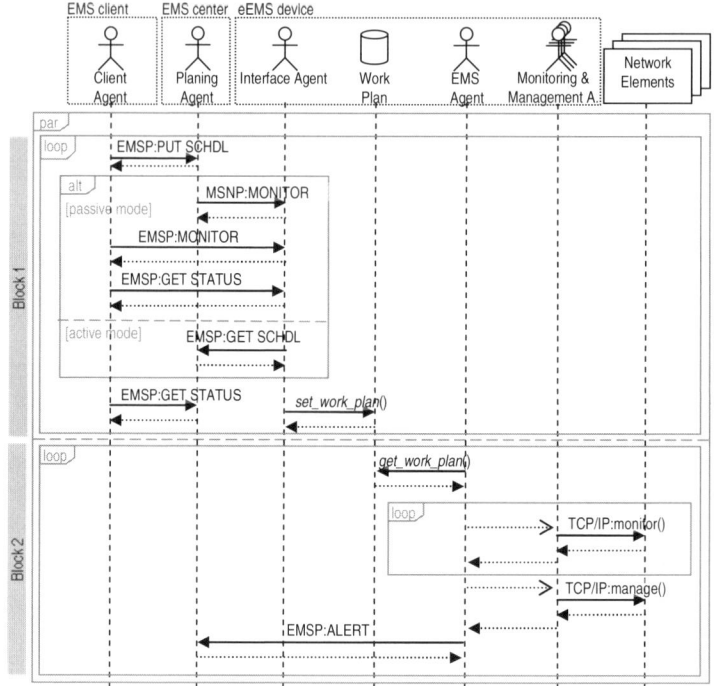

Fig. 2. Sequence diagram of the EMS main functionality

Interface Agents who have detected this lack may make a request to the *Employer Agent* programming it into its Work Plan. The *Employer Agent* then undertakes to obtain the *Monitoring Agents* required by the device. This agent is responsible for negotiating and validating the whole process. The *Monitoring & Management Agents* are mobile agents located in the agent repository in the EMS Centers.

6 eEMS Device Implementation and Test Scenario

In this section the implementation of an eEMS prototype device is presented (fig. 3). The hardware platform chosen for the prototype development is a *Lantronix Xport® AR™* device which has a 16 bit *DSTni-EX™* processor with 120MHz frequency reaching 30MIPS respectively (figure 4 shows an image of an eEMS device prototype connected to the service network). The various memory modulates provided by this device undertake specific tasks according to their intrinsic features: the execution programmes and the dates handled by the device SRAM memory reside in the (1,25MB); the ROM memory (16KB) holds the system start up application and, finally, the flash memory, with 4MB, stores information which though non-volatile, is susceptible to change, such as the set up of the eEMS device or the system applications which may be updated. These capacities are sufficient for the memory requirements of the software developed for implementing the protocol.

Among other I/O interfaces, the device has a Fast Ethernet network interface which allows suitable external communications ratios. In addition, in order to ensure the correct system operation, there are several auxiliary elements such as: a watchdog which monitors the CPU and prevents it from blocking; and a PLL frequency divider required to set up the frequency of the system clock, with an adjustable clock signal (CLK) to optimise consumption or performance according to needs.

As a real time operating system, the device incorporates version 3 of the *Lantronix* OS, *Evolution OS*™. Through a confidentiality agreement with *Lantronix*, we have had access to the different modules of the system. Given the space restrictions, this has been crucial to develop a made-to-measure version of this OS. Salient elements of this version include, a TCP/IP stack together with several client-server application protocols (HTTP, TFTP, SNMP and telnet).

In the service layer, the implementation process has been conditioned by the limited characteristics of *XPort* device. Three service blocks are implemented: the middleware that provides the communication mechanisms of the monitoring service, the EMS service kernel with the implementation of EMS instructions, and the middleware platform that provides the execution of software agents.

The communication service middleware is upheld by standard protocols and technologies included in the *Evolution OS*. In the SOA based EMSP implementation (i.e., the Web Service interface), the cSOAP library was used for development, which is appropriate for these devices [20]. However, some changes have been made to the original cSOAP library due to device limitations (restriction of memory use, proprietary libraries, etc.). These limitations have forced us to replace cSOAP XML parser, LibXML2 (over 1 MB in size), by another adapted XML parser with limited but sufficient functionalities to achieve our objective. Due to cSOAP limitations, only *RPC style* which uses the same protocol analyser used in the Client-Server version has been developed.

In addition, in order to register and to publish the services, an UDDI embedded version has been implemented based on UDDI version 2.0 which simply permits publishing the WSDL document associated with the monitoring service.

The EMS service kernel has been implemented as a functions library written in C language and offered as API for the others eEMS device modules. By means of this library, the intrinsic functionalities of the monitoring service are achieved.

In order to implement service agents, a division has been made in the implementation process between static and mobile agents. In the first case, an ad-hoc implementation for the *XPort* device has been developed in C language, using an operative system such as the agents' container. In the second case, in order to establish an execution framework for the mobile agents (the *monitoring agents*), a Python embedded engine (*ePython* version 2.5) has been adapted to the *XPort* features. These *monitoring agents* are implemented as *Python* text scripts.

In order to validate the proposal described in this research work the system and ICT infrastructures that support the Web applications of the Polytechnic University College at the University of Alicante have been chosen like test scenario. It is a replicated scenario that includes features of high availability and fault tolerance.

The Web applications provide different services for the students (9044), for the professors (609), for the administration and services staff and for the external users. These applications are available during 24 hours per day and 7 days per week

Fig. 3. eEMS device prototype architecture (left) and picture (right)

(inscription system, Web storage system, Web email system, management system, virtual classroom system, general information and others Web applications).

In the table 2 the system components are enumerated, describing the main services included and the infrastructures that support it.

Table 2. The Polytechnic University College at the University of Alicante test scenario components

Service Type	Machines	Energy Consumption
Apache Web Server 2	3 Asus RS120-E4/PA2	97,52W x 3 = 292,56W
Apache Tomcat Application Server 6	3 Asus RS120-E4/PA2	97,52W x 3 = 292,56W
MySQL Database	2 Asus RS120-E4/PA2	97,52W x 2 = 195,04W
OpenLDAP service directory	2 Asus RS120-E4/PA2	97,52W x 2 = 195,04W

In figure 4 is showed the chart that include the accesses average of all users to the applications of the Polytechnic University College and the amount of Web traffic transferred in one day. Based on the information displayed in the chart the consumption optimization strategy of the resources has been defined.

In the eEMS device a scheduling has been established that define the time intervals in which all servers have to be power on. This scheduling has been realized according to the information obtained of the users' accesses to the different applications. In the critical periods the scheduling will obligate to maintain the systems at full performance. Out of the defined periods, the eEMS, in an automatic way, will be responsible of analyzing the information traffic, the request number and accesses to the different applications. In function of the analysis, the eEMS will send the adequate commands sequence in order to power on or power off different system nodes, that is, the system capacity level will be maintained in a dynamic way based on the petition.

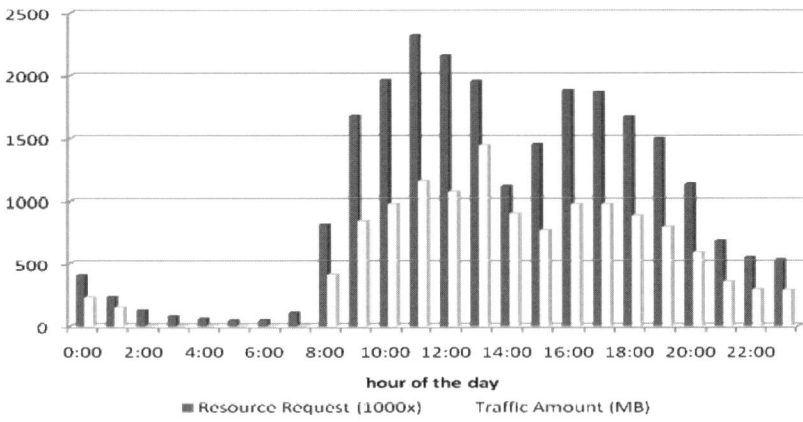

Fig. 4. Average of user requests and amount traffic per day

This strategy allows to use the system in a more efficient way obtaining energy consumption saving. During one week several tests have been realized using the management service and as a result a 13,7% reduction of the energy consumption has been observed in relation to the system without the eEMS device. The energetic saving has not been better because in this scenario there was one requirement of faults tolerance that obligate to have, minim, two servers to support each service. Obviously, if the system is more complex and there are more replicated nodes for each service the energetic saving will be greater.

Because the embedded device chosen include the PoE technology, when the eEMS is included in the system its consumption is practically negligible. If the network infrastructures where the eEMS is connected do not support PoE technology, the consumption of XPort-AR where the service EMS is included would be only 0,957W.

7 Conclusions

In this paper we have presented an energy management system for the ICT infrastructures designed to saving the energy consumption. This system is totally complementary with others approaches oriented to the energy saving and is enough flexible to adapt to different scenarios. One of the most relevant aspects of this system consists of providing these embedded management services in network devices with small size, simple, low power consumption, adjusted costs, autonomous, designed with safety criteria and robustness, and compatible with the traditional network services through the standard protocols such as: SOAP, SMTP or HTTP. In order to validate the proposal, a functional prototype has been designed and implemented. The prototype has been used in a real scenario where we have obtained satisfied results.

We are currently working with other embedded network services and integrating them all in a model based on Semantic Web Services, so that in future they will not only be compatible with existing services, but also with new services or setups which were not considered in the initial design.

Acknowledgments. This work was supported by the Spanish Ministry of Education and Science with Grant TIN2006-04081.

References

1. Gartner press release: Gartner Estimates ICT Industry Accounts for 2 Percent of Global CO2 Emissions. Gartner Symposium/ITxpo 2007 Emerging Trends, April 26 (2007), http://www.gartner.com/it/page.jsp?id=503867
2. Mines, C., Ferrusi, C., Brown, E., Lee, C., Van-Metre, E.: The dawn of green IT services. A market overview of sustainability consulting for IT organizations. Forrester Research Report (2008)
3. Commission European Report: Addressing the challenge of energy efficiency through Information and Communication Technologies, COM (2008) 241 final, http://ec.europa.eu
4. Moshnyaga, G.V., Tamaru, K.: Energy Saving Techniques for Architecture Design of Portable Embedded Devices. In: 10th annual IEEE International ASIC Conference and Exhibit, New York (1997)
5. The Green Grid, http://www.thegreengrid.org/
6. Energy Star, http://www.energystar.gov/
7. Lawton, G.: Powering Down the Computing Infrastructure. Computer 40(2), 16–19 (2007)
8. Deuty, S.: Exploring the options for distributed and point of load power in telecomm and network applications. In: 26th Annual International Telecommunications Energy Conference, INTELEC, pp. 223–229 (2004)
9. Pietilainen, J.: Improved Building Energy Consumption with the Help of Modern ICT. In: ICEBO, International Conference for Enhanced Building operations, October 13-15, Berkeley, California (2003)
10. RFC Project, http://www.rfc.net
11. Du, T.C., Li, E.Y., Chang, A.P.: Mobile Agents in Distributed Network Management. Communications at the ACM 46(7), 127–132 (2003)
12. Guo, J., Liao, Y.: B. Parviz.: An Agent-Based Network management system. 2005 Internet and Multimedia Applications (2005)
13. Topp, U., Müller, P.O., Konnertz, J., Pick, A.: Web based service for embedded devices. In: Chaudhri, A.B., Jeckle, M., Rahm, E., Unland, R. (eds.) NODe-WS 2002. LNCS, vol. 2593, pp. 141–153. Springer, Heidelberg (2003)
14. Jammes, F., Smit, H., Martinez-Lastra, J.L., Delamer, I.M.: Orchestration of Service-Oriented Manufacturing Processes. In: Proc. of the 10th IEEE International Conference on Emerging Technologies and Factory Automation, ETFA 2005, Catania, Italy, September 19-22 (2005)
15. NAGIOS, http://nagios.org
16. MON, http://www.kernel.org/software/mon/
17. MUNIN, http://munin.projects.linpro.no/
18. MONIT, http://www.tildeslash.com/monit/
19. nPULSE, http://www.horsburgh.com/h_npulse.html
20. cSOAP, http://csoap.sourceforge.net/

A Garbage Collection Technique for Embedded Multithreaded Multicore Processors

Sascha Uhrig and Theo Ungerer

Institute of Computer Science
University of Augsburg
86159 Augsburg
Germany
{uhrig,ungerer}@informatik.uni-augsburg.de

Abstract. Multicore processors get more and more popular, even in embedded systems. Due to the deeply integrated threading concept, Java is a perfect choice to deal with the necessary thread-level parallelism required for the performance potential of a multicore. Accordingly, the software developers are familiar with the threading concept, which means that single core applications already fit very well on a multicore processor and are able to utilize its advantage. Nevertheless, a drawback of Java has to be mentioned: the required garbage collection. Especially in multicore environments the most often used stop-the-world collectors reach their limits because all cores have to be suspended at the time a single thread requires a garbage collection cycle. Hence, the performance of the other cores is harmed tremendously. In this paper we present a garbage collection technique that runs in parallel to the application threads within a multithreaded multicore without any stop-the-world behavior.

1 Introduction

The benefits of Java in desktop applications are well-known, e.g. platform independence, type safety, a high number of established libraries, many highly educated software developers, and of course the garbage collection. Moreover, due to these advantages, Java also entered the market of embedded systems several years ago. A considerable amount of Java runtime environments for embedded systems are available.

Another trend in computer design is the enhancement of single core processors to multicores. Besides the improvement of the performance, multicores promise a reduced energy consumption compared to similar processors clocked with higher frequencies. Hence, multicores are well suited for embedded systems, especially battery powered devices.

Combining both approaches, i.e. Java applications executed on a multicore processor, is an obvious advancement but it also raises a new problem, the garbage collection (gc). In single core applications, the gc is active on demand if memory runs short or at the time no Java thread has to be executed. Hence, it is guaranteed that the gc has access to the runtime stacks of the Java threads. Consequently, the gc executed on a multicore also requires access to a consistent state of all Java threads independent of the core on which they are running. Assuming that it is not possible to access the register set of one core by another one, complicated object management strategies have to be developed or all cores have to be stopped at the gc phase.

In this paper, we propose a different approach which requires multithreaded cores within a multicore processors. Using multithreaded cores, we assume that it is possible to access the register set of one hardware thread slot from another slot within the same core. A gc thread is now executed in one thread slot on each core while the application Java threads are executed in the other slots in parallel. We evaluated our parallel gc for multithreaded multicore processors using the *jamuth* embedded Java environment for FPGAs.

In the next section, we discuss several related work. Section 3 describes our gc algorithm for multicores and section 4 describes the architecture of the SoPC (System on Programable Chip) used for the evaluation. The evaluations are shown in section 5 followed by the conclusions in section 6.

2 Related Work

In recent years, several multithreaded and multicore processor architectures have been established on the market of server, desktop and portable computers. A comparison of single and multicore desktop architectures based on Intel's Smithfield and Prescott architectures is given by Sibai [9].

A simulator for simultaneous multithreaded single core processors was developed by D.M. Tullsen [10]. He reported [11] a formidable speedup of multithreaded architectures. Pitter et al. [7] presents the design of a single threaded Java multicore processor for FPGAs. They evaluated multicores containing up to 8 Java cores.

Schmidt et al. [8] proposed a hardware assisted garbage collection technique for C++. A gc module works in the background concurrently to the application. It is also suitable for real-time applications and its throughput is comparable to a software-based dynamic memory management. Meyer [4] describes a gc coprocessor which supports the gc cycle of the processor. Due to upper bounds of the stop-the-world phases this technique is also suitable for real-time systems. Bacon et al. [1] presented the *Recycler* gc algorithm for multiprocessor servers. It is based on reference counting together with a method to recognize unreferenced cycles.

A special garbage collection for a multithreaded Java processor is described by Fuhrmann and Pfeffer et al. [2,6]. Our gc extends this algorithm for multicores and is demonstrated with the help of the further developed *jamuth* [12] Java processor core. It was formerly known as *Komodo* [3].

3 Garbage Collection for Multithreaded Multicores

The garbage collection described in this paper requires multithreaded processor cores within a multicore. Nevertheless, it is also suitable for a single-core multithreaded processor. A processor-internal thread scheduling that guarantees a certain thread progress is also necessary (see section 2). The basic algorithm is a mark and sweep collector extended to run on multiple cores synchronously and also in parallel to the application(s). Additionally, we avoided nearly any kind of synchronization between the application

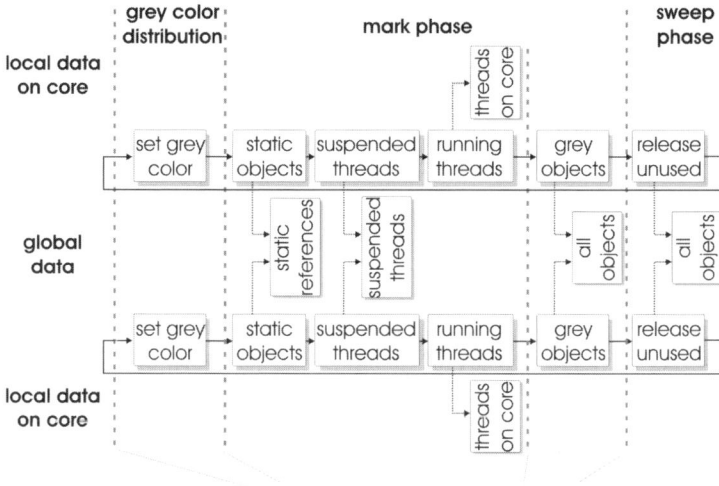

Fig. 1. Flow diagram of the garbage collection for multithreaded multicores

threads and the garbage collection threads. The only exception is the allocation of new objects because it requires the same resources as the gc: a list of new objects and the memory management structure. Neither read barriers nor write barriers are required during object access.

3.1 General Functionality

The original mark phase is divided into four sub phases whereof three handle the same data concurrently and the fourth deals with the private data of the corresponding processor core. During the sweep phase, all cores work in parallel on releasing the unreachable memory areas. In addition to the two phases *mark* and *sweep*, we put a third phase in front of them: the *grey distribution* phase. Figure 1 shows a flow diagram of the garbage collection. The six phases and sub phases are in detail:

Grey distribute: During this phase, a new *grey* color is determined just by increasing a global counter. The value of this counter is distributed to all cores and is used by the application threads to mark objects as *used*. At each reference write accesses, the grey value is written to the corresponding object and hereby it is marked as used. No synchronization is necessary for this operation.

Check static: Within the first mark phase the objects reachable from static references are marked. Additionally, all further linked objects are marked recursively. All cores work concurrently on the static references. Already marked objects are ignored.

Check suspended threads: After checking static objects, the currently not executed threads are checked. Also the currently swapped out parts of the stacks of the executed threads are checked. Here again all cores work in parallel on this task.

Check running threads: In contrast to stop-the-world garbage collectors, several application threads are executed in parallel to the gc. Hence, the gc has to take the active runtime stacks into account. At this phase, the gc thread on every core is responsible only for the threads running on the same core. No cooperation takes place. The gc scans the application threads from the start of the swapped-in stack to the top of the stack. If the application moves an object from an upper position to a lower one while the gc is in between these two locations, the corresponding object could be not marked. The same problem exists if a part of the stack is just on the way to be swapped out. To get rid of these problems, the application marks its objects as *grey* at the *move down* as well as the *swap out* operations.

Check late objects: At the end of the marking phases, this gc sub phase deals with the objects not found at the *check suspended threads* and the *check running threads* phases. Again, all cores work on that issue in parallel.

Sweep: During the sweep phase, all unmarked objects released. This is done by all cores in parallel.

In-between the *grey distribution* phase, the first three parts of the *mark* phase and its last phase as well as before and after the *sweep* phase barriers guarantee a homogenous progress of all gc threads. Moreover, these barriers are required to ensure proper access to the management data structures of the memory management.

3.2 Synchronization

Because we use a multithreaded multicore processor, several application threads run in parallel to the gc threads. Hence, many memory allocation operations can take place within a short period. Each allocation as well as the sweep phase of the gc require exclusive access to the memory management structures. To ease this bottleneck, we partitioned the memory in homogenous parts. The release operations of the gc are bounded to the partition in which the concerned memory areas are located, whereas new objects can be created in any partition, if there is enough free memory.

As a result, memory management operations do not concentrate on a single exclusive structure but on multiple ones. Increasing the number of partitions leads to less competition at the management structure while it reduces the maximum size of objects because they has to fit completely within a single partition. For our evaluation, we chose two partitions with 8MB each.

3.3 Fragmentation

A general problem in memory management issues is the fragmentation of the memory. Most Java virtual machines use compactification after the garbage collection cycles to reduce or even eliminate memory fragmentation. Unfortunately, it is either required that the JVM uses an redirection table to locate the objects or all references to the moved objects have to be updated.

Because the proposed gc algorithm focuses on embedded systems, we avoided the indirection of an additional table. However, updating the object references is not possible because our gc is executed in parallel to the also running application. Hence, we cannot get a consistent snapshot of the memory, modify it, and release it for the execution. A hardware based redirection technique like it is proposed by Schmidt et.al. [8] would be a solution for this topic if it is required.

But, due to the fact that the gc continuously collect unreferenced objects, objects with short lifetime will be released faster and new object can be placed at the same location. Thus, we expect not to have such a heterogeneous mixture of long and short lifetime objects distributed all over the memory and fragmentation should be lower than within systems with stop-the-world behavior. Because fragmentation is not a topic of this paper, we will discuss it in future work.

4 Architecture of the Java Multicore

Within this section, we shortly describe our Java multicore processor used for the evaluation. Because the cores are no standard RISC processors, we firstly give an overview of a single core itself. Afterwards, the multicore system with the interconnection network and the synchronization technique is described.

4.1 The Java Core Architecture

The processor core used for the evaluation (see figure 2) is the *jamuth* Java processor which contains a multithreaded five stage pipeline (*instruction fetch, instruction decode, operand fetch, execute,* and the *stack cache*) together with an integrated *real-time scheduler*. It is responsible for a real-time capable thread schedule if the core is used in real-time applications. We used the scheduler for guaranteeing a steady progress of the gc without impeding the application threads too much (see the guaranteed percentage scheduling later in this section).

Most of the Java integer as well as several long, float, and double bytecodes are executed directly in hardware, mostly within a single execution cycle. Instructions with

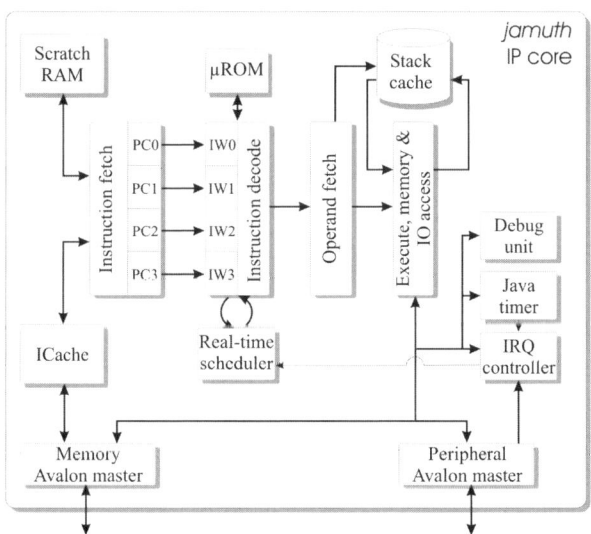

Fig. 2. Block diagram of a single processor core

medium complexity are realized by microcodes and the complex operations, such as *new*, *athrow*, *monitorenter*, and most floating point commands, call trap routines. As operand stack, a 2k-entry stack cache is integrated within the pipeline which is shared between the hardware thread slots.

Each thread slot possesses an instruction window (*IW*) into which up to six bytecodes can be prefetched. These instruction windows decouple fetching and decoding of the bytecodes. Instructions can be fetched from three different sources: external memory, instruction cache, and scratch RAM. The instruction cache and the scratch RAM are integrated within each processor core whereas the external memory has to be connected via appropriate interfaces.

The integrated real-time scheduler supports two scheduling schemes: a simple fixed priority preemptive (FPP) scheduling scheme and the so-called guaranteed percentage (GP [3]) scheduling scheme. Each hardware thread slot is assigned to one of these scheduling schemes. For the FPP scheduling a priority in the range from 0 to #$threadslots - 1$ and for GP a percentage between 0 to 100 is required. A special *jamuth* Java class supports the handling of the hardware thread slots and the scheduling policies. In our case, the scheduler performs the simple fixed priority scheduling for the application threads and the gp scheduling for the garbage collection.

The IP core contains three additional units: the *Debug unit*, the *Java timer*, and an *IRQ controller*. The first unit is responsible for debugging and observing functionalities, the timer is required for the JVM (*System.currentMillis()* and the *Sleep* methods), and the IRQ controller translates interrupt requests from the peripheral components to wake-up signals for the thread-slots resp. interrupt signals for already running threads.

4.2 Interconnection and Synchronization of the MultiCore

Multiple *jamuth* cores (see figure 3) can be combined easily to a multicore by the SoPC builder from Altera. The available Avalon master memory interfaces of the *jamuth*s must be connected to the same Avalon bus. As slave components, at least one memory controller like Altera's standard SDRAM controller must be available to establish a connection to an external shared main memory. Within the current implementation, we have not integrated any data cache, yet, nor any second level cache.

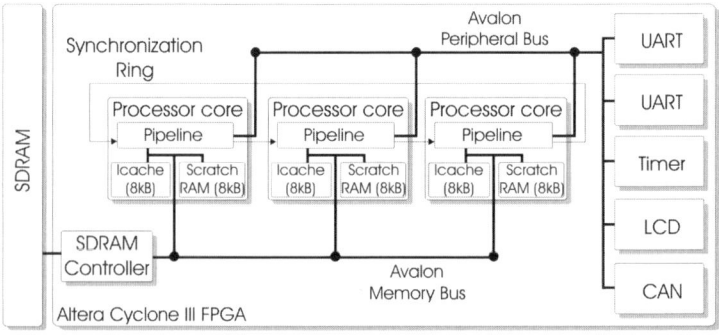

Fig. 3. Block diagram of the multicore SoPC

To connect peripheral components, each core offers a second Avalon master interface. Again, these interfaces should be connected to a second shared bus which features access to peripheral devices. Using two separated busses, memory and peripheral accesses do not interfere.

Due to the multithreading capability of *jamuth*, special synchronization instructions are already available. The *atom_lock* instruction allocates a unique lock tag which grants exclusive access to a critical section for one thread. The *atom_unlock* releases the lock tag. Within the multicore, the lock tag moves from one core to the next on a ring. If a core requires the lock, it takes it from the ring until it is freed by the application. Figure 3 shows the block diagram of the multicore used for the evaluation.

5 Evaluation

In our evaluations, we compare multicore SoPCs with two and three multithreaded *jamuth* Java processor cores with a single multithreaded core. We keep track of several multicore related parameters like the synchronization overhead, the throughput of loads, the pipeline utilization as well as the performance of the garbage collection and its behavior.

As benchmarks, we used a self-made merge sort program (*Merge*) to stress the gc as well as the *Caffeine Embedded Benchmark* suite [5]. In all evaluations, we execute a single benchmark thread on one core in parallel to the gc which is executed on a single core, a dual core, or three cores. On all cores, the gc gets only the assigned amount of processor performance. If connected, the second and the third core are idle at the remaining time.

During the *Merge* benchmark, the characters of an arbitrary string will be sorted within the string in an ascending order. The algorithm is implemented intentionally very inefficient so that it always allocates new *String* objects together with a *char* array.

Our first measurements concern the performance of the gc dependent on the number of cores and the assigned computing time. We took the time after which the *Merge* has finished and additionally the time the gc requires to collect all unused objects. Both periods begin at the start of the benchmark. The benchmark is executed 28 times with a gc running at 3% to 30% of the computing power. Figure 4 shows the runtime of the *Merge* with the three processor configurations and figure 5 presents the time required to collect all objects formerly used by the benchmark program.

It can be recognized in figure 4 that the benchmark is fastest with only one processor. This behavior is obvious because the benchmark is only a single threaded workload. The performance drawback using two and three cores originates from the synchronization at object allocation and the conflicts at the memory bus. The figure is presented in a very high scale to show the differences in the performance but it should be mentioned that the longest execution time (at 30% gc) is only 12%, 18% resp. 26% higher than the best case with one, two, and three cores.

Concerning the execution time, another very interesting observation can be made: The benchmark's best performance is not at the time the gc runs at its least performance as we would expect it. In fact, we can observe a minimum execution time at about 9% gc in the single core case and at 7% gc with more than one core. Two effects lead to

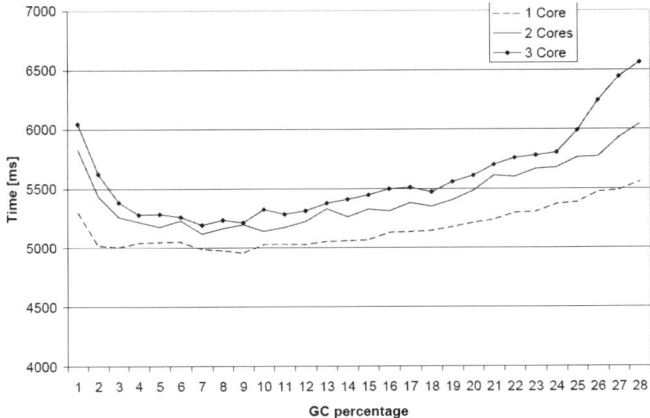

Fig. 4. The execution time of *Merge* depending on the number of cores and the gc's computing performance

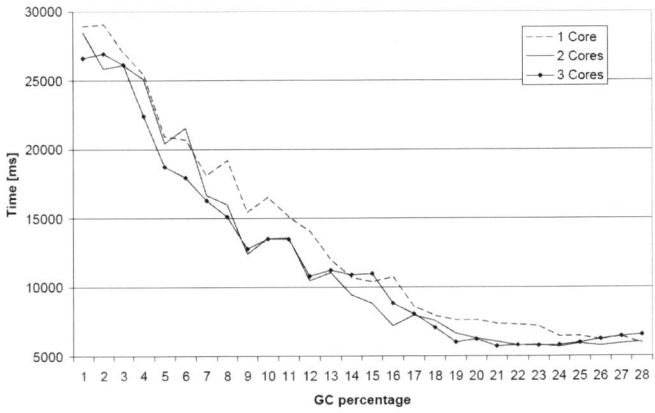

Fig. 5. The time required by the gc to collect all objects depending on the number of cores and the gc's computing performance

this behavior: With increasing gc performance, the computing time available for the application clearly decreases. But, on the other hand, the more objects the gc releases the more simple the object allocation process gets. This is due to the memory management algorithm and its block merge and divide technique. Hence, object allocation is faster which leads to a better overall performance.

Regarding the time required to collect all objects not used after the benchmark has finished, a discontinuous behavior occurs. This is because of the different overlapping of the application's object allocation and the phases of the gc, especially the *sweep* phase. Hence, objects are located in different areas and garbage collection is a little bit faster or slower. Nevertheless, a general trend is that a mentionable improvement of the gc is reached by the second processor compared to a single processor solution. In

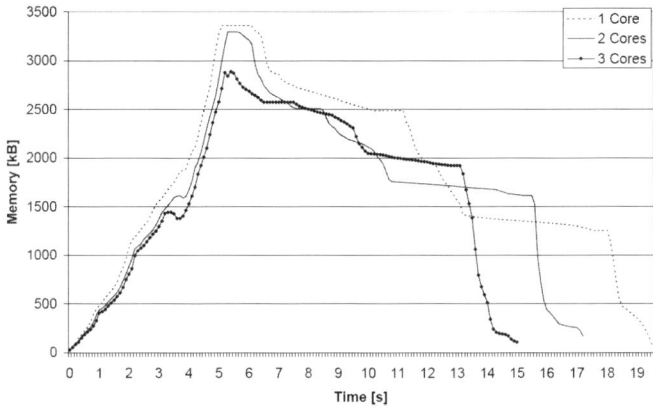

Fig. 6. Allocated memory of the *Merge* benchmark while gc is executed with 9% (1 core) and 7% (2 and 3 cores) resp

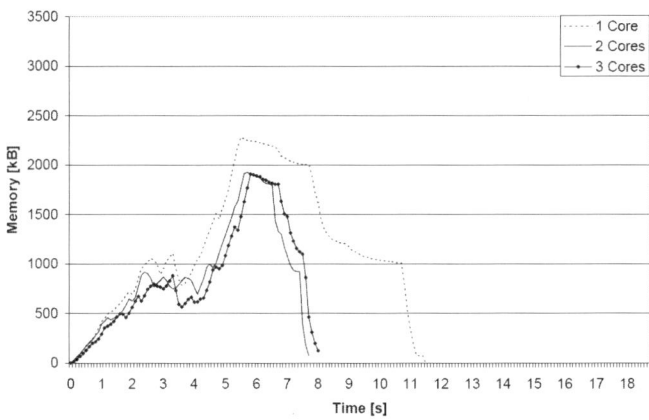

Fig. 7. Allocated memory of the *Merge* benchmark while gc is executed with 30% (1 core), 28% (2 cores), and 25% (3 cores)

contrast, the advancement of the third processor is negligible especially in the important range of 7% gc to 13% gc where the benchmark performs best.

Another very interesting topic concerning the execution time and the collection time is, that with three cores and 25% gc, the gc finishes at the same time as the benchmark. I.e. the gc collects the unreferenced objects as fast as the application produces new ones. Anyway, using two cores this point is reached at 28% gc but with only one core, we could not reach it even with 30%.

Besides the execution time of the gc to collect an amount of objects, we measured the memory consumption of the *Merge* benchmark. Figure 6 and 7 show the amount of allocated memory measured every 100ms. The first figure shows the allocation running the gc at the optimal percentage, i.e. 9% for the single core and 7% for two and three

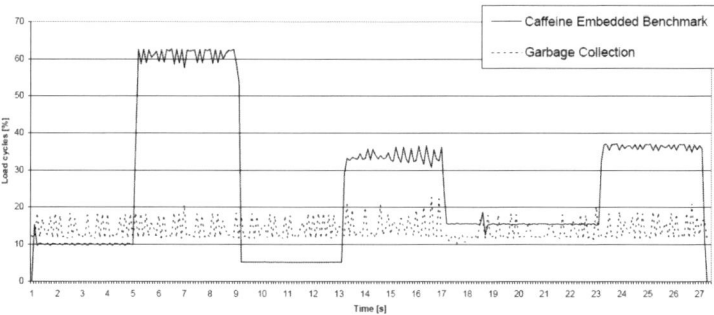

Fig. 8. Percentage of cycles a thread waits until a load is finished using 10% gc

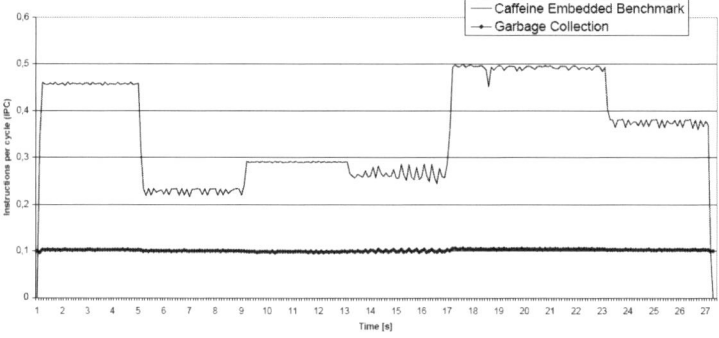

Fig. 9. Instructions per cycle of the CEB and the GC using 10% gc

cores. Additionally to the shorter collecting time, also the maximum memory consumption is reduced using a higher number of cores: with three cores about 500kB are saved compared to a single core. Assuming a gc percentage that allows a nearly simultaneous termination of the benchmark and the gc (30%, 28%, resp. 25%), the amount of required memory can further be reduced (see figure 7).

A special problem of multithreaded and multicore processors is the synchronization between different threads and concurrent memory accesses. We evaluated both, the amount of cycles a thread has to wait until it gets the atomic lock tag and the amount of cycles a thread is executing a load access from the memory. Store accesses are not taken into account. As benchmark, we used the *Caffeine Embedded Benchmark* suite (CEB) which consists of six parts with different characteristics.

Figure 8 presents the amount of clock cycles a threads is stalled until the result of a load is ready measured at the first processor core. The different phases of the CEB can be recognized by their unique load behavior. The load level of the gc is distributed more homogenously and is not affected by the application as it is intended by the guaranteed percentage scheduling. Same is valid for the gc's IPC as it is shown in figure 9. But, the IPC of the CEB is highly influenced by the number of loads. The reason is the missing

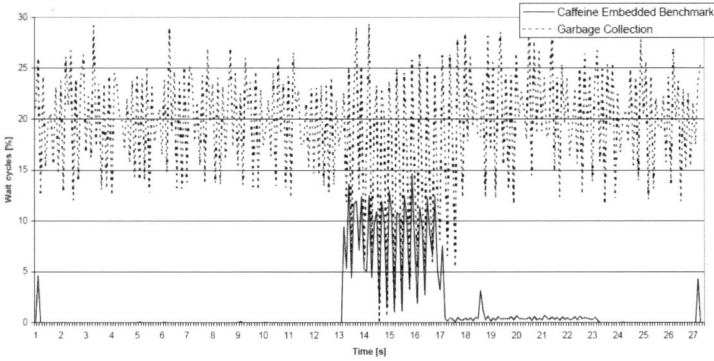

Fig. 10. Wait cycles of the CEB and the GC using 10% gc

data cache and the resulting memory latency with an average of about 8-10 clock cycles (because we use an SDRAM with row and column selection, the latency is not fixed).

Our last evaluation concerns the wait time because of a missed entry into a critical section. Especially in multicore environments, where multiple threads need access to critical data structures, a deeper look into the synchronization time is required. A central data structure in Java environments is doubtless the memory management structure. Because the proposed gc technique requires one gc thread per core, at least three threads require atomic access to the memory management (in case of three cores). Figure 10 shows the fraction of cycles a thread is stalled until it can enter a critical section, i.e. it gets the atomic lock token. Obviously, the gc thread has several problems with the synchronization because it has to synchronize itself with the gc threads executed on the other two cores. However, the application is mentionable affected only during its fourth part which is the *String* benchmark. It is the only one that intensively allocates new objects. The other benchmark affected in a marginal way is the *Float* benchmark (fifth one) which allocates and releases some very small arrays during its execution time. The benchmarks not allocating memory are not harmed in any way (the peaks at $1s$ and $27s$ stem from the startup and termination sequence). Hence, the proposed gc for multithreaded multicore processors can also be used for mixed applications where the real-time threads only use statically allocated objects.

6 Conclusions

In this paper, we proposed a garbage collection for embedded multithreaded multicore processors. One gc thread is executed within its own thread slot on each processor core. The gc threads are scheduled using the guaranteed percentage scheduling scheme, which assigns a predefined amount of execution cycles to the gc thread within a short period (100 clock cycles). We showed that the gc is able to release unreferenced objects nearly as fast as the application allocates new ones. For this purpose, the gc has to be executed with about $1/4$ to $1/3$ of the processor's computing power. We also found out, that the application's performance is best if the gc is running with about 7% to 9%.

These values have been obtained using a gc stress benchmark with a high amount of object allocations and releases.

Because of the synchronization overhead of the gc threads on the different cores, we also evaluated the stall time before entering a critical section. We found out that only application threads creating new objects suffer from the synchronization but threads using only statically allocated objects are executed absolutely independent. Hence, the proposed gc is also suitable for mixed applications with some real-time requirements.

References

1. Bacon, D.F., Attanasio, C.R., Lee, H.B., Rajan, V.T., Smith, S.: Java without the coffee breaks: A nonintrusive multiprocessor garbage collector. In: Proceedings of the ACM SIGPLAN Conference on Programming Language Design and Implementation (PLDI), Snowbird, pp. 92–103. ACM Press, New York (2001)
2. Fuhrmann, S., Pfeffer, M., Kreuzinger, J., Ungerer, T., Brinkschulte, U.: Real-time Garbage Collection for a Multithreaded Java Microcontroller. In: Int. Symposium on Object-Oriented Real-Time Distributed Computing (ISORC 2001), Magdeburg, Germany, May 2001, pp. 69–76 (2001)
3. Kreuzinger, J., Brinkschulte, U., Pfeffer, M., Uhrig, S., Ungerer, T.: Real-time Eventhandling and Scheduling on a Multithreaded Java Microcontroller. Microprocessors and Microsystems 27(1), 19–31 (2003)
4. Meyer, M.: An on-chip garbage collection coprocessor for embedded real-time systems. In: RTCSA 2005: Proceedings of the 11th IEEE International Conference on Embedded and Real-Time Computing Systems and Applications, Washington, DC, USA, pp. 517–524. IEEE Computer Society Press, Los Alamitos (2005)
5. Pendragon Software. CaffeineMark 3.0 Benchmark (1997)
6. Pfeffer, M., Ungerer, T., Fuhrmann, S., Kreuzinger, J., Brinkschulte, U.: Real-Time Garbage Collection for a Multithreaded Java Microcontroller. Journal of Real Time Systems 26(1), 89–106 (2004)
7. Pitter, C., Schoeberl, M.: Performance evaluation of a java chip-multiprocessor. In: 3rd IEEE Symposium on Industrial Embedded Systems, Montpellier, France (June 2008)
8. Schmidt, W.J., Nilsen, K.D.: Performance of a hardware-assisted real-time garbage collector. SIGOPS Oper. Syst. Rev. 28(5), 76–85 (1994)
9. Sibai, F.N.: Evaluating the performance of single and multiple core processors with pcmark05 and benchmark analysis. In: ACM SIGMETRICS Performance Evaluation Review archive, March 2008, pp. 62–71 (2008)
10. Tullsen, D.M.: Simulation and modeling of a simultaneous multithreading processor. In: The 22nd Annual Computer Measurement Group Conference (December 1996)
11. Tullsen, D.M., Eggers, S.J., Emer, J.S., Levy, H.M., Lo, J.L., Stamm, R.L.: Exploiting choice: Instruction fetch and issue on an implementable simultaneous multithreading processor. In: 23rd International Symposium on Computer Architecture (ISCA 1996), Philadelphia, PA, USA, May 1996, pp. 191–202 (1996)
12. Uhrig, S., Wiese, J.: Jamuth – an IP Processor Core for Embedded Java Real-Time Systems. In: The 5th International Workshop on Java Technologies for Real-time and Embedded Systems - JTRES 2007, Vienna, Austria (September 2007)

Empirical Performance Models for Java Workloads

Pradeep Rao and Kazuaki Murakami

Department of Informatics, ISEE, Kyushu University, Japan
Institute of Systems and Information Technologies/Kyushu, Japan
{pradeep.rao,murakami}@isit.or.jp

Abstract. Java is widely deployed on a variety of processor architectures. Consequently, an understanding of microarchitecture level Java performance is critical to optimize current systems and to aid design and development of future processor architectures for Java. Although this is facilitated by a rich set of processor performance counters featured on several contemporary processors, complex processor microarchitecture structures and their interactions make it difficult to relate observed events to overall performance. This, coupled with the complexities associated with running Java over a virtual machine, further aggravates the situation. This paper explores and evaluates the effectiveness of empirical modeling for Java workloads. Our models use statistical regression techniques to relate overall Java system performance to various observed microarchitecture events and their interactions. Multivariate adaptive *regression splines* effectively capture non-linear and non-monotonic associations between the response and predictor variables. Our models are interpretable, easy to construct and exhibit high correlation/low errors between predicted and measured performance. Furthermore, empirical models afford additional insights into the characteristics of Java performance and the use of statistical techniques throughout this study allow us to assign confidence levels to our estimates of performance.

1 Introduction

The Java programming paradigm and its associated software engineering benefits have led to its deployment on a variety of computing platforms and the emergence of this class of workload is also recognized by several organizations, software vendors and research groups that have released benchmarks over the past few years to represent this space [1,2]. The execution characteristics of Java applications have been shown to differ significantly from general purpose workloads [3], thus motivating a closer examination of Java performance components at the microarchitecture level. Performance analyses of Java workloads on a production platform enable optimizations and help identify performance bottlenecks to be addressed during the design and development of future systems for Java.

To facilitate performance analysis at the processor microarchitecture level, most modern processors provide access to a performance monitoring unit (PMU) to track a wide variety of processor events. However, the complex microarchitecture of contemporary processors obfuscate interpretation of microarchitecture events and their relation to overall performance. The additional complexities associated with running Java over a virtual machine only aggravates the situation. While recent papers [4,5,3] study and highlight the influence of low-level processor events on overall Java performance, the approach adopted inherently ignores higher order *interactions* that may exist between parameters that affect performance, thus leading to skewed and possibly incorrect conclusions.

To address these issues, this study evaluates the effectiveness of statistically rigorous empirical models for Java performance analysis. Specifically, we use regression models to relate overall Java system performance to the observed microarchitecture events and their interactions. An *interaction* is said to exist when two events occur at the same time and the performance impact attributed to one event depends on the occurrence of the other event. For example, the performance impact of cache misses would depend on the magnitude of TLB misses since software page-table walk routines tend to pollute the cache. Our approach teases out several such nuances of production environments and quantifies their effect on overall performance. This paper highlights the importance of accounting for higher order interaction effects in performance analyses and shows how this can be facilitated by empirical models. We check for non-linear and non-monotonic influences in our workload and approximate it using models based on *regression splines*. Spline functions are piecewise polynomials used in curve fitting [6] and can be used to approximate a wide variety of functions.

We model Java workloads on a production platform based on the AMD Opteron processor and a recent 64bit Sun JavaSE virtual machine. We also investigate model *transferability* across virtual machines (VM) on our platform, *i.e.*, how accurately models built using a particular VM represent observed behavior using a different VM. Our results indicate that our models are able to faithfully predict performance on an alternate VM (IBM J9 JVM) with an average prediction error of 8±0.6% at 95% confidence. While we demonstrate the construction and use of empirical models for Java performance analyses on the Opteron processor, the methodology is generic enough to extend to other platforms and workloads.

2 Preliminaries

This section presents the background required to understand the experiments and results presented in this paper. Further details may be found in several texts on statistical methods [6,7].

Regression analysis is a statistical tool that expresses the relationship between a *response* variable and its *predictors* over a sample space. In its simplest generalized form, the response variable y may be related *linearly* to p independent predictors or *regressor* variables $(Z_1, Z_2, .., Z_p)$ as expressed by the model in Eq. 1.

$$y = \beta_0 + \sum_{i=1}^{p} \beta_i Z_i + \epsilon \tag{1}$$

The parameters $\{\beta_i | 0 \leq i \leq p\}$ are called the *regression coefficients* and represent the expected change in response y per unit change in $\{Z_i | 1 \leq i \leq p\}$ when all the remaining variables $\{Z_j | j \neq i\}$ are held constant. The *residual* or the error due to lack of fit is denoted by ϵ. The model describes a hyperplane in the k-dimensional space of the regressor variables Z_i and β_0 can be interpreted as the intercept of the response surface with the y-axis. Linear regression models are commonly used to estimate parameter significance and also to predict the response variable at arbitrary points in the design space.

Often, the predictors *interact*, i.e., the response of y to a change in Z_i depends on the value of Z_j. In such cases the model in Eq. 1 can be easily extended to model such two-factor interactions as follows:

$$y = \beta_0 + \sum_{i=1}^{p} \beta_i Z_i + \sum_{i=1}^{p} \sum_{j=i}^{p} \beta_{ij} Z_i Z_j + \epsilon \tag{2}$$

Similarly, higher order interactions can be included in the equation above and the complete linear regression model can be represented as a sum of p terms with the generic form:

$$y = \beta_0 + \beta_1 X_{n1} + \beta_2 X_{n2} + ... \beta_p X_{np} + \epsilon_n \tag{3}$$

where, the subscript n identifies the *trial* and the subscript p denotes the predictor variable X. In matrix terms, the above equation can be written as:

$$\mathbf{y} = \mathbf{X}\beta + \epsilon \tag{4}$$

Hence, given the linear model with p terms, the data set from the design matrix $\mathbf{X}$ and the response vector $\mathbf{y}$, the *least squares* estimates of the partial regression coefficients $\hat{\beta} = (\beta_0, \beta_1, ..., \beta_{p-1})$ can be computed using Eq.5.

$$\hat{\beta} = (\mathbf{X}'\mathbf{X})^{-1}\mathbf{X}'\mathbf{y} \tag{5}$$

2.1 Multivariate Adaptive Regression Splines (MARS)

Spline functions are piecewise polynomials used in curve fitting [6], i.e., they are polynomials within connected intervals of $\mathbf{X}$, the endpoints of which are called *knots*. MARS [8] exploit recursive partitioning techniques to derive functions that approximate arbitrarily complex relationships. The domain is recursively partitioned into disjoint subspaces and the response in each region is described using simple functions of predictor variables. The final model is a linear combination of these *basis* functions.

Assume that the predictor X is divided into p regions. The model is represented using the basis functions B_i and the regression coefficients β_i in the form:

$$\hat{y} = \beta_0 + \sum_{i=1}^{p} \beta_i B_i(X) \tag{6}$$

The MARS approach uses *q-order splines* [8] as basis functions and the normalized coefficients are estimates of the influence of the variables and their interactions on the overall response. Consequently, these models are not only highly accurate, but also interpretable.

2.2 Model Building

We fit a model consisting of appropriate main effects and their second order interactions using both linear regression and MARS. Two or more interacting terms are indicated using an asterisk '*' between them. Since not all interactions are meaningful, based on microarchitectural insights (*e.g.*, l2.imiss*l2.dmiss, dl1.miss*l2.imiss *etc.*), we remove these terms from our model.

Model Simplification/Pruning: Overfitting refers to a model that fits the data well, but is unable to generalize beyond that. To avoid overfitting, we reduce model complexity using metrics that estimate the ability of a model to generalize. Our model simplification uses stepwise search based on the *Bayesian Information Criterion* (BIC) which penalizes overfit models. The criterion is defined by the following relation:

$$BIC = \frac{n + p(log(n) - 1)}{n(n-p)} SSE \quad (7)$$

where, $SSE = \sum_{i=1}^{p}(y_i - \hat{y}_i)^2$ is the error sum of squares, p is the number of parameters in the model, and n is the number of samples. The model with the minimal BIC tries to find an optimal compromise between model fit and model complexity. MARS models use the modified cross-validation procedure developed in [9] to determine the basis functions to be included in the model.

2.3 Model Diagnostics

The *residuals* $\{\mathbf{r}|\mathbf{r} = \mathbf{y} - \mathbf{X}\hat{\beta}\}$, are the differences between the data and the fitted values. As a consequence of least squares estimation of β, the residuals will be uncorrelated with all predictors (and intercept, if any) and can be used to diagnose problems with the model. The fit of the model can be summarized by the residual standard deviation, $\hat{\sigma} = \sqrt{\sum_{i=1}^{n} r_i^2/(n-p)}$ and R^2 in Eq.8, the fraction of variation 'expressed' by the model, and

$$R^2 = 1 - \frac{\hat{\sigma}^2}{s_y^2} \quad (8)$$

where, s_y is the standard deviation of data, and $(n-p)$ are referred to as the *degrees of freedom*.

The *goodness of fit* of a reduced model (R^2) with respect to an original model(R_o^2) can be estimated with the F-test using the statistic F in Eq. 9.

$$F_{k,n-p-1} = \frac{(R^2 - R_o^2)/k}{(1-R^2)/(n-p-1)} \quad (9)$$

where, k is the difference between the degrees of freedom of the original model and that of the reduced model. Given that the statistic follows the F-distribution with $(k, n - p - 1)$ degrees of freedom, the *p-value* is defined as the probability $P(X > |c|)$, where c is a constant. Thus, a small p-value for the F-test leads us to reject the *null-hypothesis*, suggesting that additional predictors in the larger model are statistically significant in predicting the response.

Prediction Accuracy. Measuring the accuracy of model predictions is a good way to determine the quality of the models built. Prediction accuracy for a given model is determined using *cross validation* as in other modeling studies [10]. Cross validation involves randomly partitioning the observations into n sets ($n = 5$ here). The models are then built using $n - 1$ sets and the last set is used for testing the prediction accuracy. This process is repeated n times, using a different set each time. Overall accuracy is determined by averaging the prediction metrics across all sets/folds. We use the following metrics to evaluate model prediction.

1. *Prediction error*, expressed as a percentage of the observed performance ($100 * |y_i - \hat{y}_i|/y_i$). While this metric captures the central tendency, we also capture the variation in errors using the confidence interval metric [11] (CIM). CIM is the ratio of the confidence interval for the mean prediction error expressed as a percentage of the mean observed test case performance. This is evaluated using the *paired t-test* at a confidence level of $\alpha = 0.95$.
2. *Correlation metrics* capture the degree of linear association between the model predicted performance and observed performance using statistical tests. Specifically, we use: (a) Pearson's product moment correlation coefficient (r), and (b) Spearman's rank correlation coefficient (ρ), a metric similar to Pearson's correlation, except that the samples are converted into ranks before computing the coefficient. Additionally, Spearman's statistic does not assume that the variables are normally distributed. The coefficients range from $+1$, indicating a perfect positive linear relationship, to -1, indicating a perfect negative linear relationship between the variables. A score of zero implies that there is no linear relation between the two variables

3 Experimental Methodology

Measurement Methodology. The models we build are based on measurements on the 64bit AMD Opteron processor which features a performance monitoring unit (PMU) that can be configured to measure various microarchitecture events using four 48bit counters [12]. The Linux kernel v2.6.25 is modified to support access to the processor performance monitoring unit (PMU) using the *perfmon2* [13] interface. The *perfmon2* interface provides additional features which include (1) extending the 48bit physical counters into 64bit virtual counters, (2) aggregating counts across *threads, forks* and *execs* and (3) low-overhead PMU sampling support. We choose 27 processor microarchitecture events (Tab.1) to measure and model Java applications. These metrics are similar to those used in

Table 1. Processor events measured

Event description	abbreviation
General	
Number of unhalted clock cycles	cycles
Number of retired operations	ops
Number of all data prefetches	d.prefetch
Branch prediction events	
Number of branch instructions retired	br
Number of retired mispredicted branch instructions	br.mispred
Number of return stack overflows	rs.ovfl
Stall events	
Number of instruction fetch unit stalls	if.stall
Number of dispatch stalls (combined)	dispatch.stall
Number of reorder buffer full stall cycles	rob.full
Number of reservation station full stall cycles	rs.full
Number of floating point unit (FPU) full stall cycles	fpu.full
Number of load-store unit full stall cycles	ls.full
Cache, TLB and page miss events	
Number of data cache accesses	dc.access
Number of data cache misses	dc.miss
Number of I-cache fetches	ic.access
Number of I-cache misses	ic.miss
Number of all L2 cache misses	l2.miss
Number of L2 cache misses due to instructions	l2.imiss
Number of L2 cache misses due to data	l2.dmiss
Number of L2 cache misses due to TLB walk	l2.tlbmiss
Number DC fills	d.fills
Number of IC fills	i.fills
Number of L1 I-TLB misses but L2 I-TLB hits	l2itlb.hit
Number of L1 I-TLB misses and L2 I-TLB misses	l2itlb.miss
Number of L1 D-TLB misses but L2 D-TLB hits	l2dtlb.hit
Number of L1 D-TLB misses and L2 D-TLB misses	l2dtlb.miss
Number of page misses	pg.miss

earlier Java performance analysis studies referred to in Section 6. These events and their acronyms used in this paper are shown in Tab.1. These events can be roughly classified, based on the aspect of the microarchitecture that they characterize, into general, branch, processor core and cache/memory hierarchy events.

Measurements are taken at both user and kernel level. Samples are collected at intervals of every 10M retired instructions to capture fine grain behavior [14]. Consequently, all counts are effectively normalized to the number of instructions (per 10M). Program execution is blocked on counter overflows and during sample processing. All experiments employ the following techniques to reduce measurement noise due to extraneous factors: (1) all experiments are performed in single user mode with all unnecessary processes and services turned off, and (2) we disable processor voltage/frequency scaling in the Linux kernel.

Since the Opteron PMU supports only four event counts at a time, multiple runs are required to capture the complete event set listed in Tab.1. Since the JVMs exploit several dynamic/runtime techniques, we performed the following experiment to determine if there was any significant statistical difference between runs under our experimental conditions: we took three random PMU sampled runs as described above for each benchmark and used a statistical test [7] (paired t-test) to test for the null hypothesis that the difference between the means, for each pair of sampled runs, is zero. Our experiments showed that there was

Table 2. SPEC JVM 2008 benchmark applications

Benchmark (BM)	Description	H_{min}
compiler	OpenJDK front end compiler	51MB
compress	Modified Lempel-Ziv compression	29MB
crypto	Encryption/Decryption {aes/rsa/signverify}	2625KB
derby	open source database	250MB
mpegaudio	mp3 decoding	2625KB
serial	serialize/deserialise primitives and objects using JBoss data	69MB
startup	starts each benchmark (except derby) for one operation	2625KB
sunflow	multithreaded global illumination rendering system	2625KB
xml	Application and verification of style sheets to XML documents	15MB

insufficient evidence to reject the null hypothesis that the difference between the means for the two runs is zero, thus asserting the validity of our approach.

Benchmarks and Virtual Machine. We use the fixed size (`--lagom`) workload from the recently released SPEC JVM 2008 benchmark [1] suite. The constituent applications and their brief descriptions are indicated in Tab.2.

For our model construction experiments we use the Sun JavaSE runtime environment v1.6.0. The JVM is forced to run in the 64bit server mode All experiments consider a per benchmark heap size as recommended in [5] and the minimum heap size, H_{min} is indicated in Tab.2. We take measurements at three heap sizes – H_{min}, $3H_{min}$ and $6H_{min}$. The minimum heap size is determined empirically to be the least heap size at which the Java application can execute without any `OutOfMemory` errors. However, this is subject to the caveat that the least heap allowed by the Sun^{TM}JVM is 2625kB. We also determine model transferability using measurements from an alternate virtual machine. For this purpose we use v1.6.0 of the IBM J9 VM for the AMD x86_64 platform.

4 Statistical Analyses

We first use descriptive and inferential statistics to examine and summarize measurement data. Such analyses also help identify relevant predictors for modeling.

The interrelation between the key events is illustrated in the dendrogram in Fig.1(a). These are arrived at using hierarchical variable clustering based on squared Spearman's rank correlation coefficients as similarity measures [6]. This statistic is a measure of similarity and a larger ρ^2 indicates higher correlation between the predictors connected on the figure. The horizontal line connecting the predictors marks the value of ρ^2 when extended to the vertical axis.

In cases where overfitting is a concern (defined in Section 2.2), redundant predictors can be eliminated by choosing only one predictor from a pair of highly correlated predictors. This is also effective when the predictors are collinear, since *multicollinearity* [6] influences effect estimation by artificially inflating p-values even though the variable is significant. However, multicollinearity doesn't pose a problem while predicting and the predictions will still be accurate with R^2 (Sec.2.3) capturing how well the model predicts the response y (*cycles*).

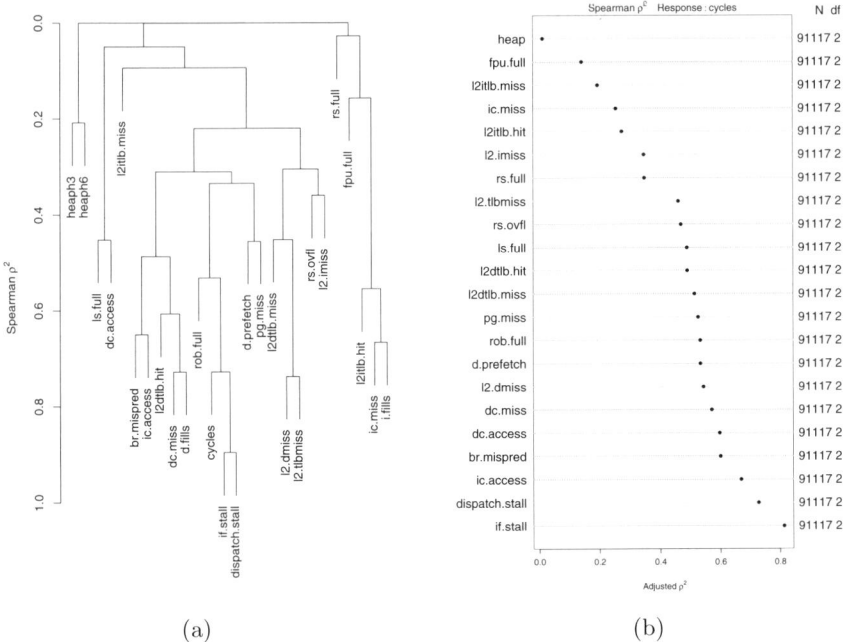

Fig. 1. (a) Predictor clustering and (b) Marginal relationship between predictors and response (cpu cycles)

Analyzing the clusters in Fig.1(a), we find that *if.stalls* and *dispatch.stalls* are highly correlated to each other and also to overall performance (cpu cycles). We also find that *if.stalls* are indeed a significant component affecting overall performance in the models that we develop in the following section. This suggests that Java application performance would benefit considerably from processor front-end engineering and from latency hiding techniques. A few other highly correlated predictor pairs are intuitive – *e.g.*, *dc.miss* and *d.fills* are expected to be correlated as most D-cache misses would typically be hits in the L2 cache (d.fills are equivalent to L2 cache hits due to data and i.fills are the equivalent for instructions). Hence, we do not include *i.fills, d.fills and dispatch.stalls* while modeling.

Fig.1(b) shows the strength of marginal relationships between predictors and the performance response using the non-monotonic (quadratic in rank) generalization of the Spearman's rank correlation [6]. The lack of fit for predictors with higher ρ^2 will have a larger negative impact on performance predictions. In cases where its difficult to assess how the predictor bears on overall performance based on microarchitectural insights, it is helpful to allocate larger number of *knots* (see Sec.2.1) to predictors that have a higher impact on the response. The figure indicates that for microarchitectural predictors, a lack of fit will be more consequential (in decreasing order of impact) for *if.stall, ic.access, br.mispred, dc.access,* etc.

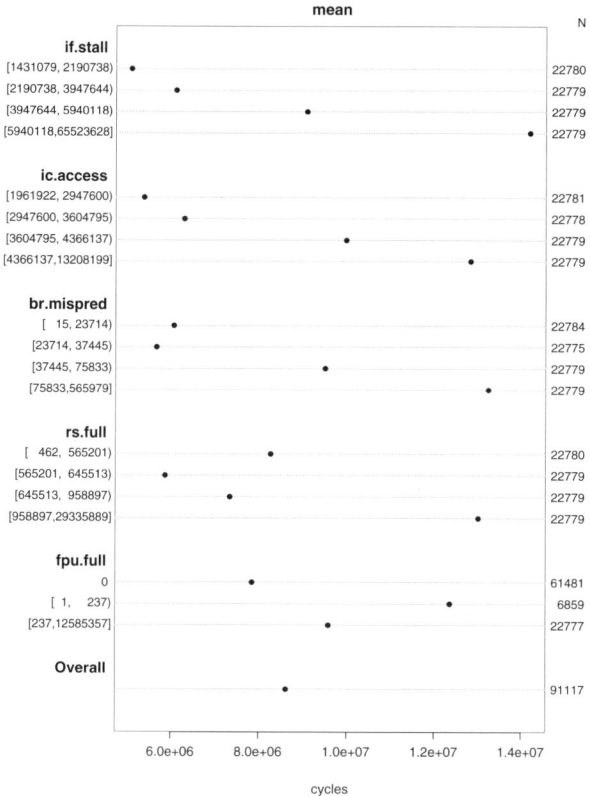

Fig. 2. Summary statistics for selected predictors

Fig.2 examines descriptive associations of the predictors by stratifying the mean response by quartiles for each predictor. The left axes indicate the quantiles and the right indicate the average number of measurements in that range. The x-axis corresponds to the mean response (cycles) in each quartile. Such a plot helps identify strong associations, linearity and monotonic and non-monotonic behaviors. For the sake of brevity, we indicate only a few selected predictors and the overall response. The plots indicate that the predictors *if.stalls* and *ic.access* have strong monotonic response while the stall parameters *br.mispred*, *rs.full*, *fpu.full*, *rs.full* all have non-monotonic behaviors. This is also consistent with the non-monotonic behavior reported by [15] for stall parameters for general purpose applications using the IBM Power processor simulator.

5 Model Evaluation

Model building and evaluation routines are written using the *R language* and its associated environment to leverage the rich set of statistical functions and packages available in that environment. To build MARS models, we use routines from the *polspline* package [9].

The Java workload used in this study produce over 1.8M samples (over 1.5GB of data) when sampling at a granularity of 10M instructions. To enable greater flexibility when experimenting with model building, we examine if sampling at lower frequencies or using fewer samples affects the quality of the models produced. We determine this by subsampling, *i.e.*, we take a random sample from the collected samples which constitutes a small percentage of the overall samples. We then build MARS models for each subsample and evaluate the model errors using cross-validation (Sec.2.3). The sample sizes chosen for subsampling are {0.5, 1, 2, 4, 8, 10, 15, 20}% of all samples for each benchmark.

We find that the mean prediction errors are $< 1\%$ for all Java applications considered across our chosen subsample sizes. Furthermore, the error confidence intervals are within $\pm 4\%$ at 95% confidence levels. This observation can be used to either reduce the number of samples used for analysis or alternately, the frequency at which the PMU is sampled can be lowered to reduce the measurement interference that arises due to frequent sample collection. In general we observe that (not shown) 400-500 samples per benchmark provide MARS models with prediction errors $< 5\%$. To make multiple model construction tractable we conservatively choose the 5% subsample level for further analyses, unless mentioned otherwise.

Effect of higher order interactions. We evaluate the effect of higher order interactions by comparing mean prediction error and its confidence interval for linear regression models with and without interactions between predictors. A model consisting of main effects only is designated as a I-order model, a model with main effects and interactions (Sec.2)between two predictors is designated as a II-order model. Finally, a II-order model with interactions between 3 predictors is designated as a III-order model. The prediction errors are evaluated on a common test unit consisting of 200 random samples for each benchmark and all confidence intervals and statistical tests are specified at 95% ($\alpha = 0.95$) unless mentioned otherwise.

The average R^2 value for the I-order model is 0.67, while that for the II-order model is 0.82. The R^2 measure indicates that the II-order model does a better job (by 22%) of *explaining* the measured variance. An F-test (Sec.2.3), comparing the II-order model and the model with only main effects indicates strong statistical evidence suggesting a lack of fit from some two way interaction term(s) (*i.e.*, null hypothesis stands rejected, Sec.2.3, Eq.9). The significant two way interaction terms can be deduced using the procedure described in Sec.2.2. These tests indicate the importance of accounting for second order effects in performance analysis studies. However, we note that a model with all II-order effects blindly included is significantly overfit as they exhibit high prediction errors. Hence, it is imperative to prune the model using the method described in Sec.2.2.

We also perform a F-test between a III-order model and a II-order model (only main effects and two-way interactions). The results indicate the presence

Table 3. Model accuracy

Benchmark	MARS models					LR models				
	R^2	error %	CIM %	ρ	r	R^2	error %	CIM %	ρ	r
compiler	0.14	0.78	1.44	0.13	0.37	0.25	0.58	1.33	0.47	0.51
compress	0.56	0.46	0.83	0.56	0.68	0.98	0.35	0.79	0.73	0.75
crypto	0.66	0.32	0.69	0.55	0.76	0.91	0.27	0.64	0.73	0.81
derby	0.66	0.31	0.76	0.56	0.77	0.64	0.27	0.71	0.74	0.82
mpegaudio	0.72	0.27	0.65	0.48	0.81	0.95	0.22	0.61	0.65	0.85
serial	0.76	0.23	0.57	0.53	0.84	0.87	0.23	0.57	0.63	0.86
startup	0.75	0.27	0.70	0.56	0.84	0.64	0.32	0.72	0.66	0.85
sunflow	0.71	0.26	0.67	0.54	0.82	0.48	0.29	0.69	0.63	0.83
xml	0.70	0.28	0.74	0.56	0.82	0.66	0.30	0.75	0.66	0.83

of third-order effects that should be included in the models. Though the large number of samples collected at 10M instruction intervals can afford building models with third-order effects, we do not analyze them further here since the prediction errors for the pruned model with only second order interactions are already close to the measurement error.

Comparing MARS and Linear Regression Models. Tab.3 indicates the prediction accuracies for the two regression algorithms considered in this paper, using the metrics described in Sec.2.3. We observe that the MARS model accuracies are comparable to those of II-order LR models suggesting that interaction effects are able to reasonably explain non-linear and non-monotonic behavior of the predictors observed in Sec.4. We note that the stepwise reduction algorithm used a maximum of 100 pruning steps (Sec.2.2). We are currently investigating the effect of increasing the number of steps on the prediction accuracy of the pruned LR model. II-order models that are not simplified result in high prediction errors due to overfitting (Sec.2.2). We also highlight the significant difference in model build times for the two algorithms. The MARS algorithm is, on an average, 7x faster to build than the linear regression algorithm (100 steps) on the same computation platform (based on Opteron 254 processor). Most of the time for the linear regression algorithm is spent in model simplification as described in Sec.2.2.

Interpreting the Model. Several techniques [6] are available to interpret the models and carry out sensitivity analyses. We estimate the effect of a predictor using the difference in the predicted response ($\hat{y}$) at the lower and upper quartiles of X, holding all other X's at their median values. Fig.3 shows the summary of the predictor effects and the 0.95 confidence intervals for the mean effects. We find that the front-end parameters (*if.stall* and *br.mispred*) are predominant factors that influence Java performance. Further analyses are detailed in [16].

Model Transferability. The usefulness of the models developed on a particular platform can be enhanced if they can also be used to estimate/predict performance for alternate VMs. We evaluate MARS model transferability for one other production VM on our platform – the 64bit IBM J9 JVM. The prediction errors and the 95% confidence intervals for the errors are indicated in Tab.4. The

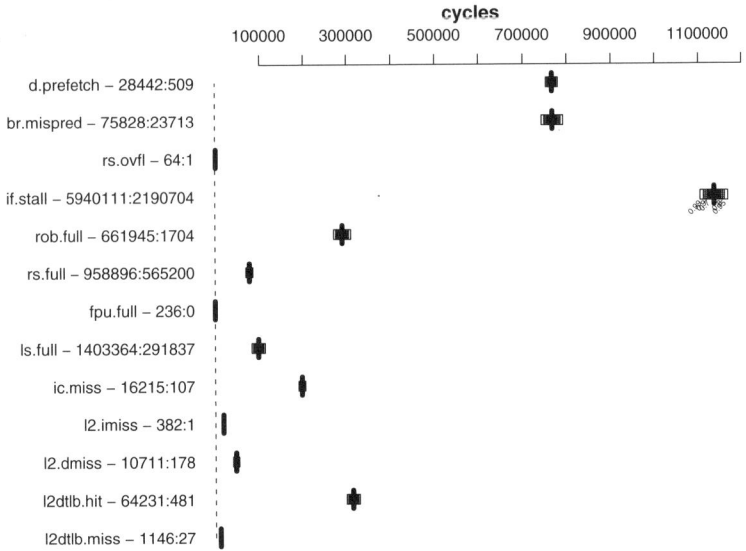

Fig. 3. Summary of predictor effects using interquartile ranges

Table 4. MARS model transferability to IBM J9 JVM

Benchmark	compiler	compress	crypto	derby	mpegaudio	serial	startup	sunflow	xml
Error %	5.31	5.09	11.01	10.12	9.39	9.11	8.48	7.55	6.99
CIM %	0.53	0.62	0.54	0.63	0.57	0.59	0.61	0.59	0.64

errors average 8% across all benchmarks with the confidence intervals at ±0.6%. Though one cannot generalize this result, it is useful to know that models are transferable across a similar class of virtual machines. This is in conformance with the results presented in [4] that shows the existence of VM clusters using principal component analysis.

6 Related Work

This section places the contributions of this study in perspective with respect to related work. Georges et.al. [17] propose rigorous measurement methodologies for Java performance evaluation, but do not model reasons for observed performance. We adopt the recommendations made in [17] and also extend the statistical toolbox to include empirical models and regression splines for Java performance analysis.

Studies on processor performance modeling [18,15] are based on software simulation of general purpose workloads using a processor model. Due to the complexity of the workload, these studies use partial traces and reduced input data sets respectively. We perceive several drawbacks while applying the methodology adopted by these papers to model Java performance: (1) contemporary processors are far too complex to be modeled accurately in a simulator and thus, the generated models may not be representative of actual performance, (2) a microarchitecture simulator typically needs to implement several additional features [19] to support the Java virtual machine and to make it feasible to use simulation for model construction, (3) the use of reduced input data sets with Java workloads has been shown [4] to poorly represent Java execution on a real machine. In contrast, our work (a) uses measurements from real machine execution using a recent production JVM, (b) uses large and realistic data inputs and all Java applications are run to completion. Further, to the best of our knowledge, this is the first study that extends rigorous statistical modeling to advance accurate Java workload performance analysis and characterization.

Since our focus is on model interpretability, we do not consider models based on neural networks and support vector machines proposed in [20,21] for workload characterization. We also do not consider model tree based approaches for performance analysis as proposed in [10], since model trees partition each predictor space into exactly two disjoint subspaces, while our approach using splines can assign subspaces to predictors based on the amount of data available to fit the function and also based on examining the strength of the predictor on the response. In our approach a highly non-linear predictor can be assigned more subspaces to approximate the function based on its bearing on the response and the impact of this decision is evident in the low prediction errors evaluated at high confidence levels (typically at 95% unless mentioned otherwise).

7 Summary and Outlook

In this paper, we develop empirical models based on performance counter data for Java performance analysis. We show that a small sample of a few events can lead to highly accurate performance predictions. We adopt several guidelines listed in [17] for Java performance analysis and extend the statistical toolbox to include empirical modeling for complex workloads in general and Java applications in particular. We show the importance of accounting for higher order effects during performance evaluation studies, especially for Java applications and we evaluate model transferability across an alternate VM. A variation of MARS [9] can also be used to model multiple responses (e.g., performance and power) and our current work investigates the possibility of joint models for power and performance estimation/prediction.

Acknowledgments. The authors wish to thank ISIT/Kyushu (JET Programme) for supporting this research, Prof. Nandy, Prof. Matthew Jacob (IISc) and the anonymous reviewers for their comments.

References

1. Standard Performance Evaluation Corporation: JVM 2008 (2008), http://www.spec.org/jvm2008/
2. Blackburn, S., Garner, R., McKinley, K.: The DaCapo benchmarks: Java benchmarking development and analysis. In: Proc. OOPSLA, pp. 169–190 (2006)

3. Georges, A., Eeckhout, L., De Bosschere, K.: Comparing low-level behavior of SPEC CPU and Java workloads. In: Proc. Asia-Pacific Computer Systems Architecture Conference, pp. 669–679 (2005)
4. Eeckhout, L., Georges, A., Bosschere, K.D.: How Java programs interact with virtual machines at the microarchitectural level. In: Proc. OOPSLA, pp. 169–186 (2003)
5. Blackburn, S.M., Cheng, P., McKinley, K.S.: Myths and realities: The performance impact of garbage collection. In: Proc. SIGMETRICS, pp. 25–36 (2004)
6. Harrell, F.: Regression modeling strategies. Springer, Heidelberg (2001)
7. Canavos, G.: Applied probability and statistical methods. Little Brown and Company (1984)
8. Friedman, J.: Multivariate adaptive regression splines. The Annals of Statistics 19 (1991)
9. Kooperberg, C., O'Connor, M.: Polymars (2001)
10. Ould-Ahmed-Vall, E., Woodlee, J., Yount, C., Doshi, K.A., Abraham, S.: Using model trees for computer architecture performance analysis of software applications. In: Proc. ISPASS, pp. 116–125 (2007)
11. Kodakara, S., Kim, J., Lilja, D., Hawkins, D., Hsu, W., Yew, P.: CIM: A reliable metric for evaluating program phase classifications. IEEE Computer Architecture Letters 6(1) (2007)
12. AMD: BIOS and kernel developer's guide for AMD Opteron processors (2006)
13. Perfmon2, http://perfmon2.sourceforge.net/
14. Sherwood, T., Perelman, E., Hamerly, G., Sair, S., Calder, B.: Discovering and exploiting program phases. IEEE MICRO, 84–93 (2003)
15. Lee, B., Brooks, D.: Accurate and efficient regression modeling for microarchitectural performance and power prediction. In: Proc. ASPLOS, pp. 185–194 (2006)
16. Rao, P., Murakami, K.: Empirical performance models for Java workloads. Technical Report, System LSI Laboratory, Kyushu University (2008)
17. Georges, A., Buytaert, D., Eeckhout, L.: Statistically rigorous Java performance evaluation. In: Proc. OOPSLA, pp. 57–76 (2007)
18. Joseph, P., Vaswani, K., Thazhuthaveetil, M.: Construction and use of linear regression models for processor performance analysis. In: Proc. HPCA, pp. 99–108 (2006)
19. Rao, P., Murakami, K.: A sampling microarchitecture simulator for Java workloads. In: Proc. Workshop on TIMERS-1 held in conjunction with IEEE ISPASS (2008)
20. Yoo, R., Lee, H., Chow, K., Lee, H.: Constructing a non-linear model with neural networks for workload characterization. In: Proc. IEEE International Symposium on Workload Characterization, pp. 150–159 (2006)
21. Ould-Ahmed-Vall, E., Woodler, J., Yount, C., Doshi, K.A.: On the comparison of regression algorithms for computer architecture performance analysis of software applications. In: Proc. Workshop on SMART co-located with HiPEAC (2007)

Performance Matching of Hardware Acceleration Engines for Heterogeneous MPSoC Using Modular Performance Analysis

Hritam Dutta, Frank Hannig, and Jürgen Teich

Hardware/Software Co-Design, Department of Computer Science,
University of Erlangen-Nuremberg, Germany
{dutta,hannig,teich}@cs.fau.de

Abstract. In order to meet demanding challenges of increasing computational requirements and stringent power constraints, there is a gradual trend towards heterogeneous multi-processor system-on-chip (MPSoC) designs integrating application specific acceleration engines. One major problem faced by the design tools for mapping of algorithms onto MPSoC architectures is the dimensioning of system components through performance analysis. In this paper, we propose a fast and accurate methodology for rate matching of statically scheduled acceleration engines using modular performance analysis. Given a set of Pareto-optimal hardware accelerator designs and an input workload behavior, the proposed methodology determines cost efficient hardware accelerators that can handle the workload. A motion JPEG case study illustrates the benefit of coupling high level synthesis tools with performance analysis.

1 Introduction and Related Work

MPSoC architectures are realized either as homogeneous tiled core architectures or as heterogeneous architectures containing application specific acceleration engines. Examples of homogeneous multi-processor architectures are Intels' dual and quad-core architectures or Tilera's TILE64 processor. Heterogeneous multi-core architectures are also ubiquitous in consumer devices (e.g., Cell Broadband Engine, TI's OMAP3, Nexperia multimedia processors from NXP Semiconductors) [1]. The differing proponents of both implementations, however, agree on the challenges faced by MPSoC community. Two major challenges to be surmounted for future MPSoC architectures are: (a) lack of parallelization and mapping tools, that is, absence of compilers for the automatic generation of RTL descriptions of specialized application acceleration engines and programs for multiple cores, respectively, (b) efficient performance analysis and exploration of the vast design space because of the numerous mapping possibilities.

In this context, we developed a design tool [2] that aims at the automatic generation of application specific accelerators for computationally intensive algorithms. The major problem faced by such tools is the explosion in the number of *Pareto-optimal* hardware designs (in terms of multiple objectives such as area, throughput, and power) of the corresponding algorithms because of the freedom in major transformations of partitioning (e.g., tile size, shapes) and scheduling (e.g. number of functional units in

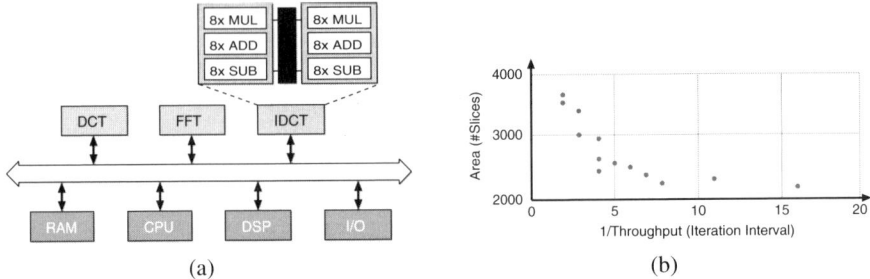

Fig. 1. (a) Example of an MPSoC architecture including several potential acceleration engines. (b) Design space exploration of an IDCT accelerator engine.

the architecture model) [3]. Fig. 1a shows a typical template of a heterogeneous MPSoC containing an inverse discrete cosine transform (IDCT) IP core. The trade-off between area and throughput for different possible designs of the IDCT accelerator with varying resource allocation is illustrated in Fig. 1b. The proper matching of the area and performance requirements of the accelerator to the overall system is important, in particular with respect to the communication behavior. Hence, the *fastest* implementation of the IDCT is an overkill if the worst case rate of input events requires much smaller throughput. In fact, we need to treat the problem of coupling such design tools with performance analysis tools to iteratively identify an optimal *rate-matched* acceleration engine leading to significant savings in area and power cost. Existing popular approaches for performance analysis are based on "Excel Sheet" analysis or simulation (e.g., with SystemC) [4]. A simulation based performance analysis of MPSoC is presented in [5]. In [6], an overview of different analytic methods for performance analysis is presented. In this paper, we use modular performance analysis based on real-time calculus providing worst case guarantees because it is orders of magnitude faster than simulation approaches and more accurate than "Excel Sheet" analysis as it accounts bursts and resource sharing [7].

In particular, we address the following problem: As we are concerned with a multi-objective optimization problem (cost and throughput), there is not only one optimal solution but typically a set of optimal solutions, so called *Pareto-optimal* solutions. Let a set of Pareto-optimal hardware accelerator designs and different workload scenarios for these hardware accelerators be given. Then the question is: What is the cheapest hardware accelerator that can handle this workload? Different load scenarios from simulation approaches are used to obtain worst case traffic which is used as input workload along with service models of accelerators for modular performance analysis. In summary, our contributions are: (a) Selection of an optimal hardware accelerator engine in terms of area and throughput with worst-case guarantees using modular performance analysis. (b) Fast and accurate characterization of hardware accelerator performance in form of service curves using polyhedral theory. (c) Presentation of a motion JPEG (M-JPEG) case study application for illustrating the benefits of the proposed methodology.

The reminder of the paper is organized as follows. In Section 2, we present basics of the hardware compiler design flow and the performance analysis methodology based on real-time calculus. Subsequently, algorithms for the characterization of the accelerator performance and their selection are presented in Section 3. In Section 4, a multimedia application is analyzed in a case study. Finally, we conclude the paper in Section 5.

2 Background

In this section, we present an overview of the design tool [2] for the automatic generation of acceleration engines along with a framework for modular performance analysis.

2.1 Design Flow

It is a known fact that about 90% of the execution time of high performance streaming applications are spent in nested loop programs which offer a tremendous potential of acceleration because of the inherent parallelism. Numerous examples from fields of signal processing, medical imaging, and financial computing require high performance computing. The major goal of our tool is the automatic generation of hardware accelerators from algorithm descriptions, especially nested loops. These hardware accelerators, often in form of processor arrays (PA), can be used inside an MPSoC. The typical design trajectory to generate such an accelerator is shown in Fig. 2. For design entry, a language for dataflow-based algorithm description and modeling of architecture resource constraints is used. Standard compiler optimizations such as common subexpression elimination and other transformations as hierarchical partitioning (also known as tiling) are also available in the high level transformation toolbox for obtaining an amenable algorithm description in terms of data reuse and resource usage. Subsequently, scheduling and resource allocation are carried out to define the place and time of execution of the loop iterations. Finally, the hardware synthesis produces an intermediate RTL representation which is currently retargeted to VHDL by the backend.

The freedom in choosing partitioning and scheduling transformations cause an explosion in the number of *Pareto-optimal* designs implementing a given algorithmic specification. The problem is which design is to be chosen. Before explaining a solution, we explain the details of partitioning and scheduling for understanding their effect on the service behavior of the accelerator.

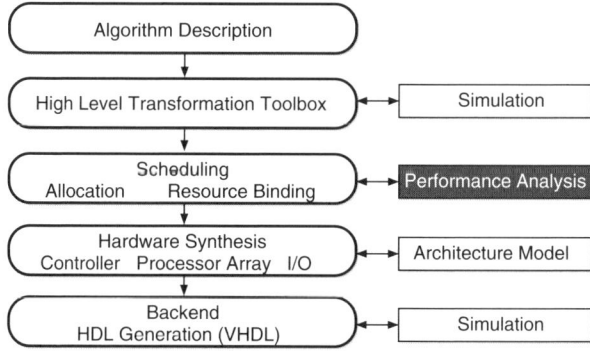

Fig. 2. Design flow for mapping algorithms to hardware accelerators with performance analysis as a plug-in

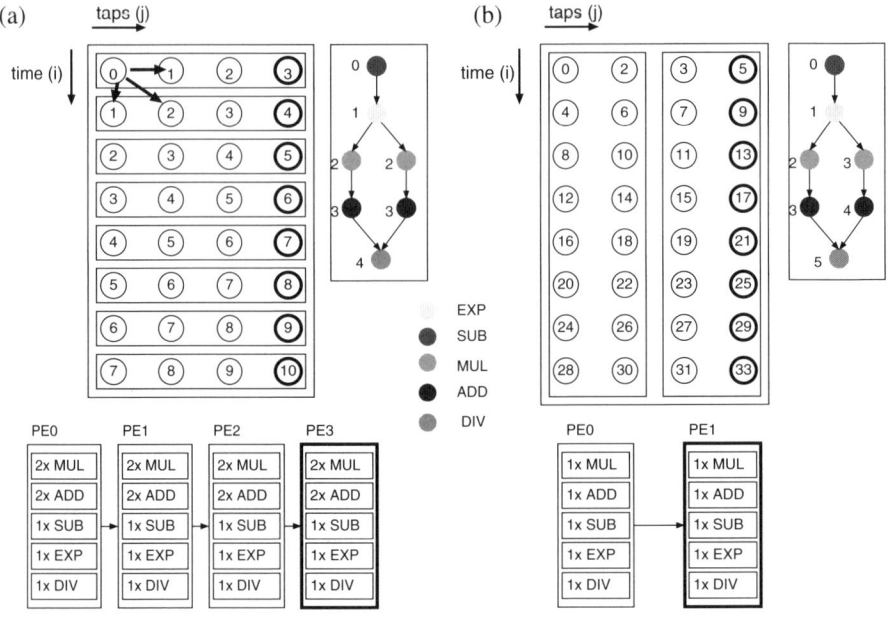

Fig. 3. (a) Dependence graph of a bilateral filter after clustering (LPGS) with tile (1 × 4) and its corresponding accelerator consisting of four PEs executing iterations within a tile. (b) Dependence graph of the bilateral filter after tiling (LSGP) the iteration space with tile (8 × 2). The numbers in/at the nodes denote the start times of the iterations and their operations, respectively. The accelerator consists of 2 PEs corresponding to each tile.

2.1.1 Design Parameters

Partitioning is a source-to-source transformation which covers the iteration space of a given nested loop specification using congruent tiles. For processor array accelerators, it is carried out in order to match a loop nest implementation to resource constraints in terms of available number of the processing elements, amount of local memory, and communication bandwidth. Well known partitioning techniques are known as multiprojection, LSGP (local sequential global parallel, often also referred as tiling or blocking) and LPGS (local parallel global sequential, also referred as clustering). In tiling, all index points within a tile are executed sequentially by the same processor and the index points in different tiles are executed in parallel by different processors (see Fig. 3b). The tiles are typically defined by a tiling matrix, P. In clustering, all index points within a tile are executed in parallel whereas the tiles are executed sequentially (see Fig. 3a). In Fig. 3a, for a 4-tap bilateral filter, the output ($j = 3$) is produced by PE3 (2 MUL, 2 ADD) every cycle. Whereas, in Fig. 3b the output is produced by PE1 (1 MUL, 1 ADD) only every fourth cycle. There exists also a 2-level hierarchical partitioning where the index space is first partitioned into LS (local sequential) tiles, this tiled index space is tiled once more using GS (global sequential) tiles as shown in Fig. 4. The start time of iterations of the output variable of a 2-level hierarchical partitioned matrix multiplication shown in Fig. 4. It illustrates the bursty nature of outputs, as 16 outputs are produced in 8 cycles with a period of 32 cycles. Obviously, the choice of tiling matrices

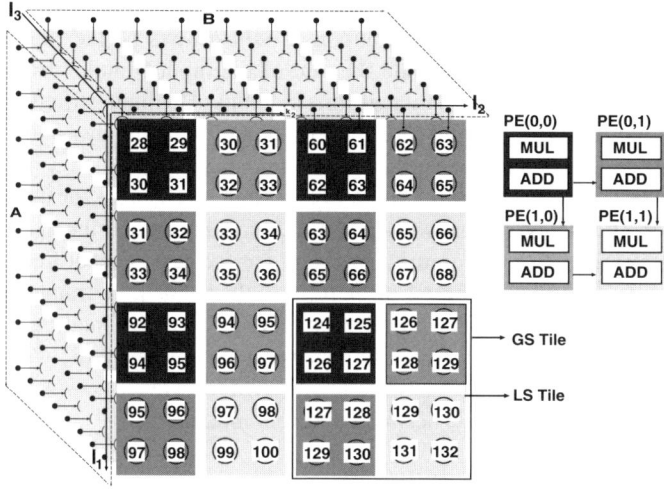

Fig. 4. The output space of the matrix multiplication with 8×8 matrices on a 2-hierarchical partitioning. The output data are produced in bursts.

P directly influences the number of PEs. Further, the allocation information on resource constraints (functional units) for each PE is specified in the architecture model of the input program. Linear transformations as in Eq. (1) are used for allocation and scheduling in order to assign a *processor index p* (space) and a *sequencing index t* (time) to index vectors $I \in \mathcal{I}$ of the iteration space $\mathcal{I}$ defined by the loop program.

$$\begin{pmatrix} p \\ t \end{pmatrix} = \begin{pmatrix} Q \\ \lambda \end{pmatrix} I \qquad (1)$$

Q is determined by the type of partitioning and tiling matrices. A schedule vector λ is obtained by solving a latency minimization problem formulated as a mixed integer linear program similar as in [8]. As a result we obtain:

- The minimal latency L and a corresponding optimal schedule vector λ. The start times of each operation within one loop iteration and their resource binding.
- The iteration interval (II): The iteration interval II is the number of time steps (clock cycles) between the evaluation of two successive instances of a variable within one processing element [8].

In Figs. 3 and 4, one observes different partitioning strategies and matrices leading to hardware accelerators with different number of PEs, resources, and performance. Therefore, selection of an optimal accelerator hardware requires a framework for performance analysis.

2.2 Modular Performance Analysis

Modular performance analysis (MPA) denotes a framework based on real-time calculus for performance investigation of time-critical embedded systems. Assume a component in an embedded system with a given input event stimulus emerging from another component. The processing rate on this component will always be the minimum of the service capacity of the component and the rate of the input stimulus from the source component. This principle is used by real-time calculus. The input stimulus is modeled using $\alpha^u(\Delta)$ and $\alpha^l(\Delta)$ denoting the maximum and minimum number of input events in any time interval Δ. The service capacity of a component is modeled using $\beta^u(\Delta)$ and $\beta^l(\Delta)$ denoting the maximum and minimum available service rate for the input events in a time interval Δ. Outgoing arrival/service curves, delay and buffer size for the component are determined from incoming arrival and service curves according to equations defined by real-time calculus based on *min-plus algebra* [7]. A framework[1] for the computation with such equations is available as Matlab implementation. The toolbox includes several models for describing typical event streams (periodic with jitter, periodic with burst, etc.) and service models (e.g., TDMA). This allows the modeling of various types of communications between different modules.

3 Optimal Accelerator Configuration

In this section, a methodology for exploring accelerator configurations and selection of optimal design depending on a given input workload behavior is presented.

3.1 Parameter Estimation for Accelerators

A large design space of hardware accelerators is spanned by numerous tiling parameters, partitioning strategies, and the choice of resource constraints of the architecture model. The following algorithm determines the Pareto-optimal designs in terms of area cost, throughput, and their corresponding performance characterization as service curve for modular performance analysis.

```
ALGORITHM 1: EXPLORE
    IN:    Intermediate representation (dependence graph) of algorithm, set P of
           tiling matrices, set R of resource constraints in architecture model
    OUT:   set of service curves β of Pareto-optimal set of hardware designs
    BEGIN
      FOR each candidate (P,R) ∈ P × R
        (L,II,λ) ← Scheduling(P,R)
        C ← AnalyzeRTLCost(P,R)
        IF (C,II) is non-dominated THEN
           β ← β ∪ ServiceCurve(P,R,λ)
        ENDIF
      ENDFOR
    END
```

For all input design parameters, the above algorithm performs scheduling. As results of scheduling, the minimal latency L, the corresponding iteration interval II, and the schedule vector λ are derived. Subsequently, an area cost estimation is performed. The

---

[1] http://www.mpa.ethz.ch/rtctoolbox

service curve of Pareto-optimal designs in terms of area and throughput is determined as discussed in next subsections.

3.1.1 Area Cost and Throughput

After scheduling, enough information is available for the generation of an intermediate RTL description of the accelerator. The cost estimation is performed by adding up annotated estimated area size of the RTL components from a database [9]. The iteration interval of an output is used for rating the performance as it is inversely proportional to the throughput.

3.1.2 Efficient Curve Estimation of Accelerators

An important question for modeling the performance is: What can be characterized as an event? For streaming applications, a single problem instance can be viewed as an event (e.g., a single frame for a streaming video filter application). A partition of the problem instance defined by the algorithm specification can also be viewed as an event (e.g., in IDCT, one macro-block or one row of a macro-block can be an event). An event at finest level of granularity represents the iteration outputs of the application, for instance, each pixel of a frame in a video streaming application. Therefore, modeling by curves requires event definition. Because of static scheduling, it is not necessary to derive the service curves from simulation traces. Here, we can consider two methods.

Method 1 is a fast estimation of the service curve of an accelerator that can be generated during scheduling as follows.

If the number of output events N_O can be processed within a latency period L. In this case, the service curve $\beta(\Delta)$ can be represented as the following piecewise linear approximation.

$$\beta(\Delta) = r\Delta, \text{ where } r = \frac{N_O}{L} \qquad (2)$$

However, the above curve models average throughput and does not represents the bursty behavior caused by partitioning. The delay of the accelerator is not considered as its influence on analysis is negligible.

Method 2: For more accurate modeling, the service curve of each PE needs to be calculated. The final service curve is given by the sum of the individual service curves of all output PEs. For calculating the service curve for a 2-level hierarchical partitioning, the following steps need to be carried out.

– Determination of output processors, $PE_1, PE_2, \ldots, PE_n$: Let $\mathcal{I}_O$ be the iteration space of the output variables. Then, the n distinct elements of intersection of processor space $\mathcal{P}(= \{Q \cdot I \mid I \in \mathcal{I}\})$ and $Q \cdot \mathcal{I}_O$ gives the set of output processor, $PE_1, PE_2, \ldots, PE_n \in \mathcal{P}$. Q defines the allocation of processor space determined by the partitioning strategy. In matrix-matrix multiplication example in Fig. 4, all the four processors are output processors due to chosen partitioning.
– Determination of service curves for each output processor: For each processor PE_i, the following parameters need to be determined to find the arrival curve.
  - N_{PE_i} gives the number of output iterations for the processor.
  - $N_{PE_i}(LS)$ be the maximum number of outputs in the corresponding sequential tile executed by processor PE_i.

- γ_{min} is the difference between the first and last output time of the local sequential tile. The value is dependent on the chosen scheduling.
- γ_{max} is the time difference between the execution of two successive scheduled LS tiles.

Then, the upper service curve, represented as piecewise curve with three segments is

$$\beta_i(\Delta) = \min\{r\Delta, r_1\Delta + q_1, N_{p_i}\} \qquad (3)$$

where $r = \frac{N_{p_i}(LS)}{\gamma_{min}}$ limit short term burstiness of output [10]. The long term bursts have been approximated with slope, $r_1 = \frac{N_{p_i}(LS)}{\gamma_{max}}$. For the matrix multiplication example in Fig. 4, $N_{PE_i}(LS) = 4, N_{PE_i} = 16, \gamma_{min} = 4, \gamma_{max} = 32$. The output is produced only in the shown face of matrix multiplication in Fig. 4. The obtained upper service curve, $\beta_i(\Delta)$ of a single PE is represented by dotted line in Fig. 5.
– Find final service curve as function of individual arrival curves of each processor: The output service curve is given by $\beta(\Delta) = \sum_i^n \beta_i(\Delta)$. The service curve of entire accelerator for matrix multiplication example is shown in Fig. 5. The service behavior is repeated periodically for larger intervals in case of streaming workloads.

LSGP and LPGS are a special case of a 2-level hierarchical partitioning. In LSGP $\gamma_{min} = \gamma_{max}$ as the LS tile is the only one to be executed by corresponding processor. For the same reason $N_{PE_i}(LS) = N_{PE_i}$. For LPGS $N_{p_i}(LS) = 1$ and $\gamma_{min} = \gamma_{max}$ as each iteration can be considered as local sequential tile. The important problem to be solved for the accurate derivation of service curves is to find the required variables N (number of output iterations) and γ (dependent on schedule). The first problem is solved counting the index points lying within the polytope formed by intersection of the output space and the processor space (defined by the space-time mapping). The counting problem

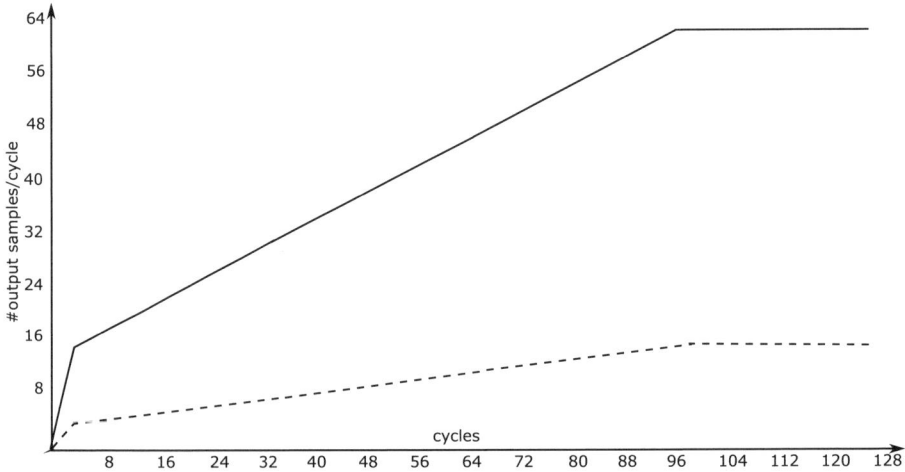

Fig. 5. The upper service curve of the matrix multiplication accelerator. The dotted service curve is of a single PE. The curves repeat periodically.

is solved by computing the iteration space volume [11]. As approximation of γ, the following term is used $\lceil \lambda \cdot (I_2 - I_1) \rceil$. I_2, I_1 are the corner output iteration and λ is the schedule vector. The results is rounded off to nearest integer.

The arrival curves must also be modified, since in realistic systems with accelerators more than one event from different input streams trigger the output event. Therefore, if an accelerator consumes n_i ($i = 1...m$) events from m streams to produce one output event, then the bound on arrival curves must be modified as $[\lceil \alpha_i^u / n_i \rceil, \lfloor \alpha_i^l / n_i \rfloor]$ and then taken as input for an abstract AND component [12]. For example in matrix multiplication, one has inputs from two different streams (matrices). n_i is the number of input events (iterations, tiles) to produce one output event.

3.2 Selection of Optimal Configuration

The modeling of the service behavior of a hardware accelerator is simplified because of static scheduling as shown in previous subsection. Furthermore, the worst-case input throughput is obtained by analyzing several simulation traces or estimated by an experienced system architect, and is modeled as an arrival curve α. The following algorithm can then use available arrival and service information to select the optimal design based on the trade-off between buffer size and delay.

ALGORITHM 2: MATCH
    IN: Input arrival curve,α,
            set B of service curve of Pareto-optimal hardware
    OUT: Optimal set B of service curves β
    BEGIN
      $B_{opt} \leftarrow \{\}$
      FOR each candidate $\beta \in B$ DO
          $DELAY \leftarrow \text{RTCDEL}(\alpha, \beta)$
          $BUFFER \leftarrow \text{RTCBUF}(\alpha, \beta)$
          $UTILIZATION \leftarrow \text{RTCUTIL}(\alpha, \beta)$
          IF $UTILIZATION < 100$ THEN
            $B_{opt} \leftarrow B_{opt} \cup \beta$
          ENDIF
      ENDFOR
    END

The above algorithm finds the delay, buffer size, and utilization for a given arrival curve and a given service curve for each Pareto-optimal hardware accelerator. The delay and buffer size are realized using min-plus algebra operations integrated as RTCDEL, RTCBUF (intuitively maximum horizontal and vertical distance between arrival and service curve) in the RTC toolbox. The utilization can be calculated as $U = \frac{\alpha^u(t)}{\beta(t)}$ where t is the end time. If the resource utilization is less than 100% and the solution is optimal w.r.t. buffer size and delay then the corresponding hardware accelerator is added to set of solutions. The accelerator is completely dedicated to the processing of input stimuli. The optimal configuration is not the fastest implementation but a rate-matched implementation. The rate-matched implementation satisfies the throughput requirement corresponding the worst case input stimulus and also results in smaller area because of resource sharing in the accelerator.

4 Case Study

In this section, we will apply the presented approach of performance analysis to match the throughput of an IDCT accelerator of a motion JPEG decoder to the requirements of a given MPSoC.

4.1 Motion JPEG Decoder

The sequence of algorithms in the M-JPEG decoder algorithm is illustrated in Fig. 7. The IDCT is a data-intensive stage which is usually implemented in hardware. Our design tool is used to synthesize the IDCT accelerator for ASICs and FPGAs with different resource constraints which gives different throughput. The fastest IDCT contains 3562 slices on a Xilinx Virtex1000 FPGA whereas an IDCT with iteration interval of 8 contains 2224 slices because of the resource sharing of 4 multipliers, 4 adders, and 4 subtracters. For obtaining a realistic estimation of input simulation traces to the IDCT, a SystemC model annotated with the execution times of the M-JPEG pipeline was written. The input for the M-JPEG simulation are sequences of encoded 176×144 QCIF

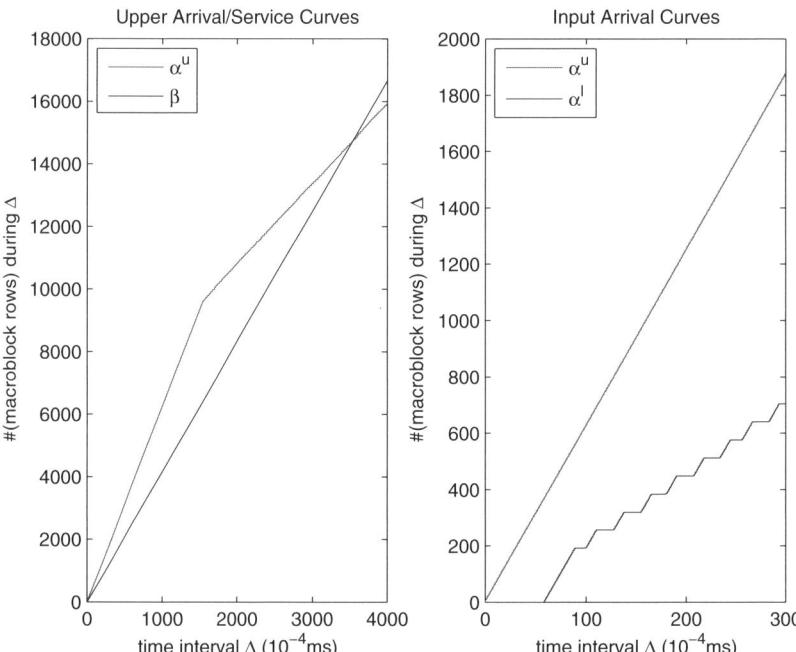

Fig. 6. (a) Arrival and service curve (II=8) for IDCT stage in M-JPEG (b) zoomed view of arrival curves

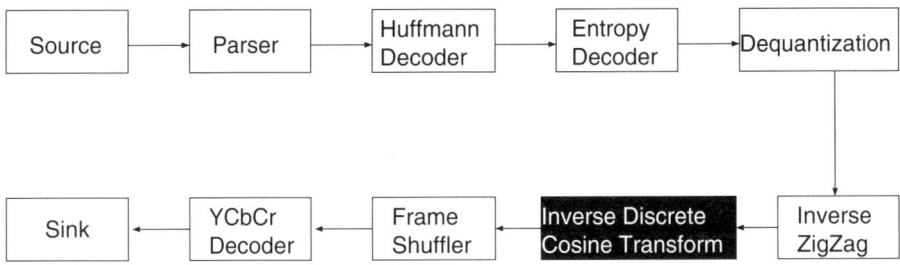

Fig. 7. M-JPEG decoder. All algorithms are implemented in hardware. Therefore, there is no output service curve.

Table 1. Trade-off between buffer size, utilization, delay, and area reduction for IDCT butterfly implementation

II (cycles)	Utilization (%)	Delay (ns)	Buffer	Area Reduction(%)
1	7.33	14	7	0
2	14.65	28	7	14.2
4	29.31	56	7	31.2
8	58.62	19292	1072	37.6
16	-	-	-	-

"-" indicates resource utilization of more than 100 percent.

images with varying degree of compression. Fig. 6b shows the upper and lower output arrival curves from the inverse zig-zag level of M-JPEG as obtained from the SystemC simulation traces (worst-case) of the complete hardware solution. The curves illustrate the bursty nature of the IDCT input. These curves are then taken as input arrival curve α for the IDCT. Afterwards, they are matched with service curves β obtained by the EXPLORE algorithm for the set of Pareto-optimal hardware accelerators. The Pareto-optimal set contains only five hardware designs (II=1,2,4,8,16). Fig. 6a shows the service curve for II=8. The results of the MATCH algorithm are shown in Table 1. The consideration of worst-case input event streams in the simulation setup shows only a resource utilization of 7% for the butterfly implementation (II=1) of the IDCT. Therefore, one cannot only increase the resource utilization by incorporating an IDCT accelerator with larger iteration interval (i.e., lower throughput), but also reduce the total SoC area (37.6% using II=8) by resource sharing within the synthesized hardware. The computed delay and buffer sizes are also optimization objectives which need to be compared. The jump in the computed delay and buffer size in Table 1 is because of the worst-case behavior which requires storage of bursts in FIFO buffers. On close observation, the Pareto-optimal hardware design ($II = 4$) can be selected on the basis of area, delay, and buffer sizes. The results hold for a particular implementation of all other components in the M-JPEG pipeline. In case of other components use different implementations (i.e., different iteration intervals), a new SystemC simulation needs to be executed for obtaining new arrival curves. This is because *back pressure* due to finite buffer sizes is currently a research topic. The simulation of a single design containing a complete hardware implementation of M-JPEG takes 62s time as compared to 0.07s using the MPA toolbox. Therefore, the combination of functional simulation with analytic methods can considerably fasten the design space exploration by orders of magnitude.

5 Conclusions and Future Work

Applying modular performance analysis can be used to find optimal hardware accelerator engines in terms of area and throughput for MPSoC with worst-case performance guarantees. A motion JPEG case study application was chosen to validate the benefits of the novel methodology in combination with simulation showing 31% area reduction. Our future work entails measurements to consider power as an objective function for matching of hardware. The matching of hardware accelerator performance by service curves using polyhedral theory indicates that similar work on optimal cache and functional unit usage can be extended and used to model software performance [13]. Therefore, a combination of modular performance analysis as plug-in for the use within HW/SW compiler tools is an important step towards optimized MPSoC designs.

References

1. Wolf, W.: The Future of Multiprocessor Systems-on-Chips. In: Proceedings of Design Automation Conference (DAC), San Diego, CA, USA, pp. 681–685 (2004)
2. Hannig, F., Ruckdeschel, H., Dutta, H., Teich, J.: PARO: Synthesis of Hardware Accelerators for Multi-Dimensional Dataflow-Intensive Applications. In: Woods, R., Compton, K., Bouganis, C., Diniz, P.C. (eds.) ARC 2008. LNCS, vol. 4943, pp. 287–293. Springer, Heidelberg (2008)
3. G. Abraham, S., R. Rau, B.: Efficient Design Space Exploration in PICO. In: Proceedings of the 2000 International Conference on Compilers, Architecture, and Synthesis for Embedded Systems (CASES), San Jose, CA, USA, pp. 71–79 (2000)
4. Benini, L., Bertozzi, D., Bruni, D., Drago, N., Fummi, F., Poncino, M.: SystemC Cosimulation and Emulation of Multiprocessor SoC Designs. Computer 36(4), 53–59 (2003)
5. Pimentel, A.D., Erbas, C., Polstra, S.: A Systematic Approach to Exploring Embedded System Architectures at Multiple Abstraction Levels. IEEE Transactions on Computers 55(2), 99–112 (2006)
6. Perathoner, S., Wandeler, E., Thiele, L., Hamann, A., Schliecker, S., Henia, R., Racu, R., Ernst, R., Harbour, M.G.: Influence of different system abstractions on the performance analysis of distributed real-time systems. In: EMSOFT 2007: Proceedings of the 7th ACM & IEEE international conference on Embedded software, pp. 193–202 (2007)
7. Thiele, L., Wandeler, E., Chakraborty, S.: A Stream-Oriented Component Model for Performance Analysis of Multiprocessor DSPs. IEEE Signal Processing Magazine 22(3), 38–46 (2005)
8. Thiele, L.: Scheduling of Uniform Algorithms with Resource Constraints. Journal of VLSI Signal Processing 10, 295–310 (1995)
9. Brandolese, C., Fornaciari, W., Salice, F.: An Area Estimation Methodology for FPGA Based Designs at SystemC-Level. In: Proceedings of Design Automation Conference (DAC), San Diego, CA, USA, pp. 129–132 (2004)

10. Van der Wolf, P.: Performance Contracts for Modular MPSoC Integration. In: 8th International Forum on Application-Specific Multi-Processor SoC, June 2008, pp. 8.10.1–8.10.12 (2008)
11. Avis, D.: lrs: A Revised Implementation of the Reverse Search Vertex Enumeration Algorithm. Polytopes – Combinatorics and Computation. DMV Seminar Band 29, 177–198 (2000)
12. Haid, W., Thiele, L.: Complex task activation schemes in system level performance analysis. In: Proc. 5th Intl. Conf. on Hardware/Software Codesign and System Synthesis (CODES+ISSS), Salzburg, Austria, pp. 173–178. ACM Press, New York (2007)
13. Catthoor, F., Danckaert, K., Wuytack, S., Dutt, N.: Code Transformations for Data Transfer and Storage Exploration Preprocessing in Multimedia Processors. IEEE Design & Test 18(3), 70–82 (2001)

Evaluating CMPs and Their Memory Architecture

Chris Jesshope, Mike Lankamp, and Li Zhang

Institute for Informatics, University of Amsterdam
{c.r.Jesshope,m.lankamp,l.zhang1}@uva.nl

Abstract. Many-core processor architectures require scalable solutions that reflect the locality and power constraints of future generations of technology. This paper presents a CMP architecture that supports automatic mapping and dynamic scheduling of threads leaving the binary code devoid of any explicit communication. The thrust of this approach is to produce binary code that is divorced from implementation parameters, yet which still gives good performance over future generations of CMPs. A key component of this abstract processor architecture is the memory system. This paper evaluates the memory architectures, which must maintain performance across a range of targets.

1 Introduction

Although on-chip frequencies have hit a power wall, functional density is still expected to grow exponentially for at least the next decade, maybe more [1], which means explicit concurrency in processor architectures is no longer optional. Hence, attention is being placed on Chip Multiprocessors (CMPs), which appear to be the only way to utilise this surplus of on-chip resources in the future. The issue of programming model now becomes paramount if these are to become truly general purpose. Users of commodity processors have come to expect binary compatibility across generations of the same processor and the ability to program them safely, without dealing with concurrency issues. To translate these advantages to CMPs is a big challenge. In this paper, we use a model that provides these advantages when implemented in the ISA of a regular core. This implementation shows very promising results but the model is disruptive and requires a whole new generation of tools to fully exploit it. However, at the ISA level, we can then exploit concurrency down to the instruction level and we believe that fine-granularity is important in the long term when scaling to thousands or even tens of thousands of cores.

The model defines a Self-adaptive Virtual Processor (SVP) and combines concurrency model with operating system kernel services, e.g. pre-emption and task termination. It was developed in the EU AETHER project (http://www.aether-ist.org/) and tools are being developed for it in the EU Apple-CORE project (http://www.apple-core.info). We adopt this new model, as those proposed to date do not meet the requirements of future technologies, i.e. concurrent composition of programs without deadlock, locality of communication, low power and fault tolerance.

Transactional Memory (TM) [2] has attracted a lot of interest recently. It provides a lock-free programming model, which divides programs into parallel transactions but ignores dependencies between them. An implementation then detects dependencies dynamically when transactions commit. Any conflict will cause one or more transactions to roll back and be re-executed. Thus, although TM provides a simple model for writing correct programs, obtaining efficiency is another matter. TM is speculative and this has significant power implications. In contrast, SVP instructions are issued conservatively, i.e. only when their data is available. When an SVP program starves of data, this can be recognised and power-saving measures taken such as stopping the clocks. Normal resumption of activity is then asynchronous, e.g. a decoupled memory requests completing.

Implementing a thread-based model in hardware is not new. For example, Niagara II [7] supports threads in hardware in multi-core chips and supports fine-grained scheduling of threads based on access to shared memory. It does not provide virtualisation or structuring of threads, as found in SVP. Multithreading has also been used to provide virtual concurrency, Niagara II provides fine-grained temporal multithreading with its multi-core implementation. Each core supports eight logical threads with four threads to each pipeline in a single core. The threads in each core are issued in an interleaved manner, where different threads can be selected for execution on each cycle. When one thread stalls, e.g. for a branch or load, further instructions are not issued until the thread is reactivated.

Other related architectures are Cell and Tilera. The Cell [9] adopts a non-threaded approach but provides high performance by incorporating a conventional processor with eight high-performance vector units, which handle the computational workload. This architecture puts a lot of responsibility on the programmer and/or compiler in managing the explicit distributed memory and computation. Tilera is a homogeneous architecture with 64 cores (http://www.tilera.com) on one die, where each core has a 3-way VLIW pipeline and where all cores are connected by a packet-routed network. Like the work described here, Tilera is programmed to share register variables. However, whereas SVP restricts communication, there are no such restrictions in Tilera meaning more responsibility on the part of the programmer or compiler again.

2 The SVP Model

SVP is based on more than 10 years of research, starting with the dynamic RISC processor [5]. This supported a large number of fine-grain threads (microthreads), to tolerate high memory latency. Based on this initial work, the model was developed and refined and is now quite general. It solves the problem of the interaction between concurrency model and the operating system as SVP model can be considered an operating system kernel, implemented in a core's ISA. The instructions implemented abstract the notion of a processing resource and implement remote job execution to resources. They also provide control and reflection on the concurrency created by fully identifying the units of work created.

SVP is captured by the language μTC [3], which can be compiled [4] into instructions that capture the model's parameterised concurrency. The instructions and their support structures implement a dynamically scheduled RISC core (DRISC) [5]. Parallelising compilers for higher-level languages such as C and SaC [6] are also being developed. We do not have space in this paper to deal with the OS aspects of SVP and the reader is referred to [10] for further information.

The most important addition to an SVP core's ISA is an instruction that creates a family of indexed threads at a place (a cluster of cores). There is no mapping or scheduling implied by this instruction and the minimum resource needed is that required for a single thread, in which case the threads will execute sequentially. However,

```
thread void si(int * a, shared int sum) {
    index i;
    sum = sum + a[i];
}

thread void main() {
    int * a;
    family fid; place pl; int s_in
    create(fid;pl;0;9;1;;) si(a, s_in);
    ...
    s_in = ...
    ...
    sync(fid);
    ...
}
```

Fig. 1. μTC code generating a family of dependent threads using a shared variable; the si thread sums an array of integers to a scalar value

if there are multiple cores available the threads will be automatically mapped to them. In addition, if there are multiple threads available per core, then many threads will be automatically interleaved on each core to provide latency tolerance. This gives SVP binary code that is independent of where it executes and independent of the number of cores used for its execution. Moreover, existing binary code for the base ISA can be executed on a single core using this instruction.

Threads in SVP are blocking and suspend when waiting on data, such as loads from memory, resources, family termination etc. or when waiting for data from another thread. This dataflow-like communication is constrained in order to provide model-based locality in the binary code. The first thread created may read data from the creating thread and any other thread may read data from its predecessor. This linear dependency chain imposes a constraint on the compiler, which can be satisfied statically when transforming loops to execute concurrently. This then allows threads to be mapped to rings of processors with only local communication. This constraint also guarantees freedom of deadlock under composition, due to its acyclic nature and also provides the bound on resources required in order to avoid resource deadlock.

In addition to this communication between threads, families of threads may communicate using shared memory but there are no guarantees on the timing of this memory. Memory consistency is weak and the data written by a family of threads may only be safely read on the termination of that family. Because SVP offers hierarchical composition, i.e. any thread may create a subordinate family, complex data-flow patterns can be established using a combination of inter-thread synchronisation and bulk synchronisation on family termination.

The aspect of the model that supports self-adaptation is the model's abstraction of a resource, the *place*. The create instruction takes a place parameter, which defines where on chip (or in a larger environment) the family will be created. The threads are statically created on the specified place, (consisting of one or more cores), but scheduled and managed dynamically at run time within that place.

2.1 Creating Families of Threads

The default mechanism for program composition in SVP is to do so concurrently using the *create* instruction, which replaces both function calls and loop constructs in this model. It defines an indexed family of blocking threads that are created asynchronously subject to available resources (e.g. thread table entries and registers, which are heap allocated). The create instruction takes one pipeline cycle and completes out of order by writing a return code to a register on termination of all its threads.

When creating functions as threads, dataflow concurrency is exploited, as parameters to functions are passed via synchronising registers called *shared variables* in μTC. This means the thread function can be created before its parameters are defined. Each register implements a dataflow i-store, which is allocated empty, i.e. undefined, blocks a reading thread if read when empty and reschedules a blocked thread when written to. Thus, parameters may be undefined when the family is created as a thread, which blocks until the shared register is set.

Threads in a family are created from a single thread definition, which may contain an *index* to distinguish different instances of it. This allows loops to be defined. The index value is initialised in hardware on thread creation to a value in the range defined by the create parameters and the threads are automatically distributed to the place where they are created (a cluster of cores configured into a ring network).

Blocking on threads is illustrated in figure 1. Note the shared variable, *sum*, in the thread definition. This identifies a value the thread may read from its predecessor's context and which, when set, may be read by its successor thread. In practice, it identifies two registers in a thread's context, one that is read-only and one that is write-once, that the thread must set - if it does not, the program will deadlock! For the first thread, its predecessor is the creating thread and for subsequent threads, it is the prior-thread in index sequence. Note that if two threads are mapped to the same core, a thread and its successor will share a physical register location, in a manner similar to the registers windows in the SPARC architecture. If however, the threads are mapped to adjacent cores (the only other alternative) a register read and/or write to a shared register will initiate a communication between adjacent core's register files. This happens automatically and makes all inter-thread communication implicit in the binary code.

In figure 1, the shared variable is equivalent to a scalar value in the body of the equivalent sequential loop in C. This μTC code does not capture much real concurrency as the thread comprises only two instructions, one to read a[i] and one that adds this value to the prior thread's shared variable and sets its own shared variable. An observant reader may ask "what is gained by this?" The answer is that by specifying this loop concurrently with a shared variable, all of the memory accesses are specified concurrently and may be issued from multiple threads on a single core in any order. This provides a mechanism to tolerate latency in memory access.

In summary then, the create action can be used to implement both independent and dependent loops as concurrent families of threads, and to replace a function call and to capture it concurrently due to the blocking nature of the shared variables used as arguments.

2.2 Places, Delegation and Mutual Exclusion

As illustrated in figure 1, the threads in a family, and its subordinate threads if required, can be executed at a specified remote place (the variable pl in figure 1). The place abstraction is implementation dependent and defines a set of processing resources. In the context of this paper, a place is a cluster of processors on the CMP, configured into a ring. Two model-defined places are *local* and *default* (no place specified). Local forces creation on the same processor (i.e. virtual concurrency only) and default distributes the family to the same cluster as the creating thread. All other places must be set by a place-server, in a very similar manner to allocating dynamic memory in C. As memory in SVP is asynchronous and cannot be used for implementing a mutex, we introduce the concept of a mutex place in SVP, which serialises any create requests sent to it. This is required to implement the place server.

The place abstraction solves a number of difficult issues. It provides an address for the delegation of work over the on-chip packet network making communication in SVP dynamically defined and implicit in the binary code. It optionally provides virtualisation of physical places. As an example, up to 32 legacy-code threads may be executed on a single SVP core described here and as described above, it supports mutual exclusion on families created at the same place.

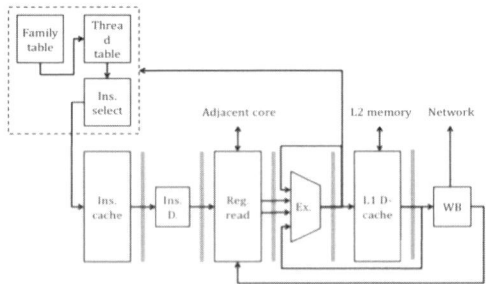

Fig. 2. SVP DRISC pipeline showing the major additional components required to support interleaved thread execution.

3 Chip and Processor Architecture

We have designed a core based on an Alpha, in-order issue pipeline, which is augmented with instructions that support the SVP model. This is illustrated in Figure 2. We also have a reference implementation of a single cluster of such cores. It emulates every interaction in each stage of the pipeline as well as implementing a full memory interface. With this C++ emulator, we can vary parameters such as cache sizes, thread and family table sizes and number of cores configured in the ring network. Reasonable parameters have been chosen for implementation delays based on an evaluation of the silicon implementation [11]. The emulator therefore gives us a very realistic estimation of the processor's expected performance.

In the configuration used in this paper, each core is able to execute up to 256 threads and the thread table is indexed by the thread's identifier (0..255). It contains a program counter and information about the location of the thread's registers in the local register file, i.e. *globals* (accessed by all threads in a family), *locals*, *dependents* (read only from the predecessor's shareds) and *shareds* (write once). It also contains other housekeeping information such as link fields for creating queues of threads, e.g.

the queue of active threads, which hold all threads currently able to execute at least one instruction.

Similarly the family table contains 32 entries and the table index is a part of the family identifier, other components of the identifier are processor number and security key. Up to 16 families may be distributed between the cores in a cluster, using a common identifier between cores the other 16 family identifiers are for local creates.

Thread creation is very efficient, requiring only a few processor cycles to acquire a family table entry, initialise it and initiate thread creation, which is independent of pipeline operation and occurs at a rate of one thread per cycle, until either resources or block size are exhausted. It takes zero cycles to context switch and threads may do so every cycle, i.e. execute a single instruction from a thread and yield.

With up to 256 threads, a large register file is required for each thread's context of synchronising variables. In this paper we evaluate a core with 1024 Integer and 512 floating-point registers for their contexts, where registers are allocated in multiples of 32 for a block of threads. Each register in the register file has a fixed number of ports, three for normal pipeline operations and an additional two for asynchronous read and writes. These include operations that complete out of order, sharing registers between cores, initializing the index value, etc. More detail on implementation of the SVP core is given in [11] with area estimates for a core.

3.1 Register File and Asynchronous Operations

The register file and its synchronisation state need some further explanation. This synchronisation allows threads to be scheduled at the instruction level as when a register is empty, a thread attempting to read the register will suspend by writing its identifier to the empty register. This occurs on the write-back of the failed instruction. Now when data is written to the empty thread, the suspended thread will be reactivated and added to the active queue.

On creation, a thread's context of register variables is set to empty. This is also the case when asynchronous operations are executed, for example on the execution of a family create, the write-back stage will set the register to empty and then the register will be written asynchronously when the family has terminated. Any instruction trying to read the control code returned would suspend on the creating thread until that happens (the sync in figure 1).

3.2 L1 Caches

Both the L1 I-cache and D-cache are similar in principal to their counterparts in conventional processors, but with some significant changes to deal with the blocking nature of microthreads and their scheduling. Lines in the I-cache are extended with a reference count and fields to maintain a list of threads waiting on the cache line. This is required as threads are only scheduled when their instructions are present in the cache. Thus on a branch or when the PC increments over a cache line boundary, a context switch will be forced. Only on a hit to the cache will these threads be rescheduled. Threads suspended on a register will also touch the cache before being rescheduled.

The L1 D-cache is also modified to keep track of outstanding memory reads on a line. A line is allocated on a cache miss, the request is sent to the next level of memory and the memory read request (which gets stored in the target register) is put on a linked list of requests for that line. When the data returns, these requests are serviced one by one after which the line can be reused. Finally, note that the D-cache can also be much smaller than in a conventional processor since the architecture supports as many outstanding reads as there are registers and the core will not stall as long as there are active threads.

3.3 Memory Architecture

In this paper, we evaluate a number of on-chip memory systems for the SVP CMP. We evaluate only on-chip memory at this stage and assume that some percentage of the chip area will be dedicated to level-2 cache, which must provide the abstraction of a shared memory and achieve this across potentially thousands of cores. Moreover, it must provide scalable throughput. Because SVP cores have good tolerance to latency, of the order of 100s of cycles in the configuration described above, our aim is to evaluate a COMA memory [13]. This has a relatively high latency due to its coherency protocol but which should provide a transparent mechanism to achieve locality of access due to the way in which cache lines are attracted to the cores using the data. This COMA memory is evaluated against a number of alternative designs. These are:

An ideal memory. This provides parallel, conflict-free, multi-ported access to all locations in memory. It takes 10 cycles to read a cache line and each CPU has concurrent, non-arbitrated access to any line.

A multi-bank memory. This assumes a non-blocking, fully connected, multi-stage switch to connect processors and memory banks. Cache lines are interleaved to banks on low-order address bits. Because it is assumed channels from the memory are relatively narrow, the memory has the following characteristics: the time for a request to get to or from memory is $\log_2$(number of banks) plus one cycle for each 8 bytes of data plus 10 cycles to read the cache line. So a read to 16 banks would take 5 cycles to get to memory, 10 to read a cache line and 13 to return the complete cache line, 28 in total. Conflicts may occur when multiple requests are routed to the same bank. Such requests are buffered at the bank and serviced in order of arrival. Conflicts decrease throughput and increase latency.

A randomised multi-bank memory, with similar network and characteristics but where the bank address is computed using a hash function of the address bits. Such a memory avoids systematic conflict patterns at the expense of losing any locality of access. Both multi-bank systems are non-coherent and distributed across the chip.

The COMA memory is similar to that in the KSR 1 [12], although our protocol has intermediate states to avoid the caches blocking on uncompleted transactions [13]. In this paper a single ring of L2 caches is evaluated where each cache is shared by four cores using a snoopy bus and the ring also has a top-level directory, directing requests to off-chip backing store. All other on-chip memories evaluated are pre-loaded with data, but this is not possible in the COMA, we therefore implement a low-latency interface to external memory in this evaluation (1 cycle per cache line). This architecture scales up by using a hierarchy of rings but in this paper a single ring is evaluated.

4 Results and Evaluation

The results presented here were measured using the cycle-accurate reference implementation of an SVP CMP, based on the specification of the model as described in [11]. It uses the Alpha ISA and each core in the cluster executes Alpha machine code with SVP extensions. Due to the unavailability of the compiler at current moment, the benchmarks were manually compiled into assembly and validated to ensure they generate correct results. Note that for each benchmark, the same binary code is executed unchanged on each memory configuration and for all cluster sizes.

Additional parameters for the results presented here include 1Kbyte, 4-way set associative L1 I and D caches; a 6-stage pipeline with asynchronous floating point operations taking 2, 8 and 10 cycles for add/mult, div and sqrt respectively; and a ring network that broadcasts a create to all cores in P+k cycles for P cores and k parameters and takes 5 cycles for a remote read and 3 for a remote write.

4.1 Inner Product

The first benchmark evaluated was an integer inner product (Livermore loop 3). This "sequential" algorithm was so that a distributed sequential reduction of one thread per core locally creates a family of threads to compute a partial reduction. The distributed reduction combines these results. This parallel algorithm has good performance so long as the number of cores is small compared to the number of elements to be reduced.

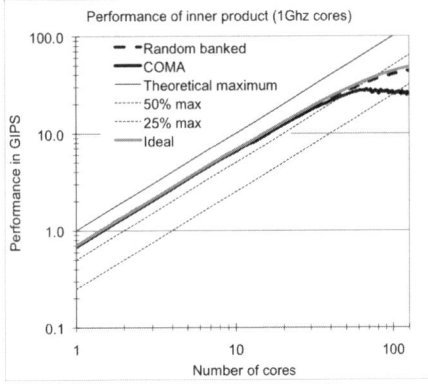

Fig. 3. Performance in GIPS for the inner product benchmark, for a 1GHz core. The diagonal bands show the 100%, 50% and 25% efficiency performance for for this problem.

The benchmark implements a reduction over a 40960-element array on from 1 to 128 cores and the results are given in figure 3. As can be seen, the performance of all memories scales linearly but saturate at between 60 and 100 cores. This is not caused by a lack of threads, as there are more threads than resources available for the largest place evaluated. The saturation is due to the distributed reduction, which requires 10 cycles per core (1 cycle to reschedule a thread, 6 cycles for the pipeline latency and 3 cycles to write to the adjacent register file). This contributes 1 µsec to a 5µsec execution time with a 100-core ring. The reduction has a relatively low efficiency as only one thread is active at a time during the reduction operation.

The COMA memory, saturation occurs earlier and is harder than the other two memories and we believe this is due to bandwidth sharing on the cache-coherency ring network (64-core place shares the ring bandwidth between 16 L2 cache banks.) Note that unlike the ideal and random banked memories, the COMA memory sources all data from off chip in this emulation. We do not simulate a hierarchy of rings in this paper, which could limit this saturation in larger CMPs.

4.2 Matrix Multiplication

The next results are for integer matrix multiplication. In the reduction, the code only reads data mapped by rows, matrix multiplication on the other hand combines both row and column mapped data in its inner product computation without any optimization. In this code, concurrency is found from the combination of outer and middle loop and the reduction is implemented sequentially. Figure 4 shows results for 64x64 matrices.

Both ideal and COMA memory give an 87.5% efficiency in the use of the pipeline cycles up to about 30 cores. The random banked memory however, is only 50% efficient, although this scales quite well. Given the fact that COMA system is simulated even without any pre-loading, the COMA is the clear winner for small number of cores. The COMA as expected saturates early and by 100 cores the performance of COMA and random banked memories are the same.

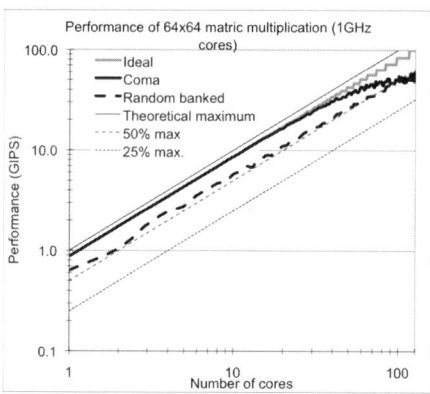

Fig. 4. Performance of 64x64 matrix multiplication in GIPS on clusters of from 1 to 128 cores. Again the bands indicate maximum, 50% and 25% efficiency.

4.3 The 256 Point FFT

With FFT, the combination of power-of-two data access with concurrent banks seems to result in memory-bank conflict. The 256-point version comprises a sequence of 8 families of 128 threads (using theCooley Tukey algorithm). Each thread computes a complex butterfly operation using pre-computed roots of unity. No reordering is performed during the FFT execution, so results are produced in bit reverse order.

The results in figure 5 show that for a single core, the banked memory has an efficiency of 90%, the COMA 97.5% and the randomised banked memory 98%. This is based on the number of floating point instructions in the thread code and peak instruction issue rate. This is significant and shows that the core is able to tolerate significant latency through instruction-level scheduling for both floating point and memory operations.

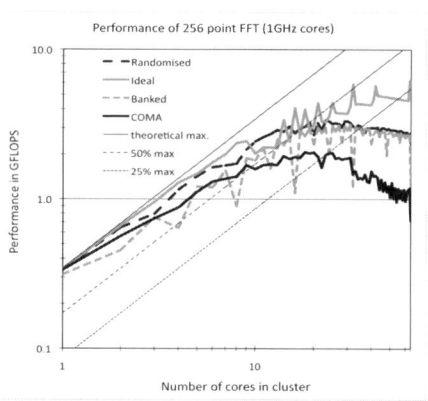

Fig. 5. Performance on 256 point FFT for clusters of from 1 to 64 cores

Peaks in performance for the ideal memory occur when the number of cores is a power of 2, i.e. when the 128 threads are distributed perfectly to cores. In this code, there is no surplus of threads and load-balancing issues are visible. However, it can also be seen that the same points give the worst performance for the banked memory. This conflict situation is investigated in figure 6 using the pipeline's statistics.

As the number of cores increases, the performance of all memories saturates due to the limited by the number of threads available. Not surprisingly the ideal memory, which has a low base latency and no queuing latency on conflicts, scales the best and is still within 25% of the theoretical maximum at 64 cores. The COMA on the other hand has the highest latency and this falls below 25% efficiency at around 12 cores. With 128 threads per stage, with more than two cores, the number of threads per core will decrease in inverse proportion to the number of cores (see figure 6 for the average active-queue length, which reflects this). Hence, performance will decrease as the pipelines begin to stall waiting for memory accesses and floating-point operations. Figure 6 also shows the maximum time in cycles for which the pipeline is stalled during the execution, which increases from around 20 for a single core to almost 1000 cycles, with clear peaks at all powers of 2. This clearly indicates memory bank conflict, as it can be seen that the peaks correspond to peaks in execution time, with load balancing only contributing smaller fluctuations.

4.4 The 4096-Point FFT

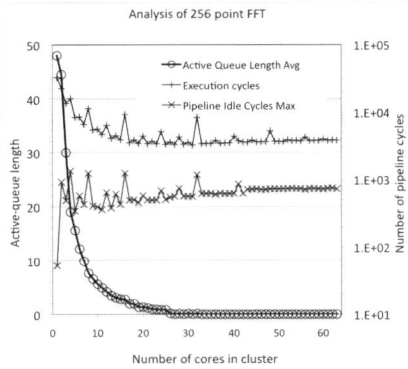

Fig. 6. Analysis of the 256-point FFT for different number of cores executing on a banked memory with M=P. This shows the average active-queue length for the execution of this code, the number of cycles required for its execution and the maximum length of time the pipeline is stalled waiting for memory.

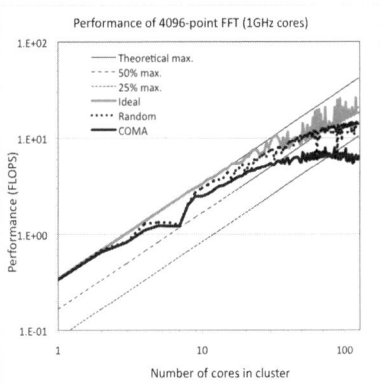

Fig. 7. Performance on 4096-point FFT for clusters of SVP cores from 1 to 128. The diagonal bands show the maximum theoretical performance, 50% of that performance and 25%. For clarity the banked-memory results are not shown.

From figure 6 and 7, it is clear that the lack of threads limits performance significantly. Figure 7 shows the performance for the 4096-point FFT. In these results, we compare the ideal, random banked and COMA memory systems. This code executes a sequence of twelve families of 2048 threads, one at each stage of the algorithm. This means that for 128 cores, a maximum of 16 threads may be active on any core (ignoring the main thread). As expected, the COMA memory system saturates first, followed by the randomised banked memory. What is important to note is that with sufficient threads, the COMA memory system is able to give a performance that comes very close to the ideal memory and unlike the random banked memory uses only local wires in its implementation, a key issue in any future silicon systems.

The anomalous step between 4 and 8 processors seems to be memory related, as it occurs for both real memory systems although not the ideal memory. We assume this is due to interactions between scheduling and memory delay. This situation is being investigated further.

5 Conclusions

In this paper, we have presented a model of concurrency and its implementation on ring-connected clusters of SVP cores. We have implemented a cycle-accurate software emulator for this MCCMP and have explored the performance of this micro-grid for a variety of memory architectures using a limited number of applications. The applications were chosen to have a range of concurrent memory access patterns. The inner product has entirely-local access patterns to distributed data, whereas the matrix multiplication accesses data by row and by column, so if data is distributed by either row or by column, some form of global access will be required. Finally, the FFT algorithm has access patterns that range from local to offsets of N/2 in powers of 2.

Our aim with the microgrid is to provide a concurrent architecture that can be used for a wide range of applications and where systems engineering and compilation issues should be a matter of matching bandwidth rather than relying on the detail of scheduling and execution latencies. This goal, we feel, has been demonstrated by our results. Across a wide range of cluster sizes, we achieve an efficient and consistent performance without changing the binary code.

We have identified a number of areas that contribute to the saturation of results as we scale up problem sizes. The most important issue is the lack of threads providing virtual concurrency, which is essential if an asynchronous schedule is to be achieved. We have also identified thread creation overheads and bandwidth saturation on the coherency network as cluster sizes scale up. The question of which memory system to implement on such a microgrid is also answered to some extent. The COMA memory system has the highest latency and hence requires more virtual concurrency than the other memory systems to maintain its performance. However, this memory system had the most consistent performance in its non-saturated region across the range of benchmarks. In particular, it outperformed the randomised banked memory in matrix multiplication by almost a factor of two. Moreover, it does so with a significantly smaller cost in terms of area and delay when implementing the communications required on chip. Whereas the randomised memory requires a wire whose length is determined by the overall dimension of the switch, all COMA communication on the other hand is in ring networks and good floor planning and layout can keep these wires fast and short.

Acknowledgements

We acknowledge support for this work from NWO in the project Microgrids and from the EU in the project Apple-CORE.

References

1. Semiconductor Industry Association, International technology roadmap for semiconductors update. Technical report (2006)
2. Hammond, L., Carlstrom, B.D., Wong, V., Chen, M., Kozyrakis, C., Olukotun, K.: Transactional coherence and consistency: Simplifying parallel hardware and software. IEEE Micro. 24(6), 92–103 (2004)
3. Jesshope, C.: μTC – an intermediate language for programming chip multiprocessors. In: Jesshope, C., Egan, C. (eds.) ACSAC 2006. LNCS, vol. 4186, pp. 147–160. Springer, Heidelberg (2006)
4. Bernard, T.A.M., Jesshope, C., Knijnenburg, P.M.W.: Strategies for Compiling μTC to Novel Chip Multiprocessors. In: Vassiliadis, S., Berekovic, M., Hämäläinen, T.D. (eds.) SAMOS 2007. LNCS, vol. 4599, pp. 127–138. Springer, Heidelberg (2007)
5. Bolychevsky, C.R.J., Muchnick, V.B.: Dynamic scheduling in RISC architectures. IEE Trans. E, Computers and Digital Techniques 143, 309–317 (1996)
6. Scholz, S.B.: Single Assignment C - efficient support for high-level array operations in a functional setting. Journal of Functional Programming 13, 1005–1059 (2003)
7. McGhan, H.: Niagara 2 opens the floodgates. Microprocessor Report 20(11), 1–12 (2006)
8. Kahle, M.N., Day, H.P., Hofstee, C.R., Johns, T.R.M., Shippy, D.: Introduction to the Cell multiprocessor. IBM Journal of Research and Development 49(4), 589–604 (2005)
9. Jesshope: Operating systems in silicon and the dynamic management of resources in many-core chips. Parallel Processing Letters (PPL) 18(2), 257–274 (2008)
10. Bousias, K., Guang, L., Jesshope, C.R., Lankamp, M.: Implementation and evaluation of a microthread architecture, Journal of System Architecture (2008), http://dx.doi.org/10.1016/j.sysarc.2008.07.001
11. K.S.R. Corporation. KSR1 technical summary, Technical report (1992)
12. Zhang, L., Jesshope, C.R.: On-chip COMA cache-coherence protocol for microgrids of microthreaded cores. In: Bougé, L., Forsell, M., Träff, J.L., Streit, A., Ziegler, W., Alexander, M., Childs, S. (eds.) Euro-Par Workshops 2007. LNCS, vol. 4854, pp. 38–48. Springer, Heidelberg (2008)

Author Index

Abdullah, Tariq 108
Alima, Luc Onana 108
Amano, Hideharu 171

Bertels, Koen 108
Bomel, Pierre 72
Buchty, Rainer 60

Calomme, David 108
Chen, Yupeng 40
Crenne, Jeremie 72

Diguet, Jean-Philippe 72
Dutta, Hritam 16, 233

Fiethe, Björn 50
Flautner, Krisztián 1

Gebis, Joseph 146
Gilart-Iglesias, Virgilio 195
Gogniat, Guy 72
González, Antonio 2
Guang, Liang 183

Hähner, Jörg 120
Hannig, Frank 16, 233
Hasegawa, Yohei 171
Hoffmann, Rolf 96

Jendrsczok, Johannes 96
Jesshope, Chris 246

Karl, Wolfgang 60
Kicherer, Mario 60
Koskinen, Lauri 183
Kramer, David 60

Lalis, Spyros 4
Lankamp, Mike 246
Lei, Zhao 171
Lenck, Thomas 96

Maciá-Pérez, Francisco 195
Mahmoudi, Ghadi 120
Marcos-Jorquera, Diego 195
Martín-Langerwerf, Javier 159
Maskell, Douglas L. 40

Mencer, Oskar 28
Michalik, Harald 50
Moch, Sören 159
Mostaghim, Sanaz 135
Müller-Schloer, Christian 120
Murakami, Kazuaki 219

Niedermeier, Christoph 84
Nigussie, Ethiopia 183

Oliker, Leonid 146
Osterloh, Björn 50
Özturgut, Harun 84

Patt, Yale 3
Payá-Vayá, Guillermo 159
Pirsch, Peter 159

Rao, Pradeep 219

Schmeck, Hartmut 135
Schmidt, Bertil 40
Scholz, Christian 84
Seki, Naomi 171
Shalf, John 146
Sokolov, Vassiliy 108
Syrivelis, Dimitris 4

Teich, Jürgen 16, 233
Tenhunen, Hannu 183

Uhrig, Sascha 207
Ungerer, Theo 207
Usami, Kimiyoshi 171

Wieland, Thomas 84
Williams, Samuel 146
Wu, Qiang 28

Xu, Hui 171

Ye, Linfeng 72
Yelick, Katherine 146
Yoshiki, Saito 171

Zhang, Li 246

Printing: Mercedes-Druck, Berlin
Binding: Stein+Lehmann, Berlin